UNDERSTANDING AND USING

ENGLISH GRAMMAR
Second Edition

WORKBOOK

UNDERSTANDING AND USING
ENGLISH GRAMMAR
Second Edition

WORKBOOK

Betty Schrampfer Azar
Donald A. Azar

Chief contributor: Rachel Spack Koch
Contributors: Susan Jamieson
Barbara Andrews
Jeanie Francis

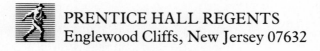
PRENTICE HALL REGENTS
Englewood Cliffs, New Jersey 07632

Publisher: *Tina B. Carver*
Managing editor, production: *Sylvia Moore*
Editorial/production supervisor: *Janet Johnston*
Prepress buyer: *Ray Keating*
Manufacturing buyer: *Lori Bulwin*
Scheduler: *Leslie Coward*
Illustrator: *Don Martinetti*
Cover supervisor: *Marianne Frasco*
Cover designer: *Joel Mitnick Design*
Interior designer: *Ros Herion Freese*
Page makeup: *Mary Fitzgerald*

 © 1992 by PRENTICE HALL REGENTS
A Division of Simon & Schuster
Englewood Cliffs, New Jersey 07632

Printed in the United States of America

10 9 8 7 6 5 4 3 2 1

ISBN 0-13-952839-3

ISBN 0-13-943986-2 {VOL. A}
ISBN 0-13-944000-3 {VOL. B}

Prentice-Hall International (UK) Limited, *London*
Prentice-Hall of Australia Pty. Limited, *Sydney*
Prentice-Hall Canada Inc., *Toronto*
Prentice-Hall Hispanoamericana, S.A., *Mexico*
Prentice-Hall of India Private Limited, *New Delhi*
Prentice-Hall of Japan, Inc., *Tokyo*
Simon & Schuster Asia Pte. Ltd., *Singapore*
Editora Prentice-Hall do Brasil, Ltda., *Rio de Janeiro*

To Chelsea,
with all our love.

Contents

Chapter 2   MODAL AUXILIARIES AND SIMILAR EXPRESSIONS

Chapter 3   THE PASSIVE

Chapter 4   GERUNDS AND INFINITIVES

Chapter 5 SINGULAR AND PLURAL

Chapter 6   ADJECTIVE CLAUSES

Chapter 7   NOUN CLAUSES

Chapter 8 SHOWING RELATIONSHIPS BETWEEN IDEAS—PART I

Chapter 9 SHOWING RELATIONSHIPS BETWEEN IDEAS—PART II

Chapter 10 CONDITIONAL SENTENCES

Appendix 1 **SUPPLEMENTARY GRAMMAR UNITS**

Answer Key

Preface

This ESL/EFL grammar workbook accompanies *Understanding and Using English Grammar (Second Edition)*. It is a place for students to explore and practice structures on their own. At the same time, the workbook provides supplementary teaching materials for the teacher to select as needed. The exercises are designated (1) SELFSTUDY PRACTICES or (2) GUIDED STUDY PRACTICES:

(1) The SELFSTUDY PRACTICES are designed for independent out-of-class use by the students, who can correct their own work by referring to the Answer Key booklet at the back of the workbook. The SELFSTUDY PRACTICES allow students ample opportunities to clarify their understandings, explore structures at their own pace, assess their proficiency, and expand their usage ability as well as their vocabulary.

(2) The GUIDED STUDY PRACTICES, for which the answers are not given, are intended primarily as additional material for the teacher to use as s/he sees the need. They can be used for classwork, homework, or individualized instruction.

The content of the exercises often seeks to inform, challenge, and pique the curiosity of students as they practice their English language skills. In addition, the workbook contains suggestions for various language-learning activities such as discussions, games, and writing topics.

The workbook is coordinated with the main text. The heading for each practice refers the students to the charts in the main text that contain explanations of the grammar being practiced. The *Teacher's Guide* that accompanies the main text includes suggestions for using the workbook, plus answers to the GUIDED STUDY PRACTICES.

The answer key to the SELFSTUDY PRACTICES is on perforated pages. The students can remove it to construct their own separate Answer Key booklet. The students can write in the workbook and then place the Answer Key booklet next to the workbook to make it easy for them to correct their answers.

Acknowledgments

My thanks go to all who have made this project possible. First of all to Don, an experienced ESL teacher and administrator, who at my urging turned his hand to writing. The enjoyment he took in his task is evident in the lively spirit of the workbook.

I also thank the contributors—Shelley Koch, Susan Jamieson, Jeanie Francis, and Barbara Andrews—for the wonderful materials they provided us to work with. They are experienced teachers who understand their students. Their understandings have greatly enhanced the workbook.

My mom and dad are also due great thanks. My mom keyboards and holds me to account for every word and punctuation mark, and my dad contributes a plethora of ideas for contexts. My thanks also to Chelsea for her help in the office and to Joy Edwards for her able and valued assistance.

And, of course, no book is possible without thoughtful editors: thanks go to Tina Carver, Ros Herion, Sylvia Moore, Janet Johnston—and all the support circle at Prentice Hall Regents.

BETTY S. AZAR
Langley, Washington

First, foremost, and above all, I want to express my appreciation to Betty. Although we worked together teaching ESL for many years, collaboration on this writing project brought our work lives together in a very different way. Her patience, her guidance, and her incredible expertise kept me from roaming too far afield from our objective. She taught me a great deal.

I also want to express my gratitude to our contributing writers: Rachel Spack (Shelley) Koch, Susan Jamieson, Barbara Andrews, and Jeanie Francis. They worked with me in developing draft material and did their part well. I also thank them for adapting to any inconsistencies in communications and schedule.

And finally, there's Chelsea Parker. She went through it all with us, and she'll have to do it again. Our work, and we, are all the better for that.

DONALD A. AZAR
Langley, Washington

CHAPTER **1**
Verb Tenses

◇ **PRACTICE 1—SELFSTUDY: Verb tenses. (Charts 1-1 → 1-5)**

Directions: Following are some dialogues between Speaker A and Speaker B. Complete the dialogues by using the correct form of the words in parentheses.

1. A: I'm going to ask you some questions so that we can practice verb tenses. Okay?

   B: Okay.

   A: What (*you, do*) _____ ***do you do*** _____ every day before you come to class? Name one thing.

   B: I (*eat*) _____ ***eat*** _____ breakfast.

2. A: What (*you, do*) _____ last night? Name three separate activities.

   B: Last night I (*eat*) _____ dinner. Then I (*visit*)

   _____ some friends, and later I (*write*) _____ a couple of letters.

3. A: What (*you, do*) _____ right now? What activity is in progress right now, at this exact moment?

   B: Right now I (*talk*) _____ to you. I (*answer*) _____ your questions.

4. A: Where were you at this exact time yesterday? And what activity was in progress yesterday at that time?

   B: Let me think. At this exact time yesterday, I was at the bookstore. I (*look*) _____

   _____ for the books I needed to buy for this class.

5. A: How many questions (*I, ask*) _____ since we began this exercise?

   B: I don't know exactly. I think you (*ask*) _____ me about five or six questions since we began this exercise.

6. A: What (*you, do*) _____ for the past five minutes? In
      other words, what activity began five minutes ago and has been in progress from that time
      to the present time?

   B: I (*talk*) _____ to you for the past five minutes. I
      started talking to you five minutes ago, and I am still talking to you.

7. A: Where (*you, be*) _____ tomorrow morning?

   B: I (*be*) _____ in class tomorrow morning.

8. A: What (*you, do*) _____ at this exact time tomorrow? In other
      words, what activity will be in progress at this exact same time tomorrow?

   B: Right now I am sitting in the classroom. And at this exact time tomorrow, I (*sit*)
      _____ in the classroom.

9. A: What (*you, do*) _____ by the time you got to class today? In
      other words, what is one activity that you had completed before you arrived in class today?

   B: Well, for one thing, I (*eat*) _____ breakfast by the time I got to class
      today.

10. A: What (*you, do*) _____ by the time you go to bed tonight?
       Name one activity that you will have completed before you go to bed tonight.

    B: I (*eat*) _____ dinner by the time I go to bed tonight.

    A: Excellent! You have a good start on understanding and using English verb tenses. In this
       chapter, we'll do a lot more practice with all the tenses.

◇ PRACTICE 2—SELFSTUDY: Names of verb tenses. (Charts 1-1 → 1-5)

   Directions: In the following dialogues, many of the verbs are in italics. Using the list of English verb
   tenses, write the names of the tenses of the italicized verbs.*

✔ *simple present*	*present progressive*	*present perfect*	*present perfect progressive*
simple past	*past progressive*	*past perfect*	*past perfect progressive*
simple future	*future progressive*	*future perfect*	*future perfect progressive*

   1. A: What *do* you *do* every morning?

      B: I *catch* a bus to school.

      _____**simple present**_____

   2. A: What *did* you *do* last night?

      B: Last night I *watched* a movie on television.

      _____

---

*Words that are "*italized*" or "*in italics*" have a slanted print.

   Regular print looks like this. *Italic print looks like this.*

3. A: What *are* you *doing* right now?

   B: Right now I *am working* on English grammar.

   _____

4. A: What *were* you *doing* at this time yesterday?

   B: At this exact time yesterday, I *was walking* from the bookstore to the classroom building.

   _____

5. A: *Have* you *met* many people since you came here?

   B: Yes, I*'ve met* a lot of people.

   _____

6. A: What *have* you *been doing* for the past few minutes?

   B: I *have been working on* this grammar practice.

   _____

7. A: What *will* you *do* if you miss the bus tomorrow morning?

   B: I*'ll walk* to school.

   _____

8. A: What *will* you *be doing* at this exact moment tomorrow?

   B: I *will be attending* my English class at this same time tomorrow.

   _____

9. A: What *had* you *done* by the time you got to class today?

   B: I *had bought* two books at the bookstore.

   _____

10. A: What *will* you *have done* by the time you go to bed tonight?

    B: I *will have finished* my homework.

    _____

11. A: Were you asleep when your friend called last night?

    B: Yes. I *had been sleeping* for almost an hour when the phone rang.

    _____

12. A: How long have you been working in this workbook?

    B: By the time I finish this practice, I *will have been working* on this grammar for ten minutes.

    _____

◇ PRACTICE 3—SELFSTUDY: Verb tenses. (Charts 1-1 → 1-5)

Directions: Complete the sentences with the correct form of the words in parentheses.

| | SIMPLE | PROGRESSIVE |

SIMPLE — **PROGRESSIVE**

PRESENT

1. Tom has regular habits. He (*eat*) _____ dinner every day. He has eaten dinner every day since he was a child. He ate dinner every day last month. He ate dinner yesterday. He will eat dinner tomorrow. He will probably eat dinner almost every day until the end of his life.

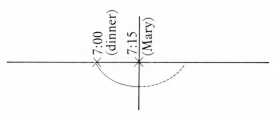

4. At 7:00 this evening, Tom started to eat dinner. It is now 7:15. Tom is on the phone because Mary called him. He says, ''Can I call you back? I (*eat*) _____ dinner right now. I'll finish soon and will call you back. I don't want my dinner to get cold.'' Tom's dinner is in progress when Mary calls.

PAST

2. Tom eats dinner every day. Usually he eats at home, but yesterday he (*eat*) _____ dinner at a restaurant.

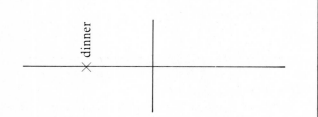

5. Last week Tom went to a restaurant. He began to eat at 7:00. At 7:15 Mary came into the restaurant, saw Tom, and walked over to say hello. Tom's dinner was still in front of him. He hadn't finished it yet. In other words, when Mary walked into the restaurant, Tom (*eat*) _____ dinner. Tom's dinner was in progress when Mary arrived.

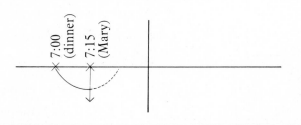

FUTURE

3. Tom ate dinner yesterday. He eats dinner every day. In all probability, he (*eat*) _____ dinner tomorrow.

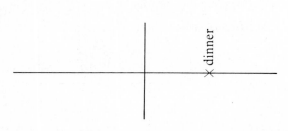

6. Tom will begin his dinner at 7:00 tonight. Mary will arrive at 7:15. It takes Tom 30 minutes to eat his dinner. In other words, when Mary arrives tonight, Tom (*eat*) _____ his dinner. Tom's dinner will be in progress when Mary arrives.

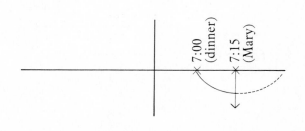

PERFECT	PERFECT PROGRESSIVE

7. Tom finished eating dinner at 7:30 tonight. It is now 8:00, and his mother has just come into the kitchen. She says, "What would you like for dinner? Could I cook something for you?" Tom says, "Thanks Mom, but I (*eat, already*) _____ dinner."

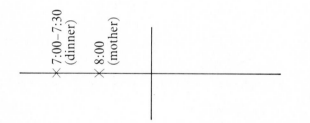

8. Yesterday Tom cooked his own dinner. He began to eat at 7:00 and finished at 7:30. At 8:00 his mother came into the kitchen. She offered to cook some food for Tom, but he (*eat, already*) _____. In other words, Tom had finished his dinner before he talked to his mother.

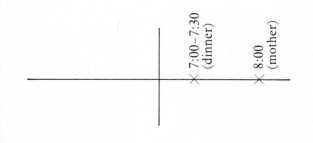

9. Tomorrow Tom will begin dinner at 7:00 and finish at 7:30. His mother will come into the kitchen at 8:00. In other words, Tom (*eat, already*) _____ dinner by the time his mother walks into the kitchen.

10. Tom began to eat dinner at 7:00 tonight. It is now, at this moment, 7:15. Tom (*eat*) _____ his dinner for fifteen minutes, but he hasn't finished yet. In other words, his dinner has been in progress for fifteen minutes. He'll probably finish soon.

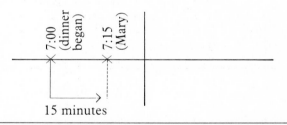

11. Last week Tom went to a restaurant. He began to eat at 7:00. At 7:15 Mary came into the restaurant, saw Tom, and walked over to say hello. Tom's dinner was still in front of him. He hadn't finished it yet. In other words, when Mary walked into the restaurant, Tom (*eat*) _____ dinner for fifteen minutes. Tom's dinner had been in progress for fifteen minutes when Mary arrived.

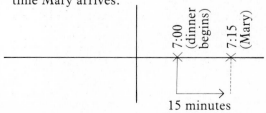

12. Tonight Tom will go to a restaurant. He will begin to eat at 7:00. At 7:15 Mary will come into the restaurant, see Tom, and walk over to say hello. Tom's dinner will still be in front of him. He won't have finished it yet. In other words, when Mary walks into the restaurant tomorrow, Tom (*eat*) _____ dinner for fifteen minutes. Tom's dinner will have been in progress for fifteen minutes by the time Mary arrives.

◇ **PRACTICE 4—SELFSTUDY:** Spelling of *-ing* and *-ed* forms. (Chart 1-6)

Part A. Directions: Write the correct *-ing* and *-ed* form for each of the following verbs.

1. shout   *shouting*   *shouted*   6. refér   ....
2. slope   ....   7. return   ....
3. stop   ....   8. enjoy   ....
4. stoop   ....   9. copy   ....
5. answer   ....   10. die   ....

Part B. Directions: Write the correct *-ing* form for each of the following verbs.

11. point   ....*pointing*.............   16. regrét   ....
12. beat   ....   17. attempt   ....
13. bet   ....   18. shout   ....
14. excite   ....   19. flit   ....
15. éxit   ....   20. interest   ....

Part C. Directions: Write the correct *-ed* form for each of the following verbs.

21. bóther   ....*bothered*   26. star   ....
22. blur   ....   27. stare   ....
23. scare   ....   28. órder   ....
24. scar   ....   29. súffer   ....
25. fear   ....   30. occúr   ....

Part D. Directions: Write the correct *-ing* form for each of the following verbs.

31. dream   ....*dreaming*.............   36. deny   ....
32. file   ....   37. scrub   ....
33. fill   ....   38. drain   ....
34. fail   ....   39. fan   ....
35. annoy   ....   40. interrupt   ....

Part E. Directions: Write the correct *-ed* form for each of the following verbs.

41. comb   ....*combed*   47. whip   ....
42. wrap   ....   48. accept   ....
43. groan   ....   49. permít   ....
44. occupy   ....   50. mérit   ....
45. spray   ....   51. whísper   ....
46. wipe   ....   52. infér   ....

◇ **PRACTICE 5—SELFSTUDY:** The simple present and the present progressive.
(Charts 1-7 → 1-10)

Directions: Use either the SIMPLE PRESENT or the PRESENT PROGRESSIVE of the verbs in the list to complete the sentences. Include any words given in parentheses. Use each verb only one time.

belong	fail	scream	tape
bite	fight	✔ shine	try
bleed	mean	shrink	whisper
blow	✔ own	sleep	

1. It's a gray day today. The sun (*not*) _____ ***isn't shining*** _____.

2. The bank lent us money for a downpayment, so now we _____ ***own*** _____ the house we used to rent.

3. Shhhh! I _____ to concentrate. I can't hear myself think with all that noise going on.

4. This book is mine. That one _____ to Pierre.

5. As a rule, I _____ until 7 o'clock in the morning, and then I get up and study for my classes.

6. A: Juan! What's the matter with your hand? It _____.

   B: I just now cut it when I was using a knife. It's not serious. I'll wash it and put a bandage on it.

7. A: My marks in school are terrible this term. I _____ three of my courses.

   B: Maybe you can improve your grades before the end of the term if you start studying harder.

8. That sweater won't fit you if you wash it in hot water. Wool _____ in hot water.

9. Look at Joan. She _____ her fingernails. She must be nervous.

10. The children can't get their kite high up in the air because the wind (*not*) _____ _____ hard enough today.

11. My two children don't get along. It seems they (*always*) _____ about something. Is that typical of siblings?

12. You can hear Tommy all over the house. Why (*he*) _____? I'd better see what's wrong.

13. I want to figure out the meaning of this saying: "The pen is mightier than the sword." I know that "mightier" _____ "more powerful," but what's a "sword?"

14. Alice and John! Why (*you*) _____ to each other? If you have something important to say, say it aloud to all of us.

15. Kareem has his tape recorder on his desk. He _____ the professor's lecture today.

◇ **PRACTICE 6—SELFSTUDY: Nonprogressive and progressive verbs. (Chart 1-9)**

Directions: Use either the SIMPLE PRESENT or the PRESENT PROGRESSIVE of the verbs in parentheses.

1. Tim (*have*) _____***has***_____ a car.

2. Tim (*have*) _____***is having***_____ trouble with his car, so he has to take the bus to work these days.

3. This box (*weigh*) _____ a lot. It's too heavy for me to lift.

4. I just handed the box to the postal worker. Right now she (*weigh*) _____ it to see how much postage it (*need*) _____.

5. I (*do*) _____ this practice at the moment. It (*consist*) _____ of both nonprogressive and progressive verbs.

6. I (*think*) _____ about the verbs in this grammar practice right now. I (*think*) _____ all of my answers are correct, but I'll use the answer key to check them when I finish just to make sure.

7. Mrs. Edwards is at the market. Right now she (*look*) _____ at the apples. They (*look*) _____ fresh.

8. Right now Martha is in the science building. The chemistry experiment she's doing is dangerous, so she (*be*) _____ very careful. She (*want, not*) _____ _____ to spill any of the acid. She (*be, always*) _____ careful when she does a chemistry experiment.

◇ **PRACTICE 7—GUIDED STUDY: The simple present and the present progressive. (Charts 1-7 → 1-10)**

Directions: Use either the SIMPLE PRESENT or the PRESENT PROGRESSIVE of the verbs in parentheses.

1. Dennis (*drink, usually*) _____***usually drinks***_____ coffee with his breakfast, but this morning he (*drink*) _____***is drinking***_____ tea instead.

2. Janet (*take*) _____ the bus to work every day. She (*wait, usually*)

   _____ for the bus at the corner of 5th and Pine.

3. This morning it (*rain*) _____. I can see Janet from my window. She

   (*stand*) _____ at the corner of 5th and Pine. She (*hold*) _____

   her umbrella over her head. She (*wait*) _____ for the bus.

4. Mike (*take*) _____ three classes this semester. Every morning he (*study*)

   _____ for two hours before he goes to school. He (*have*) _____

   French class at 9 o'clock. He (*take, also*) _____ chemistry and

   accounting. He (*like*) _____ chemistry best of all, but he (*have*)

   _____ better grades in accounting and French.

5. MOTHER: Susie! Get your fingers out of the dessert! What (*do, you*) _____?

   SUSIE: I (*taste*) _____ the cake. It (*taste*) _____

      good.

   MOTHER: Well, you'll just have to wait until dinnertime. You can have some then.

6. JANICE: What (*write, you*) _____ in your notebook?

   DIANE: I (*make*) _____ notes about questions I want to ask the teacher.

   JANICE: (*Prepare, you, always*) _____ so thoroughly for

      every class?

   DIANE: I (*try, always*) _____ to.

7. BOB: Jack really makes me angry!

   SUE: Why?

   BOB: Well, for one thing, he (*interrupt, always*) _____ me. I

      can barely get a whole sentence out of my mouth.

   SUE: Is that all?

   BOB: No. He (*ask, always*) _____ me to do his homework for him. I have

      enough homework of my own without doing his homework too!

8. ALFONSO: What's that?

   NURSE: A needle. I (*prepare*) _____

      to give you a shot.

   ALFONSO: I (*need, not*) _____ a shot!

   NURSE: Just relax and breathe deeply.
      Everything will be fine.

   ALFONSO: Ouch!

◇ **PRACTICE 8—GUIDED STUDY: Irregular verbs. (Chart 1-11)**

Directions: The following is a review of the forms of irregular verbs. The simple form is given. You are to provide the SIMPLE PAST and the PAST PARTICIPLE. *Note:* Verbs followed by an asterisk (★) are defined at the end of this practice (page 12).

GROUP 1: ALL THREE FORMS ARE DIFFERENT					
Group 1A: The vowel changes from "i" to "a" to "u":					
begin	*began*	*begun*	sink★	_____	_____
drink	_____	_____	spring★	_____	_____
ring	_____	_____	stink★	_____	_____
shrink★	_____	_____	swim	_____	_____
sing	_____	_____			
Group 1B: The vowel changes in the simple past. The past participle ends in "n":					
blow	*blew*	*blown*	get	_____	_____
draw	_____	_____	forget	_____	_____
grow	_____	_____			
know	_____	_____	mistake	_____	_____
throw	_____	_____	shake	_____	_____
fly	_____	_____	take	_____	_____
break	_____	_____	bite	_____	_____
choose	_____	_____	hide	_____	_____
drive	_____	_____			
freeze	_____	_____	be	_____	_____
ride	_____	_____	eat	_____	_____
rise	_____	_____	fall	_____	_____
speak	_____	_____	forgive	_____	_____
steal	_____	_____	give	_____	_____
swear	_____	_____	lie	_____	_____
tear	_____	_____	see	_____	_____
wear	_____	_____			
weave★	_____	_____	do	_____	_____
write	_____	_____	go	_____	_____

GROUP 2: TWO FORMS ARE THE SAME: THE SIMPLE PAST AND THE PAST PARTICIPLE

Group 2A: The simple past and the past participle end in "d":

sell	*sold*	*sold*	lay		
tell			pay		
			say		
flee★					
bleed			find		
breed★			grind★		
feed			wind★		
lead					
read			have		
speed			hear		

Group 2B: The simple past and the past participle end in "t":

creep★	*crept*	*crept*	bring		
deal★			buy		
feel			catch		
keep			fight		
kneel			seek★		
leave			teach		
mean			think		
meet					
sleep			bend		
sweep			build		
weep★			lend		
			send		
lose			spend		

Group 2C: The vowel changes to form the simple past and past participle:

cling★	*clung*	*clung*	hold		
dig			shoot		
hang			sit		
spin★			stand		
stick			understand		
sting★			win		
strike★					
swing★					

Group 2D:	Only the simple past is different:	
become	_became_	_become_
come		
run		

GROUP 3: ALL THREE FORMS ARE THE SAME

bet*	_bet_	_bet_	put		
bid*			quit		
broadcast*			shed*		
burst*			shut		
cost			slit*		
cut			split*		
hit			spread*		
hurt			upset		
let					

*Definitions of some of the less frequently used irregular verbs:

bet . . . . wager; offer to pay money if one is wrong
bid . . . . offer as a price, usually at a public sale
breed . . . . bring animals together to produce young
broadcast . . . send information by radio waves; announce
burst . . . . explode, break suddenly
cling . . . . . . hold onto tightly
creep . . . . crawl close to the ground; move slowly and quietly
deal . . . . give out playing cards to each person; give attention to (deal with)
flee . . . . escape, run away
grind . . . . crush, reducing to small pieces
seek . . . . look for
shed . . . . drop off or get rid of
shrink . . . . . . become smaller
sink . . . . drop down deeper and deeper into a liquid, usually water
slit . . . . cut a long, narrow opening along a line
spin . . . . turn rapidly around a central point
split . . . . divide into two or more parts
spread . . . . . push out in all directions (e.g., butter on bread, news)
spring . . . . . . jump or rise suddenly from a still position
sting . . . . cause pain with a sharp object (e.g., pin) or small bite (e.g., by an insect)
stink . . . . have a bad or foul odor
strike . . . . hit something with force
swing . . . . . . move back and forth
weave . . . . . . form by passing pieces of material over and under each other (e.g., baskets, cloth)
weep . . . . cry heavily
wind . . . . turn around and around

◇ PRACTICE 9—SELFSTUDY: Simple past of irregular verbs. (Chart 1-11)

Directions: Complete the sentences with the SIMPLE PAST of the irregular verbs in the list. Pay special attention to spelling. Use each verb only one time.

burst	draw	slide	stick
buy	hide	slit	✔ swear
dig	shake	spread	win

1. All of the witnesses _____**swore**_____ to tell the truth in the court of law.

2. Mike was so cold that his whole body _____.

3. Using only a pen with blue ink, Sue _____ a beautiful picture of a bird.

4. When the balloon _____, everyone was startled by the sudden noise.

5. Paul _____ his money because he was afraid it would be stolen while he was away.

6. Emily accidentally _____ her finger with a needle while she was sewing.

7. Janice _____ the top of the envelope with a knife instead of ripping it open.

8. I lost control of my car and it _____ across the ice.

9. Mary _____ butter all over her piece of toast with her knife.

10. Our team finally _____ the soccer game by one goal.

11. The small animal _____ a hole in the ground to make her nest.

12. When Fred went shopping yesterday, he _____ some car wax and a garden hose.

◇ PRACTICE 10—SELFSTUDY: Simple past of irregular verbs. (Chart 1-11)

Directions: Complete the sentences with the SIMPLE PAST of the irregular verbs in the list. Pay special attention to spelling. Use each verb only one time.

bite	cling	pay	sting
blow	feel	quit	swim
catch	mean	shed	weave

1. I broke a tooth when I _____ into a piece of hard candy.

2. The little boy _____ to his mother's hand as they walked toward the school bus.

3. Maria promised to help us. I hope she _____ what she said.

4. Arthur _____ out all of the candles on his birthday cake.

5. We both _____ smoking three months ago, and we already feel much better.

6. Douglas _____ the outside of his pocket to make sure his wallet was still there.

7. A bee _____ me on the hand while I was working in the garden.

8. Matthew Webb was the first person who _____ across the English Channel.

9. Paul _____ much more for his bicycle than I spent for mine.

10. Rita threw the ball high in the air. Daniel _____ it when it came down.

11. Each year as the snake grew larger, it formed a new skin and _____ its old skin.

12. Everyone in Ali's family has a special skill. His sister _____ that beautiful carpet.

◇ **PRACTICE 11—SELFSTUDY: Simple past of irregular verbs. (Chart 1-11)**

Directions: Complete the sentences with the SIMPLE PAST of the irregular verbs in the list. Pay special attention to spelling. Each verb is used only one time.

bet	*freeze*	*sink*	*split*
choose	*lead*	*spend*	*upset*
fly	*ring*	*spin*	*weep*

1. Dr. Perez _____ ten hours in the operating room performing the delicate surgery.

2. On my first day at the university, Sally _____ the way to our classroom. I followed.

3. We made a friendly wager on the game. I _____ a dollar on my team.

4. I _____ when I heard the tragic news. Everyone else cried too.

5. As she stood, she _____ the table, and everything on top of it fell to the floor.

6. Paul wanted to make a fire, but the logs were too big. So he _____ them with his ax.

7. When I threw a piece of wood from the shore, it floated on top of the water. When I threw a rock, it _____ immediately to the bottom of the lake.

8. In 1927, Charles Lindbergh _____ from New York to Paris in 33 hours and 30 minutes. How long does it take today on an SST? (*SST = supersonic transport*)

9. When the children _____ around and around, they became dizzy.

10. The telephone _____ several times and then stopped before I could answer it.

11. William had trouble deciding which one he liked best, but he finally _____ the blue sweater.

12. When my cat heard a noise in the bushes, she _____ in her tracks (i.e., stopped moving completely) and listened intently.

◇ **PRACTICE 12—SELFSTUDY: Simple past of irregular verbs. (Chart 1-11)**

Directions: Complete the sentences with the SIMPLE PAST of the irregular verbs in the list. Pay special attention to spelling. Each verb is used only one time.

broadcast	fall	lose	steal
cost	flee	seek	strike
deal	hold	shoot	sweep

1. Ron had a small accident. He _____ to the floor when his foot got caught in the rug.

2. The car that Barb was driving went out of control and _____ a stop sign. That's the first time Barb ever hit anything with her car.

3. All of the radio and TV stations _____ the news of the peace plan yesterday.

4. When Mrs. Grant was having trouble, she _____ help from her neighbors. She asked them for their support and advice.

5. The team played badly. They _____ the game by seven points. Oh, well. You can't win 'em all.

6. When we played cards, Jane _____ five cards to each player.

7. Sue _____ the knife in her right hand and the fork in her left hand.

8. The hunter slowly raised his rifle and _____ at the deer, but he missed.

9. Jenny wanted a color TV for her apartment, but the least expensive one _____ too much for her budget, so she decided to wait until she could save enough money.

10. When I spilled rice on the floor, I got the broom and _____ it up.

11. A thief broke into Carlos' apartment and _____ his TV and his stereo set.

12. Tommy wanted to play a little joke on his friend, Marcia. He ran up to Marcia's front door, rang the doorbell, and then _____ quickly down the street. When Marcia answered the door, no one was there.

◇ **PRACTICE 13—GUIDED STUDY: Simple past of irregular verbs. (Chart 1-11)**

Directions: Write sentences in past time using the following verbs. Be sure to use the SIMPLE PAST.

Example:
    grind → *After dinner, Maria ground some coffee beans in order to make a pot of coffee.*

1. weep	5. shake	9. creep
2. spin	6. spread	10. cling
3. seek	7. flee	11. choose
4. shed	8. split	12. sink

◇ **PRACTICE 14—SELFSTUDY:** Troublesome verbs, *rise/raise, sit/set, lie/lay.*
   (Chart 1-11)

Directions: Select the correct verb in parentheses.

1. Mr. Faust (*raises, rises*) many different kinds of flowers in his garden.

2. The student (*raised, rose*) from her seat and walked to the front of the auditorium to receive her diploma.

3. Mike (*set, sat*) a large vase with roses in it on the coffee table.

4. Claudia and Paulo (*set, sat*) next to each other at the lecture last night.

5. Hiroki is a very methodical person. Every night before going to bed, he (*lays, lies*) his clothes for the next day on his chair.

6. Wouldn't you prefer to be (*lying, laying*) on the beach right now instead of sitting in this class?

7. When Alex (*lay, laid*) down to take a nap, he ended up sleeping for the whole afternoon.

8. Where are my keys? I (*lay, laid*) them here on the desk five minutes ago.

9. Dr. Singh (*hung, hanged*) his diploma from medical school on the wall in his office.

10. Canada (*lies, lays*) to the north of the United States.

11. The fulfillment of all your dreams (*lies, lays*) within you—if you just believe in yourself.

◇ **PRACTICE 15—SELFSTUDY:** The simple past and the past progressive.
   (Charts 1-12 → 1-14)

Directions: Fill in the blanks with the SIMPLE PAST or the PAST PROGRESSIVE of the verbs in parentheses. Include any other words in parentheses.

1. We (*have*) _____*had*_____ a wonderful dinner last night to celebrate our 25th wedding anniversary.

2. We (*have, at home*) _____*were at home having*_____ our anniversary dinner when my uncle called to congratulate us last night.

3. A: Why is Henry in the hospital?

   B: He (*work, in his garage*) _____ on his car when the gas tank (*explode*) _____.

   A: What (*cause*) _____ the explosion?

   B: Henry (*light*) _____ a cigarette.

4. A: I'm sorry, Officer. I (*see, not*) _____ the stop sign. I (*think*) _____ _____ about something else.

   B: What (*think, you*) _____ about? You should have been thinking about your driving.

5. Bill asked me to come over to his apartment, but I (*want, not*) _____ to leave the house because I (*wait*) _____ for a phone call.

6. Amy (*hear, not*) _____ her parents having an argument last night. She (*listen, in her room*) _____ to music.

7. When Richard (*stop*) _____ his car suddenly, the groceries (*fall*) _____ out of the bag they were in and (*spill*) _____ all over the floor of the car.

8. When the door-to-door salesperson (*come*) _____ yesterday, Claudia (*hear, not*) _____ _____ the doorbell because she (*dry, in her room*) _____ _____ her hair with her electric hair dryer.

9. When I was a child, my mother always (*serve*) _____ cookies and milk to my friends and me when we (*go*) _____ to my house after school.

10. When we (*look*) _____ in on the baby last night, he (*sleep*) _____. I think he (*dream*) _____ about something nice because he (*smile*) _____.

◇ **PRACTICE 16—GUIDED STUDY: The simple past and the past progressive.**
(Charts 1-12 → 1-14)

Directions: Fill in the blanks with the SIMPLE PAST or the PAST PROGRESSIVE of the verbs in parentheses.

1. Yesterday David (*cross*) _____**was crossing**_____ a street when a truck (*turn*) ____**turned**____ the corner very fast and almost (*hit*) ___**hit**___ him.

2. During the study period in class yesterday, it (*be*) _____ hard for me to concentrate because the student next to me (*hum*) _____.

3. Last Monday while we (*watch, in our living room*) _____ _____ an exciting game on television, the electricity (*go*) _____ out. So we (*go*) _____ outside, (*get*) _____ into the car, (*turn*) _____ on the radio, and (*listen*) _____ to the rest of the game. The next day the car battery (*be*) _____ dead.

4. The police (*outwit*) _____ a thief yesterday. They (*surround*) _____ _____ the jewelry store while he (*stuff, still inside*) _____ _____ his pockets with diamonds.

5. Yesterday we had a houseful of children for my son's sixth birthday party. In the middle of the party, the phone (*ring*) _____, so I had to leave the children alone for a moment. When I (*come*) _____ back into the room, most of the children (*still, play*) _____ _____ together nicely. But over in the corner, Bobby (*pull*) _____ _____ Annie's hair. I quickly (*run*) _____ over and (*tell*) _____ Bobby to stop.

6. TEACHER: You're late again. You were supposed to be here ten minutes ago. Where were you?

    MICHAEL: I (*look*) _____ for a place to park.

    TEACHER: (*Find, you*) _____ one?

    MICHAEL: Yes, but it's at a parking meter that has a 15-minute limit. So every 15 minutes I'll have to go out and put some more money in the meter.

    TEACHER: Maybe you should start taking the bus to school.

MICHAEL: I (*take*) _____ the bus a couple of days ago and ended up miles from school. That's why I was absent from class.

TEACHER: Oh.

◇ **PRACTICE 17—GUIDED STUDY:** The simple past and the past progressive. (Charts 1-12 → 1-14)

Directions: Complete the sentences with the SIMPLE PAST or PAST PROGRESSIVE. Use any verb that seems right to you.

1. Last Saturday while Sandy _____*was cleaning*_____ out the attic, she ___*found*___ her grandmother's wedding dress.

2. Two days ago, Peter _____ all of his money out of the bank and _____ a new car. Yesterday, while he _____ to work, he lost control of his steering and _____ another car. He wasn't hurt, but the accident completely _____ his new car.

3. Last night we suddenly _____ up from a sound sleep when we _____ a noise about 3:00 A.M. I thought it was a burglar, but it was only a cat that _____ along the window sill.

4. Two days ago I _____ my friends Ann and Andy at their apartment. They _____ the dishes when I _____. They _____ quickly, and we all _____ down and _____ about old times.

5. When I _____ to/at the airport, Lisa _____ for me in the baggage claim area. As soon as she _____ me, she _____ her arms and _____ something that I couldn't hear because the people around me _____ so much noise.

6. Mary _____ outside _____ the flowers when it _____ to rain. So, of course, she _____ off the hose and let nature take care of her garden.

◇ **PRACTICE 18—SELFSTUDY:** The present perfect. (Chart 1-15)

Directions: Complete the sentences with the PRESENT PERFECT of the appropriate verb from the list. Use each verb only one time. Include any words given in parentheses.

cost	grow	ride	swim
drive	improve	save	win
✔ eat	know	start	write
forget	make	sweep	

1. A: How about some more pie?
   B: No, but thanks. I can't swallow another bite. I (*already*) _____*have already eaten*_____ too much.

2. Our football team is having a great season. They _____ all but one of their games so far this year and will probably win the championship.

3. Jane is expecting a letter from me, but I (*not*) _____ to her yet. Maybe I'll call her instead.

4. Jack is living in Spain now. His Spanish used to be terrible, but it _____ greatly since he moved there.

5. Our baby (*not*) _____ to talk yet. My friend's baby, who is several months older, can already say a few words in English and a few words in French.

6. A: I hear your parents are coming to visit you. Is that why you're cleaning your apartment?

   B: You guessed it! I (*already*) _____ the floor, but I still need to dust the furniture. Want to help?

7. A: I understand Tom is a good friend of yours? How long (*you*) _____ him?

   B: Since we were kids.

8. Everyone makes mistakes in life. I _____ lots of mistakes in my life. The important thing is to learn from one's mistakes. Right?

9. A: I (*never*) _____ on the subway in New York City. Have you?

   B: I've never even been in New York City.

10. A: (*You, ever*) _____ in the Atlantic Ocean?

    B: No, only the Pacific—when I was in Hawaii. I even went snorkeling when I was there.

11. Little Freddie _____ a lot since I last saw him. He's going to be tall just like his father, isn't he?

12. Let's stop at the next motel. We _____ 500 miles so far today and that's enough.

13. Simon spoke Arabic when he lived in Lebanon as a young child, but now he _____ _____ almost all of his Arabic. He remembers only a few words.

14. Maintaining this old car for the past five years _____ us much less than we would have spent if we had bought a new one. We _____ a lot of money by not buying a new car, haven't we?

◇ PRACTICE 19—SELFSTUDY: Using *since* and *for.* (Chart 1-15)

Directions: Write either *since* or *for* in the blanks.

1. I haven't seen my brother _____*for*_____ 6 months. I haven't seen my sister _____*since*_____ April.

2. My wife and I have moved three times _____ we got married.

3. We've lived here _____ three years, but we're going to move again soon.

4. The Smiths have lived here _____ a long time. They've lived here _____ 1970.

5. My sister's husband got a job on a fishing boat in Alaska. He's been there _____ eleven weeks, but he should be coming home soon.

6. The International Olympic Games have continued almost without interruption _____ 1896.

7. The world has enjoyed Beethoven's music _____ nearly 200 years.

8. They have been married _____ last summer.

9. The first sections of the Great Wall of China have endured _____ a long time. They have endured _____ more than 2,200 years.

10. Overall, Ed hasn't learned very much _____ the term began. He needs to study harder.

11. The clock on the campus tower hasn't moved _____ 3:13 on March 2, 1966. Nobody has been able to fix the clock _____ that time.

12. Argentina won The World Cup in 1986 for the second time _____ the cup was first awarded in 1930. Soccer is a popular sport there.

◇ **PRACTICE 20—SELFSTUDY: The simple past and the present perfect. (Charts 1-12 and 1-15)**

Directions: Complete the sentences with the SIMPLE PAST or PRESENT PERFECT of the verb in parentheses.

1. I ___*knew*___ Tim when he was a child, but I haven't seen him for many years. I ___*have*___ ___*known*___ Larry, my best friend, for more than 20 years. (*know*)

2. The company and the union finally _____ on salary raises two days ago. Since then, they _____ on everything, and the rest of the negotiations have gone smoothly. (*agree*)

3. Mark _____ a trip to Asia last October. He _____ many trips to Asia since he started his own import–export business. (*take*)

4. Ivan _____ the violin with the London Symphony since 1985. Last year he _____ a Beethoven violin concerto at one of the concerts. (*play*)

5. When she was in college, Julia _____ home at least once each week. Now she has a job and is living in Chicago. In the last six months, she _____ only three letters to her parents. (*write*)

6. Our university _____ 121 students to study in other countries last year. In total, we _____ 864 students abroad over the last ten years. (*send*)

7. Masaru is a pilot for JAL. He _____ nearly 8 million miles during the last 22 years. Last year, he _____ 380,000 miles. (*fly*)

8. Mark missed his physics examination this morning because he _____. He _____ a lot since the beginning of the semester. He'd better buy a new alarm clock. (*oversleep*)

9. Alex is an artist. He _____ many beautiful pictures in his lifetime. Last week, he _____ a beautiful mountain scene. (*draw*)

10. Jack really needs to get in touch with you. Since this morning, he _____ here four times trying to reach you. He _____ at 9:10, 10:25, 12:15, and 1:45. (*call*)

11. Janet _____ her new blue dress only once since she bought it. She _____ it to her brother's wedding. (*wear*)

12. The night has ended and it's daylight now. The sun _____. It _____ at 6:08. (*rise*)

◇ PRACTICE 21—GUIDED STUDY: The present perfect. (Chart 1-15)

Directions: Write answers to the following questions.

1. What significant changes have taken place in your life since you were thirteen years old?
2. What are some interesting experiences you have had in your lifetime?
3. What are some things you have not yet done in your lifetime but would like to do?
4. Who are some of the people you've met and what are some of the things you have done since the beginning of the term?
5. Where are some of the places you've visited in the world or in your country, and when did you visit them?

◇ PRACTICE 22—SELFSTUDY: The present perfect and the present perfect progressive. (Charts 1-15 and 1-16)

Directions: Use either the PRESENT PERFECT or the PRESENT PERFECT PROGRESSIVE of the given verbs.

1. The children are at the park. They (*play*) ___**have been playing**___ ball for the last two hours, but they don't seem to be tired yet.

2. Jim (*play*) ___**has played**___ soccer only a couple of times, so he's not very good at it. He's much better at tennis.

3. A: Janice (*sleep*) _____ for almost eleven hours. Don't you think we should wake her up?

   B: I guess we probably should.

4. Tim (*sleep*) _____ in the downstairs bedroom only once. He usually sleeps upstairs in the bedroom he shares with his brother.

5. I (*fly, not*) _____ on a plane since last year when I was on a plane that had a fire in one of its engines. Now I'm afraid to even think about getting on an airplane.

6. A: How much longer until we arrive at the Singapore airport?

   B: Let me see. It's about 9:15. We (*fly*) _____ for almost six hours. We should be there in another couple of hours.

7. A: Is the rescue crew still looking for survivors of the plane crash?

   B: Yes, they (*search*) _____ the area for hours, but

   they haven't found anybody else. They'll keep searching until night falls.

8. Karl (*raise*) _____ three children to adulthood. Now they are educated and

   working in productive careers.

9. Sally is falling asleep at her desk. Dr. Wu (*lecture*) _____

   since ten and it's now past noon.

10. Virginia is a law student. Ever since she enrolled in law school, she (*miss, never*) _____

    _____ a day of class due to illness.

11. The club members (*make, finally*) _____ their decision. The

    election is over, and they (*choose*) _____ a new president. Ann Andrews

    is now the club leader.

12. Since I bought my son a set of drums, the noise (*drive*) _____

    my wife and me crazy, but I suppose we'll get used to it pretty soon.

◇ **PRACTICE 23—GUIDED STUDY:**   **The present perfect and the present perfect progressive.
                                      (Charts 1-15 and 1-16)**

Directions: Complete the sentences by using the PRESENT PERFECT or PRESENT PERFECT
PROGRESSIVE of the words in the list. Include any words in parentheses. Each verb is used only
one time.

cook	hear	spend	✔ understand
dig	meet	stand	wait
grow	paint	travel	want

1. They have never gotten along with each other. I (*never*) _____*have never understood*_____ why they agreed to be roommates in the first place.

2. Al just introduced me to his sister. Now I _____ everyone in his family.

3. Ms. Erickson is a sales clerk in a large department store. It's almost closing time. Her feet hurt, as they do every day, because she _____ at the sales counter since eight o'clock this morning.

4. A: I am so happy! I finally got the one thing that I (*always*) _____

   B: What's that?

5. My uncle _____ the outside of his house for three weeks and he's still not finished. He's being very careful. He wants his house to look just right.

6. The Smiths are presently in Tunisia. They _____ throughout North Africa since the middle of May. They'll return home in another month.

7. My brother's daughter _____ nearly six inches (15 cm) since I last saw her two years ago.

8. A: How much money do you have to buy clothes with?

   B: Sixty dollars.

   A: I thought you had a hundred dollars.

   B: I did. But I (*already*) _____ forty.

9. A: Isn't the rice ready to eat yet? It _____ for over an hour, hasn't it? Are you sure you know how to cook rice?

   B: Of course I do! I've watched my mother make rice for years.

10. I'm surprised that George apologized for what he said. As far as I can remember, I (*never*) _____ him say "I'm sorry" before.

11. A: We _____ to hear about the new baby since 5 A.M. Isn't there any word yet?

    B: Not yet.

12. A: I've been watching Mr. Tuttle in his front yard across the street. He _____ a long trench across the middle of his yard for the last two hours. I wonder why.

    B: He's uncovering the water pipes so he can repair a leak and put in new plumbing.

◇ PRACTICE 25—SELFSTUDY: The simple past and the past perfect. (Charts 1-12 and 1-17)

Directions: Use the PAST PERFECT or the SIMPLE PAST of the verbs in the list to complete the sentences. Include any words in parentheses. Use each verb only once.

be	✔ finish	invent	sting
burn	fly	leave	teach
design	help	spend	✔ turn on

1. By the time Jason arrived to help, we (already) _____**had already finished**_____ moving everything.

2. The apartment was hot when I got home, so I _____**turned on**_____ the air conditioner.

3. Alexander Graham Bell (already) _____ the telephone by the time I was born.

4. The farmer's barn caught fire some time during the night. By the time the firefighters arrived, the building _____ to the ground. It was a total loss.

5. The suit I bought cost more than a week's salary. Until then, I (never) _____ _____ so much on one outfit.

6. Yesterday a hornet _____ me under my arm. That really hurt! When I put on my shirt after working in the garden, I hadn't seen that there was a hornet in it.

7. We were not happy with the plans that the architect showed us for our new house. Obviously, he (never) _____ a home like the one we wanted.

8. When I saw that Mike was having trouble, I _____ him. He was very appreciative.

9. My wife and I went to Disneyland when we visited Los Angeles last spring. Prior to that time, we (never) _____ to such a big amusement park. It was a lot of fun.

10. Last year I experienced how tedious long plane trips can be. I _____ in an airplane for fairly long distances before, but never as long as when I went to Australia last June.

11. Mr. Khan has had experience teaching chemistry and physics, but he (not) _____ _____ mathematics until this year. He's found that he enjoys teaching math.

12. Promptly at five, I went to Iris' office to offer her a ride home from work, but when I got to her office, I couldn't find her. She (already) _____.

◇ PRACTICE 26—SELFSTUDY: The simple past and the past perfect. (Charts 1-12 and 1-17)

Directions: Use the SIMPLE PAST or the PAST PERFECT of the verbs in parentheses. In some cases, both forms are correct.

1. Yesterday I (go) _____**went**_____ to my daughter's dance recital. I (be, never) _____**had never been**_____ to a dance recital before. I (take, not) _____**didn't take**_____ dancing lessons when I (be) _____**was**_____ a child.

2. Last night, I (eat) _____ four servings of food at the "all-you-can-eat" special dinner at The Village Restaurant. Until that time, I (eat, never) _____ so much in one meal. I've felt miserable all day today.

3. A friend of mine, Judith Nelson, is presently working in the international sales division at an electronics firm. She's just returned from a trip to Japan. She was asked to go to Japan because she can speak Japanese. When she (*be*) _____ a business student at Boston University, she (*study*) _____ Japanese for four years. She (*have, never*) _____ the opportunity to use her Japanese until she went to Tokyo last month. While she was there, she (*speak*) _____ Japanese every day and (*enjoy*) _____ every minute of it. She's anxious to return.

4. A: I (*see*) _____ you in the school play last night. You (*do*) _____ a terrific acting job. (*Act, you, ever*) _____ in a play before this one?

   B: Yes. I (*start*) _____ acting when I was in elementary school.

5. Last year, I (*go*) _____ mountain climbing for the first time. It was exciting and terrifying at the same time. We (*move*) _____ slowly and carefully, and it (*take*) _____ three days to get to the top. Imagine our surprise when we climbed onto the summit and found another group of climbers. They (*arrive*) _____ several hours ahead of us. They were having dinner and listening to Beethoven. We (*laugh*) _____, and they (*invite*) _____ us to join them. The climb (*be*) _____, to say the least, an unforgettable experience.

6. When I first (*travel*) _____ abroad to study, I (*live, never*) _____ in a dormitory before. During the first year, I (*have*) _____ a roommate from Switzerland who (*become*) _____ a very good friend. Prior to that time, I (*live, never*) _____ with anyone from another culture.

7. In 1955, my parents (*emigrate*) _____ to the United States from Turkey. They (*travel, never*) _____ outside of Turkey and were, of course, excited by the challenge of relocating in a foreign country. Eventually, they (*settle*) _____ in California. My sister and I were born there and (*grow*) _____ up there. Last year, I (*go*) _____ to Turkey for the first time to visit my relatives. I (*want, always*) _____ to visit Turkey and learn more about my own family background. My dream was finally realized.

◇ PRACTICE 27—GUIDED STUDY: The past perfect. (Chart 1-17)

Directions: Complete the following sentences with your own words.

1. I had never...before I....
2. By the time..., he had already....
3. In 1987, I....   Prior to that time, I had....
4. When I..., someone else had already....
5. Last January, I....   Before that, I had never....
6. I had never...until I....
7. The movie had...by the time we....
8. My...after I had already....

◇ PRACTICE 28—SELFSTUDY: The present perfect progressive and the past perfect progressive. (Charts 1-16 and 1-18)

Directions: Use the PRESENT PERFECT PROGRESSIVE or the PAST PERFECT PROGRESSIVE to complete the following sentences.

1. Anna (*listen to*) _____**had been listening to**_____ loud rock music when her friends arrived but turned it off so all of them could study together. When they finished, she turned it back on, and they (*dance*) _____**have been dancing**_____ and (*sing*) _____**singing**_____ for two hours now.

2. We (*wait*) _____ for Nancy for the last two hours, but she still hasn't arrived.

3. We (*wait*) _____ for Nancy for over three hours before she finally arrived yesterday.

4. Oscar (*train*) _____ for the Olympics for the last three years and wants to make the national team next year.

5. The marathon runner (*run*) _____ for almost two hours when she collapsed to the pavement. She received immediate medical attention.

6. Tom had a hard time finding a job. He (*try*) _____ to get a new job for six months before he finally found a position at a local community college. Now he has a two-year contract. He (*teach*) _____ there for only a few weeks, but he likes his new job very much.

7. Dr. Sato (*perform*) _____ specialized surgery since she began working at the university hospital ten years ago. She still does many operations each year, but now her work is so famous that she travels all over the world lecturing to other surgeons on her technique.

8. The Acme Construction Company is having problems. They (*work*) _____ _____ on a new office building for the last seven months, and everything seems to be going wrong. Earlier, they stopped work on a smaller structure that they (*build*) _____ _____ so they could take on this job. Now both projects are in jeopardy.

◇ **PRACTICE 29—GUIDED STUDY:** Writing.

Directions: Choose one of the following topics and write a composition.

1. Write a brief history of your country.
2. Write a brief history of your family.
3. Write a brief history of your education since early childhood.

◇ **PRACTICE 30—SELFSTUDY:** *Will* vs. *be going to*. (Charts 1-19 and 1-20)

Directions: Complete the sentences with *will* or *be going to*, as appropriate. Include any words in parentheses.

1. A: Excuse me, waiter! This isn't what I ordered. I ordered a chicken sandwich.
   B: Sorry, sir. I _____*will*_____ take this back and get your sandwich.
   A: Thank you.

2. A: Would you like to join Linda and me tomorrow? We _____*are going to*_____ visit the natural history museum.
   B: Sure. I've never been there.

3. A: Where's the mustard?
   B: In the refrigerator, on the middle shelf.
   A: I've looked there.
   B: Okay. I _____ find it for you.

4. A: What's all this paint for? (*You*) _____ paint your house?
   B: No, we _____ paint my mother's house.

5. A: Paul, do you want to go with me to the shopping mall?
   B: No thanks. I have some things I have to do today. I _____ wash my car and then clean out the basement.

6. A: Someone needs to take this report to Mr. Day's office right away, but I can't leave my desk.
   B: I _____ do it.
   A: Thanks.

7. A: Let's make something easy for dinner. Got any ideas?

B: I _____ make some hamburgers. Why don't you make a salad?

A: Sounds good.

8. A: Why did you buy so many tomatoes?

B: I _____ make a lot of spaghetti sauce.

◇ PRACTICE 31—GUIDED STUDY: *Will* vs. *be going to.* (Charts 1-19 and 1-20)

Directions: Complete the sentences with *will* or the correct form of *be going to*, as appropriate. Include any words in parentheses.

1. A: Who'd like to take the VCR back to the visual aids room? Any volunteers?

B: I _____ do it.

2. A: Why did you buy so many vegetables?

B: I _____ make a large salad for the potluck dinner tonight.

3. A: Why is Carlos wearing a suit and tie? He usually wears jeans to class.

B: He _____ give a speech at the faculty lunch today.

A: Really? What (he) _____ speak about?

B: About university study in his country.

4. A: I wonder what the weather is like in Chicago now. I need to know what kind of clothes to pack for my trip there.

B: I don't know, but it just so happens that I have a cousin who lives in Chicago, and I have to call her tonight. I _____ ask her about the weather and tell you what she says.

5. A: Jack, I need a favor.

B: What can I do, Andy?

A: I _____ go to a job interview this afternoon, and I don't have a decent tie to wear.

B: I _____ lend you one of mine.

A: Thanks.

6. A: Are you going out?

B: I _____ go to the grocery store for some fruit, meat, and rice. Can you think of anything else we need?

A: How about some chocolate-covered nuts?

B: I said ''need''!

7. A: Janice, do you want to come with us?

B: I can't. I have to study.

A: Oh, c'mon! You can't study all day and all night.

B: All right, I _____ go with you. I guess I can finish this stuff tomorrow.

8. A: How do you spell "accustomed"?

   B: I'm not sure. I _____ look it up for you.

   A: Thanks.

   B: Here it is. It has two "c's" but only one "m".

◇ **PRACTICE 32—SELFSTUDY:** Expressing the future in time clauses. (Charts 1-19 → 1-21)

Directions: Find the time clause in each sentence. Put brackets ([. . . .]) around it. Notice the use of tenses.

1. We'll be here [when you arrive tomorrow.]

2. After the rain stops, I'm going to sweep the front porch.

3. I'm going to start making dinner before my wife gets home from work today.

4. As soon as the war is over, there will be great joy throughout the land.

5. I'm going to wait right here until Jessica comes.

6. Right now the tide is low, but when the tide comes in, the ship will leave the harbor.

◇ **PRACTICE 33—SELFSTUDY:** Expressing the future in time clauses. (Charts 1-19 → 1-21)

Directions: Complete the sentences with the SIMPLE PRESENT or with *will* and/or the correct form of *be going to*. (In some blanks, both *will* and *be going to* may be possible.)

1. The strike has been going on for over two months now. The strikers (*return, not*)

   _____**will not/are not going to return**_____ to work until they (*get*) ____**get**____ a raise

   and the benefits they are demanding.

2. When Rita (*get*) _____ her driver's license next week, she (*be*)

   _____ able to drive to school every day.

3. A: I see you're reading *The Silk Road*. I'd really like to read it sometime.

   B: I (*lend*) _____ it to you as soon as I (*finish*) _____ it.

   A: Really? Thanks!

4. A: Have you heard any news about Barbara since her car accident?

   B: No, I've heard nothing. As soon as I (*hear*) _____ something, I (*let*)

   _____ you know.

5. A: Mr. Jackson called. He'll be here at the garage to pick up his car in a few minutes. He (*be,

   not*) _____ very happy when he (*learn*) _____

   about the bill for repairs on his car. Do you want to talk to him when he (*come*)

   _____ in and (*ask*) _____ about his bill?

   B: Not especially, but I will.

6. After Ali (*return*) _____ to his country next month, he (*start*)

   _____ working at the Ministry of Agriculture.

7. According to the newspaper, the Department of Transportation (*build*) _____

a four-lane highway between here and San Francisco. In my opinion, it (*be*)

_____ obsolete before they (*complete*) _____

it. It seems to me that a six-lane highway is needed to handle the heavy traffic.

8. Relax. The plumber is on his way. He (*be*) _____ here before there (*be*)

_____ a flood in the kitchen. Let's just keep mopping up the water the best

we can.

◇ **PRACTICE 34—GUIDED STUDY:** Expressing the future in time clauses. (Charts 1-19 → 1-21)

Directions: Complete the sentences with your own words.

1. After I . . . tomorrow, I . . . .
2. I'm not going to . . . until you . . . .
3. Everything will . . . as soon as . . . .
4. When . . . next week, you . . . .
5. My friend is not going to . . . until . . . .
6. When I . . . next month, the weather . . . .
7. The committee chair will . . . as soon as . . . .
8. As soon as . . . , everyone will . . . .
9. Before I . . . , I will have to . . . .
10. Please . . . before I . . . .
11. I will . . . as soon as Mr. . . . .
12. When . . . tomorrow, ...

◇ **PRACTICE 35—SELFSTUDY:** Using the present progressive to express the future. (Chart 1-22)

Directions: Use the PRESENT PROGRESSIVE form of the verbs in the list to complete the sentences.

come	✔ meet	quit
drive	pick up	see
have	play	take

1. A: How about going across the street for a cup of coffee?

B: I can't. I __*am meeting*__ Jennifer at the library at 5:00.

2. A: Why are you in such a hurry?

   B: I have to be at the airport in an hour. I _____ the 4 o'clock plane to New York. I have an important meeting there tomorrow.

3. A: We got an invitation in the mail from Ron and Maureen. They _____ a dinner party next Saturday evening. Do you want to go? I'd like to.

   B: Sure. I always enjoy spending time with them. Let's call and tell them we _____ _____.

4. A: Your cough sounds terrible! You should see a doctor.

   B: I know. It just won't go away. I _____ Dr. Murray later this afternoon.

5. A: Have you seen Jackie?

   B: She just left. She's going to the mall, and then she _____ her sister at the airport. She should be back around 4:30.

6. A: Where are you and your family going for your vacation this summer?

   B: Ontario.

   A: Are you planning to fly?

   B: No, we _____ there so we can take our time and enjoy the scenery.

7. A: We're going to a soccer match next week.

   B: Who _____?

   A: A team from Brazil against a team from Argentina. It ought to be a really exciting game.

8. A: I see you're smoking. I thought you stopped last month.

   B: I did. I don't know why I started again. I _____ again tomorrow, and this time I mean it.

◇ **PRACTICE 36—GUIDED STUDY:** **Using the present progressive to express future time. (Chart 1-22)**

Directions: Change the verbs in italics to the PRESENT PROGRESSIVE for those sentences that express a planned event or definite intention. In some sentences, no change is possible.

1. A: The package has to be there tomorrow. Will it get there in time?
   B: Don't worry. I'*m going to send* it by express mail.
    → *Also possible: I'm sending it by express mail.*

2. A: What's the weather report?
   B: It *is going to rain* tomorrow morning.
    → *(Not possible: It's raining tomorrow morning.)*

3. A: Would you like to have dinner with me tonight, Pat?
   B: Thanks, but I'*m going to have* dinner with my sister and her husband.

4. A: What *are you going to do* this evening?
   B: I'*m going to study* at the library.

5. A: The phone is ringing.
   B: I'*ll get* it.

6. A: Did you know that Bill and Sue are engaged?
   B: No. That's great! When *are they going to get* married?
   A: In September.

7. A: You'*re going to laugh* when I tell you what happened to me today!
   B: Oh? What happened?

8. A: Have you lived here long?
   B: No, not long. Only about a year. But we'*re going to move* again next month. My father's company has reassigned him to Atlanta, Georgia.

9. A: I tried to register for Professor Stein's economics class, but it's full. *Is he going to teach* it again next semester?
   B: I think so.

10. A: Son, I'*m not going to send* you any more money this month. You're spending far too much. You need to learn to be more careful.
    B: But Dad . . . !
    A: Just do the best you can. Your mother and I *are going to come* to visit you next month. We can talk about it then.

◇ **PRACTICE 37—SELFSTUDY:** The future progressive. (Charts 1-21 and 1-23)

Directions: Complete the sentences with the FUTURE PROGRESSIVE or the SIMPLE PRESENT of the verbs in parentheses.

1. Just relax, Antoine. As soon as your sprained ankle (*heal*) ____*heals*____, you can play soccer again. At this time next week, you (*play*) ___*will be playing*___ soccer again.

2. I'll meet you at the airport tomorrow. After you (*clear*) _____ customs, look for me just outside the gate. I (*stand*) _____ right by the door.

3. Ingrid and Ruth won't be at this school when classes (*start*) _____ next semester. They (*attend*) _____ a new school in Taiwan.

4. Please come and visit today when you (*have*) _____ a chance. I (*shop*) _____ _____ from 1:00 to 2:30, but I'll be home after that.

5. I won't be here next week. I (*attend*) _____ a seminar in Chicago. Ms. Gomez will substitute teach for me. When I (*return*) _____, I will expect you to be ready for the midterm examination.

6. A: Do you think life will be very different 100 years from now?
   B: Of course. I can picture it in my mind. People (*live*) _____ in modular mobile residential units that they can take with them if they have to move, and they (*drive*) _____ air cars that can go at tremendous speeds.
   A: That sounds pretty farfetched to me. Why would people want to take their houses with them when they move?

◇ PRACTICE 38—SELFSTUDY: The future perfect and the future perfect progressive.
(Charts 1-24 and 1-25)

Directions: Complete the sentences with the FUTURE PERFECT or the FUTURE PERFECT PROGRESSIVE of the verbs in the list. Include any words in parentheses. Use each verb only once.

arrive	listen	✔ rise	smoke
fly	ride	save	teach

1. By the time I get up tomorrow morning, the sun (already) _____ **will already have risen/**
   _____ **will have already risen** _____ .

2. This is a long trip! By the time we get to Miami, we _____

   on this bus for over 15 hours.

3. We're going to be late meeting my brother's plane. By the time we get to the airport, it

   (already) _____ .

4. He's never going to stop talking. In 15 more minutes, we _____

   _____ to him lecture for three solid hours. I don't even know what he's saying

   anymore.

5. What? You're smoking another cigarette? At this rate, you _____

   a whole pack before lunchtime. Don't you think you should cut down a little?

6. This is the longest flight I have ever taken. By the time we get to New Zealand, we

   _____ for 13 hours. I'm going to be exhausted.

7. Douglas has been putting some money away every month to prepare for his trip to South

   America next year. By the end of this year, he _____ enough. It

   looks like he's going to make it.

8. Can you believe it? According to our grammar teacher, by the end of this semester she

   _____ more than 3,000 students from 42 different countries.

   She has been teaching for nearly 20 years—and she still loves it!

◇ PRACTICE 39—GUIDED STUDY: Past and future. (Charts 1-12 → 1-25)

Directions: The following sentences are descriptions of typical events in a day in the life of a person named Dick. The sentences are in the past, but all of these things will happen in Dick's life tomorrow. Change all of the sentences to the FUTURE.

1. When Dick got up yesterday morning, the sun was shining.

   → *When Dick gets up tomorrow morning, the sun will be shining.*

2. He shaved and showered and then made a light breakfast.

3. After he ate breakfast, he got ready to go to work.

4. By the time he got to work, he had drunk three cups of coffee.

5. Between 8:00 and 9:00, he dictated letters and planned his day.

6. By 10:00, he had finished his account books.

7. At 11:00, he was attending a staff meeting.

8. He went to lunch at noon and had a sandwich and a bowl of soup.

9. After he finished eating, he took a short walk in the park before he returned to the office.

10. He worked at his desk until he went to another meeting in the middle of the afternoon.

11. By the time he left the office, he had attended three meetings.

12. When he got home, the children were playing in the yard.

13. They had been playing since 3:00 in the afternoon.

14. As soon as he finished dinner, he took the children for a walk to a nearby playground.

15. Afterwards, the whole family sat in the living room and discussed their day.

16. They watched television for a while, and then he and his wife put the kids to bed.

17. By the time he went to bed, Dick had had a full day and was ready for sleep.

◇ **PRACTICE 40—SELFSTUDY: Review of tenses. (Chapter 1)**

Directions: Complete the sentences with the verbs in parentheses. Use any appropriate tense.

On June 20th, I returned home. I (*1. be*) _____ away from home for two years. My family (*2. meet*) _____ me at the airport with kisses and tears. They (*3. miss*) _____ me as much as I had missed them. I (*4. be*) _____ very happy to see them again. When I (*5. get*) _____ the chance, I (*6. take*) _____ a long look at them. My little brother (*7. be*) _____ no longer little. He (*8. grow*) _____ at least a foot. He (*9. be*) _____ almost as tall as my father. My little sister (*10. wear*) _____ a green dress. She (*11. change*) _____ quite a bit, too, but she (*12. be, still*) _____ mischievous and inquisitive. She (*13. ask*) _____ me a thousand questions a minute, or so it seemed. My father (*14. gain*) _____ some weight, and his hair (*15. turn*) _____ a little bit grayer, but otherwise he was just as I had remembered him. My mother (*16. look*) _____ a little older, but not much. The wrinkles on her face (*17. be*) _____ smile wrinkles.

◇ **PRACTICE 41—SELFSTUDY: Review of tenses. (Chapter 1)**

Directions: Complete the sentences with the verbs in parentheses. Use any appropriate tense.

On June 20th, I will return home. I (*1. be*) _____ away from home for two years by that time. My family (*2. meet*) _____ me at the airport with kisses and tears. They (*3. miss*) _____ me as much as I have missed them. I (*4. be*) _____ very happy to see them again. When I (*5. get*) _____ a chance, I (6. *take*) _____ a long look at them. My little brother (7. *be, no longer*)

_____ so little. He (8. *grow*) _____

at least a foot. He (9. *be*) _____ almost as tall as my father. My little sister (10. *wear,*

probably) _____ a green dress because that's her

favorite color. She (11. *change*) _____ quite a bit, too, but she

(12. *be, still*) _____ mischievous and inquisitive. She (13. *ask*) _____

me a thousand questions a minute, or so it will seem. My father (14. *gain, probably*)

_____ some weight, and his hair (15. *turn*)

_____ a little grayer, but otherwise he will be just as I remember

him. My mother (16. *look*) _____ a little older, but not much. The wrinkles on her

face (17. *be*) _____ smile wrinkles.

◇ **PRACTICE 42—GUIDED STUDY: Review of tenses. (Chapter 1)**

Directions: Complete the sentences with the verbs in parentheses. Use any appropriate tense.

I. A: Alex, (1. *you, know*) **do you know** where Ms. Rodriguez is? I (2. *look*)

_____ for her for the past hour.

B: She (3. *see*) _____ Mr. Frost at the moment about the shipment of parts

which we (4. *receive*) _____ earlier today. Some of the parts are missing.

A: Oh, oh. That (5. *sound*) _____ like trouble. Please tell Ms. Rodriguez to phone

me when she (6. *have*) _____ some free time. I (7. *work*) _____

in my office all afternoon.

II. A: What (1. *seem*) _____ to be the trouble, Ms. Jones?

B: I (2. *send*) _____ in my money for a subscription to your magazine, *Computer Data*,

two months ago, but to date I (3. *receive, not*) _____ any

issues.

A: I'm terribly sorry to hear that. Unfortunately, one of our main computers (4. *function, not*)

_____ at the moment. However, our engineers

(5. *work*) _____ very hard to fix it at the present time. We (6. *start*)

_____ your new subscription as soon as possible.

B: Thank you.

III. A: Where's Sonia? I (1. *see, not*) _____ her lately.

B: She (2. *recuperate, at home*) _____.

A: Oh? What's she recuperating from?

B: She (3. *hurt*) _____ her back while she (4. *play*) _____

volleyball last week in the game against South City College.

A: What happened? How (5. *she, hurt*) _____ her back?

B: She (*6. try*) _____ to spike a ball when she (*7. collide*) _____ with another player and (*8. fall*) _____ to the floor. She (*9. land*) _____ hard and (*10. twist*) _____ her back.

A: Gosh, that's too bad. I'm sorry to hear that. How's she doing?

B: Well, she's pretty uncomfortable. She (*11. wear*) _____ a special brace on her back for the last five days. Needless to say, she (*12. be, not*) _____ able to play volleyball since her injury. She probably (*13. be, not*) _____ able to play again for at least a month.

A: (*14. allow, her doctor*) _____ her to play in the national tournament at the end of the summer?

B: She (*15. have*) _____ the brace on her back for more than seven weeks by then, so I think he will.

A: I hope so. I know how much she likes to compete in volleyball games. And the team really needs her.

IV. A: Hi, Jim. How's it going?

B: Great.

A: (*1. You, enjoy*) _____ the rock concert last night?

B: You bet. I had a terrific time.

A: Tell me about it. I (*2. go, never*) _____ to a rock concert.

B: Well, I (*3. go, never*) _____ to a rock concert before either, so I
(*4. know, not*) _____ what to expect. I've been to symphony concerts
lots of times, but never a rock concert. Ten minutes before the concert was supposed to
start, hundreds of teenagers (*5. try, still*) _____ to find
their seats. The place was a madhouse. I thought that things would settle down once the
concert began. Boy, was I wrong! As soon as the lead singer (*6. appear*) _____
on the stage, everyone (*7. start*) _____ screaming at the top of their lungs. I
couldn't hear myself think. But after a while things calmed down. And the music was
great. At one time during the concert, while the lead singer (*8. sing*) _____
a famous hit song, many people in the audience knew the song so well that they sang along
with him. All in all, the concert (*9. be*) _____ a lot of fun, but very noisy.

A: It does sound like it was a lot of fun!

V. Mark Twain, the author of *The Adventures of Tom Sawyer*, is one of America's best-loved
storytellers. He (*1. grow up*) _____ in a small town on the Mississippi River. As a
young boy, he (*2. admire, greatly*) _____ the pilots of the
riverboats and dreamed about being a riverboat pilot on the mighty river. He pursued his
dream, and by the age of 22, he himself (*3. become*) _____ a riverboat pilot.
Later in life, when he (*4. become*) _____ a writer, many of his stories (*5. contain*)
_____ elements of his own experiences. He wrote many humorous stories
and articles about life on the Mississippi River before he (*6. die*) _____ in 1910 at the age
of 74. Sadly, Twain (*7. work*) _____ on a new story for several months
before his death, but he (*8. finish, never*) _____ it. Over the years since his
death, his boyhood home in Hannibal, Missouri, (*9. become*) _____ a favorite
place for Americans to visit to learn about Twain and life on the Mississippi at the turn of the
century.

◇ **PRACTICE 43—GUIDED STUDY: Review of tenses. (Chapter 1)**

Directions: Complete the sentences with the words in parentheses. Use any appropriate tense.

Almost every part of the world (*1. experience*) _____ an
earthquake in recent years, and almost every part of the world (*2. experience*) _____
_____ earthquakes in the years to come. Since the ancient Chinese (*3. begin*) _____
to keep records thousands of years ago, more than 13 million earthquakes (*4. occur*)
_____ worldwide by some estimates.

What (5. *cause*) _____ earthquakes? Throughout time, different cultures (6. *develop*) _____ myths to explain these violent earth movements.

According to a Japanese myth, a playful catfish lives in the mud under the earth. Whenever it feels like playing, it (7. *wave*) _____ its fat tail around in the mud. The result? Earthquakes. From India comes the story of six strong elephants who (8. *hold*) _____ up the earth on their heads. Whenever one elephant (9. *move*) _____ its head, the earth trembles.

Nowadays, although scientists (10. *know*) _____ more about the causes of earthquakes, they still can't prevent the terrible damage.

One of the strongest quakes in this century (11. *happen*) _____ in Anchorage, Alaska, on March 24, 1964, at about six o'clock in the evening. When the earthquake (12. *strike*) _____ that evening, many families (13. *sit*) _____ down to eat dinner. People in the city (14. *find, suddenly*) _____ themselves in the dark because most of the lights in the city went out when the earthquake occurred. Many people (15. *die*) _____ instantly when tall buildings (16. *collapse*) _____ and (17. *send*) _____ tons of brick and concrete crashing into the streets.

When (18. *occur, the next earthquake*) _____? No one really knows for sure.

Interestingly enough, throughout history, animals (19. *help, often*) _____ people to predict earthquakes shortly before they happen. At present, some scientists (20. *study*) _____ catfish because catfish swim excitedly just before an earthquake. According to some studies, snakes, monkeys, and rodents (21. *appear, also*)_____ _____ to be sensitive to the approach of violent movement in the earth's surface. Some animals seem to know a great deal more than humans about when an earthquake will occur.

In recent years, scientists (22. *develop*) _____ many extremely sensitive instruments. Perhaps someday the instruments (23. *give*) _____ us a sufficiently early warning so that we can be waiting calmly in a safe place when the next earthquake (24. *strike*) _____.

◇ **PRACTICE 44—SELFSTUDY: Error analysis. (Chapter 1)**

Directions: Find and correct the errors in the following sentences. All of the mistakes are in verb tense form and usage.

1. I am studying here since last January.

2. By the time I return to my country, I am away from home for more than three years.

3. As soon as I will graduate, I going to return to my hometown.

4. By the end of the 21st century, scientists will had discovered the cure for the common cold.

5. I want to get married, but I don't meet the right person yet.

6. I have been seeing that movie three times, and now I am wanting to see it again.

7. Last night, I have had dinner with two friends. I knew both of them for a long time.

8. I am not like my job at the restaurant. My brother wants me to change it. I am thinking he is right.

9. So far this week, the teachers are giving us a lot of homework every day.

10. There are fewer than 40 presidents of the United States since it became a country. George Washington had been the first president. He was become the president in 1789.

11. Mr. Sellers was just getting off the plane when he feels a sharp pain in his chest.

12. When I got home to my apartment last night, I use my key to open the door as usual. But the door didn't open. I trying my key again and again with no luck. So I am knocking on the door for my wife to let me in. Finally the door opens, but I don't saw my wife on the other side. I saw a stranger. I had been try to get into the wrong apartment! I quickly apologizing and am went to my own apartment.

◇ PRACTICE TEST A—SELFSTUDY: Verb tenses. (Chapter 1)

Directions: Choose the correct answer.
Example:

__C__ *I've been in this city for a long time. I _____ here sixteen years ago.*
       A. have come   B. was coming   C. came   D. had come

_____ 1. "Hurry up! We're waiting for you. What's taking you so long?"
         "I _____ for an important phone call. Go ahead and leave without me."
         A. wait   B. will wait   C. am waiting   D. have waited.

_____ 2. "Robert is going to be famous someday. He _____ in three movies already."
         "I'm sure he'll be a star."
         A. has been appearing   B. had appeared
         C. has appeared   D. appeared

_____ 3. "Where's Polly?"
         "She _____."
         A. is in her room studying   B. in her room is studying
         C. studies in her room   D. has in her room studied

_____ 4. "Hello? Alice? This is Jeff. How are you?"
         "Jeff? What a coincidence! I _____ about you when the phone rang."
         A. was just thinking   B. just thought
         C. have just been thinking   D. was just thought

_____ 5. "What _____ about the new simplified tax law?"
         "It's more confusing than the old one."
         A. are you thinking   B. do you think
         C. have you thought   D. have you been thinking

_____ 6. "When is Mr. Fields planning to retire?"
         "Soon, I think. He _____ here for a long time. He'll probably retire either next year or the year after that."
         A. worked   B. had been working
         C. has been working   D. is working

_____ 7. "Why did you buy all this sugar and chocolate?"
"I _____ a delicious dessert for dinner tonight."
  A. make   B. will make
  C. am going to make   D. will have made

_____ 8. "Let's go! What's taking you so long?"
"I'll be there as soon as I _____ my keys."
  A. found   B. will find   C. find   D. am finding

_____ 9. Next week when there _____ a full moon, the ocean tides will be higher.
  A. is being   B. is   C. will be   D. will have been

_____ 10. While I _____ TV last night, a mouse ran across the floor.
  A. watch   B. watched   C. was watching   D. am watching

_____ 11. Fish were among the earliest forms of life. Fish _____ on earth for ages and ages.
  A. existed   B. are existing   C. exist   D. have existed

_____ 12. The phone _____ constantly since Jack announced his candidacy for president this morning.
  A. has been ringing   B. rang
  C. had rung   D. had been ringing

_____ 13. The earth _____ on the sun for its heat and light.
  A. is depend   B. depending   C. has depend   D. depends

_____ 14. I don't feel good. I _____ home from work tomorrow.
  A. am staying   B. stay
  C. will have stayed   D. stayed

_____ 15. Today there are weather satellites that beam down information about the earth's atmosphere. In the last two decades, space exploration _____ great contributions to weather forecasting.
  A. is making   B. has made   C. made   D. makes

_____ 16. On July 20, 1969, Astronaut Neil Armstrong _____ down onto the moon, the first person ever to set foot on another celestial body.
  A. was stepping   B. stepped   C. has stepped   D. was step

_____ 17. The plane's departure was delayed because of mechanical difficulties. When the weary passengers finally boarded the aircraft, many were annoyed and irritable because they _____ in the airport for three and a half hours.
  A. are waiting   B. were waiting
  C. have been waiting   D. had been waiting

_____ 18. If coastal erosion continues to take place at the present rate, in another fifty years this beach _____ anymore.
  A. doesn't exist   B. isn't going to exist
  C. isn't existing   D. won't be existing

_____ 19. Homestead High School's football team _____ a championship until last season, when the new coach led them to take first place in their league.
  A. has never won   B. is never winning
  C. had never been winning   D. had never won

_____ 20. Many years of intensive language study are required for non-native speakers to be able to qualify as interpreters. By the end of this year, Chen _____ English for three years, but he will still need more training and experience before he masters the language.
  A. will be studying   B. has studied
  C. will have been studying   D. has been studying

Directions: Choose the correct answer.
Example:

__**C**__ *I've been in this city for a long time. I _____ here sixteen years ago.*
  A. *have come*   B. *was coming*   C. *came*   D. *had come*

_____ 1. "May I speak to Dr. Paine, please?"
"I'm sorry, he _____ a patient at the moment. Can I help you?"
  A. is seeing   B. sees
  C. has been seeing   D. was seeing

_____ 2. "When are you going to ask your boss for a raise?"
"_____ to her twice already! I don't think she wants to give me one."
  A. I've talked   B. I've been talking
  C. I was talking   D. I'd talked

_____ 3. "Do you think Harry will want something to eat after he gets here?"
"I hope not. It'll probably be after midnight, and we _____."
  A. are sleeping   B. will be sleeping
  C. have been sleeping   D. be sleeping

_____ 4. "Paul, could you please turn off the stove? The potatoes _____ for at least thirty minutes."
"I can't. I'm feeding the baby."
  A. are boiling   B. boiling
  C. have been boiling   D. were boiling

_____ 5. "Is it true that spaghetti didn't originate in Italy?"
"Yes. The Chinese _____ spaghetti dishes for a long time before Marco Polo brought it back to Italy."
  A. have been making   B. have made
  C. had been making   D. make

_____ 6. "I once saw a turtle that had wings. The turtle flew into the air to catch insects."
"Stop kidding. I _____ you!"
  A. don't believe   B. am not believing
  C. didn't believe   D. wasn't believing

_____ 7. "Could someone help me lift the lawnmower into the pickup truck?"
"I'm not busy. I _____ you."
"Thanks."
  A. help   B. will help
  C. am going to help   D. am helping

_____ 8. My family loves this house. It _____ the family home ever since my grandfather built it 60 years ago.
  A. was   B. has been   C. is   D. will be

_____ 9. Here's an interesting statistic: On a typical day, the average person _____ about 48,000 words. How many words did you speak today?
  A. spoke   B. was speaking   C. speaks   D. is speaking

_____ 10. I know you feel bad now, Tommy, but try to put it out of your mind. By the time you're an adult, you _____ all about it.
  A. forget   B. will have forgotten
  C. will be forgetting   D. forgot

_____ 11. It's against the law to kill the black rhinoceros. They _____ extinct.
  A. became   B. have become   C. become   D. are becoming

_____ 12. After ten unhappy years, Janice finally quit her job. She _____ along with her boss for a long time before she finally decided to look for a new position.
    A. hadn't been getting   B. isn't getting
    C. didn't get   D. hasn't been getting

_____ 13. The National Hurricane Center is closely watching a strong hurricane over the Atlantic Ocean. When it _____ the coast of Texas sometime tomorrow afternoon, it will bring with it great destructive force.
    A. reaches   B. will reach   C. is reaching   D. reaching

_____ 14. At one time, huge prehistoric reptiles dominated the earth. This Age of Dinosaurs _____ much longer than the present Age of Mammals has lasted to date.
    A. lasted   B. was lasting   C. has lasted   D. had lasted

_____ 15. Jim, why don't you take some time off? You _____ too hard lately. Take a short vacation.
    A. worked   B. work
    C. were working   D. have been working

_____ 16. The city is rebuilding its dilapidated waterfront, transforming it into a pleasant and fashionable outdoor mall. Next summer when the tourists arrive, they _____ 104 beautiful new shops and restaurants in the area where the old run-down waterfront properties used to stand.
    A. will found   B. will be finding
    C. will have found   D. will find

_____ 17. A minor earthquake occurred at 2:07 A.M. on January 3. Most of the people in the village _____ at the time and didn't even know it had occurred until the next morning.
    A. slept   B. had slept   C. were sleeping   D. sleep

_____ 18. The little girl started to cry. She _____ her doll, and no one was able to find it for her.
    A. has lost   B. had lost   C. was losing   D. was lost

_____ 19. According to research reports, people usually _____ in their sleep 25 to 30 times each night.
    A. turn   B. are turning   C. have turned   D. turned

_____ 20. Jane's eyes burned and her shoulders ached. She _____ at the computer for 5 straight hours. Finally, she took a break.
    A. is sitting   B. has been sitting
    C. was sitting   D. had been sitting

CHAPTER 2

Modal Auxiliaries and Similar Expressions

◇ **PRACTICE 1—SELFSTUDY:** Verb forms with modal auxiliaries. (Chart 2-1)

Directions: Choose the correct completion.

___**C**___ 1. Mary can _____ to the meeting.
       A. comes   B. to come   C. come

_____ 2. Jack should _____ harder.
       A. studies   B. to study   C. study

_____ 3. The whole team must _____ together in order to win the game.
       A. worked   B. to work   C. work

_____ 4. We ought _____ before we drop in on Peter and Marcia. They may be busy.
       A. called   B. to call   C. call

_____ 5. Paul can _____ Chinese very well because he studied it for six years.
       A. speaks   B. to speak   C. speak

_____ 6. May I _____ you?
       A. can help   B. to help   C. help

_____ 7. The construction crew might _____ the bridge in time for the holiday traffic.
       A. finished   B. to finish   C. finish

_____ 8. We had better _____ an umbrella when we go out. It looks like it's going to rain.
       A. taken   B. to take   C. take

_____ 9. I couldn't _____ that book because I didn't bring any money with me.
       A. bought   B. to buy   C. buy

_____ 10. The children should _____ "thank you" to you when you gave them their gifts.
       A. has said   B. to have said   C. have said

_____ 11. Tom could _____ us to help him move.
       A. had asked   B. to have asked   C. have asked

_____ 12. I can't find the grocery list. Gail must _____ it with her when she went out.
       A. has taken   B. to have taken   C. have taken

◇ **PRACTICE 2—SELFSTUDY:** Making polite requests. (Charts 2-2 → 2-5)

Directions: Change the following sentences into polite requests using the words in parentheses.

1. I want you to hand me that book. (*would*)

→ *Would you please hand me that book?*

2. I want you to give me some advice about buying a computer. (*could*)

3. I want to borrow your wheelbarrow. (*could*)

4. I want to have a cup of coffee. (*may*)

5. I want to use your bicycle tomorrow. (*can*)

6. I want you to read over my composition for spelling errors. (*would*)

7. I want you to open the door for me. (*would you mind*)

8. I want to leave early. (*would you mind*)

◇ **PRACTICE 3—SELFSTUDY:** Using *would you mind.* (Chart 2-4)

Directions: Using the verb in parentheses, fill in the blank either with *if I* + the PAST tense or with the *-ing* form of the verb, as appropriate.

1. A: It's hot in here. Would you mind (*open*) ___**opening**___ the window?

B: Not at all. I'd be glad to.

2. A: It's hot in here. Would you mind (*open*) ___**if I opened**___ the window?

B: Not at all. Go right ahead. I think it's hot in here, too.

3. A: Would you mind (*take*) _____ the book back to the library for me?

B: Not at all.

4. A: This story you wrote is really good. Would you mind (*show*) _____ it to my English teacher?

B: Go right ahead. That'd be fine.

5. A: I'll wash the dishes. Would you mind (*dry*) _____ them. That would help me a lot.

B: I'd be happy to.

6. A: I'm feeling kind of tired and worn out. This heavy work in the hot sun is hard on me. Would you mind (*finish*) _____ the work by yourself?

B: No problem, Grandpa. Why don't you go in and rest? I'll finish it up.

7. A: Would you mind (*use*) _____ your name as a reference on this job application?

B: Not at all. In fact, ask them to call me.

8. A: Would you mind (*wait*) _____ here for just a minute? I need to run back to the classroom. I forgot my notebook.

B: Sure. Go ahead. I'll wait right here.

9. A: You have an atlas, don't you? Would you mind (*borrow*) _____ it for a

   minute? I need to settle an argument. My friend says Timbuktu is in Asia, and I say it's in

   Australia.

   B: You're both wrong. It's in Africa. Here's the atlas. Look it up for yourself.

10. A: Since this is the first time you've owned a computer, would you mind (*give*) _____

   _____ you some advice?

   B: Not at all. I'd appreciate it.

◇ **PRACTICE 4—GUIDED STUDY: Imperatives. (Chart 2-5)**

Directions: Complete the sentences with an appropriate verb (affirmative or negative) in the following. All of the sentences are imperative. Use ***please*** if the sentence is a polite request.

1. _____***Look***_____ out! A car is coming.

2. _____***Please wait***_____ for me. I'll be ready in just a few minutes.

3. _____***Don't tell***_____ anyone my secret. Do you promise?

4. _____ me the salt and pepper.

5. _____ up! It's time to get up.

6. _____ that pot! It's hot. You'll burn yourself.

7. _____ busy! We don't have all day.

8. _____ carefully to my directions. I'll say them only once.

9. _____ pages 35 through 70 for tomorrow's class.

10. _____ it easy. There's no need to get angry.

11. _____ the window.

12. _____ ! I can hear you. You don't have to yell.

13. _____ this soup. It's delicious.

14. _____ me in front of the bookstore at three o'clock.

15. _____ ! I'm drowning.

16. _____ the light on. It's getting dark in here.

17. _____ a newspaper on your way home.

18. _____ it over for a few days. You don't have to make a decision now.

19. _____ to bring a No. 2 pencil to the test. You will need one.

20. _____ here tomorrow at nine o'clock.

◇ **PRACTICE 5—GUIDED STUDY: Making polite requests. (Charts 2-2 → 2-5)**

Directions: Complete the polite requests in the following with your own words. Try to imagine what the speaker might say in the given situation.

1. WAITER: Good evening. Are you ready to order?
   CUSTOMER: No, we're not. Could . . . ?   (→ *Could we have a few more minutes?*)
   WAITER: Certainly. And if you have any questions, I'd be happy to tell you about anything on the menu.

2. JACK: What's the trouble officer?
    OFFICER: You made an illegal U-turn.
    JACK: I did?
    OFFICER: Yes. May...?
    JACK: Certainly. It's in my wallet.
    OFFICER: Would you please remove it from your wallet?

3. SALLY: Are you driving to the meeting tonight?
    MIKE: Un-huh, I am.
    SALLY: Could...?
    MIKE: Sure. I'll pick you up at 7:00.

4. MECHANIC: What seems to be the trouble with your car?
    CUSTOMER: Something's wrong with the brakes, I think. Could...?
    MECHANIC: Sure. Just pull the car into the garage.

5. MR. PENN: Something's come up, and I can't meet with you Tuesday. Would you mind...?
    MS. GRAY: Let me check my calendar.

6. TOM: I've never been to your house. Will...?
    MARY: That won't be necessary. Al said that he would drive by and pick you up.

7. CLERK: May...?
    CUSTOMER: Yes, please. Could...?
    CLERK: Surely. What sort of slacks are you interested in?

8. ART: Are you enjoying the movie?
    IRIS: Yes, but I can't see over the man sitting in front of me. Would you mind...?
    ART: Not at all. I see two empty seats across the aisle.

9. CARLO: I have to leave now, but I'd like to continue this conversation later. Could...?
    ANNE: Of course. My phone number is 555-1716. I'll look forward to hearing from you.

10. MOTHER: The baby is trying to sleep. Would...?
    SON: But Mom! I've been waiting all evening to watch this show!
    MOTHER: Well, all right, but could...?
    SON: Okay.

◇ PRACTICE 6—GUIDED STUDY: Making polite requests. (Charts 2-4 → 2-5)

Directions: For the given situation, make up a short dialogue between two speakers. The dialogue should contain a polite request and a response to that request.

Example: You don't have enough money to go to a movie tonight. You want to borrow some from your roommate.

Possible Dialogue:
    ME: There's a movie I really want to see tonight, but I'm running a little low on money right now. Could I borrow a few dollars? I'll pay you back Friday.
MY ROOMMATE: Sure. No problem. How much do you need?

1. Your roommate is making a sandwich and it looks delicious. You'd like to have one, but you don't feel like going to the trouble of making one yourself.

2. You are in a fast-food restaurant and want to sit down to eat your lunch. The only empty seat you can see is at a table where three people are eating and are having a lively conversation.

3. You can't get your car started and you will soon be late for work. Your neighbor is backing out of his driveway and waves at you. You shout at him to stop and ask him for help.

4. Paul just arrived at work and remembered that he left the stove burner on under the coffee pot back in his apartment. His neighbor Jack has a key to the front door, and Paul knows that Jack hasn't left for work yet. Anxiously, he telephones Jack for help.

5. A man and a woman are having dinner in a restaurant and discussing business. The man gets up and bumps the table, spilling a plate of food onto the woman's lap. He needs help from the waiter standing nearby.

6. You have to write a research paper for your biology class. You have never used the library and don't know how to find the books you need. You need assistance from the librarian.

7. Carol and Larry are going out for the evening. They are in a hurry and don't have time to give the children baths and get them ready for bed. They would like the babysitter to do this.

8. You had been driving along the highway when suddenly you had a flat tire, so you pulled over to the shoulder and stopped the car. You opened the trunk and discovered that you had no jack and couldn't change the tire. A car pulled up behind you, and a man got out and asked if you needed help.

9. You need help in understanding some of the problems in your physics class, and your friend is the best student in the class. Likewise, she needs help in preparing for her German exam, and you are the best student in the German class. You need to work out an arrangement together.

◇ PRACTICE 7—SELFSTUDY: *Must (not)* and *(do not) have to.* (Charts 2-6 and 2-7)

Directions: Choose the correct completion according to the meaning.

_____ 1. Soldiers __*B*__ disobey a superior officer.
A. must/have to   B. must not   C. don't have to

_____ 2. To stay alive, people _____ breathe oxygen.
A. must/have to   B. must not   C. don't have to

_____ 3. You _____ finish your work on this project before you go on vacation. You'll probably lose your job if you don't.
A. must/have to   B. must not   C. don't have to

_____ 4. If you have an aquarium, you _____ give your tropical fish too much food or they'll die.
A. must/have to   B. must not   C. don't have to

_____ 5. To be a successful mountain climber, you _____ have a great deal of stamina.
       A. must/have to   B. must not   C. don't have to

_____ 6. Thank goodness we _____ eat fish again tonight. Dad didn't catch any today.
       A. must/have to   B. must not   C. don't have to

_____ 7. You _____ exert yourself. You're still not fully recovered from your surgery.
       A. must/have to   B. must not   C. don't have to

_____ 8. My room is a mess, but I _____ clean it before I go out tonight. I can do it in the morning.
       A. must/have to   B. must not   C. don't have to

_____ 9. We really _____ help Marge move to her new apartment over the weekend. Not only is it too difficult for one person, but she still has her arm in a sling from her shoulder sprain a week ago.
       A. must/have to   B. must not   C. don't have to

_____ 10. Bill is in the darkroom developing the negatives of the photos he took on his last trip to Peru. You _____ open the door while he's there because the light will ruin the pictures.
       A. must/have to   B. must not   C. don't have to

◇ **PRACTICE 8—SELFSTUDY:** _Have to_, verb form review. (Charts 2-6 and 2-7)

Directions: Complete the sentences with any appropriate form of **_have to_**. Include any words in parentheses.

1. A: (_You_) __**Do you have to**__ leave so early?

   B: I'm afraid I do. I have some work I __**have to**__ finish before I go to bed tonight.

2. Last night Jack __**had to**__ go to a meeting. (_You_)__**Did you have to**__ go to the meeting last night too?

3. Joan travels to the Soviet Union frequently. Luckily, she speaks Russian, so she (_not_) _____ rely on an interpreter when she's there.

4. I (_not_) _____ water the garden later today. Joe has agreed to do it for me.

5. I _____ write three term papers since the beginning of the semester.

6. Why (_Tom_) _____ leave work early yesterday?

7. I found some milk in the refrigerator, so we (_not_) _____ go to the store after all. There is plenty.

8. (_John_) _____ buy a round-trip ticket when he went to Egypt?

9. Matt is nearsighted. He _____ wear glasses ever since he was ten years old.

10. By the time this week is finished, I _____ take eight examinations in five days. The life of a student isn't easy!

11. (_You, not_) _____ return these books to the library today? Aren't they due?

12. If Jean stays in Brazil much longer, she _____ teach English part-time so that she'll have enough money to support herself. (_She_) _____ _____ apply for a special work visa? Or can she work part-time on a student visa?

13. Because it was Emily's birthday yesterday, she (*not*) _____ do any of her regular chores, and her mother let her choose anything she wanted to eat for dinner.

14. When I arrived in Rome last week, I was looking forward to practicing my Italian. I'm disappointed because I (*not*) _____ speak Italian very much at all since I got here. Everyone keeps talking to me in English.

◇ **PRACTICE 9—GUIDED STUDY:** *Should, ought to, had better.* (Chart 2-8)

Directions: Give advice to the people in the following situations. Use ***should, ought to,*** or ***had better***.

1. Ann would like to make some new friends. → *I think she should join some clubs so she can meet people who have similar interests.*
2. Ellen is having a lot of trouble in her chemistry class. She's failed the last two tests.
3. Sam and Tim, both teenagers, have messed up the house, and their parents are coming home soon.
4. Pierre is feeling really homesick these days.
5. Ron is wearing jeans. He's expected at a formal reception this evening.
6. Alice is planning to drive across country by herself this summer, but she's never changed a flat tire or even pumped her own gas.
7. Mike can't understand what's going on in his English class.
8. William's parents expect him to work in the family business, a shoe store, but he wants to be an architect.
9. Pam's younger brother, who is 18, is using illegal drugs. How can she help him?
10. Richard's roommate stays up very late studying. While his roommate is studying, he listens to loud music, and Richard can't get to sleep.
11. The Taylors' daughter is very excited about going to Denmark to live and study for four months. You've been an international student, haven't you? Could you give her some advice?
12. Virginia doesn't really have enough money saved for a vacation, but she wants to go someplace. Do you know of any inexpensive but wonderful place she could go?
13. Mr. Rice is behind schedule in the history class he's teaching. Should he skip some less important historical events, or should he give the students longer assignments?
14. Maria is expecting George to meet her when she arrives at the airport in an hour, but George's car won't start. What should George do?

◇ **PRACTICE 10—GUIDED STUDY:** *Should, ought to, had better.* (Chart 2-8)

Directions: Complete the following dialogues with your own words.

1. A: Oops! I spilled ____*coffee on my shirt.*____
   B: You'd better ____*change shirts before you go to your job interview.*____

2. A: Lately I can't seem to concentrate on anything, and I feel _____
   B: Maybe you should _____

3. A: The shoes I bought last week _____
   B: Oh? You ought to _____

4. A: Jimmy, you'd better _____ or I'm going to
   _____
   B: Okay, Mom. I'll do it right now.

5. A: I'd better _____

   B: I agree. It'll be winter soon.

6. A: I've been studying for three days straight.

   B: I know. You should _____

   A: I know, but _____

7. A: Kids, your dad and I work hard all day long. Don't you think you should _____
   _____

   B: _____

8. A: My doctor said I should _____, but I _____

   B: Well, I think you'd better _____ _____

9. A: Mary's always wanted to learn how to _____

   B: Isn't your brother _____

   You should _____

10. A: Have you _____

    B: No, not yet.

    A: You really ought to _____

11. A: You should _____ if you _____

    B: Thanks for reminding me. I'd better _____

12. A: Do you think I ought to _____ or _____

    B: I think you'd better _____. If you don't, _____
    _____

◇ **PRACTICE 11—GUIDED STUDY: The past form of *should*. (Chart 2-9)**

Directions: Discuss or write what you think the people in the following situations ***should have done***
and ***should not have done***.

1. Tom didn't study for the test. During the exam he panicked and started looking at other
   students' test papers. He didn't think the teacher saw him, but she did. She warned him once
   to stop cheating, but he continued. As a result, the teacher took Tom's test paper, told him to
   leave the room, and failed him on the exam.

   Tom should have studied for the test.
   He shouldn't have panicked during the test.
   He shouldn't have started cheating.
   He should have known the teacher would see him cheating.
   He should have stopped cheating after the first warning.
   The teacher should have ripped up Tom's paper and sent him out of the room the first time she
   *   saw him cheating.*

2. John and his wife, Julie, had good jobs as professionals in New York City. John was offered a
   high paying job in Chicago, which he immediately accepted. Julie was shocked when he came
   home that evening and told her the news. She liked her job and the people she worked with,
   and she did not want to move away and look for another job.

3. Ann agreed to meet her friend Carl at the library to help him with his chemistry homework. On the way, she stopped at a cafe where her boyfriend worked. Her boyfriend told her he could get off work early that night, so the two of them decided to go to a movie. Ann didn't cancel her plans with Carl. Carl waited for three hours at the library.

4. Joe was unemployed. He was desperately sad because he had no money to buy a birthday gift for his son, so he stole a bicycle from the park to give to his son. His son recognized the bike as one that belonged to a friend of his. The son refused to accept the stolen gift and was so angry that he would no longer speak to his father.

5. Donna had been saving her money for three years for a trip abroad. Her brother Larry had a good job but spent all of his money on expensive cars, clothes, and entertainment. Suddenly, Larry was fired from his job and had no money to support himself while he looked for another one. Donna lent him nearly all of her savings, and within three weeks he spent it all on his car, more clothes, and expensive restaurants.

6. Sarah often exaggerated and once told a co-worker that she was fluent in French even though she had studied only a little and could not really communicate in the language. A few days later, her boss asked her to come to his office to interpret a meeting with a French businessman who had just arrived from Paris to negotiate a major contract with the company. After an embarrassed silence, Sarah told her boss that she was feeling ill and had to go home immediately.

7. Jack discovered that ten dollars was missing from his wallet. He confronted his two sons, Mark and Jason, and found a ten-dollar bill in Jason's shirt pocket. Jack became angry, sent Jason to his room, and grounded him for a week. Mark simply walked outside, but felt very bad because he was the one who had taken the money. Jason had found out and was trying to return it to his father's wallet so that Mark wouldn't get in trouble.

◇ PRACTICE 12—GUIDED STUDY: *Be to.* (Chart 2-10)

Directions: Pretend you are taking a bus load of students (ages 12 to 16) on a trip to a nearby town. You are the supervisor. Make a list of rules you want the students to follow. Use ***be to*** in your list.

1. You don't want the students to bring glass containers onto the bus. → *For safety reasons, students are not to bring glass containers (e.g., pop bottles) onto the bus.*
2. You want the students to keep the bus clean.
3. You don't want the students to lean out of the windows.
4. You don't want the students to toss anything from the bus.
5. You want the students to store personal items under the seats.
6. You don't want the students to yell, scream, or shout on the bus.
7. You want the students to stay in their seats at all times while the bus is moving.
8. (*Make additional rules you want the students to follow.*)

◇ **PRACTICE 13—GUIDED STUDY:** Necessity, advisability, and expectations.
(Charts 2-6 → 2-10)

Directions: Choose one of the following topics for writing. Use the given words and expressions.

Words and expressions to use:

a. should	g. had better
b. have to	h. must
c. be supposed to	i. ought to
d. shouldn't	j. must not
e. be to	k. do not have to
f. be not supposed to	l. have got to

Topics:

1. Pretend that you are the supervisor of a roomful of young children. The children are in your care for the next six hours. What would you say to them to make sure they understand your expectations and your rules so that they will be safe and cooperative?
    a. *You should pick up your toys when you are finished playing with them.*
    b. *You have to stay in this room. Do not go outside without my permission.*
    c. *You're supposed to take a short nap at one o'clock.*
    d. *etc.*

2. Pretend that you are the supervisor of salesclerks in a large department store and that you are talking to two new employees. You want to acquaint them with their job and your expectations.

3. Pretend that you are a travel agent and you are helping two students who are traveling to your country/your hometown for a vacation. You want them to understand some customs as well as practical travel arrangements.

4. Pretend that you are instructing the babysitter who will watch your three children, all under the age of ten, while you are out for the evening. They haven't had dinner, and they don't like to go to bed when they're told to.

5. Pretend that you are teaching your younger sister how to drive a car. This is her first time behind the wheel, and she knows little about driving regulations and the operation of an automobile.

◇ **PRACTICE 14—GUIDED STUDY:** *Let's, why don't, shall I/we.* (Chart 2-11)

Directions: Complete the dialogues with your own words.

1. A: There's a new Japanese restaurant that just opened downtown. Let's _____ *eat there* _____ *tonight* _____.

    B: Great idea. I'd like some good sushi.

    A: Why don't _____ *you call and make a reservation?* _____ Make it for about 7:30.

    B: No, let's _____ *make it for 8:00.* _____ I'll be working until 7:30 tonight.

2. A: I don't feel like staying home today.

    B: Neither do I. Why don't _____

    A: Hey, that's a great idea! What time shall _____

    B: How about in an hour?

    A: Good.

3. A: We'll never find an apartment we can afford in the middle of the city. Why don't

_____

It's farther, but the apartments are probably less expensive.

   B: Okay. I'll drive. Let's _____

   A: We should look in the classified ads for that area. Why don't _____

   B: Good idea. Here, I have some change.

4. A: Shall _____ or _____ first?

   B: Let's _____ first, then we can take our time over dinner.

   A: Why don't _____

   B: Yes. Then we'll be sure _____

5. A: Let's _____ over the weekend. The fresh

   air would do us both good.

   B: I agree. Why don't _____

   A: No. Sleeping in a tent is too uncomfortable. Let's _____

   It won't be that expensive, and we'll have hot water and a TV in the room. All the

   comforts of home.

6. A: How are we ever going to prepare for tomorrow's exam? There's so much to know!

   B: Why don't _____

   A: All right. And then let's _____

   B: Okay, but after that we should _____

7. A: I think it's time for us to do something to fix up the apartment.

   B: Okay. Why don't _____

   A: That's a good idea. Shall _____

   B: Why not?

   A: Well then, why don't you _____ And I'll _____

   B: Well, I'd really like to help, but I have to get back to my work.

8. A: I'm worried about Barbara. She's never this late.

   B: Let's not _____ She's probably just held up in traffic.

   A: Why don't _____

   At least then we'll know if she left there on time.

   B: Okay, if it'll make you feel better, but why don't _____

   I'm sure she's okay.

9. A: This pasta is delicious! Why don't _____

   B: No, thank you. I'm full. Let's _____

   A: What? No dessert? This place is famous for its pies.

   B: I couldn't eat another bite, but I'll wait for you. Shall _____

   A: Yes, if you see him. He hasn't been back since he brought our dinner.

◇ **PRACTICE 15—GUIDED STUDY:** Using *could* and *should* to make suggestions. (Chart 2-12)

Directions: For each of the following situations, give three suggestions with *could*. Then give definite advice with *should*.

1. It's late at night. Tony is home by himself. He hears a window break. He thinks it's a burglar. Now what? What could or should he do now?
   → He **could** hide under his bed. He **could** run to the phone and call the police. He **could** pick up his baseball bat and go looking for the intruder.
   → He **should** leave the house and go to his neighbor's house to call the police.

2. You and your family are driving in the countryside, and you notice that you are almost out of gas. You manage to make it to a small town nearby and discover that the only gas station in town is closed. Now what? (*We could. . . . We could. . . . We could. . . . We should. . . .*)

3. Kim is an insomniac. She tosses and turns until 2 or 3 A.M. every night. She watches television, reads books, and listens to the radio, but nothing seems to help. It's beginning to affect her work, as she has to be in her office at 8:00 A.M. She's always tired. She needs some advice.

4. Al has invited his boss out for dinner at an expensive restaurant. The food was delicious, and they're having a final cup of coffee when the waiter brings the bill. Al reaches in his pocket and discovers that he's left his wallet at home. He fumbles nervously and breaks out in a cold sweat. Now what?

5. Bruce has helped his mother onto the train and escorted her to a seat. While he is saying goodbye, the train begins pulling away from the station. By the time he gets through the crowded aisles to the exit, the train is traveling fast. Now what?

◇ **PRACTICE 16—SELFSTUDY:** Degrees of certainty: *must* and *may/might/could.* (Chart 2-13)

Directions: Which of the two completions is the speaker most likely to say? Choose the best completion.

__***B***__ 1. "Do you know where Mary is?"
   "She _____ be at home. She was going either there or to Barbara's after work."
   A. must   B. could

_____ 2. "Look at all the children waiting for the bus. What time is it?"
"It _____ be after 3:00. That's when school is out."
   A. must   B. might

_____ 3. "I heard that Jose has received a scholarship and will be able to attend the university
in the fall."
"Wonderful! He _____ be very happy to have the matter finally settled."
   A. must   B. may

_____ 4. "Excuse me. Could you tell me which bus I should take to get to City Hall?"
"Bus number 63 _____ go there. But maybe you'd better ask the driver."
   A. must   B. might

_____ 5. "George says that we're going to have a very high inflation rate next year."
"He _____ be right. I think his view is as good as anybody's. I've heard strong
opinions on all sides of that issue."
   A. must   B. could

_____ 6. "Do you suppose Carl is sick?"
"He _____ be. Nothing else would have kept him from coming to this meeting."
   A. must   B. may

_____ 7. "Have you heard anything from Ed? Is he still in Africa?"
"He _____ be, or he _____ already be on his way home. I'm just not sure."
   A. must/must   B. could/could

_____ 8. "Is that a famous person over there in the middle of that crowd?"
"It _____ be. Everyone's trying to get her autograph."
   A. must   B. might

_____ 9. "Isn't Peter Reeves a banker?"
"Yes. Why don't you talk to him? He _____ be able to help you with your loan."
   A. must   B. may

_____ 10. "Isn't Margaret's daughter over sixteen?"
"She _____ be. I saw her driving a car, and you have to be at least sixteen to get a
driver's license."
   A. must   B. might

_____ 11. "Is that Bob's brother standing with him in the cafeteria line?"
"It _____ be, I suppose. It does look a little like him."
   A. must   B. could

_____ 12. "Overall, don't you think the possibility of world peace is greater now than ever
before?"
"It _____ be. I don't know. Political relationships can be fragile."
   A. must   B. may

◇ PRACTICE 17—GUIDED STUDY: Degrees of certainty: *must* and *may/might/could.*
                              (Chart 2-13)

Directions: Which of the following completions would the speaker probably say? Choose the best
completion.

_A_ 1. "Is Jeff a good student?"
"He _____. Although he seems to study very little, I heard he was offered a scholarship
for next year."
   A. must be   B. could be   C. is

_____ 2. "The speedometer on my car is broken."
"Do you think you're driving over the speed limit?"
"I don't know. I _____."
    A. must be   B. might be   C. am

_____ 3. "You've been on the go all day. Aren't you exhausted?"
"Yes, I _____. I can't remember when I've ever been this worn out."
    A. must be   B. may be   C. am

_____ 4. "Do you think the grocery store is still open?"
"It _____. I can't ever remember what their hours are."
    A. must be   B. could be   C. is

_____ 5. "Have you seen the new movie playing at the Bijou?"
"No, but it _____ sad. Many people leaving the theater seem to have been crying."
    A. must be   B. might be   C. is

_____ 6. "Where's the chicken we had left over from dinner last night?"
"I just saw it when I got some ice cubes. It _____ in the freezer."
    A. must be   B. might be   C. is

_____ 7. "It's supposed to rain tomorrow."
"I know, but the forecast _____ wrong. Weather forecasts are far from 100% accurate."
    A. must be   B. could be   C. is

_____ 8. "Do you hear that squeak? What is it?"
"I don't know. It _____ a mouse. Isn't that what a mouse sounds like?"
    A. must be   B. may be   C. is

_____ 9. "How old do you think Roger is?"
"I just looked at his driver's license. He _____ 33."
    A. must be   B. could be   C. is

_____ 10. "Is China the largest country in the world, or is it Brazil?"
"Neither. It _____ the Soviet Union. It has nearly three times the area of either China or Brazil."
    A. must be   B. might be   C. is

◇ **PRACTICE 18—GUIDED STUDY:** **Making conclusions: _must_ and _must not_.**
                                                    (Charts 2-13 → 2-15)

Directions: Make logical conclusions about the following situations. Use **_must_** or **_must not_** for your "best guess."

1. The Adams' house is dark and quiet. Their car isn't in the driveway.
   → _They must not be at home._

2. We had a test in class yesterday. Charles, who rarely studies and usually fails the tests, got a score of 95% this time.
   → _He must have studied for the test._

3. The man sitting behind us has been talking throughout the movie. He knows what's going to happen before it happens.

4. Anita is in bed. The lights are out, and I can hear her snoring.

5. Mrs. Jenkins has lost some of her hearing. Yesterday the children asked her several times for some cookies, but she didn't answer.

6. Everyone who had the fish for dinner at that restaurant last night got sick. Those who didn't eat the fish were fine.

7. Jeremy's car radio is always set on the classical music station. He also keeps a supply of classical music tapes in the car.

8. When Jeremy's wife is in the car with him, she always asks him to change the station or the tape.

9. Diane never seems to have enough money. I tried to call her last night and got a recording telling me that her phone had been disconnected.

10. I hear sirens and see two fire trucks speeding down the street.

11. Janet described the Eiffel Tower to some of her friends and showed them some photographs she had taken.

12. Four people had dinner together. Two of them ate wild mushrooms, and two of them didn't. The two who ate the mushrooms are now critically ill.

◇ **PRACTICE 19—GUIDED STUDY:** Degrees of certainty: *must*. (Charts 2-13 → 2-15)

Directions: Look around yourself right now and make some "best guesses" using *must* about objects, people, sounds, smells, etc. Write what you see or hear, and then make a logical conclusion.

Examples:

> *My roommate's books are on his bed. He must have come back from class and then left again.*
> *My wife is reading a letter and smiling. The letter must contain some good news.*
> *I hear a dog barking. It must be Rover, my neighbor's dog.*

◇ **PRACTICE 20—SELFSTUDY:** Degrees of certainty. (Charts 2-13 → 2-16)

Directions: Using the information about the given situation, complete the sentences.

1. *Situation:* Someone's knocking at the door. I wonder who it is.
   Information: **Tom** is out of town.
   Fred called a half an hour ago, and said he wanted to stop by this afternoon.
   Alice is a neighbor who sometimes drops by in the middle of the day.

   a. It must be _____*Fred*_____.

   b. It couldn't be _____*Tom*_____.

   c. I suppose it might be _____*Alice*_____.

2. *Situation:* Someone ran into the tree in front of our house. I wonder who did it.
   Information: **Sue** has a car, and she was out driving last night.
   Jane doesn't have a car, and she doesn't know how to drive.
   Don has a car, but I'm pretty sure he was at home last night.
   Ann was out driving last night, and today her car has a big dent in front.

   a. It couldn't have been _____.

   b. It must not have been _____.

   c. It could have been _____.

   d. It must have been _____.

3. *Situation:* There is a very small hole in the bread. It looks like something ate some of the bread. The bread was in a closed drawer until I opened it.
   Information: **A mouse** likes to eat bread and is small enough to crawl into a drawer.
   A cat can't open a drawer.
   A rat can sometimes get into a drawer, but I'm pretty sure we don't have rats in our house.

   a. It could have been _____.

   b. It couldn't have been _____.

   c. It must have been _____.

4. *Situation:* My friends Mark and Carol are in the next room with my neighbor. I hear someone playing a very difficult song on the piano. I wonder who it is.

   Information: **Mark** has no musical ability at all and doesn't play any instrument.

   Carol is an excellent piano player.

   I don't think **my neighbor** plays the piano, but I'm not sure.

   a. It couldn't be _____.

   b. I suppose it could be _____.

   c. It must be _____.

5. *Situation:* The meeting starts in fifteen minutes. I wonder who is coming.

   Information: I just talked to **Bob** on the phone. He's on his way.

   Sally rarely misses a meeting.

   Janet is out of town.

   Andy comes to the meetings sometimes, and sometimes he doesn't.

   a. _____ won't be at the meeting.

   b. _____ should be at the meeting.

   c. _____ will be here.

   d. _____ might come.

6. *Situation:* I heard a loud crash in the next room. I rushed in immediately and found our antique vase on the floor. It was broken. I wondered what had happened.

   Information: Five-year-old **Bobby** was playing quietly with his toy truck.

   The cat was leaping frantically from table to table.

   The window was open, and **the breeze** was blowing gently through the room.

   a. _____ couldn't have knocked it off the table.

   b. _____ could have knocked it off the table, but it isn't likely.

   c. _____ must have knocked it off the table.

Directions: Complete the sentences with the appropriate form of the words in parentheses. Add *not* if necessary for a sentence to make sense.

1. A: Why wasn't Pamela at the meeting last night?

    B: She (*may + attend*) _____ **may have been attending** _____ the lecture at Shaw Hall. I know she very much wanted to hear the speaker.

2. Alex has a test tomorrow that he needs to study for. He (*should + watch*) _____ **shouldn't** _____ _____ **be watching** _____ TV right now.

3. A: Why didn't Diane come to the phone? I know she was home when I called.

    B: I don't know. She (*might + wash*) _____ her hair when you called. Who knows?

4. There's Tom. He's standing at the bus stop. He (*must + wait*) _____ _____ for the 2 o'clock bus.

5. Kathy lost her way while driving to River City. She (*should + leave*) _____ _____ her road map at home.

6. A: Where's Ann?

    B: I don't know. She (*could + visit*) _____ her aunt and uncle right now. She usually visits them every Friday evening.

7. You (*should + watch*) _____ the movie on TV tonight. I highly recommend it. It's a classic.

8. I heard a loud crash in the next room. When I walked in, I found a brick on the floor, and the window was broken. Someone (*must + throw*) _____ the brick through the window.

9. Jack is in the employee lounge drinking coffee. He (*should + work*) _____ _____ on his report right now. It's due at 3:00 this afternoon. He (*should + waste*) _____ his time in the employee lounge.

10. A: Where's Jane? I haven't seen her for weeks.

    B: I'm not sure. She (*might + travel*) _____ in Europe. I think I heard her mention something about spending a few weeks in Europe this spring.

11. My tweed jacket isn't in my closet. I think my roommate (*might + borrow*) _____ _____ it. He often borrows my things without asking me.

12. Do you hear that guitar music? Carla (*must + play*) _____ her guitar.

13. A: When I arrived, Dennis looked surprised.

    B: He (*must + expect*) _____ you.

14. A: I couldn't reach Peter on the phone. I wonder where he was.

B: He told me he was going to wash his car and then go to dinner at the Bistro Cafe. He (*might + wash*) _____ his car when you called, or he (*may + leave + already*) _____ for the restaurant by then.

◇ **PRACTICE 22—GUIDED STUDY: Forms of modals. (Charts 2-13 → 2-17)**

Directions: Complete the sentences with the appropriate form of the words in parentheses. Add *not* if necessary for a sentence to make sense.

1. A: I need to see Tom. Where is he?

   B: In his room. Knock on his door softly. He (*might + take*) _____ a nap.

2. When I walked into the room, the TV was on but the room was empty. Dad (*must + watch*) _____ TV a short while before I came into the room. He (*must + forget*) _____ to turn the TV off before he left the room.

3. Michael wanted to go to the opera, but he put off buying a ticket and now they're all sold. He (*should + buy*) _____ his ticket weeks ago. He (*should + wait*) _____ until now to try to get a ticket.

4. Bob was stopped by a police officer last night. He (*must + drive*) _____ _____ too fast when she clocked him on her radar. She gave him a speeding ticket.

5. The staff (*must + plan*) _____ very well for the luncheon. There are still about ten people waiting to eat, and there's not enough food left.

6. A: Why didn't Jack answer the teacher when she asked him a question?

   B: He was too busy staring out the window. He (*must + daydream*) _____ _____. He (*should + pay*) _____ attention. He (*should + stare*) _____ out the window during class yesterday.

7. A: Where's your bicycle?

   B: I don't know. One of my friends (*may + borrow*) _____ it. Gee, I hope it wasn't stolen. Maybe Sally borrowed it.

   A: Sally? She (*could + borrow*) _____ it. She has a broken leg. Why would she want to borrow your bicycle?

8. George didn't do very well on the test because he didn't understand what he was supposed to do. He (*must + listen*) _____ very carefully when the teacher gave the directions.

9. A: Joan was really upset when she found out that someone had told Alan about the surprise birthday party she gave him last night. She thinks Joe told him.

   B: Joe (*could + tell*) _____ him about it. He was out of town until just before the party. He barely got there in time from the airport.

10. A: Art has two full-time jobs this summer to make some money for school in the fall. He (*must + have*) _____ very much time to rest and do other things.

    B: That might explain why no one answered the door when I stopped by his house a little while ago. He (*must + sleep*) _____.

11. A: Kathy just bought a new car, and now she's looking for a new apartment.

    B: She (*must + make*) _____ a lot of money in her new job.

12. A: Where's that cold air coming from?

    B: Someone (*must + leave*) _____ the door open.

13. A: The roads are treacherous this morning. In places, they're nothing but a sheet of ice. I (*should + take*) _____ the bus to work this morning instead of driving my car. I thought I'd never make it!

    B: I know. It's terrible outside. Jake still hasn't arrived. He (*must + walk*) _____ _____ to work right now. He doesn't live too far away, and I know he hates to drive on icy roads.

    A: He (*might + decide*) _____ not to come in at all. He (*could + work*) _____ on his report at home this morning. I'll check with his secretary. He (*may + call*) _____ her by now.

◇ **PRACTICE 23—GUIDED STUDY: Degrees of certainty. (Charts 2-13 → 2-17)**

Directions: Go to a public place, a place where there are people whom you do not know (a cafeteria, store, street corner, park, zoo, lobby, etc.). Choose three of these people to write a composition about. Using a paragraph for each person, describe his/her appearance briefly and then make "guesses" about this person: age, occupation, personality, activities, etc.

Example: I'm in a hotel lobby. I'm looking at a man who is wearing a blue pin-striped suit and carrying a briefcase. He is talking to someone at the registration desk, so he must be registering to stay in the hotel. He couldn't be checking out, because people have to check out at a different desk. He might be simply asking a question, but I doubt it. Judging from his clothes, I'd say he's probably a businessman. But he could be something else. He might be a doctor, or a funeral director, or a professor. He has salt-and-pepper hair and not too many wrinkles. He must be about 50 or 55. He doesn't have any luggage with him. The porter must have taken his luggage. The hotel clerk just handed the man a key. Aha! I was right. He is registering to stay at the hotel.

◇ **PRACTICE 24—SELFSTUDY:** *Used to* and *be used to*. (Chart 2-18)

Directions: Complete the sentences with *used to* or *be used to* and the correct form of the verbs in parentheses.

1. I (*live*) ____**used to live**____ in Jakarta, but now I live in Paris.

2. I (*live*) ____**am used to living**____ in Jakarta. I've lived here all my life.

3. Jane (*work*) _____ for the telephone company, but now she has a job at the post office.

4. This work doesn't bother me. I (*work*) _____ hard. I've worked hard all my life.

5. Dick (*have*) _____ a mustache, but he doesn't anymore. He shaved it off because his wife didn't like it. I (*see, not*) _____ him without his mustache. He still looks strange to me.

6. When I was a child, I (*think*) _____ anyone over 40 was old. Of course, now that I'm middle-aged, I agree with those who say, "Life begins at 40."

7. It (*take*) _____ weeks or months to cross the Atlantic Ocean from Europe to the Americas, but now it takes only a matter of hours.

8. Even though Jason is only 12, he (*fly*) _____ on airplanes. His father is a pilot and has taken Jason with him in a plane many times.

9. When I was growing up, my mother often sent me to the neighborhood store to get something for her. And each time I went there, Mr. Ditmar, the owner, (*give*) _____ me a piece of candy.

10. Michael (*take*) _____ care of himself. He left home when he was 15 and has been on his own ever since.

◇ **PRACTICE 25—GUIDED STUDY:** *Used to* and *be used to*. (Chart 2-18)

Directions: Complete the sentences with *used to* or *be used to* and the correct form of the verbs in parentheses.

1. I (*play*) _____ the piano quite well when I was younger. Now, I'm not sure I could play anything if I tried. It's been too many years.

2. I (*drive*) _____ on busy highways in big cities. I've been doing it ever since I learned how to drive.

3. The early pioneers in the United States (*rely*) _____ heavily on hunting and fishing for their food.

4. My feet are killing me! I (*stand, not*) _____ for long periods of time. Let's find a place to sit down.

5. I (*come*) _____ to work ten minutes early. I hoped that my boss would notice and give me a raise in pay. It didn't work, so I stopped coming early.

6. People (*think*) _____ the world was flat.

7. I never (*like*) _____ opera, but after seeing *Madame Butterfly* last night, I've changed my mind. I thoroughly enjoyed it.

8. I (*take*) _____ a shower every morning before I go to work. I rarely miss a morning.

9. Marge and Fred (*commute*) _____ into the city to work every day. They've been doing it for two years and don't seem to mind the one-hour drive each way.

10. I (*travel*) _____ nearly two weeks out of every month, but now I do most of my work at the home office and seldom have to go out of town.

◇ **PRACTICE 26—SELFSTUDY:** Repeated action: *would.* (Chart 2-19)

Directions: Complete the sentences using *would* and the verbs in the list. Use each verb only one time. Include any words in parentheses.

bring	drive	listen	throw
call	fall	take	wipe
✔ come	knock	tell	✔ yell

1. My father never liked to talk on the phone. Whenever it rang, he (*always*) __**would**__ ___**always yell**___, "I'm not here!" Usually, he was only joking and __**would**__ ___**come**___ to the phone when it was for him.

2. I'll always remember Miss Emerson, my fifth grade teacher. Sometimes a student _____ asleep in her class. Whenever that happened, Miss Emerson _____ a piece of chalk at the student!

3. Until we finally had a long talk about it, my Aunt Pat (*never*) _____ _____ before coming over. In fact, she (*not even*) _____ _____ on the door. She would just walk right in and catch us all by surprise.

4. I have fond childhood memories of my Uncle Joe. Whenever he came to visit, he (*always*) _____ me a little present.

5. When our kids were still living at home, I liked to go out to eat with my family. On every pay day, I _____ the family to some restaurant for dinner.

6. People acquire strange habits. For example, my Uncle Oscar, who lived with us when I was a child, (*always*) _____ his plate with his napkin whenever he sat down to a meal.

7. I'll never forget evenings spent with my grandparents when I was a child. My grandmother _____ stories of her childhood seventy years ago, and we _____ _____ intently and question her for every detail.

8. When I was a salesman, it seemed to me that I was in my car most of the time. I _____ _____ to work to pick up my schedule, and then go from place to place all day, calling on small businesses.

◇ **PRACTICE 27—GUIDED STUDY:** *Would rather.* (Chart 2-20)

Directions: Complete the sentences with your own words.

1. I went to an opera last night. I would rather _____*have gone to a movie*_____.

2. I wrecked my father's car. I'd rather not ____*face him*____, but I have to.

3. Bobby said he'd rather _____

   for his birthday than _____.

4. Sometimes teenagers would rather _____.

5. I studied French when I was in high school only because my parents wanted me to. I would

   rather _____.

6. I know you want to know, but I'd rather not _____.

   I told Marge that I'd keep it a secret.

7. I would rather _____ right after dinner at the restaurant last night,

   but my friends insisted on going back to John's apartment to listen to some music and talk.

   Tonight, I'd really rather not _____. I want to get a good night's sleep

   for the first time all week.

8. I'd rather _____ than _____

   when we go camping.

9. A: Would you rather _____ or _____

      tonight?

   B: Actually, I'd rather _____. My favorite show is on tonight.

10. I would rather _____ last night than

    _____, but _____.

◇ **PRACTICE 28—SELFSTUDY:** Past ability: *could.* (Chart 2-22)

Directions: Complete the sentences with *could* and the verb in parentheses *if possible*. If the use of
could is not possible, provide any other appropriate completion.

1. When I was younger, I ____*could stay*____ up late without getting sleepy, but now I always go to
   bed early. (*stay*)

2. Last night we ____*went*____ to a restaurant. The food was delicious. (*go*)

3. The teacher gave the students plenty of time for the test yesterday. All of them _____

   _____ it before the time was up. (*complete*)

4. I was tired, but I _____ my work before I went to bed last night. (*finish*)

5. Last night I _____ TV for a couple of hours. Then I studied. (*watch*)

6. I like to ride my bicycle. I _____ it to work when we lived on First Street,

   but now I can't. Now I have to drive because we live too far away. (*ride*)

7. Susan _____ her bicycle to work yesterday instead of walking. (*ride*)

8. The picnic yesterday was a lot of fun. All of us _____ it a lot. (*enjoy*)

9. After years of devoted work, Mr. Bailey finally _____ a raise in salary last April. (*get*)

10. I (*swim*) _____ long distances when I was a teenager.

11. I had to put together my daughter's tricycle. It came from the factory unassembled. It was a struggle and took me a long time, but in the end I _____ it together. (*get*)

◇ **PRACTICE 29—GUIDED STUDY: Modals: dialogues. (Chapter 2)**

Directions: Complete the following dialogues with your own words. Add necessary punctuation.

1. A: Why don't we _____ *go to Luigi's Restaurant for lunch?* _____

   B: Thanks, but I can't. I have to _____ *stay and finish this report over lunchtime.* _____

   A: That's too bad.

   B: I should have _____ *come to work early this morning to finish it,* _____ but _____ *I couldn't. I had to drop my daughter off at school and meet with her teacher.* _____

2. A: I _____

   B: You shouldn't have done that!

   A: I know, but _____

   B: Well, why don't _____

3. A: _____

   B: No, he had to _____

   A: Why?

   B: _____

4. A: Did you hear the news? We don't have to _____

   B: Why not?

   A: _____

   B: Well, then, why don't _____

5. A: Whose _____

   B: I don't know. It _____ or it _____

   A: Can _____

   B: I'll try.

6. A: _____

   B: Not at all. I'd be happy to.

   A: Thank you. Maybe sometime _____

7. A: _____

   B: I would have liked to, but I _____

8. A: You must not _____

   B: Why not?

   A: _____

9. A: _____

   B: Well, you'd better _____ or _____

   A: I know, but _____

10. A: _____

    B: _____ but I'd rather not have gone.

       I'd rather _____

11. A: May I _____

    B: Please do. I _____

    A: We could, but it's going to _____

12. A: _____

    B: That can't be true! She couldn't have _____

    A: Oh? Why not? Why do you say that?

    B: Because _____

Directions: Work in pairs. Using the given situations, create dialogues of 10 to 20 sentences or more. Then present your dialogues to the rest of the class. For each situation, the beginning of the dialogue is given. Try to include appropriate modals in your conversation.

1. *Situation:*   *The two of you are roommates or a married couple. It is late at night. All of the lights are turned off. You hear a strange noise. You try to figure out what it might or must be, what you should or should not do, etc.*

   Dialogue: A: Psst. Are you awake?
   B: Yes. What's the matter?
   A: Do you hear that noise?
   B: Yes, what do you suppose it is?
   A: I don't know. It . . . .
   B: . . . .

2. *Situation:*   *Your teacher is always on time, but today it is fifteen minutes past the time class begins and he/she still isn't here. You try to figure out why he/she isn't here yet and what you should do.*

   Dialogue: A: Mr./Mrs./Ms./Miss/Dr./Professor _____ should have been here fifteen minutes ago. I wonder where s/he is. Why do you suppose s/he hasn't arrived yet?
   B: Well, ...

3. *Situation:*   *The two of you are planning to go on a picnic. You are almost ready to leave when you hear a loud noise. It sounds like thunder. You are supposed to meet Nancy and Paul at the park for your picnic.*

   Dialogue: A: Is the picnic basket all packed?
   B: Yes. Everything is ready to go.
   A: Good. Let's get going.
   B: Wait. Did you hear that?
   A: . . . .

4. *Situation:*   *It is late at night. The weather is very bad. Your eighteen-year-old son, who had gone to a party with some of his friends, was supposed to be home an hour ago. (The two of you are either a married couple or a parent and his/her friend.) You are getting worried. You are trying to figure out where he might be, what might or must have happened, and what you should do, if anything.*

   Dialogue: A: It's already _____ o'clock and _____ isn't home yet. I'm getting worried.
   B: So am I. Where do you suppose he is?
   A: . . . .

◇ PRACTICE 31—GUIDED STUDY: Discussion using modals. (Chapter 2)

Directions: In small discussion groups, debate one, some, or all of the following statements. At the end of the discussion time, choose one member of your group to summarize for the rest of the class the principal ideas during the discussion.

Do you agree with the following statements? Why or why not?

1. Violence on television influences people to act violently.
2. Cigarette smoking should be banned from all public places.
3. No family should have more than two children.
4. Books, films, and news should be censored by government agencies.
5. People shouldn't marry until they are at least twenty-five years old.
6. All nuclear weapons in the possession of any nation should be eliminated.
7. The United Nations is a productive and essential organization.
8. All people of the world should speak the same language.

◇ PRACTICE 32—GUIDED STUDY: General review of verb forms. (Chapters 1 and 2)

Directions: Complete the sentences with the words in parentheses. Use any appropriate tense or modal.

A: Yesterday I (*1. have*) _____ a bad day.

B: Oh? What (*2. happen*) _____?

A: I was supposed to be at a job interview at ten, but I didn't make it because while I (*3. drive*) _____ down the freeway, my car (*4. break*) _____ down.

B: What (*5. do, you*) _____?

A: I (*6. pull*) _____ over to the side of the road, (*7. get*) _____ out, and (*8. start*) _____ walking.

B: You (*9. do, not*) _____ that. Walking alone along a highway can be dangerous. You (*10. stay*) _____ in your car until help came.

A: You (*11. be, probably*) _____ right, but I (*12. start*) _____ walking down the highway. After I (*13. walk*) _____ for about 20 minutes, I got to an exit ramp. Near the bottom of the exit ramp, there was a restaurant with a public phone. I (*14. go*) _____ to the phone and (*15. discover*) _____ that I had left my purse in the car, so I (*16. have, not*) _____ any money to make a phone call.

B: What did you do then?

A: What do you think I should have done?

B: I don't know. I (*17. think*) _____ of several things. You (*18. go*) _____ back to your car for your purse. You (*19. try*) _____ to borrow some change from a customer in the restaurant. You

(*20. ask*) _____ to use the private phone in the restaurant. What did you actually do?

A: I (*21. ask*) _____ to speak with the manager of the restaurant.

B: That was a good idea. That's exactly what you should have done. What did the manager do?

A: When I (*22. tell*) _____ her my tale of woe, she (*23. be*) _____ very sympathetic. She (*24. allow*) _____ me to use her private phone to call my friend Bill, who (*25. drive*) _____ to the restaurant.

B: You (*26. feel*) _____ really glad when you saw Bill.

A: I did. First he (*27. take*) _____ me to my job interview, and then he (*28. take*) _____ care of the car.

B: Good friends are important, aren't they?

A: They sure are.

B: Did you get the job you interviewed for?

A: I don't know yet. I (*29. get*) _____ it, or I might not. I just don't know. I (*30. know*) _____ in a couple more days.

B: Good luck!

A: Thanks! I need it! Well, I (*31. leave*) _____ now. I (*32. be*) _____ _____ at a meeting in 45 minutes. (*33. I, use*) _____ _____ your phone? I (*34. need*) _____ to call a taxi. My car is still in the garage, and I (*35. have, not*) _____ time to wait for a bus.

B: I (*36. take*) _____ you to your meeting.

A: Really? Thanks. As you said, good friends are important!

◇ PRACTICE 33—GUIDED STUDY: Review of modals. (Chapter 2)

Directions: Choose three of the following topics. Write a short paragraph on each.

1. Write about when, where, and why you should (or should not) have done something in your life.
2. Write about a time in your life when you did something you did not want to do. Why did you do it? What could you have done differently? What should you have done? What would you rather have done?
3. Look at your future. What will, might, should it be like? Write about what you should, must, can do now in order to make your life what you want it to be.
4. Write about one embarrassing incident in your life. What could, should, might you have done to avoid it?
5. Look at the world situation in relationships between nations. What could, should (or should not), must (or must not) be done to improve understanding?
6. Choose one of the environmental problems people are considering today. What could, should, may, must, might be done to solve this problem?

Directions: Choose the correct completion.

Example:

__C__   Peter _____ rather sleep on a mattress than on the floor.
       A. shall   B. could   C. would   D. must

_____ 1. Al painted his bedroom black. It looks dark and dreary. He _____ a different color.
       A. had to choose   B. should have chosen
       C. must have chosen   D. could have been choosing

X _____ 2. Tom is sitting at his desk. He's reading his chemistry text because he has a test tomorrow. He _____.
       A. could study   B. should be studying
       C. will study   D. must be studying

_____ 3. When Mr. Lee was younger, he _____ work in the garden for hours, but now he has to take frequent rests because he has emphysema.
       A. has got to   B. can
       C. should be able to   D. could

_____ 4. Whenever my parents went out in the evening, I _____ the job of taking care of my younger brother.
       A. would get   B. should get
       C. must have gotten   D. had better get

_____ 5. Yesterday I _____ to a furniture store. I bought a new lamp there.
       A. could go   B. went
       C. could have gone   D. ought to have gone

_____ 6. Jimmy and Maria were mischievous children. They _____ tricks on their teachers, which always got them into a lot of trouble.
       A. could play   B. used to play
       C. could have played   D. may have played

_____ 7. Robert has a new car. He _____ it for a very good price. He paid 30 percent less than the regular retail cost.
       A. could buy   B. had to buy
       C. was supposed to buy   D. was able to buy

_____ 8. "Did you enjoy the picnic?"
      "It was okay, but I'd rather _____ to a movie."
       A. go   B. be going   C. have gone   D. went

_____ 9. "Why are you so sure that Ann didn't commit the crime she's been accused of committing?"
      "She _____ that crime because I was with her, and we were out of town on that day."
       A. may not have committed   B. wasn't supposed to commit
       C. committed   D. couldn't have committed.

_____ 10. "Since we have to be there in a hurry, we _____ take a taxi."
      "I agree."
       A. had better   B. may
       C. have been used to   D. are able to

_____ 11. "It _____ rain this evening. Why don't you take an umbrella?"
      "That's a good idea. May I borrow yours?"
       A. had better   B. could be   C. must   D. might

_____ 12. "_____ you hand me that pair of scissors, please?"
"Certainly."
      A. May   B. Shall   C. Will   D. Should

_____ 13. "Larry drove all night to get here for his sister's wedding. He _____ exhausted by the time he arrived."
"He was."
      A. ought to be   B. could be
      C. must have been   D. will have been

_____ 14. "What are you doing here now? You _____ be here for another three hours."
"I know. We got an early start and it took less time than we expected. I hope you don't mind."
      A. couldn't   B. might not
      C. had better not   D. aren't supposed to

_____ 15. "_____ taking me downtown on your way to work this morning?"
"Not at all."
      A. Can you   B. Why don't you
      C. Would you mind   D. Could you please

_____ 16. "I locked myself out of my apartment. I didn't know what to do."
"You _____ your roommate."
      A. could have called   B. may have called
      C. would have called   D. must have called

_____ 17. "You haven't eaten anything since yesterday afternoon. You _____ be really hungry!"
"I am."
      A. might   B. will   C. can   D. must

_____ 18. "How long have you been married?"
"We _____ have been married for twenty-three years on our next anniversary."
      A. must   B. should   C. will   D. could

_____ 19. "I _____ there at 6 P.M. for the meeting, but my car won't start. Could you please give me a lift in your car?"
"Sure. Are you ready to go now?"
      A. will be   B. may be
      C. supposed to be   D. have got to be

_____ 20. "I left a cookie on the table, but now it's gone. What happened to it?"
"I don't know. One of the children _____ it."
      A. may have eaten   B. could eat
      C. had to eat   D. should have eaten

◇ PRACTICE TEST B—GUIDED STUDY: Modals and similar expressions. (Chapter 2)

Directions: Choose the correct completion.

Example:

C   *Peter _____ rather sleep on a mattress than on the floor.*
      A. shall   *B. could*   *C. would*   *D. must*

_____ 1. "My boss is always looking over my shoulder whenever I do anything."
"That _____ bother you."
"But it does."
      A. shouldn't   B. might not   C. may not   D. won't

_____ 2. "This movie is boring and too violent."
"I agree. _____ leave?"
   A. Will we   B. Why don't we   C. Must we   D. Would we

_____ 3. "Chris, you _____ the fish in the refrigerator before it spoils."
"You're right. I didn't know it was still in the shopping bag."
   A. had better put   B. had to put
   C. would rather put   D. may put

_____ 4. "What does Mr. Griffin do for a living?"
"Nothing. He's very rich. He _____ work for a living."
   A. must not   B. shouldn't
   C. doesn't have to   D. hadn't better

_____ 5. "Why are you so late?"
"I _____ my aunt to the airport. The traffic was terrible!"
   A. could take   B. must have taken
   C. should take   D. had to take

_____ 6. "I heard that Laura was offered a job at a top computer firm in Chicago."
"Oh? That's wonderful! She _____ very pleased."
   A. is supposed to be   B. might be
   C. must be   D. is

_____ 7. "The hot weather doesn't seem to bother you."
"When I had my farm, I _____ work in the hot fields for hours."
   A. used to   B. ought to   C. must   D. had better

_____ 8. "They towed my car away from the executive parking lot yesterday."
"You _____ have parked there."
   A. may not   B. should not   C. must not   D. might not

_____ 9. "Are you going to have a big birthday party for your father?"
"Not this year, but next year. He _____ 50 years old then."
   A. should be   B. must be   C. will be   D. has to be

_____ 10. "I need some help with this table. _____ you lift the other end, please?"
"Sure, just a second."
   A. May   B. Should   C. Could   D. Shall

_____ 11. "How did you get my telephone number? It's not listed in the phone book, so you _____ have found it in the directory."
"I got it from your mother."
   A. may not   B. won't   C. might not   D. couldn't

_____ 12. "Is that volcano dormant or active?"
"Active. According to the experts, it _____ erupt again in the very near future."
   A. would   B. may be   C. could   D. had better

_____ 13. "Last year I _____ this fine print in these contracts, but now I can't."
"You'd better go to the eye doctor."
   A. could read   B. must have read
   C. should have read   D. had to read

_____ 14. "Is littering against the law?"
"Yes. There's a law that says that you _____ throw trash on the streets."
   A. don't have to   B. must not   C. couldn't   D. might not

_____ 15. "Do you want to go to the seashore for vacation?"
"I think I'd rather _____ to the mountains."
   A. to go   B. going   C. go   D. have gone

_____ 16. "Barbara just told me that she can't go to the meeting tonight."
   "She _____ go! We need her there for the financial report."
   A. has got to   B. has gotten to   C. have to   D. must be

_____ 17. "_____ letting me use your bicycle for a little while?"
   "Not at all."
   A. Please to   B. Would you mind
   C. Will you   D. Could you please

_____ 18. "We _____ be here. That sign says 'No Trespassing.'"
   "It's too late now. We're already here."
   A. couldn't   B. don't have to
   C. might not   D. aren't supposed to

_____ 19. "Harry's new jacket doesn't seem to fit him very well."
   "He _____ it on before he bought it."
   A. must have tried   B. was able to try
   C. should have tried   D. may have tried

_____ 20. "Do you like to play tennis?"
   "Yes. When I worked at the embassy, I _____ meet a friend at 5 every afternoon for a game."
   A. would   B. should   C. had better   D. would rather

CHAPTER 3
The Passive

◇ **PRACTICE 1—SELFSTUDY:** Forming the passive. (Chart 3-1)

Directions: Change the active to the passive by writing the correct form of *be* in the blanks. Use the same tense for *be* in the passive sentence that is used in the active sentence.

Example:
Mrs. Bell answered my question. . . . . *My question* ___**was**___ answered by Mrs. Bell.

1. *simple present*:
   Authors write books. Books _____ **written** by authors.
2. *present progressive*:
   Mr. Brown is writing that book. . . . . That book _____ **written** by Mr. Brown.
3. *present perfect*:
   Ms. Lee has written the report. . . . . The report _____ **written** by Ms. Lee.
4. *simple past*:
   Bob wrote that letter. . . . . That letter _____ **written** by Bob.
5. *past progressive*:
   A student was writing the report. . . . . The report _____ **written** by a student.
6. *past perfect*:
   Lucy had written a memo. . . . . A memo _____ **written** by Lucy.
7. *simple future*:
   Your teacher will write a report. . . . . A report _____ **written** by your teacher.
8. *be going to*:
   Tom is going to write the letter. . . . . The letter _____ **written** by Tom.
9. *future perfect*:
   Alice will have written the report. . . . . The report _____ **written** by Alice.

10. The judges have made a decision. . . . . A decision _____ **made** by the judges.

11. Several people saw the accident. . . . . The accident _____ **seen** by several people.

12. Ann is sending the letters. . . . . The letters _____ **sent** by Ann.

13. Fred will plan the party. . . . . The party _____ **planned** by Fred.

14. The medicine had cured my illness. . . . . . . My illness _____ **cured** by the medicine.

15. The cat will have caught the mouse. . . . . . . The mouse _____ **caught** by the cat.

16. Engineers design bridges. . . . . Bridges _____ **designed** by engineers.

17. The city is going to build a bridge. . . . . A bridge _____ **built** by the city.

18. A guard was protecting the jewels. . . . . The jewels _____ **protected** by a guard.

◇ **PRACTICE 2—GUIDED STUDY:** Forming the passive: questions, negative, and affirmative. (Chart 3-1 and Appendix 1, Units B and C)

Directions: Change the following sentences to the passive.

1. a. QUESTION: Did Tom write that report? → *Was that report written by Tom?*
   b. NEGATIVE: No, he didn't write it. → *No, it wasn't written by him.*
   c. AFFIRMATIVE: Alice wrote it. → *It was written by Alice.*
2. a. QUESTION: Is Mr. Brown painting your house?
   b. NEGATIVE: No, he isn't painting it.
   c. AFFIRMATIVE: My uncle is painting it.
3. a. QUESTION: Will Steve wash the dishes?
   b. NEGATIVE: No, he won't wash them.
   c. AFFIRMATIVE: The children will wash them.
4. a. Has Sue planned the meeting?
   b. No, she hasn't planned it.
   c. The committee has planned it.
5. a. Does Mr. Parr play that violin?
   b. No, he doesn't play it.
   c. His son plays it.
6. a. Is Jack going to return the books to the library?
   b. No, he isn't going to return them.
   c. His sister is going to return them.
7. a. Did the archeologists discover the ancient skeleton?
   b. No, they didn't discover it.
   c. A farmer discovered it.
8. a. Was Sally preparing the food?
   b. No, she wasn't preparing it.
   c. Her mother was preparing it.
9. a. Will Ms. Anderson have typed the letters?
   b. No, she won't have typed them.
   c. The secretary will have typed them.

◇ **PRACTICE 3—SELFSTUDY:** Forming the passive. (Chart 3-1 and Appendix 1, Units B and C)

Directions: In the following, active sentences are changed to passive sentences. Complete the passive sentence with the appropriate verb form. Keep the same tense. Use question and negative forms as necessary.

1. Did Ann discover the mistake?

   → ___*Was*___ the mistake ___*discovered*___ by Ann?

2. A famous author wrote that book.

   → That book ___*was written*___ by a famous author.

3. Jack won't pay the bill.

   → The bill ___*won't be paid*___ by Jack.

4. The waiter refilled my glass.

   → My glass _____ by the waiter.

5. Did Sue knock that vase to the floor?

   → _____ that vase _____ to the floor by Sue?

6. Tommy didn't break the chair.

→ The chair _____ by Tommy.

7. Alan's knowledge about art doesn't impress me.

→ I _____ by Alan's knowledge about art.

8. One of the parents is taping the children's song.

→ The children's song _____ by one of the parents.

9. Is a student pilot flying that airplane?

→ _____ that airplane _____ by a student pilot?

10. The best chess player will win the match.

→ The match _____ by the best chess player.

11. Your emotional appeals will not influence the judge.

→ The judge _____ by your emotional appeals.

12. The voters are going to decide that issue.

→ That issue _____ by the voters.

13. The city attorney has discovered new evidence.

→ New evidence _____ by the city attorney.

14. Mr. Snow hasn't taught that course since 1985.

→ That course _____ by Mr. Snow since 1985.

15. Had a special messenger delivered the package before you got to the office?

→ _____ the package _____ by a special messenger before you got to the office?

16. The pollution in the city was affecting Tim's breathing.

→ Tim's breathing _____ by the pollution in the city.

◇ **PRACTICE 4—SELFSTUDY:** Using the passive: transitive vs. intransitive verbs. (Chart 3-1 and Appendix 1, Unit A-1)

Directions: In the following sentences, some of the verbs are transitive and some are intransitive. Identify the verb of the sentence. Then identify the object of the verb if there is one. If the verb has an object, change the sentence to the passive. Use the symbol Ø to indicate "none."

	VERB	OBJECT OF VERB	PASSIVE SENTENCE
1. Al will pay the bill.	*will pay*	*the bill*	*The bill will be paid by Al.*
2. Sue will come tomorrow.	*will come*	Ø	Ø
3. The hotel supplies towels.			
4. Accidents happen every day.			
5. Everyone noticed my mistake.			
6. The train arrived at three.			
7. The news didn't surprise me.			
8. Did the news surprise you?			
9. The sun wasn't shining.			
10. Ann interrupted my story.			
11. Do ghosts exist?			
12. Birds fly in the sky.			
13. Will Ed come tomorrow?			
14. Mr. Lee died last year.			
15. Did Bob throw the ball?			
16. Sue laughed loudly.			
17. An old man told the story.			
18. It hasn't rained lately.			

◇ **PRACTICE 5—SELFSTUDY:** Forming the passive. (Chart 3-1)

Directions: Change the following active sentences to passive if possible. Some of the verbs are intransitive and cannot be changed. Keep the same tense.

1. My uncle will meet you at the airport. → *You will be met at the airport by my uncle.*

2. Our plane will land at 6:03. → *(no change)*

3. The chef will prepare the food.

4. John is working at the bakery.

5. Lightning didn't cause the fire.

6. We walked downtown after work yesterday.

7. Thousands of people ride the subway every day.

8. The baby was crying in his crib.

9. I don't agree with you.

10. Joe fell down on his way to school this morning.

11. George seemed unhappy yesterday.

12. A special committee is going to settle the dispute.

13. Our houseguests are going to arrive sometime tomorrow afternoon.

14. Our plan succeeded at last.

15. Barbara traveled to Uganda last year.

16. Did the army surround the enemy?

17. What happened in class yesterday?

18. The Persians invented windmills around 1500 years ago.

◇ **PRACTICE 6—SELFSTUDY: Active vs. passive. (Chart 3-1)**

Directions: Complete the sentences with the words in parentheses. Some of the sentences are active and some are passive. Use any appropriate tense.

1. You (*notify*) ____**will be notified**____ by my secretary next week.

2. Last night I (*remember, not*) ____**didn't remember**____ to lock my front door.

3. At the present time, the oldest house in town (*restore*) _____

   by the Historical Society. When the restoration is finished, the house is sure to be a popular

   tourist attraction.

4. A: What a beautiful old wooden chest!

   B: It (*build*) _____ by my grandfather over fifty years ago.

5. At one time, the entire world (rule) _____ by dinosaurs. Some dinosaurs (walk) _____ on their hind legs and (stand) _____ as tall as palm trees.

6. Disneyland is a world famous amusement park in Southern California. It (visit) _____ _____ by more than ten million people every year.

7. Many of us take water for granted in our daily lives, but people who live in the desert (use, not) _____ water carelessly. To them, each drop is precious.

8. I (agree, not) _____ with people who say space exploration is a waste of money. What do you think?

9. Do you really think that we (invade) _____ by creatures from outer space in the near future?

10. Most insects (live) _____ for less than a year. The common housefly (live) _____ from 19 to 30 days.

11. (You, accept, already) _____ by this university when you heard about the other scholarship?

12. I got into a taxi quickly because I (follow) _____ by two strange men. As soon as I got into the taxi, I (feel) _____ a little safer.

13. The impact of the earthquake yesterday (feel) _____ by people who lived hundreds of kilometers from the epicenter.

14. When Alex was only ten, his father (die) _____.

15. Mark (influence) _____ a lot by his friends, isn't he? He should be more independent and think for himself.

16. A few days ago, my car (steal) _____ by one of the teenagers in my neighborhood. He (catch) _____ by the police a few blocks from my house. He just wanted to take it for a drive, but now he's in a lot of trouble.

◇ **PRACTICE 7—SELFSTUDY: Using the "by phrase." (Chart 3-2)**

Directions: Change the active sentences to passive. Keep the same tense. Include the "*by phrase*" only if necessary.

1. People grow rice in India. → *Rice is grown in India.* (no "*by phrase*")

2. My aunt made this rug. → *This rug was made by my aunt.*

3. They are fixing my car today. → *My car is being fixed today.* (no "*by phrase*")

4. They speak French in Quebec.

5. Mr. Eads designed that bridge in the 1870s.

6. Someone invented the wheel thousands of years ago.

7. Did Thomas Edison invent the telephone?

8. They are going to build a new hospital just outside of town.

9. How do people make candles?

10. Very few people watch that TV show.

11. Look! Someone is feeding the seals.

◇ **PRACTICE 8—GUIDED STUDY:** Using the *"by* phrase." (Chart 3-2)

Directions: Change the active sentences to passive. Keep the same tense. Include the *"by phrase"* only if necessary.

1. Someone cut down that tree last week. → *That tree was cut down last week.*   *(no "by" phrase)*

2. Sally made that pie. → *That pie was made by Sally.*

3. Someone is considering Jack for that job.

4. Three continents surround the Mediterranean Sea.

5. I got upset when someone interrupted me in the middle of my story.

6. When Robert returned home, each of his relatives embraced him.

7. People didn't build Rome in a day.

8. Where do they file that information?

9. Before we arrived, someone had chained the dog to the fence in the backyard.

10. Did the noise from the neighbor's apartment annoy you last night?

11. As soon as it happened, people broadcast the news all over the world.

12. Do they make those tractors in this country, or do they import them?

13. While I was walking down the street, a nice young man in a military uniform approached me.

14. They will not provide pencils at the test, so please bring your own.

◇ PRACTICE 9—SELFSTUDY: Indirect objects as passive subjects. (Chart 3-3)

Directions: Identify the indirect object (I.O.). Change the sentences to the passive by using the *indirect object* as the subject of the sentence. Use the *"by phrase"* only if necessary. Keep the same tense.

> **I.O.**
1. Someone is going to serve Jack breakfast in bed on his birthday.

    → *Jack is going to be served breakfast in bed on his birthday.*

2. Someone has offered Mike the opportunity to study abroad.

3. People don't pay babysitters a lot of money.

4. When I was living in Kuwait, my neighbor taught me Arabic.

5. Someone awarded Jason a medal for distinguished service in the military.

6. The real estate office will send you a copy of the sales contract.

7. Someone handed me a telegram when I answered the door.

8. The director of the museum, Ms. Cynthia Hall, is going to give the schoolchildren a special tour of the modern art exhibit.

9. People gave Mr. French a gold watch upon his retirement from the company.

◇ PRACTICE 10—SELFSTUDY: Active and passive. (Charts 3-1 → 3-3)

Directions: Complete the sentences with the given words. Some of the sentences are passive and some are active. Use any appropriate tense.

1. The examination papers are scored by machine. The students (*tell*) __***will be told***__ their results next week.

2. The project got finished early. The committee (*complete*) __***completed***__ its work three weeks ahead of schedule.

3. The teacher (*assist*) _____ by two graduate students during the exam yesterday.

4. During the family celebration, the little boy was crying because he (*ignore*) _____ _____. He needed some attention, too.

5. A: Where (*buy, you*) _____ that beautiful necklace?

    B: I (*buy, not*) _____ it. It (*give*) _____ to me for my birthday. (*like, you*) _____ it?

6. Soon after I (*apply*) _____ for a job with the United Nations two years ago, I (*hire*) _____.

7. The crocodiles at the zoo look like statues. They (*lie*) _____ perfectly still for hours at a time. They have no need to move because they don't have to hunt for their food. They (*feed*) _____ regularly by the zookeepers.

8. This lovely beach won't exist forever. Eventually, it (*erode, probably*) _____ _____ away by the sea, and there will be nothing left but bedrock. The geologic forces of nature never stop.

9. Yesterday we went to look at an apartment. I really liked it, but by the time we got there, it (*rent, already*) _____.

10. Bananas originated in Asia. They (*introduce*) _____ to the Americas in 1516. Until the 1860s, bananas (*eat*) _____ principally by people of the tropics. Today, bananas (*export*) _____ to all parts of the world, and they (*enjoy*) _____ by people who live in all climates.

11. There's going to be a story in the local newspaper about my neighbor, Mrs. Morris. Tomorrow she (*interview*) _____ by one of the local reporters about her doll collection. Over the years, she (*collect*) _____ more than 400 dolls from all over the world.

12. The sun is just one of billions of stars in the universe. As it travels through space, it (*circle*) _____ by many other celestial bodies. The nine known planets (*hold*) _____ in orbit by the sun's gravitational field. The planets, in turn, (*circle*) _____ by their own satellites, or moons.

13. Early inhabitants of this region (*worship*) _____ the sun and the moon. We know this from the jewelry, sculptures, and other art work archaeologists have found.

◇ PRACTICE 11—GUIDED STUDY: Active and passive. (Charts 3-1 → 3-3)

Directions: Complete the sentences with the given words. Some of the sentences are passive and some are active. Use any appropriate tense.

1. Ali and Mustafa (*complain*) _____ to the landlord many times since they moved into their present apartment, but to date nothing (*do*) _____ about the leak in the roof and the broken window in the bedroom.

2. Yesterday I told my teenage daughter to clean her room before she (*go*) _____ to school. After she had left the house, I looked in her room. She (*pile*) _____ all of her clothes on a chair. Everything else (*shove*) _____ under the bed.

3. Sometimes people (*intimidate*) _____ by salespeople. As a result, sometimes they (*buy*) _____ things that they don't really want.

4. Two days ago I (*put*) _____ an ad in the classified section of the newspaper so I could find a buyer for my old car. Yesterday I (*sell*) _____ it. It (*buy*) _____ by a teenager who (*look*) _____ for an old car to fix up himself. Today a friend of mine told me that he wanted to buy my old car, but he was too late. By the time he talked to me, the car (*sell, already*) _____ to the teenager.

5. The wheel (*invent*) _____ over 5,000 years ago. Throughout history, it (*assist*) _____ people in making better use of oxen, horses, and other animals in transporting goods.

6. Captain Cook, a British navigator, was the first European to reach Australia's east coast. While his ship was lying off Australia, his sailors (*bring*) _____ a strange animal on board. Cook wanted to know the name of this unusual creature, so he (*send*) _____ his men ashore to ask the native inhabitants. When the natives (*ask*) _____ to name the animal, they said, "Kangaroo." The sailors, of course, believed "kangaroo" was the animal's name. Years later, the truth (*discover*) _____. "Kangaroo" means "I don't understand." But today the animal (*call, still*) _____ a kangaroo in English.

7. A person named Carl Gauss (*recognize*) _____ as a mathematical genius at the age of 10. One day a professor decided to pose an arithmetic problem to Carl. Carl (*ask*) _____ to add up all the numbers from 1 to 100 (1 + 2 + 3 + 4 + 5, etc.). It (*take*) _____ him eight seconds to solve the problem. How?*

8. The avalanche (*occur*) _____ around ten in the morning on October 7. Six skiers (*cross*) _____ a steep slope when suddenly they (*sweep*) _____ off their feet by cascading snow. Back at the ski resort, an avalanche alert was sounded, and a rescue party (*leave*) _____ immediately. After several hours, all six skiers (*find*) _____. Four of them (*injure, seriously*) _____, but they were all alive. The rescue party (*take*) _____ the injured skiers down the mountain as quickly as they could.

---

*He knew that each pair of numbers—1 plus 100, 2 plus 99, 3 plus 98, and so on to 50 plus 51—equaled 101. So he multiplied 50 times 101 and came up with the answer: 5,050.

◇ **PRACTICE 12—SELFSTUDY:** Present participle vs. past participle. (Charts 1-2 and 3-1 → 3-3)

Directions: Use the PAST PARTICIPLE or the PRESENT PARTICIPLE of the given verbs to complete the sentences. Use each verb only one time.

breed	finance	scrub	✔ thread
broadcast	lean	shove	wind
drag	mine	smuggle	
expose	✔ redecorate	stretch	

1. The Clarks' living room is being ___**redecorated**___ in blue and white. They want it to look nice for their daughter's wedding reception.

2. Jack pricked his finger while he was ___**threading**___ a needle.

3. The police talked to an informant. According to him, the illegal drugs had been _____ into the country in a private airplane.

4. The logging industry in that country still uses animal power. After the trees are cut down, the logs are _____ to the central camp by elephants.

5. On your trip to Tahiti, you will be _____ to many interesting customs, delicious food, and delightful people.

6. My hands and knees got sore while I was _____ the floor with soap and water.

7. The old clock wasn't ticking because it hadn't been _____. Someone forgot to do it.

8. The news of the victory was _____ throughout the country over the radio and television. Everyone heard about it almost as soon as it happened.

9. The bus was extremely crowded. I was _____ this way and that by the other passengers every time the bus turned a corner.

10. Oil exploration costs a lot of money. The explorations in the southern part of the country are being _____ by the government.

11. Frank was resting. He had been _____ back on his chair for several minutes with his eyes closed when he heard a knock on the door.

12. Gold is _____ in several countries. The nugget that Elena is wearing came from Brazil.

13. We couldn't enter the street. A rope had been _____ across the street.

14. Arabian horses are _____ at the Bar X ranch. They are quite expensive.

◇ **PRACTICE 13—GUIDED STUDY:** Present participle vs. past participle.
(Charts 1-2 and 3-1 → 3-3)

Directions: Use the PAST PARTICIPLE or the PRESENT PARTICIPLE of the given verbs to complete the sentences. Use each verb only one time.

bill	erase	✔ photograph	rub
destroy	✔ memorize	predict	vaccinate
equip	perform	rehearse	whisper

1. The vocabulary list had been ___**memorized**___ by all of the students, and each one scored over 90 percent on the exam.

2. Shhhh. Don't move. Don is ___**photographing**___ that deer, and we don't want to scare it off.

3. You'll want to buy this typewriter. It has been _____ with all of the latest accessories, including a 5,000-character storage memory.

4. The earthquake that struck the village was terrible. About 75 percent of the buildings were completely _____ within 2 minutes.

5. Little Jackie was _____ her eyes because she was sleepy.

6. Anna and Susie didn't hear what the teacher said because they were _____ to each other in the back of the classroom about the new boy in fifth grade.

7. Paul drew a funny picture of the teacher on the board, but it had been _____ before she entered the classroom.

8. The dance company is having a successful tour of the United States. Their dances will have been _____ over 500 times before they return to Senegal.

9. The National Weather Service is _____ another heat wave in the coming month. I hope they're wrong.

10. Robert and Julia had been _____ against cholera before they went abroad. They traveled without worrying about becoming infected.

11. When I went to the school auditorium, the children were _____ their musical play. The play is going to be presented this coming Friday at 7:00 P.M.

12. Carl spent two hours at the dentist's office today having some fillings put in. He will be _____ for the dental work at the end of the month.

◇ **PRACTICE 14—SELFSTUDY:** Passive modals. (Chart 3-4)

Directions: Change the following active sentences to the passive.

1. People should save pandas from extinction. → *Pandas should be saved from extinction.*

2. People must obey all traffic laws.

3. Someone ought to repair this broken window.

4. Someone should have supplied the hotel guests with clean towels.

5. Someone had better take this garbage to the dump soon.

6. People can pick tomatoes before they are completely ripe.

7. Someone is supposed to divide the profits among the shareholders.

8. Someone must have hurt Bob's feelings.

9. Someone has to finish this work today.

10. Someone ought to have reported the accident to the police.

11. You shouldn't put bananas in the freezer.

◇ **PRACTICE 15—SELFSTUDY: Passive modals. (Chart 3-4)**

Directions: Complete the sentences with the appropriate forms of the verbs in the list. Use each verb only one time. Some of the sentences are active and some are passive.

consider	*pollute*	*sew*	*whisper*
cost	*read*	*sign*	*wrap*
discover	✔ *repeat*	✔ *tell*	
forget	*replace*	*wear*	

1. Jack has a right to know. He ought to __***be told***__ the news immediately. If you don't do it, I will.

2. I have no patience with gossips. What I told Bill was a secret. He shouldn't have ___***repeated***___ it to you.

3. Use this brown paper and tape. A package has to _____ carefully before it is mailed. Otherwise, the post office won't send it.

4. I don't know why Jessica wasn't at the meeting. She must have _____ about it. Next time there's a meeting, I'll be sure to remind her about it.

5. The ancient ruins may have _____ as early as 1792. The historical record is difficult to interpret.

6. You should _____ this button back on right away—before you lose it. Here's a needle and thread.

7. This burnt out light bulb should have _____ days ago. There are some new bulbs in the green cabinet. Could you get one for me?

8. Did you know that Sylvia bought a new sports car? I don't know how much she paid for it, and of course it's none of my business, but it must have _____ her a lot of money.

9. Shhhh. Let's not talk so loudly. We don't want to awaken the baby. We'd better _____.

10. You'd better not drink that river water. It could _____.

11. We have no choice in the matter. I know Tommy wants to spend the night outside in a tent with his friends, but he's sick. His well-being must _____ above all else. We have to tell him he can't do it.

12. While you are working here, you are never to greet the public in your everyday clothes. When you are on duty, your uniform must _____ at all times.

13. Your passport is supposed to _____. It is invalid without your signature.

14. I think everyone should _____ this paperback on the economic crisis. It has information that everyone should have.

◇ **PRACTICE 16—GUIDED STUDY: Passive modals. (Chart 3-4)**

Directions: Complete the sentences with the appropriate forms of the verbs in the list. Use each verb only one time. Some of the sentences are active and some are passive.

distinguish	✔ obtain	scrub	vaccinate
eat	participate	stop	win
establish	reply	teach	
kill	revise	trade	

1. A driver's license can ____*be obtained*____ from the Licensing Bureau at the corner of Pine Street and 5th Avenue.

2. Sam Smith was awarded the prize, but it should have _____ by Jennifer Watson. Her drawing was much better than his in my opinion.

3. Surgeons must _____ their hands thoroughly with disinfectant soap and hot water before they enter the operating room.

4. What are you talking about? You can't have _____ against the common cold. Small pox, maybe—but not the common cold.

5. A parrot can _____ to say words. I know a parrot that can say, ''Me want food.'' Her grammar isn't very good, but she often manages to get something to eat.

6. When Mr. Brown said "How do you do?", you should have _____ by saying "How do you do?" I know that's not an answer to a question, but that's the way people talk when they greet each other.

7. I shouldn't have _____ by the police. I'm sure I wasn't speeding, but I got a ticket anyway.

8. Maria's composition was quite good, but it still had to _____. Her introduction didn't clearly state her thesis, and some of the ideas she presented weren't supported by specifics.

9. If you don't want to work tonight, you ought to _____ work shifts with Emily. She can work for you tonight, and you can work for her tomorrow night. The boss doesn't mind as long as someone is there to serve the food.

10. The games are open to anyone who wants to join in. Everyone can _____ in them. You don't have to sign up first. We welcome all players.

11. A university may _____ in outer space before long. Ideas for such a university are presently in the planning stage.

12. Your body needs lots of vitamins and minerals. You should _____ more salads and less junk food in the future.

13. A bald eagle can _____ from other large birds by its white head and white tail.

14. Some ranchers still believe that bald eagles must _____ to protect their livestock. Research has shown, however, that eagles do little if any damage to a rancher's stock. Today eagles are a protected species. The sight of a bald eagle soaring over water and trees fills one with awe and wonder at the beauty of nature.

Directions: Complete the sentences with the verbs in the list. Use the SIMPLE PRESENT. Use each verb only one time.

bury	cover	✔ excite	insure
close	crack	exhaust	pollute
confuse	dress	finish	stick

1. The children _____ **are excited** _____ about going to the circus. They're looking forward to seeing the elephants, the clowns, and the acrobats.

2. Three of the children have the measles. Their bodies _____ with red spots. They also have fevers.

3. A: What happened to this mirror? It _____.

   B: So it is. Someone must have dropped it.

4. The kids _____ from playing soccer all afternoon. They should rest for a while now.

5. _____ you _____ with that novel yet? I'd like to borrow it to read over the weekend.

6. A: I heard that a burglar broke into your house and stole all of your jewelry!

   B: Yes, and I feel terrible about it. Some of it was my grandmother's and can't be replaced. But at least all of it _____, and I'll be reimbursed for its value. It's still not the same as having the jewelry, though.

7. You shouldn't eat any of the fish from that river. The river _____ with chemical wastes from the factory upstream.

8. A: I'm going over to the theater to get tickets for the next concert.

   B: The ticket booth _____ until 6:00 P.M. You'll have to go there after six to get the tickets.

9. What's wrong with this drawer? I can't pull it open. It _____.

10. George _____ in his best suit today because he has an important interview this afternoon.

11. Douglas gave me one set of directions to their house, and Ann gave me a different set of directions. Needless to say, I _____ very _____. I hope we don't get lost on the way.

12. I know the scissors are somewhere on this desk. I think they _____ somewhere under these piles of papers.

◇ **PRACTICE 18—GUIDED STUDY:** Stative passive. (Chart 3-5)

Directions: Complete the sentences with the appropriate form of the verbs in the list. Use the SIMPLE PRESENT. Use each verb only one time.

acquaint	*equip*	*locate*	*schedule*
cancel	*forbid*	*make*	*summarize*
clog	*list*	*overdraw*	*wrinkle*

1. Maria's family lives in New York City, and her husband's family lives in Philadelphia. They would like to live in a city which _____ between the two so that they can visit their relatives frequently.

2. Robert wrote a very good, well-organized composition. The introduction tells the reader what the composition is about, and the last paragraph reviews all of his main points. His conclusions _____ in the last paragraph.

3. I don't know how, but I've lost my brother's new telephone number. Unfortunately, it _____ not _____, so I can't look it up in the directory. I'll have to call my mother and get it from her.

4. We can't climb over the fence to walk in that field. The sign says: "Trespassing _____ _____. Violators will be prosecuted."

5. I _____ not _____ with our new neighbors. They just moved in last week, and I haven't had the opportunity to introduce myself.

6. Your dental appointment _____ for 10:00 on Saturday. Please give us 24-hour notice if you need to cancel it.

7. I have to deposit some money in the bank immediately or I'm in big trouble. I've written too many checks and there's not enough money to cover them. My bank account _____ _____.

8. Good news! Our meeting _____. Now we can go to the beach after work instead of spending the evening at a meeting.

9. I can't wear this blouse because it _____. I'd have to iron it, and I don't have time.

10. Some new automobiles _____ with air bags as well as seat belts. The air bags provide additional protection in case of an accident.

11. That table _____ of plastic, not wood. The manufacturer certainly did a good job of imitating the look of wood.

12. It takes a long time for the water to go down the drain in my kitchen sink. I think the drain _____ with grease and food particles. I'd better call the plumber tomorrow.

◇ **PRACTICE 19—SELFSTUDY: Stative passive + prepositions. (Chart 3-5 and Appendix 2)**

Directions: Complete the sentences with appropriate PREPOSITIONS.

1. Our high-school soccer team was very excited ___*about*___ going to the national finals.

2. I'm not acquainted _____ that man. Do you know him?

3. Mark Twain is known _____ his stories about life on the Mississippi.

4. A person who is addicted _____ drugs needs professional medical help.

5. This apartment comes furnished _____ only a stove and refrigerator.

6. Mr. Bellamy is discriminated _____ because of his age. When he applies for a job, he gets turned down as soon as they learn he is 61 years old.

7. Jack is married _____ Joan.

8. Could I please have the dictionary when you are finished _____ it?

9. A: Aren't you ready yet? We have to be at the ferry dock at 7:45.

   B: We'll never make it. I'm still dressed _____ my pajamas.

10. My car is equipped _____ air conditioning and a sun roof.

11. The schoolchildren were exposed _____ measles by a student who had them.

12. Gandhi was committed _____ nonviolence. He believed in it all of his life.

13. The boss is so convinced _____ Jean's ability that he's paying her more money than he paid the previous employee.

14. The large table was covered _____ every kind of food you could imagine.

15. Barbara turned off the TV because she was tired _____ listening to the news.

16. Victor is blessed _____ a good sense of humor, which has helped him get out of some very difficult situations.

17. A: Are the choices in this restaurant limited _____ pizza and sandwiches?

    B: No. If you're interested _____ other dishes, take a look at the back page of the menu.

18. A: Are you disappointed _____ the color of this room? We could repaint it.

    B: I think I'm satisfied _____ it the way it is. What do you think?

19. A: Are you in favor of nuclear disarmament, or are you opposed _____ it?

    B: I'm in favor of it. I'm terrified _____ the possibility of an accidental nuclear war. My wife, however, is against disarmament.

◇ **PRACTICE 20—SELFSTUDY: Stative passive + prepositions. (Chart 3-5 and Appendix 2)**

Directions: Complete the sentences with appropriate PREPOSITIONS.

1. The department store was filled _____ toys for the holiday sale.

2. George Washington, the first president of the United States, is remembered _____ his strong leadership during the Revolutionary War.

3. John's bald head is protected _____ the hot sun. He's wearing a straw hat.

4. The store was crowded _____ last-minute shoppers on the eve of the holiday.

5. I think you're involved _____ too many activities. You don't have enough time to spend with your family.

6. Your leg bone is connected _____ your hip bone.

7. Zoology is more closely related _____ biology than it is to botany.

8. Their apartment is always messy. It's cluttered _____ newspapers, books, clothes, and dirty dishes.

9. I'm annoyed _____ my boss. He scheduled a meeting for an hour beginning at ten o'clock, the same time I was planning to see a client.

10. As soon as you are done _____ the dictionary, I'd like to use it.

11. Last month, little Billy was bitten by a dog. Now he's scared _____ every dog he sees.

12. Don't leave those seedlings outside tonight. If they're exposed _____ temperatures below freezing, they'll die.

13. An interior decorator makes certain that the color of the walls is coordinated _____ the color of the carpets and window coverings.

14. Carol is engaged _____ Larry. Their marriage is planned for May 3.

15. We finished packing our sleeping bags, tent, first-aid kit, food, and warm clothes. We're finally prepared _____ our camping trip.

16. A: Why are you so upset _____ the children?

    B: They didn't call me when they missed their school bus, and I got very worried.

17. I was very disappointed _____ that movie. The whole first hour was devoted _____ historical background with a cast of thousands fighting endless battles. I was bored _____ it before the plot took shape.

18. A: Are you still associated _____ the International Red Cross?

    B: I was, until this year. Are you interested _____ working with them?

    A: I think I'd like to. They're dedicated _____ helping people in time of crisis, and I admire the work they've done. Can you get me some information?

◇ PRACTICE 21—GUIDED STUDY: Present vs. past participles. (Charts 1-2, 3-5, and Appendix 2)

Directions: Complete the sentences with the verbs in the list. Use the PRESENT PARTICIPLE or the PAST PARTICIPLE. Include a PREPOSITION if necessary. Use each verb only one time.

accompany	compose	✔ explain	limit
annoy	✔ concern	involve	provide
bless	connect	know	satisfy
blow	cross	laugh	

1. I am _____**concerned about**_____ your health. You're not taking good care of yourself.

2. Shhh! The teacher is _____**explaining**_____ the assignment, and I want to hear what he's saying.

3. Paris is famous for the Eiffel Tower. Bangkok is _____ its floating market, which is a favorite tourist attraction.

4. In elementary school, all of the children are _____ textbooks. They don't have to buy their own.

5. Everyone is _____ hard because Don is telling a very funny story.

6. Diane is a perfectionist when it comes to developing her photographs. She's been in the darkroom for hours and won't come out until she is completely _____ _____ the prints.

7. The Atlantic Ocean is _____ the Pacific Ocean by the Panama Canal. Ships can go from one ocean to the other without having to sail around the southern tip of South America.

8. While I was _____ the street, a car came out of nowhere and almost hit me.

9. Most teenagers are very busy after school. They are _____ many extracurricular activities, such as sports and special interest clubs.

10. An alloy is a metal compound that is _____ two or more metals.

11. Mrs. Hill doesn't have to travel alone. Her daughter is _____ her to Rome.

12. We are fortunate people. We are _____ a happy home and good health. We have many things to be thankful for.

13. The enrollment in that class is _____ 25 students. You'd better sign up for it early. Otherwise, you won't be able to get in.

14. My neighbors are quite inconsiderate. They make so much noise that I can't get to sleep at night. I am very _____ them.

15. The weather was awful. It was raining so hard it was impossible to see across the valley, and the wind was _____ so hard that it was difficult to walk.

◇ **PRACTICE 22—SELFSTUDY: The passive with *get*. (Chart 3-6)**

Directions: Complete the sentences by using an appropriate form of *get* and the PAST PARTICIPLE of the verbs in the list.

break	*hurt*	*start*	✔ *tear*
bury	*lose*	*stick*	*worry*
hire	*soak*		

1. I had a terrible day. First the heel of my shoe broke off, then my dress ___**got torn**___ in the elevator door. I'm glad the day is over!

2. Oh! Look at that beautiful vase on the floor. How did it _____?

3. A: You're late. What happened?

   B: We _____. We took the wrong exit from the highway, and it took a long time to figure out where we were.

4. A: I really need a job.

   B: Why don't you apply for a job at the fast-food restaurant? They're looking for help. I'm
   sure you'll _____.

5. A: Did Susan _____ when she fell down the stairs?

   B: Not badly. Just a few bumps and bruises. She'll be fine.

6. A: You're here! I _____ about you. What happened
   that made you so late?

   B: I couldn't start my car. The battery was dead.

7. Maureen _____ thoroughly _____ when her canoe tipped over and she fell into
   the river. She looked like a drowned rat.

8. In two weeks the school term will be finished. I'd better _____ on my
   term paper before it's too late. I've been procrastinating too long.

9. It was a real tragedy. The rains were torrential, and the mudslide completely covered
   everything. Three houses _____ in the mud when it rolled down the
   hillside. We could barely see the rooftops.

10. A: I heard about your embarrassing situation last night.

    B: It was awful! I put my big toe in the faucet while I was taking a bath, and it
    _____! I couldn't pull it out no matter how hard I tried.

◇ PRACTICE 23—GUIDED STUDY: The passive with *get*. (Chart 3-6)

Directions: Complete the sentences by using an appropriate form of ***get*** and the PAST
PARTICIPLE of the verbs in the list.

accept	*dress*	*embarrass*	*invite*
catch	*elect*	*fire*	*mug*
cheat	*electrocute*	✔ *hit*	*ruin*

1. I shouldn't have parked my car near the construction site. It ___***got hit***___ by falling rocks.
   Now it's full of dents and scratches.

2. Tom has applied to three top universities. Since he's an excellent student, I'm sure he'll

_____ by at least one of them. If he doesn't, there are other good

schools he can attend.

3. Alex thought he had gotten a good deal when he bought a diamond ring from some guy on the

street, but the "stone" turned out to be glass and was practically worthless. Alex

_____.

4. A: I can't believe Paul _____ from his job. I thought he was doing well.

B: He was, but then he had a major disagreement with his boss, and tempers were flying. I

hope he gets his job back.

5. A: Let's take the subway.

B: Not me. The last time I was on the subway, I _____. A man

knocked me down and stole my wallet.

6. A: Did you _____ to the Saunder's dinner party tonight?

B: Yes, but I can't go.

7. A: You're all out of breath!

B: I was late getting home and had to _____ quickly. Then I ran all the

way over here.

A: Well, that explains why your collar is up and your tie is crooked.

8. The animal was running through the woods when it suddenly _____ in

the hunter's trap.

9. It was a close election. The new president _____ by a very small

margin.

10. What are you doing?!! Don't let the cord to your electric hair dryer fall into the sink. You'll

_____!

11. We managed to save some of the furniture, but many of our things _____

when the floodwaters poured into our house.

12. During the school play, little Annie _____ when she couldn't

remember the lines she was supposed to say.

◇ **PRACTICE 24—SELFSTUDY: Participial adjectives. (Chart 3-7)**

Directions: Complete the sentences with the correct form (PRESENT or PAST PARTICIPLE) of
the italicized word.

1. The book *interests* me. (a) It is an ___*interesting*___ book. (b) I am ___*interested*___ in it.

2. That chemical *irritates* your skin. (a) The chemical is _____. (b) Your

skin is _____.

3. The trip *tired* everybody. (a) Everyone was _____. (b) The trip was _____.

4. Ann *boiled* an egg. (a) She took the egg out of the _____ water. (b) She had a

_____ egg for breakfast.

5. The news *upset* us.   (a) We were _____.   (b) The news was _____.

6. The instructions on the box for assembling the tool *confuse* me.   (a) They are _____.   (b) I am thoroughly _____.

7. Bob's grades *disappointed* his parents.   (a) His grades were _____.
(b) His parents were _____.

8. My father often *reassured* me.   (a) He was a very _____ person.   (b) I always felt _____ when I was around him.

9. I waited for two hours to see the doctor, and it really *frustrated* me!   (a) Long waits such as that can be very _____.   (b) I was _____.

10. Anna has a noise in her car that *disturbs* her.   (a) It is a _____ noise.
(b) She is _____ when she hears it.

11. Jessica's arguments *convinced* us.   (a) She presented _____ arguments.
(b) We were _____.

12. The tender love story *moved* the audience.   (a) It was a _____ story.   (b) The audience felt _____.

13. Their behavior *shocked* us.   (a) It was _____ behavior.   (b) We were _____.

14. The sad movie *depressed* me.   (a) I was _____.   (b) It was a _____ movie.

15. The unkind teacher's harsh words *humiliated* the student.   (a) The _____ student hung his head in shame.   (b) The student never forgot that _____ experience.

16. The newspaper account of the new medical discovery *intrigued* me.   (a) It was an _____ account.   (b) Other _____ people wrote the newspaper to get more information.

◇ **PRACTICE 25—SELFSTUDY: Participial adjectives. (Chart 3-7)**

Directions: Complete the sentences with the correct form of the word in parentheses.

1. (*Pollute*) __**Polluted**__ water is not safe for drinking.

2. I don't have any furniture of my own. Do you know where I can rent a (*furnish*) _____ apartment?

3. The equator is the (*divide*) _____ line between the Northern and Southern Hemispheres.

4. The poor people who live in shacks south of the city don't have (*run*) _____ water.

5. No one may attend the lecture except (*invite*) _____ guests.

6. We all expect our (*elect*) _____ officials to be honest.

7. The (suggest) _____ remedy for the common cold is to rest and to drink plenty of fluids.

8. Because we have a (write) _____ agreement, our landlord won't be able to raise our rent for two years.

9. After an (exhaust) _____ trip of twelve hours, Jason fell asleep at the dinner table.

10. There are many (stimulate) _____ activities in a large city.

11. The anthropologist recorded the tribe's (speak) _____ language with a small tape recorder.

12. I like to hear the sound of gently (fall) _____ rain.

13. (Freeze) _____ fish is as nutritious as fresh fish, but it doesn't taste quite as good.

14. The (invade) _____ army plundered the villages of food and valuables.

15. Skydiving is a (thrill) _____ experience.

◇ PRACTICE 26—GUIDED STUDY: Participial adjectives. (Chart 3-7)

Directions: Complete the sentences with the correct form of the word in parentheses.

1. The invention of the (print) _____ press was one of the most important events in the history of the world.

2. (Experience) _____ travelers pack lightly. They carry little more than necessities.

3. Ben's tasteless jokes didn't produce the (intend) _____ effect. Instead, his guests were offended.

4. The professor dispelled the tense atmosphere in the classroom by beginning her lecture with some (amuse) _____ anecdotes.

5. That country is highly industrialized but has very little arable land. Its economy depends upon the export of various (manufacture) _____ goods in exchange for imported agricultural products.

6. When I get home from work, I'm going to take a long, (relax) _____ bath.

7. The psychologist spoke to us about some of the (amaze) _____ coincidences in the lives of twins living apart from each other from birth.

8. The scientist reviewed all of his procedures for the experiment after the (expect) _____ results did not occur.

9. When Brenda heard the news of the (approach) _____ hurricane, she bought flashlight batteries, candles, and canned food to prepare for it.

10. Bright children have (inquire) _____ minds.

11. The game was played in our stadium. The (*visit*) _____ team scored the (*win*) _____ goal in the last seconds of the soccer game. Nevertheless, the (*disappoint*) _____ fans continued to cheer our team.

12. I heard some (*encourage*) _____ news.

13. Sally spends her vacations in the mountains. The fresh air invigorates her. She likes the cool, (*invigorate*) _____ air.

14. Waste from the factory poured into the river and contaminated it. Some of the villagers got sick from eating (*contaminate*) _____ fish.

◇ **PRACTICE 27—GUIDED STUDY: Verb form review, active and passive. (Chapters 1 and 3)**

Directions: Complete the sentences with the words in parentheses.

1. Only coffee and dessert (*serve*) __***were served***__ at the reception yesterday.

2. Kim wants very badly to make the Olympic team next year. She (*train*) __***has been training***__ hard for the last two years.

3. I've looked in my purse, on the dresser, in my coat pocket, and on all of the tables in the house, but I can't find my keys anywhere. They (*lose*) _____.

4. Some people in my country don't take politics seriously. In a recent parliamentary election, a cartoon character named Donald Duck (*receive*) _____ 291 votes.

5. According to present company policy, bonuses for the most sales (*give*) _____ to the sales staff at the end of July every year.

6. According to our Constitution, everyone is equal. But in truth, some minorities (*discriminate*) _____ against in our country. In the last 20 years, new laws (*enact*) _____ to help ensure equality in housing and job opportunities.

7. Mark is a genius. By the time he graduated, he (*offer*) _____ jobs by a dozen computer companies.

8. When I (*finish*) _____ my work, I'm going to take a walk.

9. After the test papers (*return*) _____ to the students in class tomorrow, the students (*give*) _____ their next assignment.

10. Since the beginning of the modern industrial age, many of the natural habitats of plants and animals (*destroy*) _____ by industrial development and pollution.

11. The Olympic Games began in 776 B.C. in Olympia, a small town in Greece. At that time, only Greeks (*allow*) _____ to compete in them.

12. I (*fool, not*) _____ when Linda told us she'd won a million dollars at the racetrack. I knew she was only kidding.

13. There are certain (*establish*) _____ procedures that must (*follow*) _____ in conducting a scientific experiment.

14. Due to his abrasive, (*irritate*) _____ manner, Mr. Morrow has difficulty getting along with his co-workers. He (*replace*) _____ by Mr. Han next month as the co-ordinator of the production plans.

15. Ever since it (*build*) _____ three centuries ago, the Taj Mahal in Agra (*describe, often*) _____ as the most beautiful building in the world. It (*design*) _____ by a Turkish architect, and it (*take*) _____ 20,000 workers 20 years to complete it.

16. The photography competition that is taking place at the art museum today (*judge*) _____ by three well-known photographers. I've entered three of my pictures and have my fingers crossed. The results (*announce*) _____ later this afternoon.

17. When Jake put a coin in the (*vend*) _____ machine for a can of soda pop, nothing came out. So in a fit of temper, he (*kick*) _____ it hard. Suddenly, it (*fall*) _____ over, right on top of Jake, who (*injure, seriously*) _____. Jake (*end*) _____ up in the hospital for three weeks, and today he (*wear, still*) _____ a cast on his arm. I bet that's the last time he ever kicks a (*vend*) _____ machine.

18. I have a serious problem with my (*propose*) _____ class schedule this semester. The chemistry class that I need for my science requirement (*offer, not*) _____ _____ this semester. I don't know what to do. I need that class in order to graduate in June.

19. A: Arthur (*jog*) _____ for a full hour. He must be tired.

    B: Why is he jogging so much these days?

    A: He (*plan*) _____ to run in the 10k race in Chicago next month, and he wants to be ready for it.

20. A census is a survey of the population of a country. In the United States, a population census (*conduct*) _____ by the government every ten years. Questionnaires (*send*) _____ to every household in the country. People (*ask*) _____ about such things as their employment, education, housing, and family size. After the information (*collect*) _____, it (*publish*) _____ by the Census Bureau. Many government agencies (*use*) _____ this information to make plans for the future about housing, agriculture, urban development, public transportation, and schools.

◇ **PRACTICE 28—SELFSTUDY: Error analysis. (Chapter 3)**

Directions: Find and correct the errors in the following sentences.

1. The children were frightening by the thunder and lightning.
2. Two people got hurted in the accident and were took to the hospital by an ambulance.
3. The movie was so bored that we fell asleep after an hour.
4. The students helped by the clear explanation that the teacher gave.
5. That alloy is composing by iron and tin.
6. The winner of the race hasn't been announcing yet.
7. If you are interesting in modern art, you should see the new exhibit at the museum. It is fascinated.
8. Progress is been made every day.
9. When, where, and by whom has the automobile invented?
10. My brother and I have always been interesting in learning more about our family history.
11. I am not agree with you, and I don't think you'll ever be convince me.
12. Each assembly kit is accompany by detailed instructions.
13. Arthur was giving an award by the city for all of his efforts in crime prevention.
14. It was late, and I was getting very worry about my son.
15. The problem was very puzzled. I couldn't figure it out.
16. Many strange things were happened last night.

◇ PRACTICE 29—GUIDED STUDY: Writing.

Directions: In writing, describe how something is made. Choose one of the following:

1. Use a reference book such as an encyclopedia to find out how something is made, and then summarize this information. It's not necessary to get into technical details. Read about the process and then describe it in your own words. *Possible subjects:* paper, a candle, a pencil, glass, steel, silk thread, bronze, leather, etc.
2. Write about something you know how to make. *Possible subjects:* a kite, a ceramic pot, a bookcase, a sweater, a bead necklace, a special decoration, a special kind of food, etc.

Notice the use of the passive in the following example.

Paper is a common material that **is used** throughout the world. It **has been made** from various plants, such as rice and papyrus, and used **to be made** by hand. Today wood is the chief source of paper, and most of the work **is done** by machines. Paper **can be made** from wood pulp by either a mechanical or a chemical process.

In the mechanical process, the wood **is ground** into small chips. During the grinding, it **is sprayed** with water to keep it from burning from the friction of the grinder. Then the chips **are soaked** in water.

In the chemical process, first the wood **is washed**, and then it **is cut** into small pieces by a chipping machine. The wood **is** then **cooked** in certain chemicals. After cooking, the wood **is washed** to get rid of the chemicals.

The pulp that results from either the mechanical or chemical process **is** then **drained** to form a thick mass. Next it **is bleached** in chlorine and then thoroughly **washed** again. Then the pulp **is put** through a machine that squeezes the water out and forms the pulp into long sheets. Next the pulp sheets pass through a drier and a press. Then they **are wound** into rolls.

Remember: You are writing a general description of how something is made. You are not giving your reader instructions to follow. Do not write in the second person (*e.g., If you want to make paper, first you grind the wood into small chips. Be sure to spray the chips during the grinding so they don't burn. Then you soak the chips in water.*). Write a description, not instructions.

◇ PRACTICE TEST A—SELFSTUDY: The passive. (Chapter 3)

Directions: Choose the correct answer.
Example:

___**D**___ Ms. Haugen _____ at the Ajax Company.
    A. is employing   B. employed   C. employing   D. is employed

_____ 1. I still can't believe it! My bicycle _____ last night.
    A. was stolen   B. was stealing   C. stolen   D. stole

_____ 2. The current constitutional problem is _____ by the top legal minds in the country.
    A. studying   B. being studying   C. being studied   D. been studied

_____ 3. Something funny _____ in class yesterday.
    A. happened   B. was happened   C. happens   D. is happened

_____ 4. The child's arm was swollen because he _____ by a bee.
   A. stung   B. had stung
   C. had been stung   D. had being stung

_____ 5. Today, many serious childhood diseases _____ by early immunization.
   A. are preventing   B. can prevent
   C. prevent   D. can be prevented

_____ 6. I _____ with you on that subject.
   A. am agree   B. am agreed   C. agreeing   D. agree

_____ 7. Many U.S. automobiles _____ in Detroit, Michigan.
   A. manufacture   B. have manufactured
   C. are manufactured   D. are manufacturing

_____ 8. Let's go ahead and do it now. Nothing _____ by waiting.
   A. accomplishes   B. accomplished
   C. has accomplished   D. will be accomplished

_____ 9. "When _____?"
   "In 1928."
   A. penicillin was discovered   B. did penicillin discovered
   C. was penicillin discovered   D. did penicillin discover

_____ 10. In recent years, the government has imposed pollution controls on automobile
   manufacturers. Both domestic and imported automobiles must _____ anti-pollution
   devices.
   A. equip with   B. be equipped with
   C. equip by   D. be equipped by

_____ 11. A shortage of water is a problem in many parts of the world. In some areas, water _____
   from the ground faster than nature can replenish the supply.
   A. is being taken   B. has been taking
   C. is taking   D. has taken

_____ 12. Vitamin C _____ by the human body. It gets into the blood stream quickly.
   A. absorbs easily   B. is easily absorbing
   C. is easily absorbed   D. absorbed easily

_____ 13. "When can I have my car back?"
   "I think it'll _____ late this afternoon."
   A. finish   B. be finished   C. have finished   D. be finish

_____ 14. I didn't think my interview went very well, but I guess it must have. Despite all my
   anxiety, I _____ for the job I wanted. I'm really going to work hard to justify their
   confidence.
   A. was hiring   B. hired   C. got hiring   D. got hired

_____ 15. My country _____ the pursuit of world peace.
   A. is dedicating to   B. is dedicated to
   C. is dedicating by   D. is dedicated by

_____ 16. About 15,000 years ago, northern Wisconsin _____ under ice a mile deep.
   A. buried   B. was burying   C. was buried   D. had buried

_____ 17. Ed was new on the job, but he quickly fit himself into the _____ routine of the office.
   A. established   B. establishing   C. establishes   D. establish

_____ 18. The Mayan Indians _____ an accurate and sophisticated calendar more than seven
   centuries ago.
   A. were developed   B. developed
   C. are developed   D. have been developed

_____ 19. George is _____ Lisa.
        A. marry with   B. marry to   C. married with   D. married to

_____ 20. The rescuers _____ for their bravery and fortitude in locating the lost mountain climbers.
        A. were praised   B. praised   C. were praising   D. praising

◇ PRACTICE TEST B—GUIDED STUDY: The passive. (Chapter 3)

Directions: Choose the correct answer.

Example:

_D_ *Ms. Haugen _____ at the Ajax Company.*
        A. is employing   *B. employed*   *C. employing*   *D. is employed*

_____ 1. "Can't we do something about the situation?"
"Something _____ right now."
        A. is doing   B. is done
        C. is being done   D. has been doing

_____ 2. "Are you interested in scuba diving?"
"Very. Undersea life is _____."
        A. fascinated   B. fascinating
        C. being fascinating   D. being fascinated

_____ 3. The university _____ by private funds as well as by tuition income and grants.
        A. is supported   B. supports   C. is supporting   D. has supported

_____ 4. My car made strange noises, sputtered to a stop, and then wouldn't start again. Fortunately, the mechanic at my garage _____ the source of the problem.
        A. was discover   B. discovered
        C. was discovered   D. has been discovered

_____ 5. "Ms. Jones, please type those letters before noon."
"They've already _____, sir. They're on your desk."
        A. typed   B. been typed
        C. being typed   D. been being typed

_____ 6. "Has the committee made its decision yet?"
"Not yet. They are still _____ the proposal."
        A. considering   B. been considered
        C. being considered   D. considered

_____ 7. In some rural areas of the United States, health care _____ by only a small number of doctors, nurses, and other health professionals. It's often more than they can handle.
        A. is providing   B. is being provided
        C. provides   D. provided

_____ 8. "How did that window _____?"
"I don't know."
        A. get broken   B. broke   C. got broken   D. broken

_____ 9. Renoir is one of the most popular French impressionist painters. His paintings _____ masterpieces all over the world.
        A. had considered   B. are considering
        C. are considered   D. consider

_____ 10. As the fairy tale goes, the prince _____ into a frog by an evil magician, and only a kiss from a beautiful princess could restore him to his original state.
    A. turned   B. was turning
    C. was turned   D. had been turning

_____ 11. When I woke up and looked outside, the landscape had changed. The ground had been lightly _____ with a dusting of snow during the night.
    A. covering   B. cover   C. covers   D. covered

_____ 12. We can't even walk in this storm. Let's wait in the hallway where we'll be _____ the strong winds until things quiet down.
    A. protected from   B. protected by
    C. protecting from   D. protecting by

_____ 13. "_____ about the eight o'clock flight to Chicago?"
        "Not yet."
    A. Has been an announcement made   B. Has an announcement made
    C. Has an announcement been made   D. Has been made an announcement

_____ 14. Last night a tornado swept through Rockville. It _____ everything in its path.
    A. destroyed   B. was destroyed
    C. was being destroyed   D. had been destroyed

_____ 15. Be sure to wash these vegetables thoroughly. A lot of pesticide residue _____ on unwashed produce.
    A. can find   B. can found   C. can be found   D. can be finding

_____ 16. The building of the bridge had been delayed for three years because of political problems on both sides of the river. Finally, it _____ because the public demanded action, and now many hours of driving have been saved for daily commuters.
    A. was constructed   B. gets constructed
    C. constructed   D. has constructed

_____ 17. On Friday afternoon before a three-day holiday weekend, the highways _____ people on their way out of the city.
    A. are crowding by   B. are being crowd with
    C. are crowded with   D. crowd by

_____ 18. Fortunately, the hospital's new air-conditioning system _____ when the first heat wave of the summer arrived.
    A. had installed   B. installed
    C. had been installed   D. had been installing

_____ 19. It's hard to believe that my application for a scholarship _____. I was sure I'd get it. I don't know now if I'll go to school next year.
    A. was denied   B. denied   C. was denying   D. has denied

_____ 20. The man died because medical help was not summoned. A doctor should _____ immediately.
    A. have called   B. been called
    C. called   D. have been called

CHAPTER *4*
Gerunds and Infinitives

◇ **PRACTICE 1—SELFSTUDY:** Gerunds as objects of prepositions. (Chart 4-2)

Directions: Complete the sentences with PREPOSITIONS followed by GERUNDS. Use the verbs in the given list. Use each verb only once.

✔ *ask*	*have*	*make*	*see*
break	*kill*	*open*	*talk*
finish	*lock*	*practice*	*wash*

1. Instead ___ ***of asking*** ___ for help on each arithmetic problem, you should use your book and try to figure out the answers yourself.

2. I look forward _____ you the next time I'm in town. I'll be sure to let you know ahead of time so that we can plan to get together.

3. Alice told us that she was tired _____ the dishes every night.

4. The four-year-old was blamed _____ the glass candy dish.

5. Because of the bomb scare, no one was allowed in the building. People were prevented _____ the front door by a guard who was stationed there.

6. You should listen to other people instead _____ about yourself all the time.

7. What do you feel _____ for dinner? Does chicken and rice sound good?

8. Frank is an environmental conservationist who believes animals should be protected from hunters. He objects _____ wild animals for sport.

9. Please don't argue _____ your homework. Just do it.

10. Marie is responsible _____ all the doors and windows and _____ sure all the lights are turned off before she leaves work in the evening.

11. Mario spent all month preparing for the tennis match, but in spite _____ for many hours each day, he lost the match to Ivan.

◇ PRACTICE 2—GUIDED STUDY: Gerunds as objects of prepositions. (Chart 4-2)

Directions: Using the verbs in parentheses, complete the sentences with your own words.

1. (*help*)   I thanked my friend . . . *for helping me with my homework.*
2. (*collect*)   The treasurer is responsible . . . .
3. (*work*)   The employees objected . . . .
4. (*be*)   I apologized . . . .
5. (*win*)   Mark is capable . . . .
6. (*get*)   I'm not used . . . .
7. (*go to*)   The rainy weather prevented us . . . .
8. (*clean up*)   All of the children participated . . . .
9. (*enter*)   Unauthorized persons are prohibited . . . .
10. (*attend*)   She was excited . . . .
11. (*bring*)   I thanked the flight attendant . . . .
12. (*hire*)   Mr. Smith is opposed . . . .
13. (*have to do*) The students complained . . . .

◇ PRACTICE 3—GUIDED STUDY: Verbs followed by gerunds. (Charts 4-3 and 4-4)

Directions: Make sentences using the given verbs.
Examples:
    enjoy + watch → *Do you enjoy watching old movies on television?*
    mind + have to be → *I don't mind having to be in class at 8:00 A.M.*
    put off + pack → *Dan usually puts off packing his suitcase until the very last minute.*

1. talk about + take
2. avoid + eat
3. go + jog
4. finish + do
5. mind + have to stay
6. consider + go + swim
7. stop + cry
8. discuss + go + shop
9. mention + have to go
10. delay + put
11. suggest + change
12. keep + ask
13. quit + worry about
14. postpone + take

◇ PRACTICE 4—SELFSTUDY: Gerund vs. infinitive. (Charts 4-1 → 4-5)

Directions: Select the correct answer for each sentence.

___*B*___   1. Whenever we met, Jack avoided _____ at me.
                A. to look   B. looking

_____   2. Most people enjoy _____ to different parts of the world.
                A. to travel   B. traveling

_____   3. Marjorie needs _____ another job. Her present company is going out of business.
                A. to find   B. finding

_____   4. May I change the TV channel, or do you want _____ more of this program?
                A. to watch   B. watching

_____   5. Joan is considering _____ her major from pre-med studies to psychology.
                A. to change   B. changing

_____ 6. Although Joe slammed on his brakes, he couldn't avoid _____ the small dog that suddenly darted out in front of his car.
　　　A. to hit　　　　　　B. hitting

_____ 7. I hope _____ my autobiography before I die. Do you think anyone would read it?
　　　A. to write　　　　　B. writing

_____ 8. Joyce thanked us for _____ them to dinner and said that they wanted to have us over for dinner next week.
　　　A. to invite　　　　　B. inviting

_____ 9. If you delay _____ your bills, you will only incur more and more interest charges.
　　　A. to pay　　　　　　B. paying

_____ 10. My lawyer advised me not _____ anything further about the accident.
　　　A. to say　　　　　　B. saying

_____ 11. A procrastinator is one who habitually postpones _____ things—especially tasks that are unpleasant.
　　　A. to do　　　　　　B. doing

_____ 12. You should plan _____ at the stadium early or you won't be able to get good seats.
　　　A. to arrive　　　　　B. arriving

_____ 13. My mom asked me _____ up some eggs at the supermarket on my way home from work.
　　　A. to pick　　　　　B. picking

_____ 14. Nobody has offered _____ the house next door, so I think they're going to lower the price.
　　　A. to buy　　　　　　B. buying

_____ 15. The highway patrol advises _____ the old route through the city because the interstate highway is under major repairs.
　　　A. to take　　　　　B. taking

_____ 16. Would you mind _____ that apple for me? My arthritis is acting up in my right hand.
　　　A. to peel　　　　　B. peeling

_____ 17. Stop _____ me! I'll get everything finished before I go to bed.
　　　A. to nag　　　　　B. nagging

_____ 18. When the university suggested _____ the tuition again, the student senate protested vigorously.
　　　A. to raise　　　　　B. raising

_____ 19. Are we permitted _____ guests to the ceremony? I'd like to invite my friend to join us.
　　　A. to bring　　　　　B. bringing

_____ 20. The city council agreed _____ the architect's proposed design for a new parking garage.
　　　A. to accept　　　　　B. accepting

◇ **PRACTICE 5—SELFSTUDY:** Verbs followed by infinitives. (Chart 4-5)

Directions: Restate the given sentences. Choose the most appropriate reporting verb in parentheses. Make it active or passive as appropriate. Include an INFINITIVE in the completion and any other necessary words.

1. The teacher said to Jim, "Would you give your book to Mary, please?
　　(ask, tell, order)
　　→ The teacher _____*asked Jim to give*_____ his book to Mary.

2. The sign said, "No parking in this area. Violators will be towed away."
   (*invite, warn, force*)
   → Drivers _____ ***were warned not to park*** _____ in the area.

3. Before Bobby went to bed, his father said, "Don't forget to brush your teeth."
   (*invite, allow, remind*)
   → Before Bobby went to bed, his father _____
   his teeth.

4. Under the law, drivers and all passengers must wear seat belts while in a moving vehicle.
   (*encourage, require, permit*)
   → Drivers and passengers _____ seat belts while in
   a moving vehicle.

5. When I asked the nurse about my skin rash, she said, "You should consult a dermatologist."
   (*ask, permit, advise*)
   → The nurse _____ a dermatologist.

6. The fire chief said, "Everyone must leave the building immediately."
   (*order, remind, allow*)
   → Everyone _____ the building immediately.

7. The instructor said to the students, "You will have exactly one hour to complete the exam."
   (*order, expect, warn*)
   → The students _____ the exam in one
   hour.

8. Because he forgot last year, I told my husband several times that he should buy some flowers
   for his mother on Mother's Day.
   (*remind, require, allow*)
   → I _____ some flowers for his
   mother on Mother's Day.

9. My garage mechanic said, "You should get a tune-up every 5,000 miles."
   (*ask, order, advise*)
   → My garage mechanic _____ a tune-up every 5,000
   miles.

10. The factory manager said to the employees, "Do not come late. If you do, you will lose your
    jobs."
    (*ask, warn, encourage*)
    → The employees _____ late.

11. The sign on the side door says, "Do not enter," so we have to use a different door.
    (*ask, permit, force*)
    → Nobody _____ the side door.

12. The little girl said to her father, "Daddy, I really like this tricycle. Can we buy it?"
    (*require, ask, advise*)
    → The little girl _____ a tricycle for her.

13. We often told our grandfather, "Your experiences as a sailor in the navy were fascinating. You
    should write a book about them."
    (*remind, encourage, require*)
    → We _____ a book about his
    experiences in the navy.

14. The judge said to the defendant, "You must not shout in the courtroom again."
    (*ask, order, encourage*)
    → The defendant _____ in the courtroom again.

◇ **PRACTICE 6—GUIDED STUDY:** Verbs followed by infinitives. (Chart 4-5)

Directions: Report what the speakers say by using a verb from the following list and an INFINITIVE phrase. Use each verb in the list one time only. Make your sentence passive if the speaker is not specifically identified.

advise	✔ ask	invite	remind
allow	encourage	order	warn

1. During the water shortage, someone in authority said to the public, "Curtail your use of water as much as possible."
   → *During the water shortage, the public was asked to curtail its use of water as much as possible.*
2. Laura said to her roommate, "Don't forget to set your alarm clock for 6:00 A.M."
3. Mrs. Jones said to the children, "Each of you may have one piece of candy."
4. The doctor said to my father, "It would be best if you limited your sugar consumption."
5. My parents often said to me, "Good for you! It's good to be independent!"
6. Someone said to the children, "Don't swim in the lake without an adult present."
7. The police officer shouted to the reckless driver, "Pull over!"
8. Rose said to Gerald, "I'd like you to come to my house Sunday night to meet my parents."

◇ **PRACTICE 7—SELFSTUDY:** Gerund vs. infinitive. (Chart 4-6)

Directions: Choose the best answer or answers. In some cases, BOTH answers are correct.

B 1. John was trying _____ the door with the wrong key.
   A. unlocking   B. to unlock

A, B 2. The audience began _____ before the curtains closed.
   A. clapping   B. to clap

_____ 3. The soccer teams continued _____ even though it began to snow.
   A. playing   B. to play

_____ 4. We like _____ outside when the weather is warm and sunny.
   A. eating   B. to eat

_____ 5. We began _____ to the news when we heard the Olympics mentioned.
   A. listening   B. to listen

_____ 6. I was just beginning _____ asleep when the phone rang.
   A. falling   B. to fall

_____ 7. I really hate _____ late for appointments.
   A. being   B. to be

_____ 8. The cake was starting _____ when I took it out of the oven.
   A. burning   B. to burn

_____ 9. She's so impatient! She can't stand _____ in line for anything.
   A. waiting   B. to wait

_____ 10. I prefer _____ my bicycle to work because the automobile traffic is too heavy.
   A. riding   B. to ride

_____ 11. Lillian prefers _____ to taking the bus.
   A. walking   B. to walk

_____ 12. Tim prefers _____ than to jog for exercise.
   A. walking   B. to walk

_____ 13. The baby loves _____ in the car.
   A. riding   B. to ride

_____ 14. Near the end of the performance, the audience began _____ their feet on the floor.
   A. stamping   B. to stamp

_____ 15. The audience began to clap and _____ their feet on the floor.
   A. stamping   B. (to) stamp

_____ 16. The audience began clapping and _____ their feet on the floor.
   A. stamping   B. (to) stamp

_____ 17. My son sometimes forgets _____ the stove when he's finished cooking.
   A. turning off   B. to turn off

_____ 18. Alex will never forget _____ his first helicopter ride.
   A. taking   B. to take

_____ 19. Would you please remember _____ away all the tapes when you're finished listening to them?
   A. putting   B. to put

_____ 20. I remember _____ them away when I finished with them last night.
   A. putting   B. to put

_____ 21. I remember _____ Bolivia for the first time. It's a beautiful country.
   A. visiting   B. to visit

_____ 22. What am I going to do? I forgot _____ my calculus text, and I need it for the review today.
   A. bringing   B. to bring

_____ 23. My boss regrets _____ his secretary now that she is gone.
   A. firing   B. to fire

_____ 24. The letter said, "I regret _____ you that your application has been denied."
   A. informing   B. to inform

_____ 25. I haven't been able to get in touch with Shannon. I tried _____ her. Then I tried _____ her a letter. I tried _____ a message with her brother when I talked to him. Nothing worked.
   A. calling/writing/leaving   B. to call/to write/to leave

_____ 26. I always try _____ my bills on time, but sometimes I'm a little late.
   A. paying   B. to pay

◇ **PRACTICE 8—GUIDED STUDY:** Gerund vs. infinitive. (Charts 4-3 → 4-6)

Directions: Use the correct form of the verbs in parentheses and complete the sentence with your own words. Include a (PRO)NOUN OBJECT between the two verbs if necessary.

Examples:
   The fire marshal (*tell + unlock*) → *The fire marshal told us to unlock the back doors of the school to provide a fast exit in the event of an emergency.*
   (. . .) (*be asked + lead*) → *Maria was asked to lead a group discussion in class yesterday.*

1. Mr. (. . .) (*remind + finish*)
2. The teacher (*postpone + give*)
3. Students (*be required + have*)
4. The counselor (*advise + take*)
5. I (*try + learn*)
6. Ms. (. . .) (*warn + not open*)
7. I (*like + go + camp*)
8. (. . .) (*invite + go*)

9. (. . .) (*promise + not tell*)
10. We (*not be permitted + take*)
11. My friend (*ask + tell*)
12. When the wind (*begin + blow*)
13. I (*remember + call*)
14. (. . .) (*tell + wash*)
15. (. . .) (*be told + be*)
16. I (*avoid + get*)

◇ **PRACTICE 9—SELFSTUDY: Gerund vs. infinitive. (Charts 4-7 and 4-8)**

Directions: Work with another person. One of you should read the beginning of the sentence, and the other, without looking at the book, should supply the correct response: **to do it** or **doing it**. (If you are studying alone, cover up the answers in parentheses and check yourself as you go.)

Example: A: *I enjoy . . . .*
            B: *. . . doing it.*

1. I dislike . . . . (doing it)
2. She was ordered . . . . (to do it.)
3. I urged my friend . . . . (to do it.)
4. Can he afford . . . . (to do it?)
5. We all discussed . . . . (doing it.)
6. The institute requires us . . . . (to do it.)
7. We will eventually complete . . . . (doing it.)
8. The whole class practiced . . . . (doing it.)
9. I really don't care . . . . (to do it.)
10. Do you recommend . . . . (doing it?)
11. She was expected . . . . (to do it.)
12. Bill resented his roommate . . . . (doing it.)
13. Did the little boy admit . . . . (doing it?)
14. Please allow us . . . . (to do it.)
15. The whole family anticipated . . . . . . (doing it.)
16. No one recollected . . . . (doing it.)
17. Did you risk . . . . (doing it?)
18. Did they recall . . . . (doing it?)
19. My friend challenged me . . . . (to do it.)
20. Our director postponed . . . . (doing it.)
21. Do you mind . . . . (doing it?)
22. Why did he pretend . . . . (to do it?)
23. The teacher arranged . . . . (to do it.)
24. The regulations permit us . . . . (to do it.)
25. The dentist wanted to delay . . . . (doing it.)
26. Can anyone learn . . . . (to do it?)
27. Did someone offer . . . . (to do it?)
28. He doesn't deny . . . . (doing it.)
29. Somehow, the cat managed . . . . (to do it.)
30. Everyone avoided . . . . (doing it.)
31. The boy dared Al . . . . (to do it.)
32. Our teacher threatened . . . . (to do it.)
33. The contestant practiced . . . . (doing it.)
34. My friend consented . . . . (to do it.)
35. I miss . . . . (doing it.)

◇ **PRACTICE 10—SELFSTUDY: Gerund vs. infinitive. (Charts 4-2 → 4-8)**

Directions: Complete the sentences with the correct form, GERUND or INFINITIVE, using the words in parentheses.

1. The store offered ____*to refund*____ the money I paid for the book I returned. (*refund*)

2. Don't pretend ___*to be*___ what you aren't. (*be*)

3. I persuaded my brother-in-law not _____ that old car. (*buy*)

4. Annie denied _____ the brick through the window. (*throw*)

5. My father expects me _____ high marks in school. (*get*)

6. According to the sign on the restaurant door, all diners are required _____ shirts and shoes. (*wear*)

7. We are planning _____ several historical sites in Moscow. (*visit*)

8. There appears _____ no way to change our reservation for the play at this late date. (*be*)

9. For some strange reason, I keep _____ today is Saturday. (*think*)

10. All of the members agreed _____ the emergency meeting. (*attend*)

11. I've arranged _____ work early tomorrow. (*leave*)

12. Even though Anna had never cut anyone's hair before, she readily consented _____ her husband's hair. (*cut*)

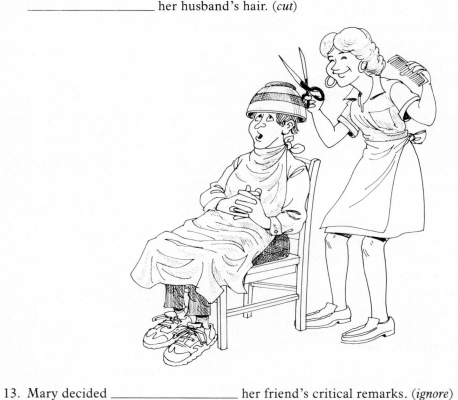

13. Mary decided _____ her friend's critical remarks. (*ignore*)

14. My roommate says I have a terrible voice, so I stopped _____ in the shower. (*sing*)

15. Did the doctor mention _____ any foods in particular? (*avoid*)

16. The cashier always remembers _____ the money in her cash register each day before she leaves work. (*count*)

17. Let's hurry! We must finish _____ the office before 3:00 this afternoon. (*paint*)

18. The student with the highest average deserves _____ an "A". (*get*)

19. I appreciate your _____ for my dinner. I'll buy next time. (*pay*)

20. The physically handicapped child struggled _____ up with the other children on the playground, but she couldn't. (*keep*)

21. Janice misses _____ walks with her father in the evening now that she has moved away from home. (*take*)

22. The customs official demanded _____ what was inside the gift-wrapped box. (*know*)

23. We've discussed _____ to New York in the fall, but I'm worried about our children having to adjust to a new school system and new friends. (*move*)

24. Children shouldn't be allowed _____ violent programs on TV. (*watch*)

25. In a fit of anger, I ordered my neighbor _____ his mule off my property. (*keep*)

◇ **PRACTICE 11—SELFSTUDY:** Gerund vs. infinitive. (Charts 4-2 → 4-8)

Directions: Complete the sentences with the correct form, GERUND or INFINITIVE, using the words in parentheses.

1. The doctor was forced __***to operate***__ immediately to save the patient's life. (*operate*)

2. The newspaper hired Bill _____ pictures of the championship match between the two boxers. (*shoot*)

3. Most passengers dislike _____ to sit in small, uncomfortable seats on transoceanic flights. (*have*)

4. I chose _____ to Stanford University for my undergraduate studies. (*go*)

5. I must drive more carefully. I can't risk _____ another speeding ticket. (*get*)

6. All of the members agreed _____ the emergency meeting. (*attend*)

7. Jack promised _____ to the meeting. (*come*)

8. The sign warns you not _____ right on a red light. (*turn*)

9. Did Dick mean _____ Sue about the surprise party, or did it slip out accidentally? (*tell*)

10. You must keep _____ on the computer until you understand how to use all of the programs. (*practice*)

11. Our class volunteered _____ the classroom during the maintenance workers' strike. (*clean*)

12. When you get through _____ the newspaper, I could use your help in the kitchen. (*read*)

13. I think we should delay _____ these reports to the main office. (*send*)

14. The judge demanded _____ the original document, not the photocopy. (*see*)

15. After hearing the weather report, I advise you not _____ skiing this afternoon. (*go*)

16. George is interested in _____ an art class. (*take*)

17. I was furious. I threatened never _____ to him again. (*speak*)

18. My parents appreciated _____ the thank-you note you sent them. (*receive*)

19. The committee is planning _____ next Friday. (*meet*)

20. If I don't leave on the 15th, I will miss _____ home in time for my mother's birthday party. (*get*)

21. I know you're anxious to get out of here and get back home, but you should seriously consider _____ in the hospital a few more days. (*stay*)

22. Alex refused _____ for his rude behavior. (*apologize*)

23. When I was in the army, I had to swear _____ my senior officers' orders. (*obey*)

24. I don't recall _____ your dictionary anywhere in the apartment. Maybe you left it in the classroom. (*see*)

25. Mrs. Lind required the children _____ off their muddy boots before they came into the house. (*take*)

◇ **PRACTICE 12—SELFSTUDY: Gerund vs. infinitive. (Charts 4-7 and 4-8)**

Directions: Choose the correct answer.

___**A**___ 1. The groom anticipated _____ the wedding ceremony.
　　　　　A. enjoying　　B. to enjoy

_____ 2. The department store agreed _____ back the damaged radio.
　　　　　A. taking　　B. to take

_____ 3. Would the doctor mind _____ some time talking to me after the examination?
　　　　　A. spending　　B. to spend

_____ 4. We miss _____ Professor Sanders in Asian history this quarter.
　　　　　A. having　　B. to have

_____ 5. Dan failed _____ the firefighter's examination and was quite upset.
　　　　　A. passing　　B. to pass

_____ 6. The travelers anticipated _____ safely at their destination.
　　　　　A. arriving　　B. to arrive

_____ 7. She expects _____ her baby at the new hospital.
　　　　　A. delivering　　B. to deliver

_____ 8. The bad weather caused us _____ our connecting flight to Rome.
　　　　　A. missing　　B. to miss

_____ 9. We dislike _____ dinner at 9:00 P.M.
　　　　　A. eating　　B. to eat

_____ 10. Most of the students completed _____ their research papers on time.
　　　　　A. writing　　B. to write

_____ 11. My niece hopes _____ with me to Disneyland next April.
　　　　　A. traveling　　B. to travel

_____ 12. This note will remind me _____ the chicken for dinner tomorrow night.
      A. defrosting   B. to defrost

_____ 13. Willy denied _____ a whole bag of chocolate chip cookies before lunch.
      A. eating   B. to eat

_____ 14. You must swear _____ the truth in a court of law.
      A. telling   B. to tell

_____ 15. I didn't mean _____ him.
      A. interrupting   B. to interrupt

◇ **PRACTICE 13—GUIDED STUDY:** Gerund vs. infinitive. (Charts 4-7 and 4-8)

Directions: Make sentences from the following verb combinations. Select any tense for the first verb but use a GERUND or INFINITIVE for the second verb. Include a (PRO)NOUN OBJECT if necessary.

Examples:
    can't afford + buy → *I can't afford to buy a new car for at least another year.*
    dare + dive → *My friends dared me to dive into the pool.*

1. keep + play
2. direct + save
3. regret + tell
4. manage + get
5. remind + take
6. be used to + stay
7. persuade + not buy
8. mention + give
9. suggest + go
10. can't imagine + travel
11. recommend + take
12. convince + go + swim
13. miss + be
14. not appreciate + hear
15. fail + tell
16. resent + be
17. resist + eat
18. claim + know
19. deserve + get
20. not recall + say
21. look forward to + see
22. beg + give
23. agree + hire + work
24. remember + tell + be
25. urge + practice + speak
26. tell + keep + try + call

◇ **PRACTICE 14—GUIDED STUDY:** Using gerunds as subjects. (Chart 4-10)

Directions: Using your own words, complete the sentences using GERUND phrases as subjects.

Examples:
    ...isn't easy. → *Climbing to the top of a mountain isn't easy.*
    ...is a demanding job. → *Managing a major corporation is a demanding job.*

1. ...wears me out.
2. ...can be difficult.
3. ...turned out to be a mistake.
4. ...will only add to your problems.
5. ...has changed my life.
6. ...requires great skill and concentration.
7. ...demands patience and a sense of humor.
8. ...is a complicated process.
9. ...is very frustrating.
10. ...was a real disappointment.
11. ...looks easy.
12. ...never works.

◇ PRACTICE 15—GUIDED STUDY: Using *it* + infinitive. (Chart 4-9)

Directions: Make sentences beginning with **it**. Use a form of the given expression in your sentence, followed by an INFINITIVE phrase.

Examples:
   be dangerous → *It's dangerous to ride a motorcycle without wearing a helmet.*
   be difficult → *It was difficult for me to quit my job and go back to school.*

1. be important	6. be always a pleasure
2. be boring	7. be clever of you
3. not be easy	8. not cost much money
4. be foolish	9. be necessary
5. must be interesting	10. might be a good idea

◇ PRACTICE 16—SELFSTUDY: *(In order) to.* (Chart 4-10)

Directions: Add *in order* wherever possible. If nothing should be added, write the Ø.

1. I went to the garden center _____*in order*_____ to get some fertilizer for my flowers.

2. When the teacher asked him a question, Jack pretended _____Ø_____ to understand what she was saying.

3. My roommate asked me _____ to repair the leaky faucet.

4. I bought a new screwdriver _____ to repair my bicycle.

5. Emily likes _____ to go ice skating every weekend.

6. Please open the door _____ to let some fresh air in.

7. My mother always said I should eat lots of green vegetables _____ to make my body strong.

8. John climbed onto a chair _____ to change a light bulb in the ceiling.

9. I really want _____ to learn Italian before I visit Venice next year.

10. Elizabeth has to practice at least four hours every day _____ to be ready for her piano recital next month.

11. I jog three times a week _____ to stay healthy.

12. It is a good idea _____ to know where your children are at all times.

13. Jim finally went to the dentist _____ to get some relief from his toothache.

14. I need to find her _____ to talk to her.

15. Claudia has to work at two jobs _____ to support herself and her three children.

16. It's easier for me _____ to understand written English than spoken English.

17. The students were practicing speaking English into a tape recorder _____ to improve their pronunciation.

18. It isn't important _____ to speak English without any accent at all as long as people understand what you're saying.

◇ **PRACTICE 17—GUIDED STUDY:** Adjectives followed by infinitives. (Chart 4-11)

Directions: Complete the sentences with the expressions in the list and with your own words. Use INFINITIVE phrases in your completions. Use any expression in the list that is appropriate, and use it more than once if you wish.

ashamed to	*delighted to*	*fortunate to*	*ready to*
careful to	*determined to*	*likely to*	*reluctant to*
certain to	*eager to*	*not prepared to*	*willing to*

1. Mary always speeds on the expressway. She's . . . .
   → *She's certain to get stopped by the police.* OR:
   → *She's likely to get a ticket.*

2. There have been a lot of burglaries in my neighborhood recently, so I have started taking precautions. Now I am always very. . . .

3. I've worked hard all day long. Enough's enough. I'm . . . .

4. Next month, I'm going to a family reunion—the first one in 25 years. I'm very much looking forward to it. I'm . . . .

5. Some children grow up in unhappy homes. My family, however, has always been loving and supportive. I'm . . . .

6. Joe's run out of money again, but he doesn't want anyone to know his situation. He needs money desperately, but he's . . . .

7. Rosalyn wants to become an astronaut. That has been her dream since she was a little girl. She has been working hard toward her goal and is . . . .

8. Peter was offered an excellent job in another state, but his wife and children don't want to move. He's not sure what to do. Although he would like the job, he's . . . .

9. At the street market, I bartered with the seller over the price of the garment. He wanted $20. I offered $10. In the end, he was . . . .

10. Jason is going fishing today. He's . . . .

11. Our neighbors had extra tickets to the ballet, so they invited us to go with them. Since both of us love the ballet, we were . . . .

12. It takes maturity and understanding to make wise decisions. Thomas is only seventeen years old. He's . . . .

◇ **PRACTICE 18—SELFSTUDY:** *Too* vs. *very*. (Chart 4-12)

Directions: Add *too* or *very* to the sentences, as appropriate.

1. The box is ___**very**___ heavy, but I can lift it.

2. John dropped his physics course because it was ___**too**___ difficult for him.

3. I think it's _____ late to get tickets to the concert. I heard they were all sold.

4. It's _____ cold today, but I'm still going to take my daily walk.

5. Our cat is fourteen years old. Now he's _____ old to catch mice in the field across the street.

6. It's _____ dark to see in here. Please turn on the lights.

7. She was _____ ill. Nevertheless, she came to the family reunion.

8. The boys were _____ busy to help me clean out the garage, so I did it myself.

9. Learning a second language is _____ difficult, but most of the students are doing well.

10. We enjoyed our dinner at that restaurant last night. It was _____ good.

11. Professor Andrews is always _____ interesting, but I'm _____ tired to go to the lecture tonight.

12. He's _____ young to understand. He'll understand when he's older.

13. The meal was _____ good. I enjoyed every morsel.

14. I'm _____ sleepy to watch the rest of the TV movie. Let me know how it turns out.

15. Sally was running _____ fast for me to keep up with her, so I lagged behind.

◇ **PRACTICE 19—SELFSTUDY: Passive infinitives. (Chart 4-13)**

Directions: Choose the correct answer.

_____ 1. When I told Tim the news, he seemed _____.
       A. to surprise   B. to be surprised

_____ 2. Ms. Thompson is always willing to help, but she doesn't want _____ at home unless there is an emergency.
       A. to call   B. to be called

_____ 3. The children agreed _____ the candy equally.
       A. to divide   B. to be divided

_____ 4. Janice is going to fill out an application. She wants _____ for the job.
       A. to consider   B. to be considered

_____ 5. I expected _____ to the party, but I wasn't.
       A. to invite   B. to be invited

_____ 6. The mail is supposed _____ at noon.
       A. to deliver   B. to be delivered

_____ 7. I expect _____ at the airport by my uncle.
       A. to meet   B. to be met

_____ 8. Mr. Steinberg offered _____ us to the train station.
       A. to drive   B. to be driven

_____ 9. The children appear _____ about the trip.
       A. to excite   B. to be excited

_____ 10. Your compositions are supposed _____ in ink.
        A. to write   B. to be written

◇ **PRACTICE 20—SELFSTUDY: Passive gerunds. (Chart 4-13)**

Directions: Choose the correct answer.

_____ 1. I don't appreciate _____ when I'm speaking.
   A. interrupting   B. being interrupted

_____ 2. Avoid _____ your houseplants too much water.
   A. giving   B. being given

_____ 3. The mountain climbers are in danger of _____ by an avalanche.
   A. killing   B. being killed

_____ 4. Does Dr. Johnson mind _____ at home if his patients need his help?
   A. calling   B. being called

_____ 5. I'm interested in _____ my communication skills.
   A. improving   B. being improved

_____ 6. Mrs. Gates appreciated _____ breakfast in bed when she wasn't feeling well.
   A. serving   B. being served

_____ 7. Jack Welles has a good chance of _____. I know I'm going to vote for him.
   A. electing   B. being elected

_____ 8. Sally's low test scores kept her from _____ to the university.
   A. admitting   B. being admitted

_____ 9. Mr. Miller gave no indication of _____ his mind.
   A. changing   B. being changed

_____ 10. Sometimes adolescents complain about not _____ by their parents.
   A. understanding   B. being understood

◇ **PRACTICE 21—SELFSTUDY: Passive infinitives and gerunds. (Chart 4-13)**

Directions: Choose the correct answer.

_____ 1. Instead of _____ about the good news, Tom seemed to be indifferent.
   A. exciting   B. being excited   C. to excite   D. to be excited

_____ 2. The new students hope _____ in many of the school's social activities.
   A. including   B. being included   C. to include   D. to be included

_____ 3. The owner of the building supply store doesn't mind _____ his customers discounts when they buy in large quantities.
   A. giving   B. being given   C. to give   D. to be given

_____ 4. Jack got into trouble when he refused _____ his briefcase for the customs officer.
   A. opening   B. being opened   C. to open   D. to be opened

_____ 5. Barbara didn't mention _____ about her progress report at work, but I'm sure she is.
   A. concerning   B. being concerned
   C. to concern   D. to be concerned

_____ 6. The City Parks Department is putting in several miles of new trails because so many people have said that they enjoy _____ on them.
   A. walking   B. being walked   C. to walk   D. to be walked

_____ 7. You'd better save some money for a rainy day. You can't count on _____ by your parents every time you get into financial difficulty.
     A. rescuing   B. being rescued   C. to rescue   D. to be rescued

_____ 8. Please forgive me. I didn't mean _____ you.
     A. upsetting   B. being upset   C. to upset   D. to be upset

_____ 9. I don't remember _____ of the decision to change the company policy on vacations. When was it decided?
     A. telling   B. being told   C. to tell   D. to be told

_____ 10. Ms. Drake expects _____ about any revisions in her manuscript before it is printed.
     A. consulting   B. being consulted
     C. to consult   D. to be consulted

_____ 11. Sally gave such a good speech that I couldn't resist _____ loudly when she finished.
     A. applauding   B. being applauded
     C. to applaud   D. to be applauded

_____ 12. Tommy admitted _____ the rock through the window.
     A. throwing   B. being thrown   C. to throw   D. to be thrown

_____ 13. If you want to develop inner tranquility, you have to stop _____ by every little thing that happens.
     A. bothering   B. being bothered
     C. to bother   D. to be bothered

_____ 14. Paul really didn't mind _____ by the party to celebrate his fortieth birthday, although he told his friends that they shouldn't have done it.
     A. surprising   B. being surprised
     C. to surprise   D. to be surprised

_____ 15. Anne hoped _____ to join the private club. She could make important business contacts there.
     A. inviting   B. being invited   C. to invite   D. to be invited

◇ PRACTICE 22—SELFSTUDY: Past and past-passive infinitives and gerunds. (Chart 4-13)

Directions: Choose the correct answer.

_____ 1. Are you sure you told me? I don't recall _____ about it.
     A. having told   B. having been told
     C. to have told   D. to have been told

_____ 2. Dan appears _____ some weight. Has he been ill?
     A. having lost   B. having been lost
     C. to have lost   D. to have been lost

_____ 3. Tom made a bad mistake at work, but his boss didn't fire him. He's lucky _____ a second chance.
     A. having given   B. having been given
     C. to have given   D. to have been given

_____ 4. Dr. Wilson is a brilliant and dedicated scientist who had expected to be selected as the director of the institute. She was very surprised not _____ the position.
     A. having offered   B. having been offered
     C. to have offered   D. to have been offered

_____ 5. By the time their baby arrives, the Johnsons hope _____ painting and decorating the new nursery.
     A. having finished   B. having been finished
     C. to have finished   D. to have been finished

_____ 6. We would like _____ to the president's reception, but we weren't.
    A. having invited   B. having been invited
    C. to have invited   D. to have been invited

_____ 7. The stockbroker denied _____ of the secret business deal.
    A. having informed   B. having been informed
    C. to have informed   D. to have been informed

_____ 8. George mentioned _____ in an accident as a child, but he never told us the details.
    A. having injured   B. having been injured
    C. to have injured   D. to have been injured

_____ 9. The Smiths wanted to give their son every advantage. However, they now regret
    _____ him by providing too many material possessions.
    A. having spoiled   B. having been spoiled
    C. to have spoiled   D. to have been spoiled

_____ 10. The spy admitted _____ some highly secret information to enemy agents.
    A. having given   B. having been given
    C. to have given   D. to have been given

◇ **PRACTICE 23—SELFSTUDY:**   Using a possessive to modify a gerund. (Chart 4-15)

Directions: Combine the following. Change ''that fact'' to a GERUND phrase. Use formal English.

Example:
   We answered all of the exam questions correctly. The teacher was pleased with that fact.
    → _The teacher was pleased with our answering_ (OR: _having answered) all of the exam questions correctly._

1. I lost my new watch. My mother was angry about that fact.

2. They are going to spend their vacation with us. We look forward to that fact.

3. Tony failed the economics test even though he studied hard. No one can understand that fact.

4. The students are required to pay an extra fee to use the laboratory. I am upset about that fact.

5. Mary worked late to finish the project. The supervisor appreciated that fact.

6. You are late to work every morning. I will no longer tolerate that fact.

◇ **PRACTICE 24—SELFSTUDY:**   Gerunds and infinitives. (Charts 4-1 → 4-15)

Directions: Choose the correct answer.

_____ 1. Alice didn't expect _____ to Bill's party.
    A. asking   B. being asked   C. to ask   D. to be asked

_____ 2. I finally finished _____ at 7:00 P.M. and served dinner.
    A. cooking   B. being cooked   C. to cook   D. to be cooked

_____ 3. Sam always remembers _____ in the garage so that the driveway is free for other cars.
    A. parking   B. being parked   C. to park   D. to be parked

_____ 4. The nurse suggested _____ two aspirin.
    A. taking   B. being taken   C. to take   D. to be taken

_____ 5. Would you mind not _____ the radio until I've finished with this phone call?
    A. turning on   B. being turned on
    C. to turn on   D. to be turned on

_____ 6. They were fortunate _____ from the fire before the building collapsed.
      A. rescuing
      B. to have rescued
      C. to rescue
      D. to have been rescued

_____ 7. The mouse family avoided _____ by coming out only when the house was empty and the two cats were outside.
      A. catching
      B. being caught
      C. to have been caught
      D. to be caught

_____ 8. The baby continued _____ even after she was picked up.
      A. being crying
      B. having cried
      C. to cry
      D. having been crying

_____ 9. Arthur pretended not _____ hurt when his younger sister bit him.
      A. having   B. be   C. to have   D. to have been

_____ 10. We were shocked to hear the news of your _____.
      A. having fired
      B. having been fired
      C. to be fired
      D. to have been fired

_____ 11. Even though she was much younger than the other children, Alexis demanded _____ in the game they were playing.
      A. including   B. being included   C. to include   D. to be included

_____ 12. Our mechanic said that he expects _____ the brakes on the car before we pick it up.
      A. fixing
      B. being fixed
      C. to have fixed
      D. to have been fixed

_____ 13. Marge's children are used to _____ after school every day. They don't have to walk home.
      A. picking up
      B. being picked up
      C. be picked up
      D. pick up

_____ 14. The bus driver was so tired of _____ the same route every day that he asked for a transfer.
      A. to drive   B. being driven   C. driving   D. drive

_____ 15. I'm sure it's not my fault that Peter found out what we were planning. I don't remember _____ anyone about it.
      A. having told   B. being told   C. to tell   D. to be told

◇ **PRACTICE 25—GUIDED STUDY:** Gerunds and infinitives. (Charts 4-1 → 4-15)

Directions: Complete the sentences. Each sentence should contain a GERUND or INFINITIVE.

Example: You are required . . . .
→ *You are required to stop at the border when entering another country.*

1. Your not wanting . . . .
2. It's important for . . . .
3. I'll never forget . . . .
4. Jack advised not . . . .
5. I'm not willing . . . .
6. My apartment needs . . . .
7. . . . enough energy . . . .
8. . . . in order to save . . . .
9. . . . to be told about . . . .
10. . . . had just begun . . . when . . . .
11. Do you think it is easy . . . .
12. . . . my having been . . . .
13. Have you ever considered . . . .
14. . . . is likely . . . .
15. Most people object . . . .
16. . . . try to avoid . . . .

◇ **PRACTICE 26—SELFSTUDY:** Using verbs of perception. (Chart 4-16)

Directions: Complete the sentences with the words in the list. Use each word only one time. Use the SIMPLE form or the *-ing* form, whichever seems better to you.

arrive	*emerge*	*open*	*prevent*
chirp	*explain*	*perform*	*snore*
climb	*melt*	✔ *practice*	*win*

1. Whenever I have free time, I like to watch the basketball team __***practice***__.

2. When I heard the front door _____, I got up to see if someone had come in.

3. A few years ago, I saw a dog _____ a child from wandering into a busy street by standing in front of her and not letting her get by.

4. It was a thrill to see my brother _____ the chess tournament last year.

5. Uncle Jake is in his bedroom right now. I can hear him _____.

6. I was amazed to see the firefighters _____ so soon after my call.

7. The boy watched the butterfly _____ from its cocoon.

8. It is educational for children to observe adults _____ their daily tasks.

9. When I look at my gym teacher _____ the rope, it looks easy, but when I try it, it is hard.

10. Hearing the birds _____ tells us that spring has indeed arrived.

11. I listened to the teacher _____ how to solve the math problem.

12. I held out my hand and watched each snowflake _____ as soon as it touched my skin.

◇ PRACTICE 27—GUIDED STUDY: Using verbs of perception. (Chart 4-16)

Directions: Make sentences from the given verb combinations. Use the **-ing** form for the second verb if appropriate.

Examples:
hear + shout at → *At work yesterday, I heard someone shouting at Mr. Lewis in the next room.*
listen to + speak → *Lionel has a wonderful British accent. I enjoy listening to him speak.*

1. hear + ring
2. see + hit
3. watch + take
4. look at + sail
5. observe + march

6. see + sink
7. listen to + howl
8. watch + do
9. see + put
10. watch + throw

◇ PRACTICE 28—SELFSTUDY: *Let, help,* and causative verbs. (Charts 4-17 and 4-18)

Directions: Choose the correct answer(s).

__C__   1. Instead of buying a new pair of shoes, I had my old ones _____.
A. repair   B. to repair   C. repaired

__A, B__   2. I helped my daughter _____ her homework.
A. finish   B. to finish   C. finished

_____   3. I made my son _____ the windows before he could go outside to play with his friends.
A. wash   B. to wash   C. washed

_____   4. Maria had her landlord _____ the broken window before winter.
A. fix   B. to fix   C. fixed

_____   5. To please my daughter, I had her old bicycle _____ bright red.
A. paint   B. to paint   C. painted

_____   6. Sam was reluctant, but we finally got him _____ his guitar for us.
A. play   B. to play   C. played

_____   7. When I had to make an emergency phone call, the secretary let me _____ her phone.
A. use   B. to use   C. used

_____   8. Jack, could you help me _____ a place in the garden to plant some tomatoes?
A. dig   B. to dig   C. dug

_____ 9. Before we leave, let's have Shelley _____ a map for us so we won't get lost.
       A. draw   B. to draw   C. drawn

_____ 10. Are you going to let me _____ that last piece of blueberry pie?
       A. eat   B. to eat   C. eaten

◇ **PRACTICE 29—GUIDED STUDY:** _Let, help,_ and causative verbs. (Charts 4-17 and 4-18)

Directions: Make sentences from the given combinations.

Examples:
    let (_someone_) + play → _When I was a child, my older brother wouldn't let me play with him and his friends._
    get (_someone_) + help → _I got my roommate to help me prepare for my final exam in physics._
    have (_something_) + repaired → _I had the brakes on my car repaired at Morgan's Garage._

1. let (_someone_) + cook
2. make (_someone_) + sit
3. get (_someone_) + buy
4. have (_something_) + filled
5. have (_someone_) + bring

6. help (_someone_) + feed
7. let (_someone_) + show
8. make (_someone_) + stop
9. get (_something_) + closed
10. have (_someone_) + find out

◇ **PRACTICE 30—GUIDED STUDY:** Special expressions followed by the _-ing_ form of a verb. (Chart 4-19)

Directions: Make sentences from the given combinations.

Examples:
    have a difficult time + understand → _I have a difficult time understanding the teacher's explanations in calculus._
    spend (_time_) + polish → _The soldier spent an hour polishing his boots._

1. have trouble + remember
2. stand (_place_) + wait
3. have a hard time + learn
4. sit (_place_) + think
5. have a good time + play
6. lie (_place_) + dream

7. have difficulty + say
8. have fun + sing and dance
9. find (_someone_) + study
10. spend (_time_) + chat
11. waste (_money_) + try
12. catch (_someone_) + take

◇ **PRACTICE 31—SELFSTUDY:** Verb form review. (Charts 4-1 → 4-19)

Directions: Choose the correct answer.

_____ 1. I enjoy _____ to the park on summer evenings.
     A. to go   B. going   C. being gone   D. go

_____ 2. Don't forget _____ home as soon as you arrive at your destination.
     A. to call   B. calling   C. having called   D. to be called

_____ 3. When I kept getting unwanted calls, I called the phone company and had my phone number _____. The process was easier than I expected it to be.
     A. change   B. changed   C. to change   D. changing

_____ 4. Jean should seriously consider _____ an actress. She is a very talented performer.
     A. to become   B. become   C. becoming   D. will become

_____ 5. _____ television to the exclusion of all other activities is not a healthy habit for a growing child.

        A. To be watched   B. Being watched   C. Watching   D. Watch

_____ 6. After their children had grown up, Mr. and Mrs. Sills decided _____ to a condominium in the city. They've never been sorry.

        A. to have moved   B. moving   C. move   D. to move

_____ 7. I truly appreciated _____ to give the commencement address, but I wasn't able to accept the honor because of a previous commitment.

        A. asking   B. to have asked
        C. to ask   D. having been asked

_____ 8. The store manager caught the cashier _____ money from the cash register and promptly called the police. They discovered that it had been going on for a long time.

        A. to sneak   B. sneaking
        C. to have sneaked   D. being sneaked

_____ 9. My roommate's handwriting is very bad, so he had me _____ his paper for him last night.

        A. to type   B. type   C. to have typed   D. typed

_____ 10. The municipal authorities advised _____ all drinking water during the emergency.

        A. to boil   B. to be boiled   C. boiling   D. boil

_____ 11. If we leave now for our trip, we can drive half the distance before we stop _____ lunch.

        A. having   B. to have   C. having had   D. for having

_____ 12. Out schedule is not working out. We should discuss _____ our daily routine. I don't feel as though we're getting enough accomplished.

        A. changing   B. to change
        C. to have changed   D. being changed

_____ 13. I can't recall _____ that old movie, but maybe I did many years ago.

        A. having seen   B. to have seen
        C. to see   D. having been seen

_____ 14. Our school basketball team won the championship game by _____ two points in the last five seconds. It was the most exciting game I have ever attended.

        A. being scored   B. to score   C. scoring   D. score

_____ 15. The flight attendants made all the passengers _____ their seat belts during the turbulence.

        A. to buckle   B. to have buckled
         C. buckling   D. buckle

_____ 16. It has become necessary _____ water in the metropolitan area because of the severe drought.

        A. rationing   B. ration
        C. to have rationed   D. to ration

_____ 17. You can't blame Ralph for _____ to eat that dessert. It looked delicious.

        A. to be tempted   B. tempted
        C. be tempted   D. having been tempted

_____ 18. Let's leave early, so we'll be ahead of the rush of commuters. We can't risk _____ in heavy traffic during rush hour.

        A. holding up   B. being held up
        C. having held up   D. to hold up

_____ 19. It is always interesting _____ people in airports while you're waiting for a flight.
   A. being observed   B. observe
   C. to have observed   D. to observe

_____ 20. I got everyone in the family _____ Jane's birthday card before I sent it to her.
   A. sign   B. signed   C. to sign   D. having signed

◇ **PRACTICE 32—SELFSTUDY: Verb form review. (Charts 4-1 → 4-19)**

Directions: Complete the sentence with an appropriate form of the verb in parentheses.

1. Bill decided (*buy*) __*to buy*__ a new car rather than a used one.

2. We delayed (*open*) _____ the doors of the examination room until exactly 9:00.

3. I really dislike (*ask*) _____ to answer questions in class when I haven't

   prepared my lesson.

4. I certainly didn't anticipate (*have*) _____ to wait in line for three hours for tickets to

   the baseball game!

5. When I was younger, I used (*wear*) _____ mini-skirts and bright colors. Now I am

   accustomed to (*dress*) _____ more conservatively.

6. My children enjoy (*allow*) _____ to stay up late when there's

   something special on TV.

7. Skydivers must have nerves of steel. I can't imagine (*jump*) _____ out of a plane

   and (*fall*) _____ to the earth. What if the parachute didn't open?

8. We are looking forward to (*take*) _____ on a tour of Athens by our Greek friends.

9. (*Observe*) _____ the sun (*climb*) _____ above the horizon at dawn makes one (*realize*) _____ the earth is indeed turning.

10. I told the mail carrier that we would be away for two weeks on vacation. I asked her (*stop*) _____ (*deliver*) _____ our mail until the 21st. She told me (*fill*) _____ out a form at the post office so that the post office would hold our mail until we returned.

11. The elderly man next door is just sitting in his rocking chair (*gaze*) _____ out the window. I wish there were something I could do (*cheer*) _____ him up.

12. I don't understand how you got the wrong results. When I look over your notes, your chemistry experiment seems (*perform*) _____ correctly. But something is wrong somewhere.

13. My mother always made me (*wash*) _____ my hands before every meal. She wouldn't let me (*come*) _____ to the dinner table until she had inspected my hands.

14. I resent (*have*) _____ to work on this project with Fred. I know I'll end up with most of the work falling on my shoulders.

15. John admitted (*surprise*) _____ by the unexpected birthday party last night. We had a lot of fun (*plan*) _____ it.

16. Rick moved from a big city to a small town. He appreciates (*be*) _____ able to drive to work in five minutes with very little traffic congestion.

17. The power lines outside my house were dangerous. I finally got the power company (*move*) _____ them to a safer place.

18. I wanted (*help*) _____ them (*resolve*) _____ their differences, but Sally persuaded me (*interfere, not*) _____.

19. The witness to the murder asked not (*identify*) _____ in the newspaper. She wanted her name kept secret.

20. Sara was encouraged by her teachers (*apply*) _____ for study at the Art Institute.

21. I was happy (*learn*) _____ of your new position in the company, but I was disappointed (*discover*) _____ that you had recommended (*promote*) _____ Carl to your old position instead of me.

22. I don't mind (*remind*) _____ you every day (*lock*) _____ the door when you leave the apartment, but I would appreciate your (*try*) _____ (*remember*) _____ on your own.

23. It is generally considered impolite (*pick*) _____ your teeth at the dinner table.

24. I don't recall (*meet*) _____ Mr. Parker before. I'm sure I haven't. I'd like (*introduce*) _____ to him. Would you do the honors?

25. Now I remember your (*ask*) _____ me to bring sandwiches to the picnic. Your complaints about my (*forget*) _____ things seem justified. I'm sorry.

26. Ed's boss recommended him for the job. Ed was pleased (*consider*) _____ _____ for the job even though he didn't get it.

27. After our automobile accident, the insurance company had a stack of papers for us to sign, but our lawyer advised us (*sign, not*) _____ them until she had a chance to study them very carefully.

28. I wasn't tired enough (*sleep*) _____ last night. For a long time, I just lay in bed (*think*) _____ about my career and my future.

29. John was responsible for (*notify*) _____ everyone about the meeting, but he apparently failed (*call*) _____ several people. As a result, not enough people showed up, and we have to try to get everybody together again soon.

30. Art smelled something (*burn*) _____. When he ran into the kitchen, he saw fire (*come*) _____ out of the oven and panicked. If Barbara hadn't come running in with the fire extinguisher, I don't know what would have happened.

◇ **PRACTICE 33—GUIDED STUDY: Verb form review. (Charts 4-1 → 4-19)**

Directions: Complete the sentence with the appropriate form of the verb in parentheses.

1. After I decided (*have*) _____ a garage (*build*) _____ next to the house, I hired a carpenter (*do*) _____ the work.

2. The coach didn't let anyone (*watch*) _____ the team (*practice*) _____ before the championship game. He wanted to keep the opposing team from (*find*) _____ out about the new plays he had devised.

3. Jeff applied to medical school many months ago. Now he's so concerned about (*accept*) _____ into medical school that he's having a difficult time (*concentrate*) _____ on the courses he's taking this term.

4. My son is playing in his first piano recital this evening. I'm looking forward to (*hear*) _____ him (*play*) _____, but I know he's worried about (*forget*) _____ the right notes and (*make*) _____ a fool of himself. I told him just (*relax*) _____ and (*enjoy*) _____ himself.

5. It may be impossible (*persuade*) _____ my mother (*give*) _____ up her job even though she's having health problems. We can't even get her (*cut*) _____ down on her working hours. She enjoys (*work*) _____ so much that she refuses (*retire*) _____ and (*take*) _____ it easy. I admire her for (*dedicate*) _____ to her work, but I also want her to take care of her health.

6. There's not much point in (*waste*) _____ a lot of time and energy on that project. It's likely (*fail*) _____ no matter what we do. Spend your time (*do*) _____ something more worthwhile.

7. Traffic has become too heavy for the Steinbergs (*commute*) _____ easily to their jobs in the city. They're considering (*move*) _____ to an apartment close to their places of work. They don't want (*give*) _____ up their present home in the suburbs, but they need (*live*) _____ in the city and (*be*) _____ closer to their work so they can spend more time (*do*) _____ the things they really enjoy (*do*) _____ in their free time.

8. Last week I was sick with the flu. It made me (*feel*) _____ awful. I didn't have enough energy (*get*) _____ out of bed. I just lay there (*feel*) _____ sorry for myself. When my father heard me (*sneeze*) _____ and (*cough*) _____, he opened my bedroom door (*ask*) _____ me if I needed anything. I was really happy (*see*) _____ his kind and caring face, but there wasn't anything he could do to make the flu (*go*) _____ away.

9. Fish don't use their teeth for (*chew*) _____. They use them for (*grab*) _____, (*hold*) _____, or (*tear*) _____. Most fish (*swallow*) _____ their prey whole.

10. (*Attend*) _____ the dance proved to be an (*embarrass*) _____ experience for me, especially since I don't know how to dance. I felt like a fish out of water. I wanted (*hide*) _____ someplace or (*get*) _____ out of there, but my friend wouldn't let me (*leave*) _____.

11. I'm over sixty now, but I enjoy (*recall*) _____ my high-school days. I remember (*choose*) _____ by my classmates as "Most Likely to

Succeed" when I was a senior. My best friend was chosen as "Least Likely to Succeed," and he is now the president of an electronics company. Once in a while when we get together, we have a good time (*look*) _____ through the high-school yearbook and (*laugh*) _____ at the way we looked then. We reminisce about (*act*) _____ in school dramas and (*play*) _____ on the basketball team. We remember (*be*) _____ serious young men who knew how to have fun. We congratulate ourselves for (*achieve*) _____ more than we had thought we could when we were eighteen.

12. I can't seem (*get*) _____ rid of the cockroaches in my apartment. I see them (*run*) _____ all over my kitchen counters every night. It drives me crazy. I'm considering (*have*) _____ the whole apartment (*spray*) _____ by a professional pest control expert.

13. The employees were unhappy when the new management took over. They weren't accustomed to (*treat*) _____ disrespectfully by the managers of the production departments. By (*threaten*) _____ (*stop*) _____ (*work*) _____, they got the company (*listen*) _____ to their grievances. In the end, a strike was averted.

14. Our house needs (*clean*) _____. The floors need (*sweep*) _____ _____. The dishes need (*wash*) _____. The furniture needs (*dust*) _____. However, I think I'll read a book. (*Read*) _____ is a lot more interesting than (*do*) _____ housework.

15. According to some estimates, well over half of the world's population is functionally illiterate. Imagine (*be*) _____ a parent with a sick child and (*be*) _____ unable to read the directions on a medicine bottle. We all know that it is important for medical directions (*understand*) _____ clearly. Many medical professionals are working today (*bridge*) _____ the literacy gap by (*teach*) _____ health care through pictures.

16. As an adult, I very much appreciate (*give*) _____ the opportunity to travel extensively with my parents when I was a child. Those experiences were important in (*form*) _____ my view of the world. I learned (*accept*) _____ different customs and beliefs. At times, I would resist (*go*) _____ away on another trip, especially when I was a teenager. In the end, I always accompanied my parents, and I am grateful that I did. I didn't understand at that time how those trips would influence my later life. My (*be*) _____ a compassionate and caring adult is due in large part to my (*expose*) _____ to many different ways of life as a child.

17. (*Find*) _____ a cure for the common cold does not appear (*be*) _____ imminent. Colds are caused by hundreds of different viruses. You can possibly avoid (*expose*)

_____ to the viruses by (*stay*) _____ away from those with colds, but it's almost impossible (*avoid*) _____ the viruses completely. If you want (*minimize*) _____ the risk of (*get*) _____ a cold, it is prudent (*get*) _____ enough rest and (*eat*) _____ properly. Some people believe in (*take*) _____ large amounts of Vitamin C. In the long run, it is probably easier (*prevent*) _____ (*catch*) _____ a cold than it is to cure one.

18. Modern cars have systems that protect us from (*inconvenience*) _____ _____ or (*hurt*) _____ by our own carelessness. In most cars, when the keys are left in the ignition, a buzz sounds in order (*remind*) _____ the driver (*remove*) _____ them. In some models, if the driver does not remember (*turn*) _____ off the lights, it does not matter because the lights go off automatically. In some cases, when the seat belts are not buckled, the ignition does not start and then the driver is actually forced (*buckle*) _____ up. Often when the driver has failed (*shut*) _____ a door properly, another signal noise may be given. A few cars emit sounds to warn us (*fill*) _____ the tank before it is completely empty.

It is easy (*forget*) _____ (*do*) _____ many routine tasks in (*drive*) _____ a car. The automatic warning systems help drivers (*avoid*) _____ (*make*) _____ some common mistakes. While some people may resent (*instruct*) _____ by their own automobiles (*perform*) _____ certain procedures, many others do not mind at all (*remind*) _____ (*carry*) _____ out these easily overlooked procedures.

◇ **PRACTICE 34—SELFSTUDY: Error analysis. (Chapter 4)**

Directions: Correct the errors in the following sentences.

1. Please promise not telling anybody my secret.

2. I would appreciate having heard from you soon.

3. Parents should never let very young children to stay at home alone.

4. Maria has never complained about have a handicap.

5. Mr. Lee didn't remember bring his passport when he went to the consulate.

6. Lillian deserves to be tell the truth about what happened last night.

7. Ali no speak Spanish, and Juan not know Arabic. But they communicate well by speak English when they be together.

8. I enjoyed to talk to her on the phone. I look forward to see her next week.

9. During a fire drill, everyone is required leaving the building.

10. Attend the premiere of the new musical play was a big thrill for me.

11. Don't keep to be asking me the same questions over and over.

12. I anticipate to arrive at the airport about 3:00 P.M.

13. Let me to help you carrying that table upstairs.

14. When I entered the room, I found my young son stand on the kitchen table.

◇ **PRACTICE 35—GUIDED STUDY:** Verb forms.

Directions: Write a composition for me, your reader, in which you explain exactly how to do something. Choose any topic that you know well. Assume that I know almost nothing about your topic. I have not had the experiences you have had. I don't know what you know. You must teach me. In your composition, use the words ''I'' and ''you''. Explain why/how you know about this topic. Address your information directly to your reader.

Possible topics follow.

How to:	buy a used car	prepare a meal
	travel to a particular place	write a story
	open a bank account	paint a room
	get a job	repair a car
	take care of someone who has the flu	design a bridge
	plant a garden	study a language
	rent an apartment	organize a meeting
	register at a hotel	decorate a home
	breed dairy cows	teach a class
	interpret an X-ray	maintain a farm
	change a flat tire	start a business
	play a guitar	live abroad
	catch a fish	play a game

Example of an introductory paragraph:

Have you ever thought about buying a used car? When I was in my late teens, I decided I had to have a car. I worked hard and saved my money. When the time came, I convinced my best friend to accompany me to a used car lot. I didn't really know what I was doing, so I knew I needed him to help me. When we got to the lot, the salesman had us look at lots of cars. Suddenly we came upon the car of my dreams: a small, black sports convertible. It was classy, comfortable, shiny, and had leather seats, not to mention a powerful engine and lots of speed. My friend urged me to think it over, but I was so excited I handed the salesman my check for the first of many payments. Of course, I had no idea that the car was simply a beautiful pile of junk. I learned that later when everything started to go wrong with it. I'm older and wiser now, and even though I'm not a connoisseur of automobiles, I'd like to share my experiences with you and discuss what you should consider before you buy a used car.

Directions: Choose the correct answer.

Example:

__C__   *The office staff decided _____ a retirement party for Dolores.*
          A. having had   B. to have had   C. to have   D. having

_____   1. I don't blame you for not _____ outside in this awful weather.
          A. wanting to go   B. wanting go   C. want to go   D. to want go

_____   2. I think I hear someone _____ the back window. Do you hear it, too?
          A. trying open   B. trying to open   C. try opening   D. try to open

_____   3. When Alan was questioned by the police, he admitted knowing about the embezzlement of funds from his company, but denied _____ in any way.
          A. to be involved   B. involving
          C. having involved   D. being involved

_____   4. Mr. Lee was upset by _____ him the truth.
          A. our not having told   B. us not tell
          C. we didn't tell   D. not to tell

_____   5. We considered _____ after work.
          A. to go shop   B. going shopping
          C. going to shop   D. to go to shop

_____   6. Jack offered _____ care of my garden while I was out of town.
          A. take   B. taking   C. to have taken   D. to take

_____   7. Could you please come over? I need you _____ the refrigerator.
          A. help me moving   B. helping me to move
          C. to help me move   D. help me to move

_____   8. I just heard that there's been a major accident that has all of the traffic tied up. If we want to get to the play on time, we'd better avoid _____ the highway.
          A. having taken   B. take   C. to take   D. taking

_____   9. The painting was beautiful. I stood there _____ it for a long time.
          A. for admiring   B. being admired   C. admire   D. admiring

_____   10. Jim should have asked for help instead _____ to do it himself.
          A. of trying   B. to try   C. try   D. from trying

_____   11. A plane with an engine on fire approached the runway. _____ was frightening. There could have been a terrible accident.
          A. Watch it landing   B. Watching it land
          C. To watch it to land   D. Watching to land it

_____   12. The customs officer opened the suitcase _____ if anything illegal was being brought into the country.
          A. seeing   B. for seeing   C. see   D. to see

_____   13. Sometimes very young children have trouble _____ fact from fiction and may believe that dragons actually exist.
          A. to separate   B. separating
          C. to be separated   D. for separating

_____   14. Do you have an excuse _____ late to class two days in a row?
          A. for to be   B. for being   C. to be   D. being

_____   15. Jack made me _____ him next week.
          A. to promise to call   B. to promise calling
          C. promise to call   D. promise calling

_____ 16. I got Barbara _____ her car for the weekend.
A. to let me to borrow   B. let me borrow
C. to let me borrow   D. let me to borrow

_____ 17. I'll never forget _____ that race. What a thrill!
A. to win   B. win   C. being won   D. winning

_____ 18. No one has better qualifications. Carol is certain _____ for the job.
A. to choose   B. having chosen   C. to be chosen   D. being chosen

_____ 19. I was enjoying my book, but I stopped _____ a program on TV
A. reading to watch   B. to read to watch
C. to read for watching   D. reading for to watch

_____ 20. Who is the woman talking to Mr. Quinn? I don't recall _____ her around the office before.
A. to have seen   B. seeing   C. to see   D. being seen

◇ PRACTICE TEST B—GUIDED STUDY: Gerunds and infinitives. (Chapter 4)

Directions: Choose the correct answer.

Example:

__C__   _The office staff decided _____ a retirement party for Dolores._
A. having had   B. to have had   C. to have   D. having

_____ 1. Roger proved that the accident wasn't his fault by _____ two witnesses who testified in his favor.
A. produce   B. produced   C. to produce   D. producing

_____ 2. The front door is warped from the humidity. We have a difficult time _____ it.
A. open   B. to open   C. having opened   D. opening

_____ 3. I stood up at the meeting and demanded _____. At last, I got the chance to express my opinion.
A. to be heard   B. to hear   C. to have heard   D. to have heard

_____ 4. Did you ever finish _____ the office for that new client of yours?
A. to design   B. designing
C. designed   D. having designed

_____ 5. It's a beautiful day, and I have my brother's boat. Would you like to go _____?
A. to sail   B. sailing   C. to sailing   D. for sailing

_____ 6. I called a plumber _____ the kitchen sink.
A. for repairing   B. for to repair   C. to repair   D. to be repaired

_____ 7. I'm angry because you didn't tell me the truth. I don't like _____.
A. deceiving   B. to deceive
C. being deceived   D. having deceived

_____ 8. A good teacher makes her students _____ the world from new perspectives.
A. to view   B. viewing   C. view   D. to be viewed

_____ 9. Please remember _____ your hand during the test if you have a question.
A. raising   B. to raise   C. having raised   D. to have raised

_____ 10. It is important _____ care of your health.
A. to take   B. to be taken   C. take   D. taken

_____ 11. _____ in restaurants as often as they do is very expensive.
A. Being eaten   B. Having eaten
C. Having been eating   D. Eating

_____ 12. I expect Mary _____ here early tonight. She should arrive in the next half hour.
     A. to come   B. coming   C. having come   D. to have come

_____ 13. I advised my niece not _____ at an early age.
     A. marrying   B. to marry
     C. being married   D. to have been married

_____ 14. Shhh. I hear someone _____ in the distance. Do you hear it, too?
     A. shout   B. shouted   C. to shout   D. shouting

_____ 15. I don't understand _____ your job so suddenly. Why did you do that?
     A. your quitting   B. you to have quit
     C. to quit   D. you quit

_____ 16. Last night, we saw a meteor _____ through the sky.
     A. streaked   B. to streak
     C. streak   D. to have streaked

_____ 17. My parents wouldn't let me _____ up late when I was a child.
     A. to be stay   B. staying   C. to stay   D. stay

_____ 18. Children should be encouraged _____ their individual interests.
     A. develop   B. to be developed
     C. to develop   D. developing

_____ 19. This room is too dark. We need _____ a lighter shade.
     A. to have it painted   B. to be painted
     C. painting it   D. to have it paint

_____ 20. I'm sorry I never graduated. I've always regretted not _____ college.
     A. to finish   B. finish
     C. finished   D. having finished

CHAPTER 5
Singular and Plural

◇ **PRACTICE 1—SELFSTUDY:** Final *-s/-es*. (Charts 5-1 and 5-2)

Directions: Add final *-s/-es* where necessary. Do not change, add, or omit any other words in the sentences.

1. A bird *cares* care for its *feathers* feather by cleaning them with its beak.

2. There are many occupation in the world. Doctor take care of sick people. Pilot fly airplane. Farmer raise crop. Shepherd herd sheep.

3. An architect design building. An archeologist dig in the ground to find object from past civilizations.

4. The first modern computer were developed in the 1930s and 1940s. Computer were not commercially available until the 1950s.

5. There are several factory in my hometown. The glass factory employ many people.

6. Kangaroo are Australian animal. They are not found on any of the other continent, except in zoo.

7. Mosquito are found everywhere in the world, including the Arctic.

8. At one time, many people believed that tomato were poisonous.

9. Bird, fish, insect, and mammal are different species. Each group of these life form shares physical characteristic.

10. Most of the creature in the world possess the five sense of sight, hearing, touch, taste, and smell. However, these sense are often more highly developed in one species than another. Bird have a highly developed sense of sight. For instance, an eagle can spot a small lizard from high in the air. The lizard would be undetectable by a human being from the same distance. Animal that hunt by following a trail on the ground may have poor eyesight but a keen sense of smell. For example, dog see a blurred, gray world because they are nearsighted and cannot see colors. However, they can smell thousands of times better than human being can.

◇ **PRACTICE 2—SELFSTUDY: Plural nouns. (Charts 5-1 and 5-2)**

Directions: Write the correct form of the nouns in parentheses.

1. I met some interesting _____**men**_____ at the meeting last night. (*man*)

2. The farmer loaded his cart with _____**boxes**_____ of fresh vegetables to take to market.

   His cart was pulled by two _____**oxen**_____. (*box, ox*)

3. The baby got two new _____. (*tooth*)

4. I need some _____ to light the fire. (*match*)

5. Alex saw some _____

   running across the floor. (*mouse*)

6. We cooked some _____ for dinner. (*potato*)

7. The north side of the island has no _____. There are only steep

   _____. No one can climb these steep walls of rock. (*beach, cliff*)

8. If a houseplant is given too much water, its lower _____ turn yellow. (*leaf*)

9. Before Marie signed the contract, she talked to two _____. (*attorney*)

10. New scientific _____ are made every day in _____ throughout

    the world. (*discovery, laboratory*)

11. I caught several _____ in the lake. (*fish*)

12. On our trip in the mountains, we saw some _____, _____,

    _____, and wild _____. (*wolf, fox, deer, sheep*)

13. When the _____ were playing a game, they hid behind some

    _____. (*child, bush*)

14. When I was at the park, I saw some _____ and _____

    swimming in a pond. (*duck, goose*)

15. When we spoke in the cave, we could hear _____ of our voices. (*echo*)

16. The music building at the university has 27 _____. Students need to sign up

    for practice times. (*piano*)

◇ **PRACTICE 3—SELFSTUDY: Irregular foreign plurals. (Chart 5-2)**

Directions: Use the correct plural form of the nouns in the list to complete the sentences. Use each word only one time.

bacterium	*curriculum*	*medium*	*phenomenon*
crisis	*datum*	*memorandum*	*stimulus*
criterion	*hypothesis*	*oasis*	✔ *thesis*

1. Graduate students are often required to write long papers in which they state an opinion and give evidence to support it. These papers are often referred to as _____ **theses** _____.

2. Thunder and lightning are _____ of nature.

3. Before the students began their chemistry experiments, they stated theories to explain what was going to happen in their experiments. In other words, they made _____.

4. The government of that country is unstable. The country has faced many political _____ in the last ten years. It has had to face one problem after another.

5. The office supervisor, Ms. Hall, is well known for the large number of _____ she sends to her staff. She believes it is necessary to write many notes to remind the staff of things that need to be taken care of.

6. People get most of their news about the world through the mass _____ (that is, through radio, television, newspapers, and magazines).

7. The teacher wanted to make sure the students understood the standards by which she would make her judgments. She carefully explained the _____ she would use to judge the students' work.

8. All of the departments at the university provide descriptions of their _____ in the school catalog. Look there to find out what courses the departments offer.

9. Certain factors cause plants to grow. These _____ are light, water, and fertile soil.

10. Very small living things that can cause disease are called germs. Germs are forms of _____.

11. In a desert, there are places where water is available and a few plants grow. These areas are called _____.

12. The researcher assembled numerous facts through months of investigation. She used the _____ she had gathered to write a report for a scientific journal.*

◇ **PRACTICE 4—SELFSTUDY: Possessive nouns. (Chart 5-3)**

Directions: Make the italicized nouns possessive by adding *apostrophes* and final *-s/-es* as necessary.

1. I enjoy visiting *friend* **s'** houses.

2. When I was in Chicago, I stayed at a *friend* **'s** house.

---

*In very formal English, **data** is considered plural, but more typically it is used as a singular noncount noun. Typical use: **This data is** *not correct.* Formal use: **These data are** *not correct.*

3. My uncle is my *father*   brother.

4. I have four aunts. All of my *aunt*   homes are within walking distance of my *mother*
   apartment.

5. Tom's *aunt*   oldest son is a violinist.

6. There were five astronauts aboard the space shuttle. The *astronaut*   safe return to earth was
   a welcome sight to millions of television viewers.

7. The *children*   favorite part of the circus was the elephant act.

8. When the *child*   toy broke, I fixed it.

9. I borrowed the *secretary*   pen to finish filling out the application form.

10. It is the *people*   right to know what the city is going to do about the housing problem.

11. *Bill*   wife is a factory worker.

12. *Bess*   husband is a housepainter.

13. There are quite a few diplomats in the city. Almost all of the *diplomat*   children attend a
    special school.

14. A *diplomat*   work almost invariably involves extensive traveling.

◇ **PRACTICE 5—SELFSTUDY: Using apostrophes.**
                (Chart 5-3; Appendix 1, Charts A-7 and A-8)

Directions: Add apostrophes as necessary to mark a possessive noun or a contraction.

        Mary's   ***He's***
1. Marys father works at the Northgate Medical Center. Hes a dentist.

2. Jacks parents live in Georgia. His parents home is in Atlanta.

3. Our teachers last name is Wells. Shes one of the best teachers in the school.

4. Our teachers last names are Wells, Hunt, and Moore. Theyre all good teachers.

5. Ms. Wells husband is also a teacher. Ms. Hunts husband is an engineer.

6. Its well known that a bear likes sweet food. Its favorite food is honey.

7. Anns telephone number is 555-8989. Ours is 555-9898. People often confuse hers with ours,
   so we get frequent calls for her.

8. The tiger is a beautiful animal. Its coat is orange and white with black stripes. Although its
   found in the wild only in Asia, people throughout the world appreciate its beauty and power.
   Even though tigers are protected by laws, many scientists predict their extinction within
   twenty to thirty years. How much poorer our childrens and grandchildrens lives will be when
   the earth no longer has a place for tigers, elephants, wolves, and numerous other animals
   whose fates rely upon the wisdom and compassion of humankind.

◇ PRACTICE 6—GUIDED STUDY: Using apostrophes.
(Chart 5-3; Appendix 1, Charts A-7 and A-8)

Directions: Add apostrophes as necessary to mark a possessive noun or a contraction.

1. A polar bears sense of smell is keen. Its ability to smell prey over a mile away is important to its survival in the vast expanses of snow and ice where it lives.

2. Texas is a leading producer of petroleum and natural gas. Its one of the worlds largest storage areas for petroleum.

3. All of the performers in the play did well. The audience applauded the actors excellent performance.

4. Psychologists have developed many different kinds of tests. A "personality test" is used to evaluate an individuals personal characteristics, such as friendliness or trustworthiness.

5. Many mythological stories tell of heroes encounters with giants or dangerous animals. In one story, the heros encounter with a dragon saves a village from destruction.

6. Childrens play is an important part of their lives. It teaches them about their environment while theyre having fun. For instance, they can learn that boats float and can practice ways to make boats move across water. Toys are not limited to children. Adults have their own toys, such as pleasure boats, and children have theirs, such as miniature boats. Adults toys are usually much more expensive than childrens toys.

◇ PRACTICE 7—SELFSTUDY: Using nouns as modifiers. (Chart 5-4)

Directions: Complete the sentences with the nouns in the parentheses. Use the singular or plural form as appropriate.

1. They sell _____ *shoes* _____ at that store. It is a _____ *shoe* _____ store. (*shoe*)

2. I like _____ salads. I like salads that contain _____. (*tomato*)

3. This soup is made from black _____. It is black _____ soup. (*bean*)

4. People can buy special food in small jars for _____. It is called _____ food. (*baby*)

5. I have a _____ garden. I grow many different kinds of _____. (*vegetable*)

6. Some people are addicted to _____. They are _____ addicts. (*drug*)

7. In tropical climates, sometimes it is necessary to hang a net over a bed to protect the sleeper from _____. It is called a _____ net. (*mosquito*)

8. At a formal dinner, there are usually two forks on the table. The smaller fork is for _____. It is a _____ fork. (*salad*)

Directions: Complete the sentences with the words in parentheses. Use the singular or plural form as appropriate. Include hyphens (-) as necessary.

1. (*two + hour*) The plane was late. We had a _____*two-hour*_____ wait. We had to wait for _____*two hours*_____.

2. (*ten + year + old*) My brother is _____*ten years old*_____. I have a _____*ten-year-old*_____ brother.

3. (*two + lane*) We drove down an old, narrow highway that had only _____. We drove down a _____ highway.

4. (*five + minute*) I gave a _____ speech in class. My speech lasted for _____.

5. (*sixty + year + old*) The Watkins live in a _____ house. Any house that is _____ usually needs a lot of repairs.

6. (*ten + speed*) Joe can shift his bicycle into _____ different _____. He has a _____ bike.

7. (*six + game*) The basketball team has won _____ in a row (i.e., they haven't lost one of their last six games). They have a _____ winning streak.

8. (*three + letter*) ''Arm'' and ''dog'' are _____ words. Each of them has _____.

Directions: What do you call the following?

1. someone who robs banks → *a bank robber*
2. someone who fights bulls → *a bullfighter**
3. someone who collects stamps → *a stamp collector*†

4. someone who trains animals
5. someone who tells stories*
6. someone who collects taxes†
7. something that opens cans
8. something that wipes a windshield
9. someone who earns wages
10. someone who manages an office
11. someone who programs computers
12. someone who keeps books*

13. something that removes spots
14. something that holds pots
15. someone who makes trouble*
16. someone who reads minds
17. something that dries hair
18. something that peels potatoes
19. someone who plays tennis
20. someone who fights fires*
21. someone who carries mail

_____
*Usually spelled as one word.
†Spelled with *-or* instead of *-er*.

◇ **PRACTICE 10—SELFSTUDY: Count and noncount nouns.**
(Charts 5-5 → 5-7; Appendix 1, Charts E-1 and E-2)

Directions: Add *a/an* if necessary. Write ø in the blank if the noun is noncount. Capitalize as appropriate.

1. __*A*__ *bird* has wings.

2. __*An*__ *animal* needs a regular supply of food.

3. __*ø F*__ *food* is a necessity of life.

4. _____ *concert* is a musical performance.

5. _____ *opera* is a musical play.

6. _____ *music* consists of a series of pleasant sounds.

7. _____ *cup* is a small container used for liquids.

8. _____ *milk* is nutritious.

9. _____ *island* is a piece of land surrounded by water.

10. _____ *gold* is a metal.

11. _____ *bridge* is a structure that spans a river.

12. _____ *valley* is an area of land between two mountains.

13. _____ *health* is one of the most important things in life.

14. _____ *adjective* is a word that modifies a noun.

15. _____ *knowledge* is a source of power.

16. _____ *golf* is a sport.

17. _____ *professional golfer* has to practice long hours.

18. _____ *tree* needs water to survive.

19. _____ *water* is composed of oxygen and hydrogen.

20. _____ *homework* is a necessary part of a course of study.

21. _____ *grammar* is interesting and fun.

22. _____ *sentence* usually contains a subject and a verb.

23. _____ *English* is used in airports throughout much of the world.

24. _____ *leaf* is green until it begins to die.

25. _____ *orange* is green until it ripens.

26. _____ *fruit* is good for you.

27. _____ *iron* is a metal.

28. _____ *iron* is an instrument used to take wrinkles out of clothes.

29. _____ *basketball* is round.

30. _____ *basketball* is a sport.

◇ **PRACTICE 11—SELFSTUDY: Count and noncount nouns.**
(Charts 5-5 → 5-7; Appendix 1, Charts E-1 and E-2)

Directions: Use *a/an* or *some* in the following:

1. The teacher made _____*an*_____ announcement.

2. I saw _____*a*_____ bird.

3. I saw _____*some*_____ birds.

4. She borrowed _____*some*_____ money from her uncle.

5. I had _____ accident.

6. I have _____ homework to do tonight.

7. There is _____ table in the room.

8. There is _____ furniture in the room.

9. There are _____ chairs in the room.

10. My father gave me _____ advice.

11. She is carrying _____ suitcase.

12. She is carrying _____ luggage.

13. There was _____ earthquake in California.

14. I got _____ letters in the mail.

15. Ann got _____ letter from her mother.

16. Jerry got _____ mail yesterday.

17. A computer is _____ machine that can solve problems.

18. The factory bought _____ new machinery.

19. _____ machines are powered by electricity. Some use other sources of energy.

20. I threw away _____ junk.

21. I threw away _____ old basket that was falling apart.

22. I threw away _____ old boots that had holes in them.

◇ **PRACTICE 12—GUIDED STUDY: Count and noncount nouns. (Charts 5-5 → 5-7)**

Directions: A favorite game for adults and children alike is called ''My Grandfather's Store.'' It is played with a group of people. Each person begins his/her turn by saying, ''*I went to my grandfather's store and bought. . . .*'' The first person names something that begins with the letter ''A.'' The second person repeats what the first person said, and then names something that begins with the letter ''B.'' The game continues to the letter ''Z,'' the end of the alphabet. The people in the group have to listen carefully and remember all the items previously named.

Example:

1st person: *I went to my grandfather's store and bought **an apple**.*
2nd person: *I went to my grandfather's store and bought **an apple** and **some bread**.*
3rd person: *I went to my grandfather's store and bought **an apple**, **some bread**, and **a camel**.*
4th person: *I went to my grandfather's store and bought **an apple**, **some bread**, **a camel**, and **some dark socks**.*
5th person: *Etc.*

Assume that "grandfather's store" sells just about anything anyone would ever think of. Pay special attention to the use of *a, an,* and *some.*

Alternative beginnings:
> *Tomorrow I'm going to (name of a place). In my suitcase, I will pack . . . .*
> *If I lived on a deserted island, I would need . . . .*

◇ PRACTICE 13—SELFSTUDY: Count and noncount nouns. (Charts 5-5 → 5-7)

Directions: Add final *-s/-es* to the italicized nouns if necessary.

(no change)

1. Jackie has brown *hair* and gray *eyes* .

2. My parents gave me some good *advice* .

3. I always drink *water* when I'm hot and thirsty.

4. We ate some *sandwich* for lunch.

5. We've been having some bad *weather* lately.

6. I have a lot of *homework* to do tonight.

7. Maria took some good *photograph* at the wedding party.

8. Our country has made a lot of *progress* in the last 25 years.

9. That book has a lot of good *idea* .

10. An encyclopedia contains a lot of *information* .

11. I've learned a lot of new *vocabulary* .

12. Olga knows a lot of American *slang* .

13. Every day, I learn some more new *word* in English.

14. A gambler needs a lot of *luck* .

15. Pioneer women had a lot of *courage* .

16. We bought some new *clothing* .

17. I bought a pair of leather *glove* .

18. At rush hour there are a lot of *car* on the highway. Although normally it takes us twenty *minute* to drive from home to work, at rush hour it can take an hour because of the heavy *traffic* .

19. We received a postcard from Melissa today. She's on vacation in the country, staying in a two-hundred-*year* -old inn. She says the area has fantastic *scenery* and that there hasn't been any *rain* , although there is *fog* in the mornings. She's been playing a lot of tennis and *golf* during the day, and *bridge* at night. She's having a lot of *fun* .

20. *Traveling* can impart a great deal of *education* as well as *enjoyment* . When *people* travel to another *country* , they can learn about its *history* , *economy* , and *architecture* , as well as become acquainted with its various *custom* .

◇ **PRACTICE 14—GUIDED STUDY: Count and noncount nouns. (Charts 5-1 → 5-7)**

Directions: Add final -s/-es to the italicized nouns if necessary. Do not add, omit, or change any other words.

(no change)

1. I like to experience different *season***s** . I like both hot and cold *weather* .

2. Being a parent has brought me a lot of *happiness* . Parenting requires a lot of *patience* , but it provides many *reward* .

3. *Butterfly* begin as *caterpillar* and then are transformed into beautiful *insect* with vividly colored *wing* .

4. Although everyone believed the accused man was guilty of murder, he was acquitted. The prosecuting attorney did not have enough *evidence* to convict him, nor even any *proof* that he had been able to enter the murdered man's house.

5. You need more *calcium* in your diet, Mrs. Abbott. It is found in *milk* and milk *product* , in dark green *vegetable* such as *broccoli* , and in *fish* such as *sardine* . You need *vitamin* , too. Do you take *vitamin pill* ?

6. I don't mind hard *work* , but the *job* that I have now is too stressful. I'm going to look for another *position* . *Unemployment* in my field is low now, so there should be plenty of *job* for me to choose from.

7. Last night we heard about a new political *crisis* in our country. Do you have any more *information* about it? Are there any reports of *violence* ? We've heard a lot of rumors about what may be happening, but we're anxious to know the *truth* . We need *fact* , not *gossip* .

8. Experienced *traveler* learn to travel with minimal *luggage* . My globe-trotting aunt can pack everything she needs into two small *suitcase* , whether a trip will last for three *day* or three *month* . I'm not an experienced *traveler* . When I travel, I invariably take along too much *stuff* . Last month I took a three-*day* trip to Chicago and had twice as many clothes as I needed.

◇ **PRACTICE 15—SELFSTUDY: *Much* vs. *many*. (Charts 5-1 → 5-8)**

Directions: Write *much* or *many*. Also write the plural form of the italicized nouns as necessary. In some sentences, you will need to choose the correct verb in parentheses.

1. I haven't visited _____**many**_____ *city* **cities** in the United States.

2. I don't have _____**much**_____ *money* .

3. There (is/are) _____**is**_____ too _____**much**_____ *furniture* in our living room.

4. There (isn't/aren't) _____**aren't**_____ _____**many**_____ *hotel* **hotels** in my hometown.

5. I haven't gotten _____ *mail* lately.

6. I don't get _____ *letter*

7. There (isn't/aren't) _____ _____ *traffic* today.

8. There (isn't/aren't) _____ _____ *car* on the road today.

9. I can't go with you because I have too _____ *work* to do.

10. How _____ *side* does a pentagon have?*

11. I couldn't find _____ *information* in that book.

12. How _____ *homework* did the teacher assign?

13. I haven't met _____ *people* since I came here.

14. How _____ *postage* do I need to mail this letter?

15. I think there (is/are) _____ too _____ *violence* on television.

16. I don't have _____ *patience* with incompetence.

17. The doctor has so _____ *patient* that she has to work at least 12 hours a day.

18. How _____ *tooth* does the average person have?*

19. There (isn't/aren't) _____ _____ international *news* in the local paper.

20. How _____ *fish* (is/are) _____ there in the ocean?

21. How _____ *continent* (is/are) _____ there in the world?*

22. How _____ *progress* has your country made in improving the quality of medical care available to the average citizen?

◇ **PRACTICE 16—SELFSTUDY: Expressions of quantity. (Charts 5-5 → 5-8)**

Directions: If the given noun can be used to complete the sentence, write it in its correct form (singular or plural). If the given noun cannot be used to complete the sentence, write ø.

1. Helen bought several . . . .

lamp	**lamps**
furniture	ø
jewelry	ø
necklace	**necklaces**

2. Jack bought too much . . . .

shoe	ø
salt	**salt**
equipment	**equipment**
tool	ø

3. Sam bought a lot of . . . .

stamp	**stamps**
rice	**rice**
stuff	**stuff**
thing	**things**

4. Alice bought a couple of . . . .

bread	
loaf of bread	
honey	
jar of honey	

_____

*Look in the Answer Key at the back of this book for the answer to this question.

5. I read a few . . . .

novel _____

literature _____

poem _____

poetry _____

9. He has a number of . . . .

shirt _____

homework _____

pen _____

chalk _____

6. I bought some . . . .

orange juice _____

light bulb _____

hardware _____

computer software _____

10. I don't have a great deal of . . . .

patience _____

wealth _____

friend _____

pencil _____

7. We need plenty of . . . .

sleep _____

information _____

fact _____

help _____

11. I need a little . . . .

luck _____

money _____

advice _____

new hat _____

8. I saw both . . . .

woman _____

movie _____

scene _____

scenery _____

12. The author has many . . . .

idea _____

theory _____

hypothesis _____

knowledge _____

◇ **PRACTICE 17—SELFSTUDY:** Using *a few/few; a little/little.* (Chart 5-9)

Directions: Without substantially changing the meaning of the sentence, replace the italicized words with *a few, (very) few, a little,* or *(very) little*.

a little
1. I think that *some* lemon juice on fish makes it taste better.

(very) few
2. Many people are multilingual, but *not many* people speak more than ten languages.

3. *Some* sunshine is better than none.

4. January is a cold and dreary month in the northern states. There is *not much* sunshine during that month.

5. My parents like to watch TV. Every evening they watch *two or three* programs on TV before they go to bed.

6. I don't watch TV very much because there are *hardly any* television programs that I enjoy.

7. If a door squeaks, *several* drops of oil in the right places can prevent future trouble.

8. If your door squeaks, put *some* oil on the hinges.

9. Mr. Adams doesn't like to wear rings on his fingers. He wears *almost no* jewelry.

10. You might reach your goal if you put forth *some* more effort.

11. Even though the mountain is very steep and the climb is hazardous, *several* strong-willed people have managed to reach the top.

12. The number of people in the world who are willing to risk their lives climbing a dangerous mountain is small. *Not very many* people will actually face death to climb a mountain.

◇ PRACTICE 18—SELFSTUDY: Using *of* in expressions of quantity. (Chart 5-10)

Directions: Add *of* or write Ø.

1. When I went shopping yesterday, there were several _____Ø_____ jackets in my size.

2. Several _____*of*_____ the jackets were made of 100 percent wool.

3. Many _____ students work part-time while they are attending school.

4. Many _____ my classmates have part-time jobs.

5. Some _____ dairy products are high in cholesterol.

6. Some _____ my favorite kinds of food are not good for me to eat.

7. The teacher didn't fail any _____ the students in his class.

8. Any _____ passengers who have first-class tickets can board the plane first.

9. I picked a few _____ flowers from my garden and made a bouquet.

10. A few _____ the flowers in the bouquet have already wilted.

11. Everyone needs a little _____ luck in life.

12. Most _____ babies learn to walk before their first birthday.

13. Our company imports products from abroad. Most _____ these new products are testmarketed in selected cities.

14. Most _____ people enjoy picnics.

15. Some _____ the people we want to invite for our anniversary dinner will be on vacation.

16. Not all _____ trees lose their leaves in winter.

17. All _____ deciduous trees lose their leaves during the cold part of the year, whereas evergreen trees do not.

18. All _____ the trees in that orchard have been sprayed with pesticides.

19. Both _____ my sisters attended Harvard University.

20. Both _____ women are talented in music and drama.

21. The concert was delayed because two _____ the musicians had left their instruments on the bus.

22. A trio consists of three _____ musicians.

23. I have two _____ sisters and three _____ brothers.

24. Two _____ my brothers live in St. Louis.

25. A hundred _____ people bought tickets to the lecture.

26. Two hundred _____ people came to the public meeting.

27. Hundreds _____ people visit the Lincoln Memorial every day.

28. A thousand _____ years ago, the power of electricity had not been discovered.

29. Three thousand _____ years ago, the number of planets in our solar system was unknown.

30. Thousands _____ years ago, the wheel was invented.

◇ **PRACTICE 19—GUIDED STUDY: Using *of* in expressions of quantity. (Chart 5-10)**

Directions: Add *of* or write ø.

1. Some _____ø_____ fish are surface feeders. Others are bottom feeders.

2. Some _____*of*_____ the fish we caught were too small to keep.

3. Almost all ___*of* OR: ø___ the fish in Jennifer's aquarium died. She finally had to admit that she didn't know much about taking care of tropical fish.

4. I bought several _____ books at the used book sale.

5. Several _____ my friends and I have volunteered to clean up the litter left on the school grounds by thoughtless students.

6. A few _____ children are given their first watch by the time they are six years old. However, most _____ these children cannot tell time correctly.

7. When my parents were young, they had little _____ opportunity to travel.

8. Square dancing is a traditional folk dance in the United States. We all had a lot _____ fun learning to square dance at the party. Many _____ the people at the party had never done any square dancing before.

9. The airline was crippled by a strike last month, but now it's over. All _____ the pilots were happy to get back to work after the strike.

10. Most _____ people have a little _____ trouble using the currency in a foreign country for a few _____ days after they first arrive.

11. There's nothing I like better than a good book, but I haven't done much _____ reading for fun lately. Most _____ the reading I do is related to my work.

12. It's important for young people to have goals in their lives. My mother always told me that any _____ dream is worth pursuing if I know in my heart it is what I want to do. Few _____ people have made great accomplishments in life without first having a dream—a personal, inner vision of what is possible.

◇ **PRACTICE 20—GUIDED STUDY: Writing.**

Directions: In writing, describe your future. What are your goals and how are you going to reach them?

◇ **PRACTICE 21—SELFSTUDY: Using *one, each, every*. (Chart 5-11)**

Directions: Choose the correct word in italics.

1. Each (*student*) *students*   in the class is required to take the final examination.
2. Each of the   *student,* (*students*)   in the class is required to take the final examination.
3. There is at least one window in every   *room, rooms*   in our apartment.
4. Every one of the   *room, rooms*   in our apartment has at least one window.
5. My bedroom has only one, very small   *window, windows*   .
6. One of the smallest   *window, windows*   in our apartment is in my bedroom.
7. When John bought some supplies at the hardware store, he thought the total amount on the bill was incorrect, so he checked each   *item, items*   on his bill very carefully.
8. Each of the   *item, items*   on the bill was correct.
9. Susan has traveled widely, but she has visited only one Scandinavian   *country, countries*   .
10. Alex took an extended vacation in northern Europe last summer.   Sweden was one of the   *country, countries*   he visited when he was in Scandinavia.
11. Tom believes that there are no strangers. He views each   *person, people*   in the world as a friend he hasn't met yet.
12. I answered every   *question, questions*   on the examination. I didn't skip any.
13. Each one of the   *child, children*   in the class was given a piece of paper and a crayon. Each   *child, children*   drew a picture.
14. Hunger is one of the biggest   *problem, problems*   in the world today.
15. Each of the   *applicant, applicants*   for the scholarship is required to furnish five references (that is, names of people who are willing to write letters of recommendation).

◇ **PRACTICE 22—GUIDED STUDY: Expressions of quantity. (Charts 5-10 → 5-13)**

Directions: Make each statement clearer or more accurate by adding an expression of quantity. Add other words to the sentence or make any changes you wish. The following list suggests expressions of quantity you might use.

all (of)	many (of)	one (of)	some (of)
each (of)	much (of)	two (of)	several (of)
every	a number of	half of	(a) few (of)
almost all (of)	a great deal of	50 percent of	(a) little (of)
most (of)	a lot of	three-fourths of	hardly any (of)
not all (of)	plenty of	a majority of	none of
		hundreds of	no

Example: My classmates speak Arabic.
Possible sentences: → Most of my classmates speak Arabic.
   → All (of) my classmates speak Arabic.
   → One of my classmates **speaks** Arabic.
   → Hardly any of my classmates speak Arabic.
   → None of my classmates **speaks** Arabic.

1. The people in my class are international students.

2. People are friendly.

3. The pages in this book contain illustrations.

4. Babies are born bald.

5. The students in my class are from South America.

6. People like to live alone.

7. The people I know like to live alone.

8. The countries in the world are in the northern hemisphere.

9. The citizens of the United States speak English.

10. Children like to read scary stories.

11. The children in my country go to school.

12. Airplanes depart and arrive precisely on time.

13. The rivers in the world are polluted.

14. The pollution in the world today is caused by human beings.

15. City dwellers do not have cars.

16. The food at (*the name of the place you usually eat*) is very good.

◇ **PRACTICE 23—SELFSTUDY: Subject-verb agreement. (Charts 5-12 → 5-15)**

Directions: Choose the correct completion for the sentence.

1. Most of the mountain peaks in the Himalayan range   *is,* *are*   covered with snow the year around.

2. Nearly 40 percent of the people in our town never   *votes, vote*   in local elections.

3. A number of students   *has, have*   participated in intensive language programs abroad.

4. The number of students who knew the answer to the last question on the exam   *was, were* very low.

5. Studying a foreign language often   *leads, lead*   students to learn about the culture of the countries where it is spoken.

6. The United States of America   *consists, consist*   of fifty separate states.

7. Two hours   *is, are*   too long to wait, don't you think?

8. *Isn't, Aren't*   Portuguese spoken in Brazil?

9. A lot of Brazilians   *speaks and understands, speak and understand*   Spanish.

10. Why   *is, are*   the police standing over there?

11. Why   *does, do*   most of the television stations broadcast national news at the same hour?

12. Some of the most important books for my report   *is, are*   not available in the school library.

13. There   *has, have*   been times when I have seriously considered dropping out of school.

14. Not one of the men in the original group of U.S. astronauts   *continues, continue*   in the space program today.

15. The news on the radio and TV stations   *confirms, confirm*   that a serious storm is approaching our city.

16. Geography   *is, are*   fascinating. Mathematics   *is, are*   fascinating.

17. Mathematics and geography   *is, are*   my favorite subjects.

18. All of the windows in our house   *was, were*   broken in the earthquake.

19. By law, every man, woman, and child   *is, are*   guaranteed the right to free speech.

20. Some of the movie about the creatures from outer space   *was, were*   surprisingly funny.

21. Some of the movies these days   *contains, contain*   too much violence.

22. *Is, Are*   pineapple and sugar the leading crops in Hawaii today?

23. Why   *is, are*   there a shortage of certified school teachers at the present time?

24. How many people   *is, are*   there in Canada?*

25. What   *is, are*   the population of Canada?*

26. How many of the states in the United States   *begins, begin*   with the letter "A"?*

27. Which one of the continents in the world   *is, are*   uninhabited?*

28. Most of the water in the world is salt water. What percentage of the water in the world   *is, are*   fresh water?*

29. The most common name for dogs in the United States   *is, are*   "Rover."

30. What places in the world   *has, have*   no snakes?*

---

*Look in the Answer Key for the answer to this question.

◇ **PRACTICE 24—GUIDED STUDY: Subject-verb agreement. (Charts 5-12 → 5-15)**

Directions: Choose the correct completion for the sentence.

1. A lot of the books in my office   *is,* (*are*) very valuable to me.

2. A lot of the advice my grandparents gave me   *has, have*   proven to be invaluable.

3. All of the employees in that company   *is, are*   required to be proficient in a second language.

4. Listening to very loud music at rock concerts   *has, have*   caused hearing loss in some teenagers.

5. Many of the satellites orbiting the earth   *is, are*   used for communications.

6. The news about the long-range effects of pollution   *is, are*   disturbing.

7. *Doesn't, Don't*   everybody   *seeks, seek*   peace and contentment in life?

8. According to the poll, 53 percent of the people in the country   *doesn't, don't*   want the incumbent to be re-elected.

9. Even though the eye of the hurricane will miss our city, there   *is, are*   still the possibility of heavy rain and high winds.

10. Chinese   *has, have*   more than 50 thousand written characters.

11. About two-thirds of the Vietnamese   *works, work*   in agriculture.

12. A number of planes   *was, were*   delayed due to the inclement weather.

13. The number of passengers affected by the delays   *was, were*   great.

14. More men than women   *is, are*   left-handed.

15. Every girl and boy   *is, are*   required to have certain immunizations before enrolling in public school.

16. Politics   *is, are*   a constant source of interest to me.

17. Seventy-five percent of the people in New York City   *lives, live*   in upstairs apartments, not on the ground floor.

18. Most of the fish I caught   *was, were*   too small to keep for dinner.

19. Unless there   *is, are*   a profound and extensive reform of government policies in the near future, the economic conditions in that country will continue to deteriorate.

20. While I was in Paris, some of the best food I found   *was, were*   not at the well-known eating places, but in small out-of-the-way cafes.

21. *Was, Were*   there ever any doubt in your mind about the outcome of the election?

22. Where   *is, are*   my gloves? Have you seen them anywhere? I can't find them.

23. Where   *is, are*   Kenya? Can you find it for me on the map?

24. According to one report, approximately 80 percent of all the data in computers around the world   *is, are*   in English.

◇ **PRACTICE 25—SELFSTUDY: Agreement of pronouns. (Charts 5-16 → 5-20)**

Directions: Complete the sentences with pronouns. In some of the blanks there is more than one possibility. Choose the appropriate singular or plural verb in parentheses where necessary.

1. A student should always hand in _____*his/her; his or her; his*_____ work on time.

2. Students should always hand in _____*their*_____ work on time.

3. Teachers determine _____ students' course of study.

4. A teacher determines _____ students' course of study.

5. Each student is expected to hand in _____ work on time.

6. All students are expected to hand in _____ work on time.

7. If anyone calls, please ask _____ to leave a message.

8. Somebody left _____ raincoat in the classroom.

9. The flight crew on our long plane trip were very attentive. _____ efforts to make us comfortable were greatly appreciated.

10. My family is wonderful. _____ (*has, have*) always helped me in any way _____ could.

11. The crowd enjoyed the game. _____ got excited whenever the home team scored.

12. The crowd at the last concert broke attendance records. _____ (*was, were*) the largest audience ever to have been in that stadium to listen to a rock concert.

◇ **PRACTICE 26—SELFSTUDY: Reflexive pronouns. (Chart 5-19)**

Directions: Complete the following by using appropriate reflexive pronouns.

1. John overslept and missed his plane to San Francisco. He was angry at _____*himself*_____ for not checking his alarm clock before going to bed.

2. I was a stranger at the party. I stood alone for a while, then walked over to an interesting-looking person and introduced _____.

3. Jason has only _____ to blame for the mistake he made.

4. Sue, please help _____ to some more cake. And would you like some more coffee?

5. All of you who are successful Olympic athletes should be very proud of _____. Your achievements inspire people all over the world.

6. The math team from our high school won the state competition. They should pat _____ on the back for a job well done.

7. When I was younger, I would get embarrassed by my mistakes. Now I am more relaxed and have found it is easier to laugh at _____.

8. Children need to learn to rely upon _____.

9. My father always told me to handle my problems _____ and not to expect others to solve them for me.

10. The little girl lost her teddy bear in the park. She tried to be brave, but at bedtime she cried _____ to sleep.

11. Edward lived a lonely life as a young boy. With no one to play with, he would often sit on the front steps talking to _____ or to an imaginary friend.

12. What delicious cheesecake, Amelia! Did you make this _____?

13. Whenever we have problems in life, we have to be careful not to waste too much time feeling sorry for _____.

14. After a busy day at work, I always enjoy a little time by _____.

15. Fred wanted to be able to do something unusual, so he taught _____ to drink a glass of water while standing on his head.

◇ **PRACTICE 27—SELFSTUDY: Impersonal pronouns. (Chart 5-20)**

Directions: Complete the sentences with appropriate pronouns. Choose the correct words in italics as necessary.

1. We should ask _____**ourselves**_____ if _____**we are**_____ (*is, are*) doing everything in _____**our**_____ power in order to solve the problem of hunger in the world.

2. Each of you should ask _____ if _____ (*is, are*) doing everything in _____ power in order to solve the problem of hunger in the world.

3. All of you should ask _____ if _____ (*is, are*) doing everything in _____ power in order to solve the problem of hunger in the world.

4. People should ask _____ if _____ (*is, are*) doing everything in _____ power in order to solve the problem of hunger in the world.

5. Everyone should ask _____ if _____ (*is, are*) doing everything in _____ power in order to solve the problem of hunger in the world.

◇ **PRACTICE 28—GUIDED STUDY: Singular-plural. (Charts 5-1 → 5-20, Appendix 1)**

Directions: Choose the correct words in italics.

1. *Penguin,* (*Penguins*) are interesting *creature,* (*creatures*) . They are *bird,* (*birds*) , but *it,* (*they*) cannot fly.

2. *Million, Millions* of *year, years* ago, they had *wing, wings* . *This, These* wings changed as the birds adapted to *its, their* environment.

3. *Penquin's, Penguins'* principal food *was, were* *fish, fishes* . They needed to be able to swim to find their food, so eventually, their *wing, wings* evolved into *flipper, flippers* that enabled them to swim through water with speed and ease.

4. Penguins *spends, spend* most of their lives in *water, waters* . However, they lay their *egg, eggs* on *land, lands* .

5. Emperor penguins have interesting *habit, habits* .

6. The female *lays, lay* one *egg, eggs* on the *ice, ices* in Arctic regions, and then immediately *returns, return* to the ocean.

7. After the female lays the egg, the male *takes, take* over. *He, They* *covers, cover* the egg with *his, their* body until *she, he, it, they* hatches.

8. *This, These* process *takes, take* 7 to 8 *week, weeks* . During *this, these* time, the male *doesn't, don't* eat.

9. After the egg *hatches, hatch* , the female returns to take care of the chick, and the male *goes, go* to the ocean to find food for *himself, herself* , his mate, and their offspring.

10. Penguins generally live in polar *region, regions* , but if you want to see them, *you, one* can go to any major zoo. Penguins seem to adapt well to life in confinement, so *you, one* can enjoy watching their antics without feeling sorry about their loss of freedom.

◇ **PRACTICE 29—SELFSTUDY: Forms of *other*. (Chart 5-21)**

Directions: Use a form of *other* to complete the sentence: **other, another, others, the other, the others.**

1. I had a red pen, but I seem to have lost it. I guess I'd better buy _____*another*_____ one.

2. Some people are lazy. _____ are energetic. Most people are a mixture of both.

3. Two countries share the island of Hispañola. One is Haiti. _____ is the Dominican Republic.

4. Excuse me, waiter? Could you please bring me _____ fork? I dropped mine on the floor.

5. Only two countries in South America, Bolivia and Paraguay, are inland. All of _____ have coastlines.

6. Washington is one of the five states of the United States with borders on the Pacific Ocean. What are _____ states?*

7. A successful harvest depends largely on the weather. In some years, there is an abundant harvest. In _____ years, the harvest is lean, especially when there is a drought.

8. I enjoyed watching everyone at the beach. Some people were playing volleyball, while _____ were picnicking. Some were listening to music, some were sleeping, and _____ were just lying in the sun. _____ people were swimming in the surf.

9. I'll be finished with this report soon. Give me _____ twenty minutes and I'll be ready to go with you.

───────────

*Look in the Answer Key for the answer to this question.

10. Ali has been here studying for almost three years. In _____ six months he will have his degree and return to his country.

11. Only three of the forty-two applicants for the job possess the necessary qualifications. None of _____ will be considered.

12. I work for Mr. Anderson every _____ Saturday. I help him with chores around his house.

◇ **PRACTICE 30—GUIDED STUDY: Forms of *other*. (Chart 5-21)**

Directions: Use a form of *other* to complete the sentence: ***other, another, others, the other, the others***.

1. Scandinavia consists of four countries. One is Denmark. _____ are Finland, Norway, and Sweden.

2. Budapest, Hungary, is actually two cities. On one side of the Danube River lies Buda, and directly across from it, on _____ side of the river, lies Pest.

3. Most of the candidates who will take the qualifying examination in May will probably pass the first time. _____ will have _____ chance next month.

4. Some people like to take vacations in the mountains. _____ prefer the seashore. Some people like to drive from place to place; _____ people prefer to get to their destinations as quickly as possible. Although many people like to travel on their vacations, many _____ prefer just to stay at home.

5. The Wolcott twins are identical. They look alike, and they think alike. Sometimes when one begins a sentence, _____ finishes it.

6. One of the most important inventions in the history of the world was the printing press. _____ was the electric light. _____ were the telephone, television, and the computer.

7. To avoid competitive disadvantages, professional boxers are classified by weight groups. There are over a dozen different weight classes. One is called the flyweight group. _____ are the featherweight, middleweight, and heavyweight groups.

8. The committee meets every _____ Monday.

9. Joe and Frank, detectives in the police department, work as a team. They work well with each _____.

10. The car I bought last year has turned out to be a real lemon! I'll never buy _____ one of the same make.

11. My report is due today, but I need _____ two days to finish it.

12. Some babies begin talking as early as six months; _____ don't speak until they are more than two years old.

◇ **PRACTICE 31—GUIDED STUDY:** Forms of *other*. (Chart 5-21)

Directions: Write sentences that include the given words. Punctuate carefully.
Examples:

I . . . two . . . one . . . (+ form of *other*) . . . .
→ *I have **two** brothers. **One** of them is in high school, and **the other** is in college.*

Some . . . like coffee . . . while (+ form of *other*) . . .
→ ***Some** people **like coffee** with their breakfasts, **while others** prefer tea.*

One city . . . (+ form of *other*) is . . . .
→ ***One city** I would like to visit is Paris. **Another is** Rome.*

1. My . . . has two . . . one of them . . . (+ form of *other*) . . . .
2. Some people . . . in their free time . . . while (+ form of *other*) . . . .
3. . . . national hero . . . (+ form of *other*) . . . .
4. . . . three . . . two of . . . (+ form of *other*) . . . .
5. . . . more time . . . (+ form of *other*) . . . minutes . . . .
6. There are three . . . that I especially like . . . one is . . . (+ form of *other*) . . . .
7. I lost . . . bought (+ form of *other*) . . . .
8. Some movies . . . while (+ form of *other*) . . . .
9. . . . speak . . . (+ form of *other*) . . . .
10. . . . is one of the longest rivers in the world . . . is (+ form of *other*) . . . .
11. Some children . . . while (+ form of *other*) . . . .
12. . . . enough money to buy . . . needed (+ form of *other*) . . . .

◇ **PRACTICE 32—SELFSTUDY:** Error analysis. (Chapter 5)

Directions: Find and correct the errors.

1. In my country, there is a lots of schools.
2. Writing compositions are very hard for me.
3. The front-page articles in the daily newspaper has the most important news.
4. Besides the zoo and the art museum, I have visited many others places in this city.
5. It's difficult for me to understand English when people uses a lot of slangs.
6. A student at the university should attend class regularly and hand in their assignments on time.
7. In the past, horses was the principal mean of transportation.
8. In my opinion, the english is a easy language to learn.
9. There is many different kind of animal in the world.
10. They want to move to other city because they don't like a cold weather.
11. I like to travel because I like to learn about other country and custom.
12. Collecting stamps is one of my hobby.
13. Chicago has many of tall skyscraper.
14. I came here three and a half month ago. I think I have made a good progress in English.
15. I was looking for my clothes, but I couldn't find it.

◇ **PRACTICE 33—GUIDED STUDY: Error analysis. (Chapter 5)**

Directions: Find and correct the errors.

1. When my mother was child, she lived in a small town. Now this town is big city with tall building and many highway.

2. English has borrowed quite a few of word from another languages.

3. There is many student from differents countries in my class.

4. Thousand of athlete take part in the Olympics.

5. Almost all of the house in the town are white with red roof.

6. Education is one of the most important aspect of life. Knowledges about many different things help us live fuller lives.

7. All of the students names were on the list.

8. I live in a two rooms apartment.

9. Many of people prefer to live in small towns. Their attachment to their communities prevent them from moving from place to place in search of works.

10. Todays news is just as bad as yesterdays news.

11. Almost of the students in our class speak English well.

12. The teacher gave us several homework to hand in next Tuesday.

13. Today womans work as doctor, pilot, archeologist, and many other thing. Both my mother and father are teacher's.

14. Every employees in our company respect Mr. Ward.

15. A child needs to learn how to get along with another people, how to spend his or her time wisely, and how to depend on yourself.

◇ **PRACTICE 34—GUIDED STUDY: Writing.**

Directions: Write a paragraph on one of the topics below. Write as quickly as you can. Write whatever comes in to your mind. Try to write 100 words in ten minutes. When you finish your paragraph, exchange it with a classmate. Correct each other's errors.

1. food
2. English
3. this room
4. animals

◇ **PRACTICE TEST A—SELFSTUDY: Singular and plural. (Chapter 5)**

Directions: Choose the correct completion.
Example:
    I don't get __***B***__.
        A. *many mail*   B. *much mail*   C. *many mails*   D. *much mails*

1. The science classes at this _____ difficult.
        A. schools are   B. school is   C. school are   D. school's is

2. One of the _____ from Italy.
        A. student is   B. students are   C. student are   D. students is

3. _____ to support the case against James?
   A. Is there any proof   B. Are there any proof
   C. Is there any proofs   D. Are there any proofs

4. You have to pay extra if you take too _____ with you.
   A. much luggages   B. many luggages   C. much luggage   D. many luggage

5. _____ in your class have tickets for the lecture series?
   A. Do any of the student   B. Does any of the student
   C. Do any of the students   D. Does any of the students

6. Bob got fired. It's going to be difficult for him to find _____ job.
   A. other   B. another   C. the other   D. the another

7. There _____ available in his area of specialization.
   A. isn't a lot of job   B. aren't a lot of jobs
   C. isn't a lot of jobs   D. aren't a lot of job

8. He made the soup by mixing _____ meat with some rice.
   A. little   B. few   C. a little   D. a few

9. Many of the _____ not expect to win.
   A. participants in the race do   B. participant in the races does
   C. participants in the race does   D. participant in the race does

10. The English _____ strong traditions.
    A. has many   B. have much   C. have many   D. has much

11. _____ moved to that city recently.
    A. A number of Vietnamese have   B. A number of Vietnamese has
    C. The number of Vietnamese has   D. The number of Vietnamese have

12. Each of the reference _____ available in the school library.
    A. books on that list is   B. books on that list are
    C. book on that list is   D. book on that list are

13. Several _____ sleeping under a tree.
    A. of lions were   B. lion was   C. of the lions was   D. lions were

14. Many of the _____ not used today. They are remnants of the past.
    A. railroad tracks around here are   B. railroad's track around here is
    C. railroad tracks around here is   D. railroads' tracks around here are

15. As we walked through the jungle, the _____ unusually quiet.
    A. monkeys were   B. monkeys was   C. monkies were   D. monkies was

16. At the news conference, several reporters didn't get clear answers to _____ questions.
    A. theirs   B. their   C. his and hers   D. his and her

17. I have a _____ sister.
    A. seven years old   B. seven-years-old   C. seven-year-old   D. seven year olds

18. There _____ in the world today.
    A. is many new computer company   B. is many new computer companies
    C. are many new computers companies   D. are many new computer companies

19. Self-esteem is important. It's important for people to like _____.
    A. oneself   B. yourself   C. him/herself   D. themselves

20. What _____ you used in picking a winner in the art contest?
    A. is the criteria   B. are the criteria
    C. are the criterion   D. are the criterions

Directions: Choose the correct completion.
Example:
   I don't get __**B**__.
      A. *many mail*   B. *much mail*   C. *many mails*   D. *much mails*

1. One of the dinner _____ broken.
      A. plate is   B. plates are   C. plates is   D. plate are

2. Most _____ hard.
      A. of students work   B. students work   C. student works   D. of student works

3. Can you help me? I need _____ information.
      A. a little   B. little   C. a few   D. few

4. All of the athletes who took part in the international games should be very proud of _____.
      A. himself   B. oneself   C. themselves   D. yourselves

5. Snow and rain _____ of nature.
      A. are phenomenon   B. are phenomena   C. is phenomena   D. is phenomenon

6. I accidently broke the _____ by stepping on it. I apologized to them for my carelessness.
      A. child's toy   B. child's toys   C. children's toy   D. childrens' toys

7. Our weather is cloudy in the winter. We don't have _____.
      A. many sunshines   B. many sunshine   C. much sunshines   D. much sunshine

8. Several of my friends are _____ reporters.
      A. newspaper   B. newpapers   C. newspaper's   D. newspapers'

9. Construction workers need _____ to build a highway.
      A. an heavy equipment   B. a heavy equipment
      C. heavy equipments   D. heavy equipment

10. Our classroom is supplied with _____.
      A. plenty of chalks   B. plenty of chalk   C. several chalks   D. several chalk

11. Knowing several _____ helpful if you work for an international corporation.
      A. languages are   B. language is   C. languages is   D. language are

12. Two-thirds of my _____ from the Middle East.
      A. classmates is   B. classmate are   C. classmate is   D. classmates are

13. There _____ in my country.
      A. are a lot of prcblem   B. are a lot of problems
      C. is a lot of problems   D. is a lot of problem

14. Winning a lottery is a rare occurrence. _____ very small.
      A. A number of winners is   B. The number of winners is
      C. A number of winners are   D. The number of winners are

15. There are several means of mass communication. The newspaper is one. Television is _____.
      A. other   B. the other   C. another   D. the another

16. Each of the _____ own cage.
      A. birds has their   B. bird has its   C. birds have their   D. birds has its

17. I really need _____. Can we talk?
      A. some advice   B. an advice   C. some advices   D. advices

18. Every _____ a license plate.
   A. cars have   B. cars has   C. car has   D. car have

19. The swimming team has done well this year. All of _____ have trained very hard.
   A. their members   B. its members   C. it's members   D. theirs members

20. Next week, we're going to take a _____.
   A. three day trips   B. three-day trip   C. three days trip   D. three days' trip

CHAPTER 6
Adjective Clauses

◇ **PRACTICE 1—SELFSTUDY:** Basic patterns of adjective clauses. (Charts 6-1 → 6-4)

Directions: Underline the adjective clauses in the following sentences.

1. a. The paintings <u>that are marked with a small red dot</u> have already been sold.
   b. The paintings <u>which are marked with a small red dot</u> have already been sold.

2. a. The secretary who sits at the first desk on the right can give you the information.
   b. The secretary that sits at the first desk on the right can give you the information.

3. a. The shoes that I bought were made in Italy.
   b. The shoes which I bought were made in Italy.
   c. The shoes I bought were made in Italy.

4. a. I wrote a letter to the woman that I met at the meeting.
   b. I wrote a letter to the woman who(m) I met at the meeting.
   c. I wrote a letter to the woman I met at the meeting.

5. a. The speech we listened to last night was informative.
   b. The speech that we listened to last night was informative.
   c. The speech which we listened to last night was informative.
   d. The speech to which we listened last night was informative.

6. a. Dr. Jones is the professor I told you about.
   b. Dr. Jones is the professor who(m) I told you about.
   c. Dr. Jones is the professor that I told you about.
   d. Dr. Jones is the professor about whom I told you.

7. The student whose parents you just met is in one of my classes.

8. The pianist who played at the concert last night is internationally famous.

9. Some of the people a waiter has to serve at a restaurant are rude.

10. The restaurant Bob recommended was too expensive.

11. Thomas Raven is a physicist whose book on time and space has been translated into dozens of languages.

12. The woman who lives next door to us is a weathercaster on a local TV station.

◇ **PRACTICE 2—SELFSTUDY: Basic patterns of adjective clauses. (Charts 6-1 → 6-4)**

Directions: In the spaces, write all the pronouns possible to complete the sentence. In addition, write Ø if the sentence is correct without adding a pronoun.

1. Mr. Green is the man | **who(m)** / **that** / Ø | I was talking about.

2. She is the woman | **who** / **that** | sits next to me in class.

3. The hat [ ] Tom is wearing is unusual.

4. Hunger and poverty are worldwide problems to [ ] solutions must be found.

5. I enjoyed talking with the man [ ] I sat next to on the plane.

6. People [ ] fear flying avoid traveling by plane.

7. That is the man [ ] daughter won the spelling bee.

8. The people about [ ] the novelist wrote were factory workers and their families.

9. A barrel is a large container [ ] is made of wood or metal.

◇ **PRACTICE 3—SELFSTUDY: Basic patterns of adjective clauses. (Charts 6-1 → 6-3)**

Directions: Write all the pronouns possible to complete the sentence. In addition, write Ø if the sentence is correct without adding a pronoun.

PART I: Using Subject Pronouns in Adjective Clauses.

1. The bat is the only mammal [**which** / **that**] can fly.

2. People [____] don't get enough sleep may become short-tempered and irritable.

3. The cold weather [____] swept in from the north damaged the fruit crop.

4. Alex bought a bicycle [____] is specially designed for long-distance racing.

5. I read about a man [____] keeps chickens in his apartment.

PART II: Using Object Pronouns in Adjective Clauses.

6. We used the map │ *which* / *that* / ∅ │ my sister drew for us.

7. The teacher [   ] I like the most is Mrs. Grange.

8. Louise, tell us about the movie [   ] you saw last night.

9. The subject about [   ] Dr. Gold spoke was interesting.

10. The subjects [   ] we talk about in class are interesting.

11. The person to [   ] Ann spoke could not answer her question.

12. I enjoyed the people [   ] I talked to at the party.

◇ **PRACTICE 4—SELFSTUDY: Adjective clause patterns. (Charts 6-1 → 6-3)**

Directions: Combine the sentences, using all possible forms. Use (b) as an adjective clause.

1. (a) Louis knows the woman.   (b) The woman is meeting us at the airport.

→ *Louis knows the woman* { *who* / *that* } *is meeting us at the airport.*

2. (a) The chair is an antique.   (b) Sally inherited it from her grandmother.

3. (a) The bench was wet.   (b) I sat on it.

4. (a) The man finished the job in four days.   (b) I hired him to paint my house.

5. (a) I miss seeing the old woman.   (b) She used to sell flowers on that street corner.

6. (a) The architect is brilliant.   (b) Mario works with him.

7. (a) Mary tutors students.   (b) They need extra help in geometry.

8. (a) I took a picture of the rainbow.   (b) It appeared in the sky after the shower.

◇ PRACTICE 5—SELFSTUDY: Adjective clauses: using *whose*. (Chart 6-4)

Directions: Combine the sentences, using *whose* in an adjective clause.

1. The man's wife had been admitted to the hospital. I spoke to him.
   → *I spoke to the man whose wife had been admitted to the hospital.*

2. I read about the child. Her life was saved by her pet dog.
   → *I read about a child whose life was saved by her pet dog.*

3. The students raised their hands. Their names were called.

4. Jack knows a man. The man's name is William Blueheart Duckbill, Jr.

5. The woman's purse was stolen outside the supermarket. The police came to question her.

6. We live in a small town. Its inhabitants are almost invariably friendly and helpful.

7. The day care center was established to take care of children. These children's parents work during the day.

8. We couldn't find the person. His car was blocking our driveway.

9. Tobacco is a plant. Its large leaves are used for smoking or chewing.

10. Three students' reports were turned in late. The professor told them he would accept the late papers this time but never again.

◇ PRACTICE 6—SELFSTUDY: Adjective clauses. (Charts 6-1 → 6-4)

Directions: Choose the correct answer or answers.

1. Yoko told me about students ___**A, D**___ have taken the entrance exam 13 times.
   A. who   B. whom   C. which   D. that

2. The secretary ___**B, C, D**___ I talked to didn't know where the meeting was.
   A. which   B. whom   C. that   D. ø

3. You need to talk to a person _____ you can trust. You will feel better if you do.
   A. whose   B. which   C. whom   D. ø

4. Bob is the kind of person to _____ one can talk about anything.
   A. who   B. whom   C. that   D. him

5. He is a person _____ friends trust him.
   A. who   B. his   C. that   D. whose

6. I'm looking for an electric can opener _____ also can sharpen knives.
   A. who   B. which   C. that   D. ø

7. People _____ live in glass houses shouldn't throw stones.*
   A. who   B. whom   C. which   D. ø

8. The problems _____ Tony has seem insurmountable.
   A. what   B. he   C. that   D. ø

_____

*This is an idiom that means: People shouldn't criticize others for faults they themselves have. For example, a lazy person shouldn't criticize another person for being lazy.

9. The man _____ I introduced you to last night may be the next president of the university.
   A. which   B. whom   C. that   D. Ø

10. Cathy is trustworthy. She's a person upon _____ you can always depend.
    A. who   B. whom   C. that   D. Ø

11. Your career should focus on a field in _____ you are genuinely interested.
    A. which   B. what   C. that   D. Ø

12. People _____ outlook on life is optimistic are usually happy people.
    A. whose   B. whom   C. that   D. which

◇ PRACTICE 7—SELFSTUDY: Adjective clauses: subject-verb agreement
        (Charts 6-1 → 6-2 and Chapter 5)

Directions: Choose the correct verb in italics.

1. There are three students in my class who   *speaks,* (*speak*)   French.

2. There is one student in my class who   *speaks, speak*   Greek.

3. The patients who   *is, are*   treated at City Hospital   *doesn't, don't*   need to have private physicians.

4. The courses this school   *offers, offer*   *is, are*   listed in the catalog.

5. A pedometer is an instrument that   *measures, measure*   the distance a person   *walks, walk.*

6. People who   *suffers, suffer*   from extreme shyness can sometimes overcome their problem by taking a public speaking class.

7. The boy drew pictures of people at an airport who   *was, were*   waiting for their planes.

8. In the months that   *has, have*   passed since the accident, Robert has regained the use of his legs.

9. Malnutrition and illiteracy are among the problems in the world that   *has, have*   no simple solutions.

10. It is estimated by those who   *works, work*   in the hunger program that 3500 people die from starvation in the world every day.

11. Most advertisements are directed toward adults or teenagers, but you can see commercials on television that   *is, are*   aimed at prompting children to persuade their parents to buy certain products.

12. The requirements of the school as written in the catalog   *states, state*   that all students who   *wishes, wish*   to attend must take an entrance exam.

◇ PRACTICE 8—SELFSTUDY: Error analysis. (Charts 6-1 → 6-4)

Directions: All of the following sentences contain errors in adjective clause structures. Correct the errors.

1. In our village, there were many people didn't have much money.

   → *In our village, there were many people who/that didn't have much money.*

   OR: *In our village, many people didn't have much money.*

2. I enjoyed the book that you told me to read it.

3. I still remember the man who he taught me to play the violin when I was a boy.

4. I showed my father a picture of the car I am going to buy it as soon as I save enough money.

5. The woman about who I was talking about suddenly walked into the room. I hope she didn't hear me.

6. Almost all of the people appear on television wear makeup.

7. My grandfather was a community leader whom everyone in our town admired him very much.

8. I don't like to spend time with people which loses their tempers easily.

9. I sit next to a person who his name is Ahmed.

10. In one corner of the marketplace, an old man who was playing a violin.

◇ **PRACTICE 9—SELFSTUDY: Adjective clauses: using *where* and *when*. (Charts 6-5 and 6-6)**

Directions: Combine the sentences by using either *where* or *when* to introduce an adjective clause.

1. That is the place. The accident occurred there.

→ *That is the place **where** the accident occurred.*

2. There was a time. Movies cost a dime then.

→ *There was a time **when** movies cost a dime.*

3. A cafe is a small restaurant. People can get a light meal there.

4. Every neighborhood in Brussels has small cafes. Customers drink coffee and eat pastries there.

5. There was a time. Dinosaurs dominated the earth then.

6. The house was destroyed in an earthquake ten years ago. I was born and grew up there.

7. Summer is the time of year. The weather is the hottest then.

8. The miser hid his money in a place. It was safe from robbers there.

9. There came a time. The miser had to spend his money then.

10. His new shirt didn't fit, so Dan took it back to the store. He'd bought it there.

◇ PRACTICE 10—GUIDED STUDY: Writing adjective clauses. (Charts 6-1 → 6-7)

Directions: Write sentences in which you use the given groups of words. Do not change the given words in any way. Each sentence should contain an adjective clause.

Examples:
the people I → *Most of **the people I** have met since I came here have been very friendly.*
the people that I → *One of **the people that I** admire most in the history of the world is Gandhi.*
the people with whom I → *I enjoyed talking to **the people with whom I** had dinner last night.*

1. the things I	7. the time my	13. everything you
2. the people who	8. a person whose	14. those who
3. a person who	9. a woman I	15. the only one who
4. the man to whom I	10. employees who	16. nothing I
5. the place I	11. the restaurant where	17. everyone she
6. a book that	12. someone that I	18. the doctor he

◇ PRACTICE 11—GUIDED STUDY: Writing. (Charts 6-1 → 6-7)

Directions: In writing, define a friend. What are the qualities you look for in a friend? What does a friend do or not do? Tell your reader about your friends. Who are they and what are they like?

◇ PRACTICE 12—SELFSTUDY: Punctuation of adjective clauses. (Chart 6-8)

Directions: Circle YES if the adjective clause requires commas and add the commas in the appropriate places. Circle NO if the adjective clause does not require commas.

1. YES (NO) The newspaper article was about a man who died two years ago of a rare tropical disease.

2. (YES) NO Paul O'Grady , who died two years ago , was a kind and loving man.

3. YES NO I made an appointment with a doctor who is considered an expert on eye disorders.

4. YES NO I made an appointment with Dr. Raven who is considered an expert on eye disorders.

5. YES NO The car that Al bought had had three previous owners, but it was in excellent condition.

6. YES NO We thoroughly enjoyed the music which we heard at the concert last Sunday.

7. YES NO Bogota which is the capital of Colombia is a cosmopolitan city.

8. YES NO They climbed Mount Rainier which is in the State of Washington twice last year.

9. YES NO Emeralds which are valuable gemstones are mined in Colombia.

10. YES NO The company offered the position to John whose department performed best this year.

11. YES NO On our trip to Africa, we visited Nairobi which is near several fascinating game reserves and then traveled to Egypt to see the pyramids.

12. YES NO I think the waiter who took our order used to work at Captain Bob's Restaurant.

13. YES NO Someone who understands physics better than I do is going to have to help you.

14. YES NO Larry was very close to his only brother who was a famous social historian.
15. YES NO Violent tropical storms that occur in western Asia are called typhoons.
16. YES NO Similar storms that occur on the Atlantic side of the Americas are called hurricanes rather than typhoons.
17. YES NO A typhoon which is a violent tropical storm can cause great destruction.
18. YES NO According to the news report, the typhoon that threatened to strike the Indonesian coast has moved away from land and toward open water.

◇ **PRACTICE 13—SELFSTUDY: Punctuation of adjective clauses. (Chart 6-8)**

Directions: Choose the correct answer or answers.

1. Ms. Donaldson, ____*A*____ teaches linguistics at the university, recently received recognition for her research on the use of gestures in communication.
   A. who   B. whom   C. which   D. that   E. ø

2. A woman ___*A, D*___ teaches linguistics at the university received an award for outstanding research.
   A. who   B. whom   C. which   D. that   E. ø

3. The earth, _____ is the fifth largest planet in the solar system, is the third planet from the sun.
   A. who   B. whom   C. which   D. that   E. ø

4. A grant of $1.5 million was awarded to Dr. Sato, _____ has impressed the scientific community with his research on the common cold.
   A. who   B. whom   C. which   D. that   E. ø

5. The award for the Most Valuable Player was won by a player _____ the coaches and the entire team respect.
   A. who   B. whom   C. which   D. that   E. ø

6. The award was won by Dennis Johnson, _____ the coach highly respects.
   A. who   B. whom   C. which   D. that   E. ø

7. My accountant, _____ understands the complexities of the tax system, is doing my taxes this year.
   A. who   B. whom   C. which   D. that   E. ø

8. The school board voted to close a neighborhood elementary school. The decision, _____ affected over 200 students, was not warmly received in the community.
   A. who   B. whom   C. which   D. that   E. ø

9. Our office needs a secretary _____ knows how to use various word processing programs.
   A. who   B. whom   C. which   D. that   E. ø

10. The winner of the Nobel Prize in physics dedicated the honor to his high school physics teacher, _____ had been an inspiration during his early years.
    A. who   B. whom   C. which   D. that   E. ø

11. The consultant _____ was hired to advise us never really understood our situation.
    A. who   B. whom   C. which   D. that   E. ø

12. I gave the check to Oliver, _____ promptly cashed it and spent all the money before the day was out.
    A. who   B. whom   C. which   D. that   E. ø

13. The check _____ I gave to Oliver was for work he'd done for me.
    A. who   B. whom   C. which   D. that   E. ø

◇ PRACTICE 14—SELFSTUDY: Punctuation of adjective clauses. (Chart 6-8)

Directions: Choose the correct explanation of the meaning of each sentence.

1. The students, who attend class five hours per day, have become quite proficient in their new language.
   (a.) *All* of the students attend class for five hours per day.
   b. *Only some* of the students attend class for five hours per day.

2. The students who attend class five hours per day have become quite proficient in their new language.
   a. *All* of the students attend class for five hours per day.
   (b.) *Only some* of the students attend class for five hours per day.

3. The orchestra conductor signaled the violinists, who were to begin playing.
   a. *All* of the violinists were to begin playing.
   b. *Only some* of the violinists were to begin playing.

4. The orchestra conductor signaled the violinists who were to begin playing.
   a. *All* of the violinists were to begin playing.
   b. *Only some* of the violinists were to begin playing.

5. I put the vase on top of the TV set, which is in the living room.
   a. I have *more than one* TV set.
   b. I have *only one* TV set.

6. I put the vase on top of the TV set that is in the living room.
   a. I have *more than one* TV set.
   b. I have *only one* TV set.

7. Trees which lose their leaves in winter are called deciduous trees.
   a. *All* trees lose their leaves in winter.
   b. *Only some* trees lose their leaves in winter.

8. Pine trees, which are evergreen, grow well in a cold climate.
   a. *All* pine trees are evergreen.
   b. *Only some* pine trees are evergreen.

◇ PRACTICE 15—SELFSTUDY: Punctuation of adjective clauses. (Charts 6-8 → 6-11)

Directions: Circle YES if the adjective clause requires commas and add the commas in the appropriate places. Circle NO if the adjective clause does not require commas.

1. (YES) NO   Thirty people **,** two of whom were members of the crew **,** were killed in the ferry accident.

2. YES (NO)   I'm trying to convince my mother to buy a small car which has front-wheel drive instead of a large car with rear-wheel drive.

3. YES NO   Over 500 students took the entrance examination the results of which will be posted in the administration building at the end of the month.

4. YES NO   The newspapers carried the story of an accident in which four pedestrians were injured.
5. YES NO   The newly married couple that lives next door just moved here from California.
6. YES NO   The Caspian Sea which is bounded by the Soviet Union and Iran is fed by eight rivers.
7. YES NO   The new supervisor was not happy with his work crew none of whom seemed interested in doing quality work.
8. YES NO   My oldest brother in whose house I lived for six months when I was ten has been a father to me in many ways.
9. YES NO   Tom is always interrupting me which makes me mad.
10. YES NO   To express the uselessness of worrying, Mark Twain once said, "I've had a lot of problems in my life most of which never happened."

◇ **PRACTICE 16—SELFSTUDY: Expressions of quantity in adjective clauses. (Chart 6-9)**

Directions: Combine the sentences. Use the second sentence as an adjective clause.

1. I received two job offers. I accepted neither of them.
   → *I received two job offers, neither of which I accepted.*

2. I have three brothers. Two of them are professional athletes.

3. Jerry is engaged in several business ventures. Only one of them is profitable.

4. The United States of America is a union of fifty states. The majority of them are located east of the Mississippi River.

5. The two women have already dissolved their business partnership. Both of them are changing careers.

6. Tom is proud of his success. Much of it has been due to hard work, but some of it has been due to good luck.

◇ **PRACTICE 17—SELFSTUDY: Using *which* to modify a sentence. (Chart 6-11)**

Directions: Combine the sentences, using *which*.

1. Sally lost her job. That wasn't surprising.
   → *Sally lost her job, which wasn't surprising.*

2. She usually came to work late. That upset her boss.

3. So her boss fired her. That made her angry.

4. She hadn't saved any money. That was unfortunate.

5. So she had to borrow some money from me. I didn't like that.

6. She has found a new job. That is lucky.

7. So she has repaid the money she borrowed from me. I appreciate that.

8. She has promised herself to be on time to work every day. That is a good idea.

◇ **PRACTICE 18—GUIDED STUDY: Special adjective clauses. (Charts 6-9 → 6-11)**

Directions: Write sentences that contain the following groups of words. Do not change the order of the words as they are given. Add words only before and/or after the group of words. Add punctuation as necessary.

Examples:
. . . yesterday which surprised. . . .
→ *Tom didn't come to class **yesterday, which surprised** me.*

. . . people to my party some of whom. . . .
→ *I invited ten **people to my party, some of whom** are my classmates.*

1. . . . brothers all of whom . . .
2. . . . early which was fortunate . . .
3. . . . students three of whom . . .
4. . . . ideas none of which . . .
5. . . . jewelry the value of which . . .
6. . . . teachers some of whom . . .
7. . . . mother which made me . . .
8. . . . a little money all of which . . .
9. . . . sisters each of whom . . .
10. . . . new car the inside of which . . .
11. . . . clothes some of which . . .
12. . . . yesterday which surprised . . .

◇ **PRACTICE 19—GUIDED STUDY: Writing adjective clauses. (Charts 6-1 → 6-11)**

Directions: Combine the sentences. Use (b) as an adjective clause. Punctuate carefully. Use formal written English.

1. (a) The blue whale is considered the largest animal that has ever lived.
   (b) It can grow to 100 feet and 150 tons.
   → *The blue whale, which can grow to 100 feet and 150 tons, is considered the largest animal that has ever lived.*

2. (a) An antecedent is a word.
   (b) A pronoun refers to this word.
   → *An antecedent is a word to which a pronoun refers.*

3. (a) The plane was met by a crowd of three hundred people.
   (b) Some of them had been waiting for more than four hours.

4. (a) In this paper, I will describe the basic process.
   (b) Raw cotton becomes cotton thread by this process.

5. (a) The researchers are doing case studies of people to determine the importance of heredity in health and longevity.
   (b) These people's families have a history of high blood pressure and heart disease.

6. (a) At the end of this month, scientists at the institute will conclude their AIDS* research.
   (b) The results of this research will be published within six months.

7. (a) People may become anxious and worried.
   (b) They are forced to retire in their middle or late sixties.

8. (a) My parents look forward to retirement.
   (b) They know how to enjoy themselves and their family.

_____
*AIDS = **A**cquired **I**mmune **D**eficiency **S**yndrome

9. (a) According to many education officials, "math phobia" (that is, a fear of mathematics) is a widespread problem.
   (b) A solution to this problem must and can be found.

10. (a) The art museum hopes to hire a new administrator.
    (b) Under this person's direction it will be able to purchase significant pieces of art.

11. (a) The giant anteater licks up ants for its dinner.
    (b) Its tongue is longer than 30 centimeters (12 inches).

12. (a) The anteater's tongue is sticky.
    (b) It can go in and out of its mouth 160 times a minute.

◇ **PRACTICE 20—SELFSTUDY: Adjective phrases. (Charts 6-12 and 6-13)**

Directions: Change the adjective clauses to adjective phrases.

1. Only a few of the movies that are shown at the Gray Theater are suitable for children.
   → *Only a few of the movies shown at the Gray Theater are suitable for children.*

2. Jasmine, which is a viny plant with fragrant flowers, grows only in warm places.
   → *Jasmine, a viny plant with fragrant flowers, grows only in warm places.*

3. The couple who live in the house next door are both college professors.
   → *The couple living in the house next door are both college professors.*

4. A throne is the chair which is occupied by a queen, king, or other rulers.

5. A knuckle is a joint that connects a finger to the rest of the hand.

6. We visited Belgrade, which is the capital city of Yugoslavia.

7. Antarctica is covered by a huge ice cap that contains 70 percent of the earth's fresh water.

8. Astronomy, which is the study of planets and stars, is one of the world's oldest sciences.

9. Only a small fraction of the eggs that are laid by a fish actually hatch and survive to adulthood.

10. Our solar system is in a galaxy that is called the Milky Way.

11. Two out of three people who are struck by lightning survive.

12. Arizona, which was once thought to be a useless desert, is today a rapidly growing industrial and agricultural state.

13. Simon Bolivar, who was a great South American general, led the fight for independence in the early 19th century.

14. In hot weather, many people enjoy lemonade, which is a drink that is made of lemon juice, water, and sugar.

15. I was awakened by the sound of laughter which came from the room which was next door to mine at the motel.

16. Few tourists ever see a jaguar, which is a spotted wild cat that is native to tropical America.

◇ PRACTICE 21—SELFSTUDY: Punctuation of adjective phrases. (Charts 6-12 and 6-13)

Directions: Add commas where necessary.

1. A national holiday has been established in memory of Martin Luther King, Jr., the leader of the civil rights movement in the United States in the 1950s and 1960s.

2. Neil Armstrong the first person to set foot on the moon reported that the surface was fine and powdery.

3. Susan B. Anthony the first and only woman whose picture appears on U. S. money worked tirelessly during her lifetime to gain the right to vote for women.

4. Mark Twain is an author known far and wide as one of the greatest American humorists.

5. Many famous people did not enjoy immediate success in their lives. Abraham Lincoln one of the truly great presidents of the United States ran for public office 26 times and lost 23 of the elections. Walt Disney the creator of Mickey Mouse and founder of his own movie production company once got fired by a newspaper editor because he had no good ideas. Thomas Edison the inventor of the light bulb and phonograph was believed by his teachers to be too stupid to learn. Albert Einstein one of the greatest scientists of all time performed badly in almost all of his high school courses and failed his college entrance exam.

◇ PRACTICE 22—SELFSTUDY: Adjective phrases. (Charts 6-12 and 6-13)

Directions: Complete the sentences in *PART II* with adjective phrases by using the information in *PART I*. Use commas as necessary.

PART I:
  A. It is the lowest place on the earth's surface.
✔ B. It is the highest mountain in the world.
  C. It is the capital of Iraq.
  D. It is the capital of Argentina.
  E. It is the largest city in the western hemisphere.
  F. It is the largest city in the United States.
  G. It is the most populous country in Africa.
  H. It is the northernmost country in Latin America.
  I. It is an African animal that eats ants and termites.
  J. It is a small animal that spends its entire life underground.
  K. They are sensitive instruments that measure the shaking of the ground.
  L. They are devices that produce a powerful beam of light.

PART II:

1. Mt. Everest _____, ***the highest mountain in the world,*** _____ is in the Himalayas.

2. One of the largest cities in the Middle East is Baghdad _____.

3. Earthquakes are recorded on seismographs _____.

4. The Dead Sea _____ is located in the Middle East between Jordan and Israel.

5. The newspaper reported a minor earthquake in Buenos Aires _____.

6. Industry and medicine are continually finding new uses for lasers _____.

7. Mexico _____ lies just south of the United States.

8. Even though the nation consists of more than 250 different cultural groups, English is the official language of Nigeria _____.

9. Both Mexico City _____ and New York City _____ face challenging futures.

10. The mole _____ is almost blind. The aardvark _____ _____ also lives underground but hunts for its food above ground.

◇ **PRACTICE 23—GUIDED STUDY: Adjective phrases. (Charts 6-12 and 6-13)**

Directions: Change all of the adjective clauses to adjective phrases.

1. None of the pedestrians who were walking up and down the busy street stopped to help or even inquire about the elderly man who was slumped in the doorway of an apparently unoccupied building.
   → *None of the pedestrians walking up and down the busy street stopped to help or even inquire about the elderly man slumped in the doorway of an apparently unoccupied building.*

2. Food that passes from the mouth to the stomach goes through a tube which is called the esophagus.

3. Animals that are born in a zoo generally adjust to captivity better than those that are captured in the wild.

4. The children attended a special movie program that consisted of cartoons that featured Donald Duck and Mickey Mouse.

5. One of the most important foodstuffs in the world is flour, which is a fine powder that is made by grinding wheat or other grains.

6. My uncle Elias, who is a restaurant owner, often buys fish and shellfish from boats that are docked at the local pier. Customers come from miles around to dine on a seafood feast that is considered to be the best in all of the northeastern United States.

7. Hundreds of volunteers went to a northern village yesterday to reinforce firefighters who are trying to save a settlement which is threatened by a forest fire. The fire started when a cigarette ignited oil which was leaking from a machine which is used to cut timber.

8. Researchers have developed a way to mark genes so that they glow in the dark, which is a technique that scientists can use to follow specific genetic activity of cells which are within plants and animals. This development, which was announced by the National Science Foundation, which is the sponsor of the research, should prove useful to scientists who study the basic functions of organisms.

9. A discovery and an invention are different, but they are related. A discovery occurs when something that exists in nature is recognized for the first time. Fire is an example of a discovery. An invention is something that is made for the first time by a creator. An invention never existed before the act of creation. The telephone and the automobile, which are two examples of important twentieth century inventions, illustrate the way in which inventions give people control over their environment and enable them to live better lives.

◇ **PRACTICE 24—GUIDED STUDY: Speaking and writing. (Chapter 6)**

Directions: Either in a group or by yourself, draw up a list of inventions made in the 20th century. Discuss the inventions you have named, using the following questions as guidelines:

1. What are the three most important twentieth century inventions that you have listed? Why? In other words, why do you rate these as the most influential/important inventions?
2. What were important inventions prior to the twentieth century? Why?
3. Which invention has brought the most happiness to people? Which has caused the most unhappiness?
4. Are any of the inventions you have listed luxury items? Which of the inventions you have listed have become accepted as necessities?
5. What would your world be like without a certain invention? How has your life been influenced by these inventions? Would you like to go back to 1900 when none of these things existed? Can you visualize life as it was then?
6. What would you like to see invented now? What do you think will be one of the most important inventions that will be made in the future? What are you going to invent?

◇ **PRACTICE 25—GUIDED STUDY: Adjective clauses and phrases. (Charts 6-2 → 6-13)**

Directions: Combine each group of short, choppy sentences into one sentence. Use the <u>underlined</u> sentence as the independent clause; build your sentence around the independent clause. Use adjective clauses and adjective phrases wherever possible.

1. <u>Chihuahua is divided into two regions</u>. It is the largest Mexican state. One region is a mountainous area in the west. The other region is a desert basin in the north and east.
   → ***Chihuahua,*** *the largest Mexican state,* ***is divided into two regions,*** *a mountainous area in the west and a desert basin in the north and east.*

2. <u>Disney World covers a large area of land</u>. It is an amusement park. It is located in Orlando, Florida. The land includes lakes, golf courses, campsites, hotels, and a wildlife preserve.

3. <u>Jamaica is one of the world's leading producers of bauxite</u>. It is the third largest island in the Caribbean Sea. Bauxite is an ore. Aluminum is made from this ore.

4. <u>Robert Ballard made headlines in 1985</u>. He is an oceanographer. In 1985 he discovered the remains of the Titanic. The Titanic was the "unsinkable" passenger ship. It has rested on the floor of the Atlantic Ocean since 1912. It struck an iceberg in 1912 and sank.

5. <u>William Shakespeare's father was a glove maker and a town official</u>. William Shakespeare's father was John Shakespeare. He owned a shop in Stratford-upon-Avon. Stratford-upon-Avon is a town. It is about 75 miles (120 kilometers) northwest of London.

6. <u>The Yemen Arab Republic is an ancient land</u>. It is located at the southwestern tip of the Arabian Peninsula. This land has been host to many prosperous civilizations. These civilizations include the Kingdom of Sheba and various Islamic empires.

◇ **PRACTICE 26—SELFSTUDY: Error analysis. (Charts 6-2 → 6-13)**

Directions: All of the following sentences contain errors in adjective clauses, adjective phrases, or punctuation. Find the errors and correct them, using any appropriate form.

1. One of the people which I admire most is my uncle.

2. Baseball is the only sport in which I am interested in it.

3. My favorite teacher, Mr. Peterson, he was always willing to help me after class.

4. There are some people in the government who is trying to improve the lives of poor people.

5. I have some good advice for anyone who he wants to learn a second language.

6. My classroom is located on the second floor of Carver Hall that is a large brick building in the center of the campus.

7. When we walked past the theater, there were a lot of people waited in a long line outside the box office.

8. Students who living on campus are close to their classrooms and the library.

9. A myth is a story expresses traditional beliefs.

10. If you need any information, see the librarian sits at the central desk on the second floor.

11. My oldest sister is Anna is 21 years old.

12. Hiroko was born in Sapporo that is a city in Japan.

13. Patrick who is my oldest brother. He is married and has one child.

14. The person sits next to me is someone I've never met him.

15. My favorite place in the world is a small city is located on the southern coast of Brazil.

◇ **PRACTICE 27—GUIDED STUDY: Error analysis. (Chapter 6)**

Directions: All of the following sentences contain errors in adjective clauses, adjective phrases, or punctuation. Find the errors and correct them, using any appropriate form.

1. Last Saturday I attended a party giving by one of my friends. My friend, who his apartment is in another town, was very glad that I could come.

2. Dr. Darnell was the only person to whom I wanted to see.

3. There are eighty students, are from all over the world, study English at this school.

4. The people who we met them on our trip last May are going to visit us in October.

5. Dianne Jones that used to teach Spanish has organized a tour of Central America for senior citizens.

6. There is an old legend telling among people in my country about a man lived in the seventeenth century saved a village from destruction.

7. I've met many people since I came here who some of them are from my country.

8. An old man was fishing next to me on the pier was muttering to himself.

9. People can speak English can be understood in many countries.

10. When I was a child, I was always afraid of the beggars whom they went from house to house in my neighborhood.

11. At the national park, there is a path leads to a spectacular waterfall.

12. The road that we took it through the forest it was narrow and steep.

◇ **PRACTICE 28—GUIDED STUDY. Writing game. (Chapter 6)**

Directions: Form a group of three people. Together, make up one sentence with as many adjective clauses as possible. In other words, make the most awkward sentence you can while still using grammatically correct sentence structure. Count the number of adjective clauses you use. See which group can make the worst sentence by using the largest number of adjective clauses.

Example of a stylistically terrible, but grammatically correct, sentence:
The man who was sitting at a table which was at the restaurant where I usually eat dinner, which is something I do every evening, was talking to a woman who was wearing a dress which was blue, which is my favorite color.

◇ **PRACTICE 29—GUIDED STUDY. Writing. (Chapter 6)**

Directions: Write on one, two, or all of the following topics. Try to use adjective clauses and phrases as appropriate.

1. Write about three historical figures from your country. Give your reader information about their lives and accomplishments.
2. Write about your favorite TV shows. What are they? What are they about? Why do you enjoy them?
3. Who are some people in your country who are popular with young people (e.g., singers, movie stars, political figures, etc.)? Tell your readers about these people. Assume your readers are completely unfamiliar with them.
4. You are a tourist agent for your hometown/country. Write a descriptive brochure that would make your reader want to visit your hometown/country.
5. What kind of people do you like? What kind of people do you avoid?
6. What kind of person do you want to marry? What kind of person do you not want to marry? If you are already married, what kind of person did you marry?

◇ **PRACTICE TEST A—SELFSTUDY: Adjective clauses. (Chapter 6)**

Directions: Choose the correct answer.

Example:
Friends are people __**B**__ *close to us.*
  A. *who is*   B. *who are*   C. *which is*   D. *which are*

1. "Who is eligible for the scholarship?"
   "Anyone _____ scholastic record is above average can apply for the scholarship."
   A. who has a   B. has a   C. who's a   D. whose

2. Dr. Sales is a person _____.
   A. in whom I don't have much confidence   B. in that I don't have much confidence
   C. whom I don't have much confidence in him   D. I don't have much confidence

3. "Is April twenty-first the day _____?"
   "No, the twenty-second."
   A. you'll arrive then   B. when you'll arrive
   C. on that you'll arrive   D. when you'll arrive on

4. The severe drought _____ occurred last summer ruined the corn crop.
      A. that it   B. which it   C. it   D. that

5. Florida, _____ the Sunshine State, attracts many tourists every year.
      A. is   B. known as   C. is known as   D. that is known as

6. The new shopping mall is gigantic. It's advertised as a place _____ you can find just about anything you might want to buy.
      A. where   B. which   C. in where   D. in that

7. Lola's marriage has been arranged by her family. She is marrying a man _____.
      A. that she hardly knows him   B. whom she hardly knows him
      C. she hardly knows   D. she hardly knows him

8. People who exercise frequently have greater physical endurance than those _____.
      A. who doesn't   B. that doesn't   C. which don't   D. who don't

9. "Is this the address to _____ you want the package sent?"
   "Yes."
      A. where   B. that   C. which   D. whom

10. Ann quit her job at the advertising agency, _____ surprised everyone.
       A. which   B. that   C. who   D. that it

11. That book is by a famous anthropologist. It's about the people in Samoa _____ for two years.
       A. that she lived   B. that she lived among them
       C. among whom she lived   D. where she lived among them

12. The missing man's family is desperately seeking anyone _____ information about his activities or whereabouts.
       A. has   B. having   C. who have   D. have

13. The publishers expect that the new biography of Simon Bolivar will be bought by people _____ in Latin American history.
       A. who they are interested   B. are interested
       C. interested   D. they are interested

14. I have always wanted to visit Paris, _____ of France.
       A. is the capital   B. which the capital is
       C. that is the capital   D. the capital

15. The chemistry book _____ was a little expensive.
       A. that I bought it   B. I bought that   C. what I bought   D. I bought

16. "Have you ever met the man _____ over there?"
    "No. Who is he?"
       A. stands   B. standing
       C. is standing   D. who he is standing

17. "Do you have the book _____ the teacher?"
    "Yes, I do."
       A. that it belongs to   B. to which belongs to
       C. to which belongs   D. that belongs to

18. The voters were overwhelmingly against the candidate _____ proposals called for higher taxes.
       A. who his   B. whose   C. whom he had   D. that his

19. "Do you remember Mrs. Goddard, _____ taught us English composition?"
    "I certainly do."
       A. who   B. whom   C. that   D. which

20. I have three brothers, _____ are businessmen.
       A. that all of them   B. who they all   C. all of whom   D. who all of them

Directions: Choose the correct answer.

Example:
    Friends are people ___**B**___ close to us.
    A. who is   B. who are   C. which is   D. which are

1. "Were you able to locate the person _____ wallet you found?"
   "Luckily, yes."
   A. which   B. that his   C. whose   D. that's

2. Some fish is frozen, but _____ is best.
   A. fish is fresh   B. fresh fish
   C. fish fresh   D. fresh fish is caught

3. "Why do you get up at 4:00 A.M.?"
   "Because it's the only time _____ without being interrupted."
   A. when I can work on my book   B. when I can work on my book at
   C. when I can work on my book then   D. at when I can work on my book

4. "You seem so happy today."
   "I am. You are looking at a person _____ has just been accepted into medical school!"
   A. who   B. who she   C. whom she   D. whom

5. "The movie _____ last night was terrific."
   "What's it about?"
   A. I went   B. I went to it   C. I went to   D. that I went

6. Many people lost their homes in the earthquake. The government needs to establish more shelters to care for those _____ have homes.
   A. who doesn't   B. who don't   C. which doesn't   D. which don't

7. The problem _____ never occurred.
   A. I had expected it   B. who I had expected
   C. that I had expected it   D. I had expected

8. I had to drive to the factory to pick up my brother, _____ car wouldn't start.
   A. who his   B. who   C. who's   D. whose

9. I read a book about Picasso, _____.
   A. is a Spanish painter   B. a Spanish painter
   C. who a Spanish painter is   D. that is a Spanish painter

10. The people _____ the acrobat turn circles in the air were horrified when he missed the outstretched hands of his partner and fell to his death.
    A. watched   B. watch   C. watching   D. were watching

11. "My writing has improved a lot in this class."
    "Mine has, too. All the students _____ do well in writing."
    A. whom Mr. Davis teaches them   B. which Mr. Davis teaches
    C. that Mr. Davis teaches them   D. Mr. Davis teaches

12. "Have you seen the place _____ the graduation ceremony will be held?"
    "Yes. It's big enough to hold 5,000 people."
    A. in that   B. where   C. is where that   D. which

13. "How's your class this term?"
    "Great. I have seventeen students, most of _____ speak English very well."
    A. who   B. those   C. whom   D. which

14. "Will everyone like the book?"
    "No. Only people _____ interested in anthropology."
    A. are   B. who are   C. in whom are   D. that is

15. "How did you enjoy your dinner with Mr. Jackson?"
"It was boring. He talked only about himself, _____ almost put us to sleep."
    A. which   B. that   C. who   D. that he

16. My grandfather, _____ a wise man, has greatly influenced my life.
    A. is   B. that is   C. who is   D. who he is

17. "Is Dr. Brown the person _____ you wish to speak?"
"Yes, please."
    A. that   B. whom   C. to that   D. to whom

18. In the movie, a teenager _____ to pursue a singing career meets resistance from his strong-willed father.
    A. wants   B. wanted   C. wanting   D. who want

19. "Excuse me, but there is something about _____ immediately."
"Certainly."
    A. which I must speak to you   B. which I must speak to you about it
    C. that I must speak to you about   D. that I must speak to you

20. *Little Women*, _____ in 1868, is my sister's favorite book.
    A. is a novel published   B. a novel published
    C. a novel was published   D. was a novel published

CHAPTER 7
Noun Clauses

◇ **PRACTICE 1—SELFSTUDY:** Questions and noun clauses that begin with a question word. (Charts 7-1 and 7-2; Appendix 1, B-1 and B-2)

Directions: Look at the <u>underlined</u> part of each sentence. If the underlined part is a question, circle **Q.** If it is a noun clause, circle **N.Cl.** Then add the necessary final punctuation: a period (.) or a question mark (?).

1. (**Q**) **N.Cl.** I couldn't hear him. <u>What did he say</u>**?**
2. **Q** (**N.Cl.**) I couldn't hear <u>what he said</u>.
3. **Q N.Cl.** I need some information. <u>Where does Tom live</u>   I have to send him a letter.
4. **Q N.Cl.** I need to know <u>where Tom lives</u>   I have to send him a letter.
5. **Q N.Cl.** There's something I don't understand. <u>Why did Barb cancel her vacation plans</u>
6. **Q N.Cl.** I don't understand <u>why Barb canceled her vacation plans</u>
7. **Q N.Cl.** I can't tell you <u>what they did</u>   You'll have to ask Jim.
8. **Q N.Cl.** <u>What did they do</u>   Please tell me.
9. **Q N.Cl.** Do you know that woman? <u>Who is she</u>   She looks familiar.
10. **Q N.Cl.** Do you see that woman over there? Do you know <u>who she is</u>   She looks familiar.
11. **Q N.Cl.** <u>Where did Ann go</u>   Do you know?
12. **Q N.Cl.** <u>Where Ann went</u>   is a secret

◇ **PRACTICE 2—SELFSTUDY:** Questions and noun clauses that begin with a question word. (Charts 7-1 and 7-2; Appendix 1, B-1 and B-2)

Directions: If the given words are a question, insert a capital letter and a question mark. If the given words are a noun clause, write *"I don't know"* and a final period.

1. _____ ***W*** ~~w~~here is he **?**
2. ___ ***I don't know*** where he is.
3. ___ ***I don't know*** what he did.
4. _____ ***W*** ~~w~~hat did he do **?**
5. _____ how old is he
6. _____ how old he is
7. _____ where did he go
8. _____ where he went
9. _____ why he said that
10. _____ why did he say that
11. _____ who he is
12. _____ who is he
13. _____ when will he arrive
14. _____ when he will arrive
15. _____ who is he talking to
16. _____ which one he bought

◇ **PRACTICE 3—SELFSTUDY: Forms of information questions and noun clauses.**
(Charts 7-1 and 7-2; Appendix 1, Charts B-1 and B-2)

Directions: Make a question from the given sentence. The words in parentheses should be the answer to the question you make. Use a question word (***who, what, how,*** *etc.*). Then change the question to a noun clause.

1. Tom will be here (*next week*).

   QUESTION: ___*When will Tom be here?*___

   NOUN CLAUSE: Please tell me ___*when Tom will be here.*___

2. He is coming (*because he wants to visit his friends*).

   QUESTION: _____

   NOUN CLAUSE: Please tell me _____

3. He'll be on flight (*645, not flight 742*).

   QUESTION: _____

   NOUN CLAUSE: Please tell me _____

4. (*Jim Hunter*) is going to meet him at the airport.

   QUESTION: _____

   NOUN CLAUSE: Please tell me _____

5. Jim Hunter is (*his roommate*).

   QUESTION: _____

   NOUN CLAUSE: Please tell me _____

6. Tom's address is (*4149 Riverside Road*).

   QUESTION: _____

   NOUN CLAUSE: Please tell me _____

7. He lives (*on Riverside Road in Columbus, Ohio, USA*).

   QUESTION: _____

   NOUN CLAUSE: Please tell me _____

8. He was (*in Chicago*) last week.

   QUESTION: _____

   NOUN CLAUSE: Please tell me _____

9. He has been working for IBM★ (*since 1988*).

   QUESTION: _____

   NOUN CLAUSE: Do you know _____

10. He has (*an IBM*) computer at home.

   QUESTION: _____

   NOUN CLAUSE: Do you know _____

★IBM = the name of a corporation (**I**nternational **B**usiness **M**achines)

11. He needs (*some new disks for his computer*).

QUESTION: _____

NOUN CLAUSE: Do you know _____

12. He called (*yesterday*).

QUESTION: _____

NOUN CLAUSE: Please tell me _____

13. He wants to (*see all his friends*) after he gets here.

QUESTION: _____

NOUN CLAUSE: Do you know _____

14. It was (*his*) idea to have a party.

QUESTION: _____

NOUN CLAUSE: Can you tell me _____

◇ **PRACTICE 4—SELFSTUDY: Questions and noun clauses that begin with a question word. (Charts 7-1 and 7-2; Appendix 1, B-1 and B-2)**

Directions: Use the words in parentheses to complete the sentences. Use any appropriate verb tense. Some of the completions contain noun clauses and some contain questions.

1. A: Where _____ ***did Ruth go*** _____? She's not in her room. (*Ruth, go*)

B: I don't know. Ask Tina. She might know where _____ ***Ruth went*** _____. (*Ruth, go*)

2. A: John is searching every drawer. Do you know what _____ ***he's looking for*** _____? (*he, look for*)

B: I have no idea. Why don't I just ask him? John? What _____ ***are you looking for*** _____? (*you, look for*)

3. A: Oops! I made a mistake. Where _____? Didn't I lend it to you? (*my eraser, be*)

B: I don't have it. Ask Sally where _____. I think I saw her using it. (*it, be*)

4. A: I heard that Sam changed his mind about going on the picnic. Why _____ _____ to stay home? Is something wrong? (*he, decide*)

B: I don't know. Maybe Jane can tell us why _____ not to come with us. Let's ask her. I hope he's okay. (*he, decide*)

5. A: Whose book _____? (*this, be*)

B: It's not mine. I don't know whose _____. (*it, be*)

6. A: Did Jack get enough food when he went to the market? How much fish _____ _____? It takes a lot of fish to feed 12 people. (*he, buy*)

B: Just relax. I don't know exactly how much fish _____, but I'm sure there'll be enough for dinner for all of us. (*he, buy*)

7. A: The door isn't locked! Why _____ it before he left? (*Fred, lock, not*)

   B: Why ask me? How am I supposed to know why _____ it? Maybe he just forgot. (*he, lock, not*)

8. A: The Lee family are recent immigrants, aren't they? How long _____ in this country? (*they, be*)

   B: I have no idea. Would you like me to ask Mr. Lee how long _____ _____ here? I'll be seeing him this afternoon. (*he and his family, live*)

9. A: I need a math tutor. Do you know who _____? (*John's tutor, be*)

   B: No. Let me ask Phil. Excuse me, Phil? Who _____? Do you know? (*John's tutor, be*)

10. A: You're a student here? I'm a student here, too. Tell me what classes _____ _____ this term. Maybe we're in some of the same classes. (*you, take*)

    B: Math 4, English 2, History 6, and Chemistry 101. What classes _____ _____? (*you, take*)

11. A: Lucy, why _____ for the exam? You could have done much better if you'd been prepared. (*you, study, not*)

    B: Well, Professor Morris, why _____ for the exam is a long story. I intended to, but . . . . (*I, study, not*)

12. A: Help! Quick! Look at that road sign! Which road _____ to take? (*we, be supposed*)

    B: You're the driver! Don't look at me! I don't know which road _____ to take. I've never been here before in my entire life. (*we, be supposed*)

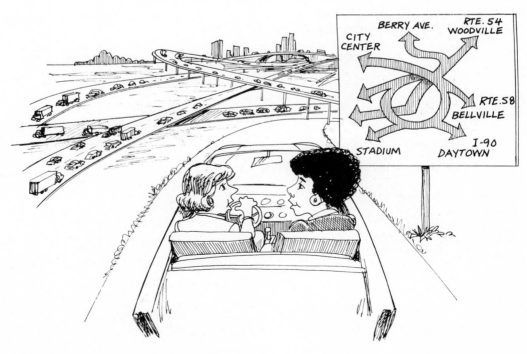

◇ **PRACTICE 5—GUIDED STUDY: Information questions and noun clauses.**
(Charts 7-2 and 7-3)

Directions: Pair up with another student.
 STUDENT A: Ask any question using the given words.
 STUDENT B: To make sure you understood Student A correctly, repeat what s/he said using a noun clause. Begin by saying: "You want to know . . . ."
Listen to each other's grammar carefully, especially word order.

Examples:

who/roommate   STUDENT A: *Who is your roommate?*
               STUDENT B: *You want to know who my roommate is.*

where/go   STUDENT A: *Where did you go after class yesterday?*
               STUDENT B: *You want to know where I went after class yesterday.*

how far/it   STUDENT A: *How far is it from Bangkok to Rangoon?*
               STUDENT B: *You want to know how far it is from Bangkok to Rangoon.*

PART I: (Appoint one of yourselves A and the other B.)

1. whose/that	6. when/you	11. who/prime minister
2. how much/cost	7. where/last night	12. which/want
3. what time/get	8. why/didn't	13. why/blue
4. how long/you	9. what/like	14. what/after
5. what kind/have	10. where/the teacher	15. from whom/borrow

PART II: (Switch roles: now B becomes A and asks the questions.)

1. where/born	6. when/get	11. what/tomorrow
2. what color/eyes	7. where/located	12. how far/it
3. whose/is	8. who/is	13. what kind/buy
4. which/you	9. who/talk	14. how often/you
5. why/ask	10. how many/go	15. to whom/give

◇ **PRACTICE 6—SELFSTUDY: Changing yes/no and information questions to noun clauses.**
(Charts 7-2 and 7-3)

Directions: Complete the sentence by changing the question in parentheses to a noun clause.

1. (*Will it rain?*) I wonder _____*if/whether it will rain*_____.

2. (*When will it rain?*) I wonder _____*when it will rain*_____.

3. (*Is Sam at home?*)

   I don't know _____ at home.

4. (*Where is Sam?*)

   I don't know _____.

5. (*Did Jane call?*)

   Ask Tom _____.

6. (*What time did she call?*)

Ask Tom _____ .

7. (*Why is the earth called "the water planet"?*)

Do you know _____ "the water planet"?

8. (*How far is it from New York City to Jakarta?*)

I wonder _____ from New York to Jakarta.

9. (*Has Susan ever been in Portugal?*)

I wonder _____ in Portugal.

10. (*Does she speak Portuguese?*)

I wonder _____ Portuguese.

11. (*Who did Ann play tennis with?*)

I wonder _____ tennis with.

12. (*Who won the tennis match?*)

I wonder _____ the tennis match.

13. (*Did Ann win?*)

I wonder _____ .

14. (*Do all creatures, including fish and insects, feel pain in the same way as humans do?*)

I wonder _____ pain in the same way as humans do.

15. (*Can birds communicate with each other?*)

Do you know _____ with each other?

16. (*How do birds communicate with each other?*)

Have you ever studied _____ with each other?

17. (*Where is the nearest post office?*)

Do you know _____?

18. (*Is there a post office near here?*)

Do you know _____ near here?

◇ **PRACTICE 7—SELFSTUDY: Error analysis. (Charts 7-2 and 7-3)**

Directions: Find and correct the errors in the following sentences.

1. Please tell me what is your name. → *Please tell me what **your name is**.*
2. No one seems to know when will Maria arrive.
3. I wonder why was Bob late for class.
4. I don't know what does that word mean.
5. I wonder does the teacher know the answer?
6. What should they do about the hole in their roof is their most pressing problem.
7. I'll ask her would she like some coffee or not.
8. Be sure to tell the doctor where does it hurt.
9. Why am I unhappy is something I can't explain.
10. I wonder does Tom know about the meeting or not.
11. I need to know who is your teacher.
12. I don't understand why is the car not running properly.

◇ **PRACTICE 8—SELFSTUDY: Question words and *whether* followed by infinitives. (Chart 7-4)**

Directions: Using the idea in the question in parentheses, complete the sentence with a question word or *whether* followed by an infinitive.

1. (*Where should I buy the meat for the lamb stew?*)

I don't know ____**where to buy**____ the meat for the lamb stew.

2. (*Should I stay home or go to the movie?*)

Tom can't decide ____**whether to stay**____ home or ___**go**___ to the movie.

3. (*How can I fix this toaster?*)

Jack doesn't know ____**how to fix**____ the toaster.

4. (*Should I look for another job?*)

Jason is wondering ____**whether (or not) to look**____ for another job.

5. (*Where can I get a map of the city?*)

Ann wants to know _____ a map of the city.

6. (*Should I go to the meeting?*)

Al is trying to decide _____ to the meeting.

7. (*What time should I pick you up?*)

I need to know _____ you up.

8. (*Who should I talk to about this problem?*)

I don't know _____ to about this problem.

9. (*Should I take a nap or do my homework?*)

I can't decide _____ a nap or _____ my homework.

10. (*How can I solve this problem for you?*)

My adviser can't figure out _____ this problem for me.

11. (*Where should I tell them to meet us?*)

I'm not sure _____ them to meet us.

12. (*How long am I supposed to cook this meat?*)

I can't remember _____ this meat.

13. (*What should I wear to the ceremony?*)

I can't decide _____ to the ceremony.

14. (*How much coffee should I make for the meeting?*)

You'll have to tell me _____ for the meeting.

15. (*Which essay should I use for the contest?*)

Susan can't decide _____ for the contest.

16. (*Should I take a year off from work and travel around the world? Or should I keep working and save my money?*)

Alice can't decide _____ a year off from work and _____ around the world, or _____ working and _____ her money.

◇ **PRACTICE 9—GUIDED STUDY: "*That* clauses." (Chart 7-5)**

Directions: Complete the sentences with your own words.

Examples:
    It is apparent that . . . .
    → *It is apparent that the weather is not going to improve.*
    That . . . is a fact that is hard to deny.
    → *That pollution diminishes the quality of our lives is a fact that is hard to deny.*

1. It is extremely important that . . . .
2. It is surprising that . . . .
3. That . . . is unfortunate.
4. That . . . indicates that . . . .
5. It is undeniably true that . . . .
6. It seems obvious to me that . . . .
7. That . . . is strange.
8. It is a pity that . . . .
9. I'm not pleased that . . . .
10. It seems necessary that . . . .
11. My biggest problem is that . . . .
12. I'm afraid that . . . . Please try to understand.
13. The reason he was fired from his job is that . . . .
14. That . . . was not made clear to me.
15. The fact that . . . does not mean that . . . .
16. That . . . is amazing.

◇ **PRACTICE 10—SELFSTUDY:** Using *the fact that.* (Chart 7-5)

Directions: Combine each pair of sentences into one sentence by using ***the fact that***.

1. I studied for three months for the examination. Regardless of that, I barely passed.
   → *Regardless of* **the fact that** *I studied for three months for the examination, I barely passed.*

2. Jim lost our tickets to the concert. There's nothing we can do about that.

3. We are going to miss one of the best concerts of the year because of Jim's carelessness. That makes me a little angry.

4. We can't go to the concert. In view of that, let's plan to go to a movie.

5. I couldn't speak a word of Italian and understood very little. Except for that, I had a wonderful time visiting my Italian cousins in Rome.

6. Many people living in Miami speak only Spanish. When I first visited Florida, I was surprised by that.

7. Bobby broke my grandmother's antique flower vase. That isn't important.

8. He lied about it. That is what bothers me.

9. Prof. Brown, who had had almost no teaching experience, was hired to teach the advanced physics courses. At first, some of us objected to that, but she has proven herself to be one of the best.

10. That automobile has the best safety record of any car manufactured this year. I am impressed by that and would definitely recommend that you buy that make.

◇ **PRACTICE 11—SELFSTUDY:** Quoted speech. (Chart 7-6)

Directions: Add the necessary punctuation and capitalization to the following. Do not change the word order or add or delete any words.

1. The athlete said where is my uniform
   → *The athlete said, ''Where is my uniform?''*

2. Who won the game asked the spectator

3. Stop the clock shouted the referee we have an injured player

4. I can't remember Margaret said where I put my purse

5. Sandy asked her sister how can I help you get through this difficulty

6. I'll answer your question later he whispered I'm trying to hear what the speaker is saying

7. As the students entered the room, the teacher said please take your seats quickly.

8. Why did I ever take this job Barry wondered aloud

9. After crashing into me and knocking all of my packages to the ground, the man stopped abruptly, turned to me and said softly excuse me

10. I'm going to rest for the next three hours she said I don't want to be disturbed
    That's fine I replied you get some rest I'll make sure no one disturbs you

11. Do we want four more years of corruption and debt the candidate shouted into the microphone no the crowd screamed

12. The woman behind the fast-food counter shouted who's next

I am three people replied all at the same time

Which one of you is really next she asked impatiently

I was here first said a young woman elbowing her way up to the counter I want a hamburger.

You were not hollered an older man standing next to her I was here before you were give me a chicken sandwich and a cup of coffee

Wait a minute I was in line first said a young man give me a cheeseburger and a chocolate shake

The woman behind the restaurant counter spotted a little boy politely waiting his turn she turned to him and said hi, Sonny what can I get for you

◇ PRACTICE 12—SELFSTUDY: Reported speech. (Chart 7-7)

Directions: Complete the sentences by changing quoted speech to reported speech. Use formal sequence of tenses.

1. Tom said, "I am busy."→ Tom said that he _____*was*_____ busy.

2. Tom said, "I need some help.→ Tom said that he _____ some help.

3. Tom said, "I am having a good time."→ Tom said that he _____ a good time.

4. Tom said, "I have finished my work."→ Tom said that he _____ his work.

5. Tom said, "I finished it an hour ago."→ Tom said that he _____ it an hour ago.

6. Tom said, "I will arrive at noon."→ Tom said that he _____ at noon.

7. Tom said, "I am going to be there at noon."→ Tom said that he _____ there at noon.

8. Tom said, "I can solve that problem."→ Tom said that he _____ that problem.

9. Tom said, "I may come early."→ Tom said that he _____ early.

10. Tom said, "I might come early."→ Tom said that he _____ early.

11. Tom said, "I must leave at eight."→ Tom said that he _____ at eight.

12. Tom said, "I have to leave at eight."→ Tom said that he _____ at eight.

13. Tom said, "I should go to the library."→ Tom said that he _____ to the library.

14. Tom said, "I ought to go to the library."→ Tom said that he _____ to the library.

15. Tom said, "Stay here."→ Tom told me _____ here.

16. Tom said, "Don't move."→ Tom told me _____.

17. Tom said, "Are you comfortable?"→ Tom asked me if I _____ comfortable.

18. Tom said, "When did you arrive?"→ Tom asked me when I _____.

◇ PRACTICE 13—SELFSTUDY: Reported speech. (Chart 7-7)

Directions: Complete the sentences by changing quoted speech to reported speech. Use formal sequence of tenses as appropriate. (Pay attention to whether the reporting verb is past or present.)

1. *I asked Martha, "Are you planning to enter law school?"*
   I asked Martha _____*if/whether she was planning*_____ to enter law school.

2. *Ed just asked me, "What time does the movie begin?"*
   Ed wants to know _____*what time the movie begins.*_____

3. *Fred asked, "Can we still get tickets for the concert?"*
   Fred asked _____*if/whether we could still get*_____ tickets for the concert.

4. *Thomas said to us, "How can I help you?"*
   Thomas wants to know _____*how he can help*_____ us.

5. *Eva asked, "Can you help me, John?"*
   Eva asked John _____ her.

6. *Charles said, "When will the final decision be made?"*
   Charles wanted to know _____

7. *Frank asked Elizabeth, "Where have you been all afternoon?"*

Frank asked Elizabeth _____ all afternoon.

8. *Bill just said, "What is Kim's native language?"*

Bill wants to know _____.

9. *Yesterday Ron said to Bob, "What's the problem?"*

Ron asked Bob _____.

10. *I asked myself, "Am I doing the right thing?"*

I wondered _____ the right thing.

11. *All of the farmers are asking, "When is this terrible drought going to end?"*

All of the farmers are wondering _____ to end.

12. *George asked me, "What time do I have to be at the laboratory in the morning?"*

George asked me _____ to be at the laboratory in the morning.

13. *Beth asked, "Who should I give the message to?"*

Beth asked me _____.

14. *Our tour guide said, "We'll be leaving around 7:00 o'clock in the morning."*

Our tour guide told us _____ around 7:00 o'clock in the morning.

15. *Nancy asked, "Why didn't you call me?"*

Nancy wanted to know _____ her.

◇ **PRACTICE 14—SELFSTUDY: Reported speech. (Chart 7-7)**

Directions: Complete the sentences using the information in the dialogue. Use the formal sequence of tenses.

1. *Fred asked me, "Can we still get tickets to the game?"*
   I said, "I've already bought them."

   When Fred asked me if we _____ ***could still get*** _____ tickets to the game, I told him

   that I _____ ***had already bought*** _____ them.

2. *Mrs. White said, "Janice, you have to clean up your room and empty the dishwasher before you leave for the game."*
   Janice said, "Okay, Mom. I will."

   Mrs. White told Janice that she _____ her room and

   _____ the dishwasher before she _____ for the

   game. Janice promised her mom that she _____.

3. *I asked Mary, "Why do you still smoke?"*
   Mary replied, "I've tried to quit many times, but I just don't seem to be able to."

   When I asked Mary why she _____, she replied that she _____

   _____ to quit many times but she just _____ to be able to.

4. *I asked the ticket seller, "Are the concerts going to be rescheduled?"*
   The ticket seller said, "I don't know, Ma'am. I just work here."

   When I asked the ticket seller if the concerts _____ to be rescheduled,

   she told me that she _____ and said that she just _____ there.

5. *The teacher asked, "Bobby, what is the capital of Australia?"*
   Bobby replied, "I'm not sure, but I think it's Sydney."

   Yesterday in class, Bobby's teacher asked him _____. He

   answered that he _____ sure but that he _____ Sydney.

6. *I asked Boris, "Where will the next chess match take place?"*
   Boris replied, "It hasn't been decided yet."

   When I asked Boris _____ place, he replied that it

   _____ yet.

7. *The children inquired of their father, "Will we be able to visit the Air and Space Museum and the*
   Natural History Museum, too?"
   Their father said, "We will if we leave the hotel before 10 o'clock tomorrow morning."

   The children asked their father whether they _____ able to visit

   the Air and Space Museum and the Natural History Museum, too. He told them they

   _____ if they _____ the hotel before 10 o'clock the next morning.

8. *I said to Alan, "I'm very discouraged. I don't think I'll ever speak English well."*
   Alan said, "Your English is getting better every day. In another year, you'll be speaking English
   with the greatest of ease."

   I complained that I _____ very discouraged, and that I _____ I

   _____ English well. Alan told me that my English _____

   _____ better every day. He assured me that in another year I _____

   _____ English with the greatest of ease.

9. *I told Jenny, "It's pouring outside. You'd better take an umbrella."*
   Jenny said, "It'll stop soon. I don't need one."

   I told Jenny that it _____ outside and that she _____ an

   umbrella. However, Jenny said she thought the rain _____ soon and that

   she _____ one.

10. *A person in the audience asked the speaker, "Are there presently available the necessary means to*
    increase the world's food supply?"
    The agronomy professor said, "It might be possible to grow 50 percent of the world's food in
    underwater cultivation if we can develop inexpensive methods."

    A person in the audience asked the agronomy professor if there _____

    presently available the necessary means to increase the world's food supply. The professor

    stated that it _____ possible to grow 50 percent of the world's food under

    water if we _____ inexpensive methods.

◇ PRACTICE 15—GUIDED STUDY: Reported speech. (7-1 → 7-7)

Directions: In the following, read a dialogue and then write a report of the dialogue. In your report, you need to give an accurate idea of the speakers' words, but you don't necessarily have to use the speakers' exact words. Study the first three examples of possible written reports carefully.

Example dialogue:
> Jack said, "I can't go to the game."
> Tom said, "Oh? Why not?"
> Jack replied, "I don't have enough money for a ticket."

Possible written reports of the above dialogue:
→ *Jack told Tom that he couldn't go to the game because he didn't have enough money for a ticket.*
→ *When Tom asked Jack why he couldn't go to the game, Jack said he didn't have enough money for a ticket.*
→ *Jack said he couldn't go to the game. When Tom asked him why not, Jack replied that he didn't have enough money for a ticket.*

Example dialogue:
> "Where are you going, Ann?" I asked.
> "I'm on my way to the market," she replied. "Do you want to come with me?"
> "I'd like to, but I have to stay home. I have a lot of work to do."
> "Okay," Ann said. "Is there anything you would like me to pick up for you at the market?"
> "How about a few bananas? And some apples if they're fresh?"
> "Sure. I'd be happy to."

Possible written report:
→ *When I asked Ann where she was going, she said she was on her way to the market and invited me to come★ with her. I said I'd like to, but that I had to stay home because I had a lot of work to do. Ann kindly asked me if there was anything she could pick up for me at the market. I asked her to pick up a few bananas and some apples if they were fresh. She said she'd be happy to.*

Write reports of the following dialogues:

1.   "What are you doing?" Alex asked.
     "I'm drawing a picture," I said.

2.   Ann said, "Do you want to go to a movie Sunday night?"
     Sue said, "I'd like to, but I have to study."

3.   "How old are you, Mrs. Robinson?" the little boy asked.
     Mrs. Robinson said, "It's not polite to ask people their age."

4.   "Is there anything you especially want to watch on TV tonight?" my sister asked.
     "Yes." I replied. "There's a show at eight that I've been waiting to see for a long time."
     "What is it?" she asked.
     "It's a documentary on green sea turtles," I said.
     "Why do you want to see that?"
     "I'm doing a research paper on sea turtles. I think I might be able to get some good information from the documentary. Why don't you watch it with me?"
     "No, thanks," she said. "I'd rather do my math homework than watch a show on green sea turtles."

_____

★See Chart 4–5 for the use of infinitives to report speech (for example, *invited me **to come**, asked her **to pick up**, told me **to finish**, promised **to do** it).*

◇ **PRACTICE 16—GUIDED STUDY: Reporting speech. (Chapter 7)**

Directions: Break up into small groups and discuss one (or two, or all) of the following topics. At the end of your discussion, make a formal written report of the main points made by each speaker in your group. (Do not attempt to report every word that was spoken.)

In your report, use words such as *think, believe, say, remark,* and *state* to introduce noun clauses. When you use *think* or *believe*, you will probably use present tenses (e.g., *John thinks that money is the most important thing in life.*) When you use *say, remark,* or *state*, you will probably use past tenses (e.g., *Ann said that many other things were more important than money.*).

Do you agree with the given statement? Why or why not?

1. Money is the most important thing in life.
2. A woman can do any job a man can do.
3. When a person decides to get married, his or her love for the other person is the only important consideration.
4. A world government is both desirable and necessary. Countries should simply become the states of one nation, the Earth. In this way, wars could be eliminated and wealth could be equally distributed.

◇ **PRACTICE 17—GUIDED STUDY: Reporting speech. (Chapter 7)**

Directions:

You are a newspaper reporter at a press conference. You and your fellow reporters (your classmates) will interview your teacher or a person whom your teacher invites to class. Your assignment is to write an article for the school newspaper. The purpose of your article is to give a professional and personal sketch of the person whom you interview.

Take notes during the interview. It is important to report information accurately. Listen to the answers carefully. Write down some of the important sentences so that you can use them for quotations in your article. Ask for clarification if you do not understand something the interviewee has said.

When you write the article, try to organize your information into related topics. For example, if you interview your teacher:

    I. General introductory information
   II. Professional life
      A. Present teaching duties
      B. Academic duties and activities outside of teaching
      C. Past teaching experience
      D. Educational background
  III. Personal life
      A. Basic biographical information (e.g., place of birth, family background, places of residence)
      B. Spare-time activities and interests
      C. Travel experiences

The above outline suggests one possible method of organization. You must organize your own article, depending upon the information you learn from the interview and whom you interview.

When you write your report, most of your information will be presented in reported speech; use quoted speech only for the most important or memorable sentences. When you use quoted speech, be sure you are presenting the interviewee's *exact words*. If you are simply paraphrasing what the interviewee said, do not use quotation marks.

◇ **PRACTICE 18—SELFSTUDY: Error analysis. (Chapter 7)**

Directions: The following sentences contain errors. Correct the errors.

1. What is the government official going to say in his speech tonight will affect all of us.
2. I asked Paul help me move the table to the other side of the room.
3. My friend asked me what you are going to do Saturday? I replied it depends on the weather.
4. What my friend and I did it was our secret. We didn't even tell our parents what did we do.
5. The doctor asked that I felt okay. I told him that I don't feel well.
6. Is clear that the ability to use a computer it is an important skill in the modern world.
7. They asked us that we will be sure to turn out the lights when we leave.
8. Is true you almost drowned? my friend asked me.

   Yes, I said. I'm really glad to be alive. It was really frightening.
9. It is a fact that I almost drowned makes me very careful about water safety whenever I go swimming.

◇ **PRACTICE 19—GUIDED STUDY: Error analysis. (Chapter 7)**

Directions: The following sentences contain errors. Correct the errors.

1. I didn't know where am I supposed to get off the bus, so I asked the driver where is the science museum. She tell me the name of the street. She said she will tell me when should I get off the bus.
2. Studying psychology last year made me realize that what kind of career did I want to have.
3. My mother said don't forget your family when you're far away from home.
4. When I asked the taxi driver to drive faster he said I will drive faster if you pay me more. At that time I didn't care how much would it cost, so I told him to go as fast as he can.
5. My mother did not live with us. When other children asked me where was my mother, I told them she is going to come to visit me very soon.
6. I asked him what kind of movies does he like, he said me, I like romantic movies.

◇ **PRACTICE 20—SELFSTUDY: Using the subjunctive. (Chart 7-8)**

Directions: Complete the sentence, using the idea of the words in parentheses.

1. (*You should organize a camping trip.*)
   The girls proposed that their scout leader _____*organize*_____ a camping trip.

2. (*Ms. Hanson thinks that the director should divide our class into two sections.*)
   Ms. Hanson recommended that our class _____*be divided*_____ into two sections.

3. (*You must call home every week.*)
   Dan's parents insisted that he _____ home every week.

4. (*Someone must tell her the truth about her illness.*)

It is essential that she _____ the truth about her illness.

5. (*Open your suitcases for inspection.*)

The customs official demanded that all passengers _____ their suitcases.

6. (*Ann, you should take some art courses.*)

The counselor recommended that Ann _____ some art courses.

7. (*All parts of the motor must work correctly.*)

It is vital that all parts of the motor _____ in proper working order.

8. (*Please mail all packages at the central office.*)

The director requests that all packages _____ at the central office.

9. (*Soldiers must obey their officers.*)

It is imperative that soldiers _____ their officers.

10. (*We must remember to give the babysitter certain phone numbers to call in case of emergency.*)

It is important that the babysitter _____ phone numbers to call in case of emergency.

◇ **PRACTICE 21—SELFSTUDY: Using *-ever* words. (Chart 7-9)**

Directions: Complete the following sentences by using *-ever* words.

1. As vice-president of international sales, Robert has complete control over his travel schedule. He can travel _____ **whenever** _____ he wants.

2. Robert is free to decide which countries he will visit during his overseas trips. He can travel _____ **wherever** _____ he wants.

3. The English professor told us that we could write our papers on _____ subject we wanted as long as it related to the topics we discussed in class this semester.

4. There are only two appointment time slots remaining. You may select _____ one you prefer.

5. To Ellen, the end justifies the means. She will do _____ she has to do in order to accomplish her objective.

6. Linda is very amiable and gregarious. She makes friends with _____ she meets.

7. It doesn't matter which class you take to fulfill this requirement. Just take _____ one fits best into your schedule.

8. _____ is the last to leave the room should turn off the lights and lock the door.

9. I know that Norman will succeed. He'll do _____ is required to succeed.

10. My wife and I are going to ride our bicycles across the country. We will ride for six to seven hours every day, then stop _____ we happen to be at the end of the day.

Directions: In each of the following, select the ONE correct answer.

Example:
He asked me where ___**B**___.
   A. *did I live*   B. *I lived*   C. *do you live*   D. *that I lived*

1. I talked to Bob two weeks ago. I thought he wanted to know about my cat, but I misunderstood him. He asked me where _____, not my cat.
   A. is my hat   B. my hat was   C. my hat is   D. was my hat

2. "The people in the apartment upstairs must have a lot of children."
"I don't know how many _____, but it sounds like they have a dozen."
   A. children do they have   B. do they have children
   C. children they have   D. they have children

3. Do you know _____? I myself have no idea.
   A. how many years the earth is   B. how old the earth is
   C. how long is the earth   D. how much time has been the earth

4. "There's too much noise in this room. I can't understand what _____."
"Neither can I."
   A. is the professor saying   B. is saying the professor
   C. that the professor is saying   D. the professor is saying

5. When I was little, my father gave me some advice. He said _____ talk to strangers.
   A. I shouldn't   B. that shouldn't   C. don't   D. that I don't

6. "I didn't expect Ann's husband to be here at the opera with her."
"I'm surprised, too. Ann must have insisted that _____ with her."
   A. he come   B. he comes   C. he came   D. he had come

7. "Ms. Wright, can you give me a little extra help typing some letters today?"
"Sorry, I can't. The boss has an urgent report for me to write. She demanded that it _____ on her desk by 5 P.M. today."
   A. was   B. will be   C. is   D. be

8. "Did you tell Carol where _____ us this evening?"
"Yes, I did. I can't understand why she is late."
   A. should she meet   B. she to meet   C. she meets   D. to meet

9. A fortune-teller predicted _____ inherit a lot of money before the end of the year.
   A. that I would   B. that I   C. what I will   D. what I

10. "Bill Frazer seems like a good person for the job, but we don't know why he left his last job."
"I know why. He told me _____ a serious policy disagreement with his boss last January."
   A. if he'd had   B. he'd had   C. what he'd had   D. that what he had

11. "Is it true that you fell asleep in class yesterday and began to snore?"
"Unfortunately, yes. _____ is unbelievable! I'm very embarrassed."
   A. That I could do such a thing it   B. That I could do such a thing
   C. I could do such a thing it   D. I could do such a thing

12. "Officer, can you tell me how to get to Springfield?"
"Sure. What part of Springfield _____ to go to?"
   A. do you want   B. you want   C. that you want   D. where you want

13. "Is it true _____ the law says there is no smoking in restaurants in this city?"
"Yes. That law was passed last year."
   A. that what   B. what   C. if   D. that

14. _____ prompt is important to our boss.
  A. A person is   B. Is a person   C. If a person is   D. Whether or not a person is

15. A scientific observer of wildlife must note every detail of how _____ in their environment: their eating and sleeping habits, their social relationships, and their methods of self-protection.
  A. do animals live   B. live animals   C. do live animals   D. animals live

16. The mystery movie was clever and suspenseful. The audience couldn't guess _____ committed the murder until the surprise ending.
  A. who he   B. who had   C. that who   D. that

17. How do you like your new school? Tell me _____.
  A. who in your class is   B. who your class is in
  C. who is in your class   D. your class who is in it

18. "What do you recommend _____ about this tax problem?"
    "I strongly suggest that we consult an expert as soon as possible."
  A. do we do   B. we will do   C. we do   D. should we do

19. The college does not grant degrees simply to _____ pays the cost of tuition; the student must satisfy the academic requirements.
  A. whoever   B. who   C. whomever   D. whoever that

20. "What are you going to buy in this store?"
    "Nothing. _____ want is much too expensive."
  A. That I   B. What I   C. That what I   D. What do I

◇ PRACTICE TEST B—GUIDED STUDY: Noun clauses. (Chapter 7)

Directions: In each of the following, select the ONE correct answer.

Example:
  He asked me where __B__.
  A. did I live   B. I lived   C. do you live   D. that I lived

1. "Does anybody know _____ on the ground?"
   "Your guess is as good as mine."
  A. how long this plane will be   B. how long will be this plane
  C. how long will this plane be   D. that how long this plane will be

2. "This restaurant is very expensive!"
   "It is, but order _____ want. Your birthday is a very special occasion."
  A. what is it you   B. what do you   C. whatever you   D. whatever you do

3. Why did Beth ask you _____ a bicycle?
  A. that if you had   B. do you have   C. that you had   D. if you had

4. "What did your grammar teacher want to talk to you about?"
   "I did badly on the last test. She _____ study for it."
  A. said why didn't I   B. asked why didn't I
  C. said why I didn't   D. asked why I didn't

5. "Why are you staring out the window? What _____ about?"
   "Nothing."
  A. you are thinking   B. you think
  C. are you thinking   D. do you are thinking

6. "I can't decide what color I want for my bedroom. What do you think?"
   "You should choose _____ color you want. You're the one who will have to live with it."
   A. whichever that   B. whatever   C. however   D. that what

7. "Did you remember to tell Marge _____ she should bring to the meeting tomorrow?"
   "Oh, my gosh! I completely forgot! I'm sorry."
   A. that   B. what   C. if   D. that what

8. "My aunt has been feeling bad since Uncle George died. Is it because she's depressed?"
   "I think so. _____ can cause debilitating physical symptoms is a medical fact."
   A. Depression   B. That depression it
   C. That depression   D. It is that depression

9. There was an earthquake on the coast yesterday. Fortunately, there was no loss of life.
   However, because of the danger of collapsing sea walls, it was essential that the area _____
   evacuated quickly.
   A. to be   B. will be   C. be   D. is

10. _____ saying was so important that I asked everyone to stop talking and listen.
    A. What the woman was   B. The woman was
    C. That the woman was   D. What was the woman

11. "This cake is terrible. What happened?"
    "It's my grandmother's recipe, but she forgot to tell me how long _____ it."
    A. did I bake   B. should I bake   C. do I bake   D. to bake

12. "Let's go to Riverton this weekend."
    "Sounds like fun. _____ from here?"
    A. How far is   B. How far it is   C. It how far is   D. How far is it

13. "Somebody forgot this hat. I wonder _____."
    A. whose is this hat   B. whose hat this is   C. whose hat is   D. is this whose hat

14. Edward's interview was very intense. The interviewer wanted to know many facts about his
    personal life, and even asked him _____ had ever used any illegal drugs of any kind.
    A. that if he   B. that he   C. if or not he   D. whether or not he

15. It is hoped that all present-day communicable diseases will be conquered. However, _____
    about certain diseases is still not sufficient to prevent them from spreading easily among the
    population.
    A. what we know   B. what do we know
    C. what we know that   D. that we know what

16. "Why didn't Henry attend the meeting this morning?"
    "He's been very sick. His doctor insisted that he _____ in bed this week."
    A. will stay   B. stayed   C. stays   D. stay

17. Nobody yet knew what _____ to cause the dam to burst, but the residents of the area organized
    quickly to protect life and property against the rising floods.
    A. happens   B. had happened   C. happen   D. did it happen

18. Did the teacher explain how _____ this problem?
    A. do we solve   B. can we solve   C. to solve   D. solve

19. _____ the National Weather Bureau predicted severe storms did not deter the fishing boats
    from going out into the open seas.
    A. The fact that   B. That fact is that   C. Is fact that   D. The fact is that

20. Tom walked into the huge hall to register for classes. At first, he simply looked around and
    wondered what _____ supposed to do.
    A. was he   B. am I   C. he was   D. I am

CHAPTER 8
Showing Relationships Between Ideas—Part I

◇ PRACTICE 1—SELFSTUDY: Parallel structure. (Chart 8-1)

Directions: Write the words that are parallel in each of the sentences.

1. These apples are fresh and sweet.

1. _____*fresh*_____ and _____*sweet*_____
      (adjective)   +   (adjective)

2. These apples and pears are fresh.

2. _____ and _____
      (noun)   +   (noun)

3. I washed and dried the apples.

3. _____ and _____
      (verb)   +   (verb)

4. I am washing and drying the apples.

4. _____ and _____
      (verb)   +   (verb)

5. We ate the fruit happily and quickly.

5. _____ and _____
      (adverb)   +   (adverb)

6. I enjoy biting into a fresh apple and tasting the juicy sweetness.

6. _____ and _____
      (gerund)   +   (gerund)

7. I like to bite into a fresh apple and taste the juicy sweetness.

7. _____ and _____
      (infinitive)   +   (infinitive)

8. Those imported apples are delicious but expensive.

8. _____ but _____
      (adjective)   +   (adjective)

9. Apples, pears, and bananas are kinds of fruit.

9. _____, _____, and _____
    (noun)   +   (noun)   +   (noun)

10. Those apples are red, ripe, and juicy.

10. _____, _____, and _____
    (adjective) +   (adjective)   +   (adjective)

◇ PRACTICE 2—SELFSTUDY: Parallel structure. (Charts 8-1 and 8-2)

Directions: Write "C" if the parallel structure is CORRECT. Write "I" if the parallel structure is INCORRECT, and make any necessary corrections. Underline the parallel elements of the sentences.

1. __*I*__ I admire him for his <u>intelligence</u>, cheerful <u>disposition</u>, and ~~he is honest~~.　　*honesty*

2. __*C*__ Abraham Lincoln was a <u>lawyer</u> and a <u>politician</u>.

3. _____ When Anna moved, she had to rent an apartment, make new friends, and find a job.

4. _____ Barb studies each problem carefully and works out a solution.

5. _____ Aluminum is plentiful and relatively inexpensive.

6. _____ Many visitors to Los Angeles enjoy visiting Disneyland and to tour movie studios.

7. _____ Children are usually interested in but a little frightened by snakes.

8. _____ Either fainting can result from a lack of oxygen or a loss of blood.

9. _____ So far this term, the students in the writing class have learned how to write thesis statements, organize their material, and summarizing their conclusions.

10. _____ The boat sailed across the lake smoothly and quiet.

11. _____ When I looked more closely, I saw that it was not coffee but chocolate on my necktie.

12. _____ Not only universities support medical research but also many government agencies.

13. _____ Physics explains why water freezes and how the sun produces heat.

14. _____ All plants need light, a suitable climate, and an ample supply of water and minerals from the soil.

15. _____ With their keen sight, fine hearing, and refined sense of smell, wolves hunt day or night in quest of elk, deer, moose, or caribou.

◇ PRACTICE 3—SELFSTUDY: Paired conjunctions, subject-verb agreement. (Chart 8-2)

Directions: Supply the correct present tense form of the verb in parentheses.

1. (know)   Neither the students nor the teacher _____*knows*_____ the answer.
2. (know)   Neither the teacher nor the students _____*know*_____ the answer.
3. (know)   Not only the students but also the teacher _____ the answer.
4. (know)   Not only the teacher but also the students _____ the answer.
5. (know)   Both the teacher and the student _____ the answer.
6. (want)   Neither Alan nor Carol _____ to go skiing this weekend.
7. (like)   Both John and Ted _____ to go cross-country skiing.
8. (have)   Either Jack or Alice _____ the information you need.
9. (agree)   Neither my parents nor my brother _____ with my decision.
10. (be)   Both intelligence and skill _____ essential to good teaching.
11. (realize) Neither my classmates nor my teacher _____ that I have no idea what's going on in class.
12. (think)   Not only Laura's husband but also her children _____ she should return to school and finish her graduate degree.

◇ PRACTICE 4—SELFSTUDY: Paired conjunctions. (Chart 8-2)

Directions: Combine the following into sentences which contain parallel structure. Use the paired conjunctions in parentheses. Pay special attention to the exact place you put the paired conjunctions in the combined sentence.

1. Many people don't drink coffee. Many people don't drink alcohol. (neither . . . nor)
   → *Many people drink neither coffee nor alcohol.*

2. Barbara is fluent in Chinese. She is also fluent in Japanese. (not only . . . but also)

3. I'm sorry to say that Paul has no patience. He has no sensitivity to others. (neither . . . nor)

4. She can sing. She can dance. (*both . . . and*)

5. If you want to change your class schedule, you should talk to your teacher, or you should talk to your academic counselor. (*either . . . or*)

6. Diana is intelligent. She is very creative. (*both . . . and*)

7. You may begin working tomorrow or you may begin next week. (*either . . . or*)

8. Michael didn't tell his mother about the trouble he had gotten into. He didn't tell his father about the trouble he had gotten into. (*neither . . . nor*)

9. Success in karate requires balance and skill. Success in karate requires concentration and mental alertness. (*not only . . . but also*)

◇ **PRACTICE 5—GUIDED STUDY: Parallel structure. (Charts 8-1 and 8-2)**

Directions: With your own words, complete the sentences using parallel structures.

1. Dennis has proven himself to be a sincere, hardworking, and _____*efficient*_____ supervisor.

2. The professor walked through the door and _____.

3. I was listening to music and _____ when I heard a knock at the door.

4. I'm planning to stay here during the summer but _____ in the winter.

5. When I was a student, I would usually _____ and then _____ after dinner.

6. _____ and attending concerts in the park are two of the things my wife and I like to do on summer weekends.

7. When you visit other countries, it is important to be able to speak at least a few words of the language, to understand the local customs, and _____.

8. I get up at seven every morning, eat a light breakfast, and _____.

9. Our whole family enjoys camping. We especially enjoy fishing in mountain streams and _____.

10. My parents want me to either call or _____ every week, but I'm so busy and _____ by the end of each day that all I want to do is go to bed and _____.

11. You can pay the bill either _____ or _____.

12. I'm going to subscribe to either _____ or _____.

◇ **PRACTICE 6—GUIDED STUDY: Parallel structure. (Charts 8-1 and 8-2)**

Directions: Choose the correct completion in parentheses.

1. *Hamlet* is one of Shakespeare's finest and most (*famous*, *famously*) plays.

2. On my vacation I lost a suitcase, broke my glasses, and (*missing*, *missed*) my plane.

3. Walking briskly for 30 minutes or (*run*, *running*) for 15 minutes will burn an approximately equal number of calories.

4. Slowly and (*cautious*, *cautiously*), the firefighter ascended the charred staircase.

5. The comedian made people laugh by telling jokes and (*making*, *make*) funny faces.

6. Tina is always understanding, patient, and (*speaks sensitively*, *sensitive*) when helping her friends with their problems.

7. Not only the post office but also all banks (*closes*, *close*) on most national holidays.

8. When tourists visit a new city, they often have trouble deciding where to go and how (*they can get*, *to get*) there.

9. Both the Indian cobra snake and the king cobra (*uses*, *use*) poison from their fangs in two ways: by injecting it directly into their prey or (*spit*, *by spitting*) it into the eyes of the victim.

10. What do people in your country think of bats? Are they mean and (*scary*, *scare*) creatures, or are they symbols of happiness and (*lucky*, *good luck*)? In western countries, many people have an unreasoned fear of bats. According to scientist Dr. Sharon Horowitz, bats are beneficial and (*harmless*, *harm*) mammals. ''When I was a child, I believed that a bat would attack me and (*tangle*, *tangled*) itself in my hair. Now I know better,'' said Dr. Horowitz.

Contrary to popular western myths, bats do not attack humans and (*be*, *are*) not blind. Though a few bats may be infected, they are not major carriers of rabies or (*give people other dread diseases*, *other dread diseases*). Bats help natural plant life by pollinating plants, (*spread seeds, and eat insects; spreading seeds, and eating insects*). If you get rid of bats that eat overripe fruit, then fruit flies flourish and (*destroying*, *can destroy*) the fruit industry. According to Dr. Horowitz, they make loving, trainable, and (*gentle*, *gently*) pets. Not many people, however, are known to have bats as pets, and bats themselves prefer to avoid people.

◇ **PRACTICE 7—SELFSTUDY: Combining independent clauses: periods and commas. (Charts 8-1 and 8-3)**

Directions: Punctuate the following sentences by adding periods (.) or commas (,) as necessary. Do not add any words. Capitalize letters where necessary. Some sentences may require no changes.

1. I like French cooking my wife prefers Italian cooking.
   → *I like French cooking. My wife prefers Italian cooking.*

2. I like French cooking but my wife prefers Italian cooking.
   → *I like French cooking, but my wife prefers Italian cooking. (optional comma)*

3. I've read that book it's very good.

4. I've read that book but I didn't like it.

5. I opened the door and asked my friend to come in.

6. I opened the door my sister answered the phone.

7. I opened the door and my sister answered the phone.

8. Minerals are common materials they are found in rocks and soil.

9. The most common solid materials on earth are minerals they are found in rocks soil and water.

10. You can travel to England by plane or you can go by ship if you prefer.

11. You can travel to England by plane or by ship.

12. Jason was going to study all night so he declined our invitation to dinner.

13. Jason declined our invitation to dinner he needed to stay home and study.

14. The wind was howling outside yet it was warm and comfortable indoors.

15. I hurried to answer the phone for I didn't want the children to wake up.

16. Last weekend we went camping it rained the entire time.

17. The highway was under construction so we had to take a different route to work.

18. No one thought we would win the championship yet our team won by a large margin.

19. We arrived at the theatre late but the play had not yet begun we were quite surprised.

20. A central heating system provides heat for an entire building from one central place most central heating systems service only one building but some systems heat a group of buildings, such as those at a military base a campus or an apartment complex.

◇ **PRACTICE 8—GUIDED STUDY: Using parallel structure. (Charts 8-1 → 8-3)**

Directions: Write two descriptive paragraphs on one of the topics below. The first paragraph should be a draft, and the second should be a "tightened up" revision of the same description. Look for places where two or three sentences can be combined into one by effective use of parallel structure. Pay special attention to punctuation and be sure all of your commas and periods are used correctly.

Topics: 1. Give a physical description of your place of residence (apartment, dorm room, etc.).
2. Describe the characteristics and activities of a successful student.
3. Give your reader directions for making a particular food dish.

Example:

First draft: *To make spaghetti sauce, you will need several ingredients. First, you will need some ground beef. Probably about one pound of ground beef will be sufficient. You should also have an onion. If the onions are small, you should use two. Also, find a green pepper and put it in the sauce. Of course, you will also need some tomato sauce or tomatoes.*

Revision: *To make spaghetti sauce you will need one pound of ground beef, one large or two small onions, a green pepper, and some tomato sauce or tomatoes.*

◇ **PRACTICE 9—SELFSTUDY: Adverb clauses. (Chart 8-4)**

Directions: Change the position of the adverb clause in the sentence. <u>Underline</u> the adverb clause in the given sentence, and <u>underline</u> the adverb clause in the new sentence. Punctuate carefully.

1. <u>As soon as a hurricane strikes land</u>, its force begins to diminish.
   → *A hurricane's force begins to diminish <u>as soon as it strikes land</u>.*

2. I didn't feel any older <u>when I reached my 21st birthday</u>.
   → *<u>When I reached my 21st birthday</u>, I didn't feel any older.*

3. I had a cup of tea before I left for work.

4. After I get home from work, I like to read the evening newspaper.

5. Since my watch broke, I have been late to work three times.

6. My cat hides under the house whenever it rains.

7. I'm going to get a job once I finish school.

8. While I was waiting for my bus, I heard a gunshot.

9. The village will have no electric power until a new generator is installed.

10. The last time I was in Taipei, I saw Mr. Wu.

11. Because I already had my boarding pass, I didn't have to stand in line at the airline counter.

12. Productivity in a factory increases if the workplace is made pleasant.

◇ **PRACTICE 10—SELFSTUDY: Periods and commas. (Charts 8-1 → 8-5)**

Directions: Add periods and commas as necessary. Do not change, add, or omit any words. Capitalize as necessary.

1. The lake was calm Tom went fishing.
   → *The lake was calm. Tom went fishing.*

2. Because the lake was calm Tom went fishing.
   → *Because the lake was calm, Tom went fishing.*

3. Tom went fishing because the lake was calm he caught two fish.

4. Tom went fishing because the lake was calm and caught two fish.

5. When Tom went fishing the lake was calm he caught two fish.

6. The lake was calm so Tom went fishing he caught two fish.

7. Because the lake was calm and quiet Tom went fishing.

8. The lake was calm quiet and clear when Tom went fishing.

◇ **PRACTICE 11—GUIDED STUDY: Periods and commas. (Charts 8-1 → 8-5; 6-8)**

Directions: Add periods and commas as necessary. Do not change, add, or omit any words. Capitalize as necessary.

1. Mr. Hood is admired because he dedicated his life to helping the poor he is well known for his work on behalf of homeless people.

2. Greg Adams has been blind since he was two years old today he is a key scientist in a computer company he is able to design complex electronic equipment because he can depend

on a computer that reads writes and speaks out loud his blindness neither helps nor hinders him it is largely irrelevant to how well he does his job.

3. Microscopes automobile dashboards and cameras are awkward for lefthanded people to use they are designed for righthanded people when "lefties" use these items they have to use their right hand to do the things that they would normally do with their left hand.

4. When you speak to someone who is hard of hearing you do not have to shout it is important to face the person directly and to speak clearly my father who is hard of hearing and wears a hearing aid can understand me if I speak distinctly as long as I enunciate clearly I do not need to shout when I speak to him.

◇ PRACTICE 12—SELFSTUDY: Verb tenses in adverb clauses of time. (Chart 8-5; Chapter 1)

Directions: Choose the letter of the correct answer.

1. After Jessica __C__ her degree, she intends to work in her father's company.
   A. will finish   B. will have finished   C. finishes   D. is finishing

2. By the time I go to bed tonight, I _____ my work for the day.
   A. will finish   B. have finished   C. will have finished   D. finish

3. When my parents _____ for a visit tomorrow, they will see our new baby for the first time.
   A. will arrive   B. arrived   C. will have arrived   D. arrive

4. Fatemah looked down to discover a snake at her feet. When she saw it, she _____.
   A. was screaming   B. had screamed   C. screamed   D. screams

5. By the time Alfonso finally graduated from high school, he _____ seven different schools because his parents moved frequently.
   A. attended   B. was attending   C. had attended   D. had been attending

6. Until you learn to relax more, you _____ your ability to speak English.
   A. haven't improved   B. aren't improving   C. don't improve   D. won't improve

7. I borrowed four books on gardening the last time I _____ to the library.
   A. go   B. went   C. had gone   D. have gone

8. Before I started the car, all of the passengers _____ their seat belts.
   A. will buckle   B. had buckled   C. buckle   D. have buckled

9. It seems that whenever I travel abroad I _____ to take something I need.
   A. forgot   B. am forgetting   C. forget   D. had forgotten

10. When I see the doctor this afternoon, I _____ him to look at my throat.
    A. will ask   B. asked   C. will have asked   D. ask

11. After ancient Greek athletes won a race in the Olympics, they _____ a simple crown of olive leaves.
    A. received   B. had received   C. were receiving   D. have received

12. After the race _____, the celebration began.
    A. had been won   B. is won   C. will be won   D. has been won

13. I'll return Bob's pen to him the next time I _____ him.
    A. see   B. will see   C. will have seen   D. have seen

14. I _____ all of the questions correctly since I began this grammar exercise on verb tenses.
    A. am answering   B. answer   C. have answered   D. answered

15. A small stone struck the windshield while we _____ down the gravel road.
    A. drive   B. were driving   C. had driven   D. had been driving

◇ **PRACTICE 13—GUIDED STUDY: Verb tenses in adverb clauses of time. (Chart 8-5; Chapter 1)**

Directions: Choose the letter of the correct answer.

1. As soon as Martina saw the fire, she _____ the fire department.
    A. was telephoning   B. telephoned   C. had telephoned   D. telephones

2. Before Jennifer won the lottery, she _____ any kind of contest.
    A. hasn't entered   B. didn't enter   C. wasn't entering   D. hadn't entered

3. Every time Prakash sees a movie made in India, he _____ homesick.
    A. will have felt   B. felt   C. feels   D. is feeling

4. Since I left Venezuela six years ago, I _____ to visit friends and family several times.
    A. return   B. will have returned   C. am returning   D. have returned

5. While he was washing his new car, Mr. De Rosa _____ a small dent in the rear fender.
    A. has discovered   B. was discovering   C. is discovering   D. discovered

6. Yesterday while I was jogging in the park, Matthew _____ on the company's annual report.
    A. was working   B. had been working C. has worked   D. works

7. Tony _____ to have children until his little daughter was born. After she won his heart, he decided he wanted a big family.
    A. didn't want   B. hadn't wanted   C. wasn't wanting   D. hasn't wanted

8. After the horse threw her to the ground for the third time, Jennifer picked herself up and said, "I _____ on another horse as long as I live."
    A. never ride   B. have never ridden C. will never ride   D. do not ride

9. The next time Paul _____ to New York, he will visit the Metropolitan Museum's famous collection of international musical instruments.
    A. will fly   B. flies   C. has flown   D. will have flown

10. Ever since Maurice arrived, he _____ quietly in the corner. Is something wrong?
    A. sat   B. has been sitting C. sits   D. is sitting

11. After Nancy _____ for twenty minutes, she began to feel tired.
    A. jogging   B. had been jogging C. has been jogging   D. has jogged

12. Peter, _____ since you got home from football practice?
    A. have you eaten   B. will you eat   C. are you eating   D. do you eat

13. By the time the young birds _____ the nest for good, they will have learned how to fly.
    A. will leave   B. will have left   C. are leaving   D. leave

14. The last time I _____ in Athens, the weather was hot and humid.
    A. had been   B. was   C. am   D. will be

15. The farmer acted too late. He locked the barn door after his horse _____.
    A. had been stolen   B. will be stolen   C. is stolen   D. has been stolen

◇ **PRACTICE 14—SELFSTUDY: Using adverb clauses to show time relationships. (Chart 8-5)**

Directions: Combine each pair of sentences into one new sentence using the word(s) in parentheses. Omit unnecessary words, make any necessary changes, and punctuate carefully. Pay special attention to verb tenses. <u>Underline</u> the adverb clause in the new sentence.

1. The other passengers will get on the bus soon. Then we'll leave. (*as soon as*)
   → <u>**As soon as** the other passengers get on the bus, we'll leave.</u>

2. I turned off the lights. After that, I left the room. (*before*)
   → *I turned off the lights <u>**before** I left the room</u>.*

3. Susan sometimes feels nervous. Then she chews her nails. (*whenever*)

4. I saw the great pyramids of Egypt in the moonlight. I was speechless then. (*the first time*)

5. The frying pan caught on fire. I was making dinner at that time. (*while*)

6. I'll finish working on the car soon. Then we'll all take a walk in the park. (*as soon as*)

7. Ceylon had been independent for 24 years. Then its name was changed to Sri Lanka. (*after*)

8. Shakespeare died in 1616. He had written more than 37 plays before then. (*by the time*)

9. Douglas fell off his bicycle last week. He has had to use crutches to walk. (*since*)

10. Ms. Johnson will return your call soon. She'll have some free time soon. (*as soon as*)

11. John will learn how to use a computer. Then he'll be able to work more efficiently. (*once*)

12. I won't return my book to the library. I'll finish my research project first. (*until*)

13. Sue dropped a carton of eggs. She was leaving the store. (*as*)

14. Sam will go to the movies again. He'll remember to take his glasses then. (*the next time*)

15. The flooding river raced down the valley. It destroyed everything in its path. (*when*)

16. Mohammad had never heard about Halloween.* Then he came to the United States. (*before*)

---

*Halloween (which occurs every year on October 31) is a U.S. holiday primarily for children, who dress up in costumes and go from house to house for a "treat" such as candy or fruit.

◇ **PRACTICE 15—GUIDED STUDY:** Using adverb clauses to show time relationships. (Chart 8-5)

Directions: Write a sentence from the given words. Do not change the order of the words. Use any appropriate verb forms and punctuate carefully.

Examples:

as soon as + I + finish + I → ***As soon as I finish*** *my report,* ***I'll*** *call you and we'll go to dinner.*
I + after + I + climb → ***I was exhausted*** ***after I climbed*** *the stairs to the eighth floor.*

1. whenever + I + go + I
2. by the time + I + get + I
3. I + since + I + leave
4. just as + I + open + I
5. I + as soon as + I + eat

6. I + when + I + be
7. the first time + I + see + I
8. I + until + I + be
9. while + I + look + I
10. I + before + I + drive

◇ **PRACTICE 16—SELFSTUDY:** Cause and effect. (Charts 8-1, 8-4, 8-6 → 8-11)

Directions: Choose **ALL** of the correct completions for each sentence. There may be more than one correct answer.

Example:

    ___**B, D**___ *the post office was closed, I couldn't mail my packages.*
    A. Therefore   *B. Because*   *C. For*   *D. Since*

1. _____ we got lost driving into the city, we were late for the meeting.
   A. Since   B. Because   C. Consequently   D. For

2. I couldn't repair my bicycle, _____ I didn't have the right tools.
   A. so   B. for   C. because of   D. therefore

3. Two of the factories in our small town have closed. _____, unemployment is high.
   A. Consequently   B. Because   C. So that   D. Therefore

4. _____ I had nothing for lunch but an apple, I ate dinner early.
   A. For   B. Since   C. Due to   D. Therefore

5. The fire raged out of control. It got _____ bad that more firefighters had to be called in.
   A. such   B. therefore   C. so   D. as

6. _____ the flood has receded, people can move back into their homes.
   A. Now that   B. Since   C. Because   D. Inasmuch as

7. Mr. Watson retired from his job early _____ his ill health.
   A. because   B. due to   C. because of   D. for

8. Bill's favorite show was on. He reached to turn on the TV _____ he could watch it.
   A. because of   B. therefore   C. so that   D. for

9. She bought the book _____ she had heard it was good.
   A. because   B. so   C. because of   D. due to the fact that

10. The Eskimo* way of life changed dramatically during the 1800s _____ the introduction of firearms and the influx of large numbers of European whalers and fur traders.
   A. because   B. due to   C. so   D. for

---

*Eskimos are people who live in the Arctic regions of northern Alaska, northern Canada, and Greenland.

11. During extremely hot weather, elephants require both mud and water to keep their skin cool _____ they have no sweat glands.

    A. and   B. so   C. because of   D. due to the fact that

12. Tommy doesn't have Ms. Simmons as his fifth grade teacher anymore. _____ the classroom was overcrowded, Tommy and several other children were assigned to a different class.

    A. Because   B. Therefore   C. For   D. Due to

◇ **PRACTICE 17—SELFSTUDY:** Using adverb clauses to show cause and effect relationships. (Chart 8-6)

Directions: Combine the sentences, using the word or phrase in parentheses. Add commas where necessary.

1. We can go swimming every day. The weather is warm. (*now that*)
   → *We can go swimming every day **now that the weather is warm.***

2. All of the students had done poorly on the test. The teacher decided to give it again. (*since*)
   → ***Since all of the students had done poorly on the test,** the teacher decided to give it again.*

3. Cold air hovers near the earth. It is heavier than hot air. (*because*)

4. Our TV set was broken. We listened to the news on the radio. (*because*)

5. Larry is finally caught up on his work. He can start his vacation tomorrow. (*now that*)

6. You have paid for the theater tickets. Please let me pay for our dinner. (*inasmuch as*)

7. 92,000 people already have reservations with Pan Am for a trip to the moon. I doubt that I'll get the chance to go on one of the first tourist flights. (*since*)

8. Our flight is going to be delayed. Let's relax and enjoy a quiet dinner. (*as long as*)

9. My registration is going to be canceled. I haven't paid my fees. (*because*)

10. Erica has qualified for the Olympics in speedskating. She must train even more vigorously. (*now that*)

◇ **PRACTICE 18—SELFSTUDY:** Using *because* and *because of.* (Charts 8-6 and 8-7)

Directions: Complete the sentences with either ***because*** or ***because of.***

1. We postponed our trip _____***because of***_____ the bad driving conditions.

2. Sue's eyes were red _____***because***_____ she had been swimming in a chlorinated pool.

3. We can't visit the museum tomorrow _____ it isn't open.

4. Jim had to give up jogging _____ his sprained ankle.

5. _____ heavy fog at the airport, we had to stay in Boston an extra day.

6. _____ the elevator was broken, we had to walk up six flights of stairs.

7. Please walk carefully _____ the walkway is slippery when wet.

8. Thousands of Irish people emigrated to the United States _____ the potato famine in Ireland in the middle of the nineteenth century.

9. The young couple decided not to buy the house _____ its dilapidated condition.

10. You can't enter this secured area _____ you don't have an official permit.

11. My lecture notes were incomplete _____ the instructor talked too fast.

12. _____ the re-opening of the only factory in town, most of the residents of Waterton are working again.

◇ **PRACTICE 19—GUIDED STUDY:** Using *because* and *therefore.* (Charts 8-6 and 8-8)

Directions: Combine the given sentences in two ways: (a) use ***because***; (b) use ***therefore***. Punctuate and capitalize as appropriate.

1. John didn't go to work yesterday. He didn't feel well.

   (a) *because → John didn't go to work yesterday **because** he didn't feel well.*
       OR: ***Because** John didn't feel well, he didn't go to work yesterday.*

   (b) *therefore → John didn't feel well. **Therefore,** he didn't go to work yesterday.*
       OR: *John didn't feel well. He, **therefore,** didn't go to work yesterday.*
       OR: *John didn't feel well. He didn't go to work yesterday, **therefore.***

2. Angela ate a sandwich. She was hungry.

3. We need to eat nutritious food. Good health is important.

4. Edward missed the final exam. He failed the course.

5. Jessica secured a good job in international business. She is bilingual.

◇ **PRACTICE 20—SELFSTUDY: Using *because* and *therefore*. (Charts 8-6 and 8-8)**

Directions: Add appropriate punctuation and capitalization as necessary.

1. Bill couldn't pick us up for the concert because his car wouldn't start. (*no changes*)

2. Bill's car wouldn't start therefore he couldn't pick us up for the concert.
   → *Bill's car wouldn't start. Therefore, he couldn't pick us up for the concert.*

3. Because young Joseph was an inquisitive student he was always liked by his teachers.

4. Emily has never wanted to return to the Yukon to live because the winters are too severe.

5. We lose 60 percent of our body heat through our head therefore it is important to wear a hat on cold days.

6. The television broadcast was interrupted in the middle of the eighth inning therefore most of the audience missed the conclusion of the baseball game.

7. When I was in my teens and twenties it was easy for me to get into an argument with my father because both of us have always been stubborn and opinionated.

8. Robert did not pay close attention to what the travel agent said when he went to see her at her office last week therefore he had to ask many of the same questions again the next time he talked to her.

◇ **PRACTICE 21—SELFSTUDY: Showing cause and effect. (Charts 8-6 → 8-9)**

PART I: Complete the sentences with *because of*, *because*, or *therefore*. Add any necessary punctuation and capitalization.

1. _____**Because**_____ it rained , we stayed home.

2. It rained _____. **Therefore,**_____ we stayed home.

3. We stayed home _____**because of**_____ the rain.

4. The hurricane was moving directly toward a small coastal town _____ all residents were advised to move inland until it passed.

5. The residents moved inland _____ the hurricane.

6. _____ the hurricane was moving directly toward the town all residents were advised to move inland.

7. Piranhas, which are found in the Amazon River, are ferocious and bloodthirsty fish. When they attack in great numbers, they can devour an entire cow in several minutes _____ their extremely sharp teeth.

8. A tomato is classified as a fruit, but most people consider it a vegetable _____ it is prepared and eaten in the same ways as lettuce, onions, and other vegetables.

9. In ancient Rome, garlic was believed to make people courageous Roman soldiers _____ ate large quantities of it before a battle.

PART II: Complete the sentences with **due to, since,** or **consequently.** Add any necessary punctuation and capitalization.

1. _____ his poor eyesight John has to sit in the front row in class.

2. _____ John has poor eyesight he has to sit in the front row.

3. John has poor eyesight _____ he has to sit in the front row.

4. Sarah is afraid of heights _____ she will not walk across a bridge.

5. Sarah will not walk across a bridge _____ her fear of heights.

6. _____ a camel can go completely without water for eight to ten days it is an ideal animal for desert areas.

7. Mark is overweight _____ his doctor has advised him to exercise regularly.

8. _____ a diamond is extremely hard it can be used to cut glass.

9. _____ consumer demand for ivory many African elephants are being slaughtered ruthlessly _____ many people who care about saving these animals from extinction refuse to buy any item made from ivory.

◇ **PRACTICE 22—SELFSTUDY:** Using *such . . . that* and *so . . . that.* (Chart 8-10)

Directions: Add *such* or *so* to the following sentences.

1. The wind was _____**so**_____ strong that it blew my hat off my head.

2. Sue is _____**such**_____ a good pianist that I'm surprised she didn't go into music professionally.

3. The radio was _____ loud that I couldn't hear what Michael was saying.

4. The food was _____ hot that it burned my tongue.

5. Alison did _____ a poor job that she was fired.

6. Professor James is _____ a stern taskmaster that lazy students won't take his class.

7. The restaurant patron at the table near us was _____ belligerent that we all felt embarrassed, especially when he swept everything off the table and demanded his money back.

8. Small animals in the forest move about _____ quickly that one can barely catch a glimpse of them.

9. The intricate metal lacework on the Eiffel Tower in Paris was _____ complicated that the structure took more than two and a half years to complete.

10. Charles and his brother are _____ hard-working carpenters that I'm sure they'll make a success of their new business.

11. The children had _____ much fun at the carnival that they begged to go again.

12. There are _____ many leaves on a single tree that it is impossible to count them.

13. _____ few students signed up for the course that it was canceled.

14. I feel like I have _____ little energy that I wonder if I'm getting sick.

15. Jan and Arlene have always been _____ good friends that it's a shame to see them not speaking to each other.

16. Indian food can be hot and spicy. Jack ate some very hot chicken curry when he was in India a year ago. In fact, it was _____ hot that smoke came out of his ears!

◇ **PRACTICE 23—GUIDED STUDY:** Using *such . . . that* and *so . . . that.* (Chart 8-10)

Directions: Add **such** or **so**, and complete the sentences with your own words.

Examples:

I'm really fond of my old car, but it's in _____ terrible shape that . . . .
→ *I'm really fond of my old car, but it's in such terrible shape that I'm going to have to get rid of it.*

When the passenger was told that his seat was no longer available on the plane, he became _____ angry that . . . .
→ *When the passenger was told that his seat was no longer available on the plane, he became so angry that he pounded his fist on the counter and threatened to sue the airline.*

1. Larry was _____ exhausted after working for ten straight hours that . . . .

2. I couldn't help it! When Al told me that joke, I laughed _____ hard that . . . .

3. Bill always snores when he sleeps. In fact, he is _____ a loud snorer that . . . .

4. I had been away from home for three years before I was finally able to return for a visit. When I first saw my family at the airport, I felt _____ happy that . . .

5. Sandra was planning to take a long vacation, but her boss suddenly gave her _____ much work to do that . . . .

6. Janet is a travel agent, and she uses her computer for nearly everything in her work. It is _____ an essential piece of equipment that . . . .

7. It was a dangerous situation. _____ many fans crowded together outside the sports arena that . . . .

8. John is the laziest person I've ever met. He is _____ lazy that . . . .

9. My neighbor has six beautiful children who are full of fun and laughter. Sometimes, however, they are _____ noisy children that . . . .

10. My sister is the world's worst cook. Her cooking is _____ bad that . . . .

11. . . . _____ exhausted that . . . .

12. . . . _____ a good time that . . . .

13. . . . _____ shy that . . . .

14. . . . _____ many people that . . . .

◇ **PRACTICE 24—SELFSTUDY: Using *so that*. (Chart 8-11)**

Directions: Complete the sentences in COLUMN A with the ideas in COLUMN B. Pay special attention to the verb forms following *so that*.

Examples:

Column A	**Column B**
1. Ali borrowed an eraser so that	A. wash my clothes
2. Jack fixed the leak in the boat so that	B. erase a mistake in his composition
3. I need to buy some laundry detergent so that	C. not sink

→ 1. *Ali borrowed an eraser so that **he could erase** a mistake in his composition.*
→ 2. *Jack fixed the leak in the boat so that **it wouldn't sink.***
→ 3. *I need to buy some laundry detergent so that **I can wash** my clothes.*

Column A	**Column B**
1. I turned up the radio so that	A. read the fine print at the bottom of the contract
2. Roberto is studying the history and government of Canada so that	B. travel in Europe
3. Carolyn put on her reading glasses so that	C. fix her own car
4. Jane is taking a course in auto mechanics so that	D. see the dancers in the street
5. Al is working hard to impress his supervisor so that	E. get expert advice on our itinerary
6. Nancy is carrying extra courses every semester so that	F. not disturb her roommate
7. Jason is tired of work and school. He wants to take a semester off so that	G. listen to the news
8. Suzanne lowered the volume on the TV set so that	H. be considered for a promotion at this company
9. During the parade, James lifted his daughter to his shoulder so that	I. become a Canadian citizen
10. Whenever we are planning a vacation, we call a travel agent so that	J. graduate early

◇ **PRACTICE 25—GUIDED STUDY: Using *so that*. (Chart 8-11)**

Directions: Complete the sentences with your own words.

Examples:

Sam took lots of pictures on his vacation so (that) . . . .
→ *Sam took lots of pictures on his vacation so (that) he could show his family where he had been.*

. . . so (that) I could see better.
→ *I moved to the front of the room so (that) I could see better.*

1. I need a pen so (that) . . . .
2. . . . so (that) he can improve his English.
3. I turned on the TV so (that) . . . .
4. Mary hurried to get the child out of the road so (that) . . . .
5. . . . so (that) he wouldn't miss his important appointment.
6. I'm taking a bus instead of flying so (that) . . . .
7. . . . so (that) I could tell him the news in person.
8. . . . so (that) his children will have a better life.
9. Martina is trying to improve her English so (that) . . . .
10. . . . so (that) the celebration would be a great success.
11. Ralph borrowed some money from his friend so (that) . . . .
12. . . . so (that) you can be ready to leave on time.

◇ **PRACTICE 26—GUIDED STUDY: Cause and effect. (Charts 8-1, 8-4, 8-6 → 8-11)**

Directions: Choose **ALL** of the correct completions for each sentence. There may be more than one correct completion.

Example:

_____**A, C, D**_____ *I was tired, I went to bed.*
  A. *Because*   B. *For*   C. *Since*   D. *Due to the fact that*

1. A small fish needs camouflage to hide itself _____ its enemies cannot find it.
  A. so that   B. so   C. therefore   D. due to

2. Josh couldn't open the door _____ the lock was broken.
  A. because   B. therefore   C. so   D. due to the fact that

3. The workers have gone on strike. _____, all production has ceased.
  A. Because   B. Therefore   C. Consequently   D. Inasmuch as

4. _____ my company's bid for building the library was the lowest, we were awarded the contract.
  A. Because   B. Since   C. For   D. Inasmuch as

5. I needed to finish the marathon race _____ I could prove that I had the strength and stamina to do it. I didn't care whether I won or not.
  A. because of   B. so that   C. for   D. therefore

6. Let's ask our teacher how to solve this problem _____ we can't agree on the answer.
  A. since   B. because of   C. consequently   D. as long as

7. Our apartment building has had two robberies in the last month, _____ I'm going to put an extra lock on the door and install a telephone in my bedroom.
    A. now that   B. so that   C. so   D. since

8. The Chippewas are Native North Americans. Their language is one of the most complex in the world, _____ it contains more than 6,000 verb forms.
    A. consequently   B. so   C. so that   D. for

9. _____ the bad grease stain on the carpet, we had to rearrange the furniture before the company arrived.
    A. Because of   B. Now that   C. Due to   D. Since

10. The price of airline tickets has gone down recently. _____ the tickets cost less, more people are flying than before.
    A. Consequently   B. Because of   C. Because   D. For

11. The mountain road was closed to all traffic _____ the heavy rainfall had caused a huge mudslide that blocked the way.
    A. therefore   B. because   C. due to   D. so

12. Janet called the security guard _____ someone had taken her briefcase while she was making a call at the public phone.
    A. so that   B. so   C. because   D. because of

13. Dolphins are sometimes caught and killed in commercial fishing nets _____ they often swim in schools with other fish, such as tuna.
    A. since   B. as   C. so   D. because

14. We can finally afford to trade in the old car for a new one _____ I've gotten the raise I've been waiting for.
    A. so that   B. now that   C. consequently   D. so

◇ **PRACTICE 27—SELFSTUDY: Reduction of adverb clauses to modifying phrases. (Charts 8-12 and 8-13)**

Directions: Change the adverb clause to a modifying phrase.

            opening
1. Since ~~he opened~~ his new business, Bob has been working 16 hours a day.

            leaving
2. I shut off the lights before ~~I left~~ the room.

3. While he was herding his goats in the mountains, an Ethiopian named Kaldi discovered the coffee plant more than 1200 years ago.

4. Before they marched into battle, ancient Ethiopian soldiers ate a mixture of raw coffee beans and fat for extra energy.

5. After I had met the movie star in person, I understood why she was so popular.

6. I found my keys after I searched through all my pockets.

7. When it was first brought to Europe, the tomato was thought to be poisonous.

8. Since it was first imported into Australia many years ago, the rabbit has become a serious pest because it has no natural enemies there.

◇ **PRACTICE 28—SELFSTUDY: Modifying phrases. (Chart 8-13)**

Directions: Underline the subject of the adverb clause and the subject of the main clause. Change the adverb clauses to modifying phrases if possible.

1. After <u>the musician</u> stopped playing, <u>the audience</u> stood and clapped enthusiastically.
   → *(no change possible)*

2. After <u>the police</u> stopped the fight, <u>they</u> arrested two men and a woman.
   → *After stopping the fight, the police arrested two men and a woman.*

3. Since <u>Bob</u> opened his new business, <u>he</u> has been working 16 hours a day.
   → *Since opening his new business, Bob has been working 16 hours a day.*

4. While Sam was driving to work in the rain, his car got a flat tire.

5. While Sam was driving to work, he had a flat tire.

6. Before Paulo returned to his country, his American friends gave him a surprise going-away party.

7. Since the Irish immigrated to the United States in large numbers in the mid-1800s, Americans have celebrated Halloween and St. Patrick's Day as holidays.

8. After Tom had worked hard in the garden all afternoon, he took a shower and then went to the movies with his friends.

9. Before a friend tries to do something hard, an American may say "Break a leg!" to wish him or her good luck.

10. Before George took his driving test, the police officer asked him a few questions about the traffic laws.

11. After Sunita had made a delicious chicken curry for her friends, they wanted the recipe.

12. Emily always straightens her desk before she leaves the office at the end of the day.

13. Before Nick left on his trip, his boss gave him a big raise.

◇ **PRACTICE 29—SELFSTUDY: Reduction of adverb clauses to modifying phrases. (Charts 8-12 and 8-13)**

Directions: Complete the sentences with the correct forms of the verbs in parentheses.

1. a. Before (*leave*) __*leaving*__ on his trip, Tom renewed his passport.
   b. Before Tom (*leave*) __*left*__ on his trip, he renewed his passport.

2. a. After Thomas Edison (*invent*) __*invented/had invented*__ the light bulb, he went on to create many other useful inventions.
   b. After (*invent*) __*inventing/having invented*__ the light bulb, Thomas Edison went on to create many other useful inventions.

3. a. While (*work*) _____ with uranium ore, Marie Curie discovered two new elements, radium and polonium.
   b. While she (*work*) _____ with uranium ore, Marie Curie discovered two new elements, radium and polonium.

4. a. Before an astronaut (*fly*) _____ on a space mission, s/he will have undergone thousands of hours of training.
   b. Before (*fly*) _____ on a space mission, an astronaut will have undergone thousands of hours of training.

5. a. After they (*study*) _____ the stars, the ancient Mayans in Central America developed a very accurate solar calendar.

   b. After (*study*) _____ the stars, the ancient Mayans in Central America developed a very accurate solar calendar.

6. a. Since (*learn*) _____ that cigarettes cause cancer, many people have stopped smoking.

   b. Since they (*learn*) _____ that cigarettes cause cancer, many people have stopped smoking.

7. a. Aspirin can be poisonous when it (*take*) _____ in excessive amounts.

   b. Aspirin can be poisonous when (*take*) _____ in excessive amounts.

8. a. When (*take*) _____ aspirin, you should be sure to follow the directions on the bottle.

   b. When you (*take*) _____ aspirin, you should be sure to follow the directions on the bottle.

9. a. I took a wrong turn while I (*drive*) _____ to my uncle's house and ended up back where I started.

   b. I took a wrong turn while (*drive*) _____ to my uncle's house and ended up back where I started.

◇ **PRACTICE 30—SELFSTUDY: Modifying phrases. (Charts 8-14 and 8-15)**

Directions: Combine the two sentences, making a modifying phrase out of the first sentence, *if possible*.

1. Anna kept one hand on the steering wheel. She opened a can of soda pop with her free hand.
   → ***Keeping*** *one hand on the steering wheel,* ***Anna*** *opened a can of soda pop with her free hand.*

2. Anna kept one hand on the steering wheel. Bob handed her a can of pop to hold in the other hand. → (*no change possible*)

3. I misunderstood the directions to the hotel. I arrived one hour late for the dinner party.

4. I misunderstood the directions to the hotel. The taxi driver didn't know how to get there either.

5. The taxi driver misunderstood my directions to the hotel. He took me to the wrong place.

6. I live a long distance from my work. I have to commute daily by train.

7. Heidi lives a long distance from her work. She has to commute daily by train.

8. Fred lives a long distance from his work. His car is essential.

9. Martha was picking strawberries in the garden. A bumblebee stung her.

10. Ann remembered that she hadn't turned off the oven. She went directly home.

11. Jim tripped on the carpet. He spilt his coffee.

12. I recognized his face but I had forgotten his name. I just smiled and said, "Hi."

13. We slowly approached the door to the hospital. The nurse stepped out to greet us.

14. I was lying by the swimming pool. I realized I was getting sunburned.

15. I met Gina after work. She suggested playing tennis.

16. My family and I live in the Pacific Northwest, where it rains a great deal. We are accustomed to cool, damp weather.

◇ **PRACTICE 31—SELFSTUDY: Modifying phrases. (Charts 8-14 and 8-15)**

Directions: Make sentences that combine a modifying phrase with a main clause. Write the capital letter of the most logical main clause to complete the sentence. Use each capital letter only one time.

Modifying phrases:

1. Trying to understand the physics problem, __*E*__

2. Since injuring my arm, _____

3. Fighting for her life, _____

4. Wanting to ask a question, _____

5. Exhausted after washing the windows, _____

6. Not wanting to disturb the manager, _____

7. Upon hearing the announcement that their plane was delayed, _____

8. Talking with the employees after work, _____

9. Attempting to enter the freeway, _____

10. Currently selling at record-low prices, _____

11. Stepping onto the platform to receive their medals, _____

12. Before turning in your exam paper, _____

Main clauses:

A. the desperate woman grasped a floating log after the boat capsized.

B. I collapsed in my chair for a rest.

C. the taxi driver caused a multiple-car accident.

D. carefully proofread all your answers.

✔ E. the students repeated the experiment.

F. the athletes waved to the cheering crowd.

G. the little girl raised her hand.

H. the manager learned of their dissatisfaction with their jobs.

I. the passengers angrily walked back to the ticket counter.

J. I haven't been able to play tennis.

K. gold is considered a good investment.

L. the worker in charge of Section B of the assembly line told the assistant manager about the problem.

◇ **PRACTICE 32—GUIDED STUDY: Modifying phrases. (Charts 8-14 and 8-15)**

Directions: Make sentences by combining the ideas in Column A and Column B. Use the idea in Column A as a modifying phrase. Show logical relationships.

Examples:

Column A	**Column B**
1. She was looking in the want ads in the Sunday newspaper.	A. Mary has a lot of responsibilities.
2. She had grown up overseas.	B. Ann found a good used car at a price she could afford to pay.
3. She is the vice president of a large company.	C. Alice enjoys trying foods from other countries.

→ 1. *Looking in the want ads in the Sunday newspaper, Ann found a used car for a good price.*
→ 2. *Having grown up overseas, Alice enjoys trying foods from other countries.*
→ 3. *Being the vice-president of a large company, Mary has a lot of responsibilities.*

Column A	**Column B**
1. They have sticky pads on their feet.	A. Sally didn't know what to expect when she went to the Thai restaurant for dinner.
2. He has worked with computers for many years	B. Mice can hide in almost any part of a house.
3. She was born two months prematurely.	C. Rhinos are protected by law from poachers who kill them solely for their horns.
4. He had done everything he could for the patient.	D. The doctor left to attend to other people.
5. She had never eaten Thai food before.	E. Nancy expects to be hired by a top company after graduation.
6. He had no one to turn to for help.	F. Diamonds are used extensively in industry to cut other hard minerals.
7. They are an endangered species.	G. Flies can easily walk on the ceiling.
8. They are able to crawl into very small spaces.	H. Sam was forced to work out the problem by himself.
9. She has done very well in her studies and is finally nearly finished.	I. Mary needed special care for the first few days of her life.
10. They are extremely hard and nearly indestructible.	J. Robert has an excellent understanding of their limitations as well as their potential.

◇ **PRACTICE 33—SELFSTUDY: Modifying phrases with *upon*. (Chart 8-16)**

Directions: Write completions using the ideas in the italicized sentences.

I heard my name called.
✔ *I arrived at the airport.*
She learned the problem was not at all serious.
She was told she got it.

He investigated the cause.
He heard those words.
He discovered it was hot.
I reached the other side of the lake.

1. It had been a long, uncomfortable trip. Upon _____**arriving at the airport**_____, I quickly unfastened my seatbelt and stood in the aisle waiting my turn to disembark.

2. I rented a small fishing boat last weekend, but I ended up doing more rowing than I did fishing. The motor died halfway across the lake, so I had to row to shore. It was a long distance away. Upon _____, I was exhausted.

3. The small child reached toward the lighted candle. Upon _____ _____, he jerked his hand back, held it in front of himself, and stared at it curiously. Then he began to scream.

4. There must have been over 300 students in the room on the first day of class. The professor slowly read through the list of names. Upon _____, I raised my hand to identify myself.

5. Captain Cook had been sailing for many weeks with no land in sight. Finally, one of the sailors shouted, ''Land ahoy!'' Upon _____, Cook grabbed his telescope and searched the horizon.

6. At first, we thought the fire had been caused by lightning. However, upon _____ _____, the fire chief determined it had been caused by faulty electrical wiring.

7. Amy felt terrible. She was sure she had some dread disease, so she went to her doctor for some tests. Upon _____, she was extremely relieved.

8. Janet wanted that scholarship with all her heart and soul. Upon _____ _____, she jumped straight up in the air and let out a scream of happiness.

◇ **PRACTICE 34—SELFSTUDY: Modifying phrases. (Charts 8-13 → 8-16)**

Directions: Change the adverb clause in each sentence to an adverb phrase *if possible*. Make any necessary changes in punctuation, capitalization, or word order.

1. After it spends some time in a cocoon, a caterpillar will emerge as a butterfly.
   → *After spending some time in a cocoon, a caterpillar will emerge as a butterfly.*

2. When the movie started, the audience suddenly got very quiet.
   → *(no change possible)*

3. When we entered the theater, we handed the usher our tickets.
   → *Upon entering the theater, we handed the usher our tickets.*

4. Because I was unprepared for the test, I didn't do well.
   → *Being unprepared for the test, I didn't do well.* OR: *Unprepared for the test, I didn't do well.*

5. Before I left on my trip, I checked to see what shots I would need.

6. Since Indians in the high Andes Mountains live in thin air, their hearts grow to be a larger than average size.

7. Because I hadn't understood the directions, I got lost.

8. My father reluctantly agreed to let me attend the game after he had talked it over with my mother.

9. When I discovered I had lost my key to the apartment, I called the building supervisor.

10. Jane's family hasn't received any news from her since she arrived in Australia two weeks ago.

11. Garcia Lopez de Cardenas accidentally discovered the Grand Canyon while he was looking for the legendary Lost City of Gold.

12. Because the forest area is so dry this summer, it is prohibited to light camp fires.

13. After we had to wait for over half an hour, we were finally seated at the restaurant.

14. Before Maria got accepted on her country's Olympic running team, she had spent most of the two previous years in training.

15. Because George wasn't paying attention to his driving, he didn't see the large truck until it was almost too late.

◇ PRACTICE 35—GUIDED STUDY: Modifying phrases. (Charts 8-13 → 8-16)

Directions: Underline the adverb clauses in the following. Change the adverb clauses to adverb phrases *if possible*. Make any necessary changes in punctuation, capitalization, or word order.

1. Alexander Graham Bell, a teacher of the deaf in Boston, invented the first telephone. One day in 1875, while he was running a test on his latest attempt to create a machine that could carry voices, he accidentally spilled acid on his coat. Naturally, he called for his assistant, Thomas A. Watson, who was in another room. Bell said, ''Mr. Watson, come here. I want you.'' When Watson heard words coming from the machine, he immediately realized that their experiments had at last been successful. He rushed excitedly into the other room to tell Bell that he had heard his words over the machine.

    After Bell had successfully tested the new apparatus again and again, he confidently announced his invention to the world. For the most part, scientists appreciated his accomplishment, but the general public did not understand the revolutionary nature of Bell's invention. Because they believed the telephone was a toy with little practical application, most people paid little attention to Bell's announcement.

2. Wolves are much misunderstood animals. Because many people believe that wolves eagerly kill human beings, they fear them. However, the truth is that wolves eagerly avoid any contact with human beings. U.S. wildlife biologists say there is no documented case of wolves attacking humans in the lower 48 states. More people are hurt and killed by buffaloes in Yellowstone Park than have ever been hurt by wolves in North America.

    Because they are strictly carnivorous, wolves hunt large animals, such as elk and deer, and small animals, such as mice and rabbits. However, wolves are also particularly fond of sheep. Their killing ranchers' livestock has helped lead to their bad reputation among people.

    Because it was relentlessly poisoned, trapped, and shot by ranchers and hunters, the timber wolf, a subspecies of the gray wolf, was eradicated in the lower 48 by the 1940s. Not one wolf remained. In the 1970s, because they realized a mistake had been made, U.S. lawmakers passed laws to protect wolves.

Long ago, wolves could be found in almost all areas of the Northern Hemisphere throughout Asia, Europe, and North America. Today, after they have been unremittingly destroyed for centuries, they are found in few places, principally in sparsely populated areas of Alaska, Minnesota, Canada, and the northernmost regions of Russia and China.

◇ **PRACTICE 36—SELFSTUDY: Error analysis: modifying phrases. (Charts 8-13→8-16)**

Directions: Write "I" if the sentence is INCORRECT. Write "C" if the sentence is CORRECT. Reminder: A modifying phrase must modify the subject of the sentence.

1. __*I*__ While taking a trip across Europe this summer, Jane's camera suddenly quit working.

2. __*C*__ When using a microwave oven for the first time, read the instructions carefully about the kind of dish you can use.

3. _____ Having been given their instructions, the teacher told her students to begin working on the test.

4. _____ After receiving the Nobel Peace Prize in 1979, Mother Teresa returned to Calcutta, India, to work and live among the poor, the sick, and the dying.

5. _____ Having studied Greek for several years, Sarah's pronunciation was easy to understand.

6. _____ Since returning to her country after graduation, Maria's parents have enjoyed having all their children home again.

7. _____ While bicycling across the United States, the wheels on my bike had to be replaced several times.

8. _____ Not wanting to interrupt the conversation, I stood quietly and listened until I could have a chance to talk.

9. _____ Being too young to understand death, my mother gave me a simple explanation of where my grandfather had gone.

10. _____ When asked to explain his mistake, the new employee cleared his throat nervously.

11. _____ While working in my office late last night, someone suddenly knocked loudly at my door and nearly scared me to death!

12. _____ After hurrying to get everything ready for the picnic, it began to rain just as we were leaving.

13. _____ When told he would have to have surgery, the doctor reassured Bob that he wouldn't have to miss more than a week of work.

14. _____ While walking across the street at a busy intersection, a truck nearly ran over my foot.

15. _____ Before driving across a desert, be sure that your car has good tires as well as enough oil, water, and gas to last the trip.

◇ **PRACTICE 37—SELFSTUDY: Error analysis. (Chapter 8)**

Directions: Find and correct the errors in the following sentences.

1. I was very tired, go to bed.
   → *I was very tired, so I went to bed.* OR: *I was very tired and went to bed.*

2. Because our leader could not attend the meeting, so it was canceled.

3. I and my wife likes to travel.

4. I always fasten my seatbelt before to start the engine.

5. I don't like our classroom. Because it is hot and crowded. I hope we can change to a different room.

6. The day was very warm and humid, for that I turned on the air conditioner.

7. Upon I learned that my car couldn't be repaired for three days, I am very distressed.

8. Having missed the final examination, the teacher gave me a failing grade.

9. Both my sister and my brother is going to be at the family reunion.

10. I hope my son will remain in school until he will finish his degree.

11. My brother has succeeded in business because of he works hard.

12. Luis stood up, turned toward me, and speaking so softly that I couldn't hear what he said.

13. I was lost. I could not find my parents neither my brother.

14. When I traveled through Europe I visited England, France, Italy, Germany, and Swiss.

◇ PRACTICE 38—GUIDED STUDY: Speaking

Directions: Pair up with another student and make up a short skit (i.e., a very short drama) that demonstrates one of the following emotions. Using both words and gestures, present your skit to the class and ask them to guess the emotion you intended to demonstrate by your skit.

1. anger	7. fear	13. disgust
2. cheerfulness	8. amusement	14. belligerence
3. sadness	9. envy	15. disappointment
4. weariness	10. impatience	16. nervousness
5. embarrassment	11. surprise	17. bewilderment
6. enthusiasm	12. delight	18. boredom

◇ PRACTICE 39—GUIDED STUDY: Writing

Directions: Using one of the following topics, try to communicate in writing an emotion you have felt. Describe the situation that caused this emotion, your actions (and those of any other people who were involved), and your feelings.

1. Describe an occasion when you felt nervous.
2. Describe an occasion when you experienced fear.
3. Describe a time when you felt completely at peace.
4. Describe an occasion when you worried needlessly.
5. Describe a time when you felt very surprised.

◇ PRACTICE TEST A—SELFSTUDY: Showing relationships between ideas. (Chapter 8)

Directions: Choose the correct answer.

Example:
___**B**___ *I get angry and upset, I try to take ten deep breaths.*
   A. Until   *B. Whenever*   *C. Therefore*   *D. For*

1. _____ Paul brings the money for our lunch, we'll go right down to the cafeteria.
   A. Since   B. As soon as   C. Now that   D. Until

2. My mouth is burning! This is _____ spicy food that I don't think I can finish it.
   A. such   B. so   C. very   D. too

3. Both my books _____ from my room last night.
   A. were stolen and my wallet   B. and my wallet were stolen
   C. and my wallet was stolen   D. were and my wallet was stolen

4. When _____ a dictionary, you need to be able to understand the symbols and abbreviations it contains.
   A. having used   B. use   C. to use   D. using

5. Bats are fascinating _____ have many interesting and amazing qualities.
   A. animals. Therefore, they   B. animals, they
   C. animals. They   D. animals. Because they

6. While _____ to help Tim with his math, I got impatient because he wouldn't pay attention to what I was saying.
   A. I am trying   B. having tried   C. I try   D. trying

7. _____ extremely bad weather in the mountains, we're no longer considering our skiing trip.
    A. Due to   B. Because   C. Since   D. Due to the fact that

8. Emily is motivated to study _____ she knows that a good education can improve her life.
    A. therefore   B. because of   C. because   D. so

9. Sonia broke her leg in two places. _____, she had to wear a cast and use crutches for three months.
    A. Inasmuch as   B. Consequently   C. For that   D. Because

10. Our village had _____ money available for education that the schools had to close.
    A. so little   B. such little   C. so much   D. such much

11. Hundreds of species of Hawaiian flowers have become extinct or rare _____ land development and the grazing of wild goats.
    A. now that   B. due to   C. because   D. for

12. Tom Booth is one of the best players in the country. We have won all of our games _____ he joined our team.
    A. when   B. the first time   C. since   D. due to

13. Joe seemed to be in a good mood, _____ he snapped at me angrily when I asked him to join us.
    A. yet   B. so   C. for   D. and

14. _____ Jan arrives, we will have finished this group project.
    A. By the time   B. Until   C. Now that   D. Since

15. For the most part, young children spend their time playing, eating, and _____ a lot.
    A. they sleep   B. sleeping   C. sleep   D. they are sleeping

16. Joan worked in a vineyard last summer _____ money for school expenses.
    A. because to earn   B. so she earns
    C. for she earned   D. so that she could earn

17. _____ unprepared for the exam, I felt sure I would get a low score.
    A. Being   B. Having   C. Because   D. Upon

18. Ever since _____ Ted the bad news, he's been avoiding me.
    A. telling   B. told   C. I told   D. having told

19. _____ my daughter reaches the age of sixteen, she will be able to drive.
    A. Having   B. Since   C. Once   D. Because

20. Matt will enjoy skiing more the next time he goes to Mt. Baker _____ he has had skiing lessons.
    A. so that   B. before   C. now that   D. and

◇ **PRACTICE TEST B—GUIDED STUDY: Showing relationships between ideas. (Chapter 8)**

Directions: Choose the correct answer.

Example:
    _B_ *I get angry and upset, I try to take ten deep breaths.*
    A. Until   B. Whenever   C. Therefore   D. For

1. _____ it's warm and sunny today, why don't we go to the park?
    A. Therefore   B. Due to   C. As long as   D. For

2. The first time I went swimming in deep water, I sank to the bottom like a rock. _____ I've learned to stay afloat, I feel better about the water, but I still can't swim well.
    A. As soon as   B. The first time   C. When   D. Now that

3. It's obvious that neither the workers _____ to fight the new rules.
    A. nor the manager intend   B. intend nor the manager
    C. nor the manager intends   D. intend nor the manager intends

4. Timmy doesn't do well in school _____ his inability to concentrate on any one thing for longer than a minute or two.
   A. as   B. due to   C. because   D. therefore

5. After _____ to 45 minutes of an extremely boring speech, I found myself nodding off.
   A. was listening   B. listen   C. listening   D. having listen

6. Why did I stay until the end? I am never going to stay and watch a bad movie again! _____ I am in that situation, I'm going to leave the theater immediately.
   A. The next time   B. Now that   C. After   D. Until

7. "Why aren't you ready to go?"
   "I am ready."
   "How can that be? It's freezing outside, _____ you're wearing shorts and a T-shirt!"
   A. for   B. so   C. because   D. yet

8. Erin likes to swim, jog, and _____ tennis.
   A. plays   B. play   C. to play   D. playing

9. Since _____ to a warmer and less humid climate, I've had no trouble with my asthma.
   A. upon moving   B. I moving   C. moving   D. I move

10. Tony spent _____ money buying movie tickets that he didn't have enought left to buy a soft drink or candy bar.
    A. such   B. a lot of   C. too much   D. so much

11. _____ I get back from my next business trip, I'm taking a few days off. I'm worn out!
    A. Once   B. Since   C. Now that   D. Every time

12. Citrus growers become anxious about losing their fragile crop of oranges _____ the temperature gets near freezing in Florida.
    A. and   B. consequently   C. until   D. whenever

13. Before _____ a promotion and transfer to another city, I will discuss it at length with my whole family to be sure that everyone will be able to adjust to the change.
    A. accept   B. accepted
    C. having been accepted   D. accepting

14. You should learn how to change a tire on your car _____ you can handle an emergency situation if necessary.
    A. so that   B. when   C. for that   D. therefore

15. Cars have become much more complicated. _____, mechanics need more training than in the past.
    A. Because   B. Therefore   C. So that   D. For

16. Not wanting to be late my first day of class, _____ to school after I missed my bus.
    A. so I ran   B. because I ran   C. I ran   D. therefore, I ran

17. It was raining _____ I couldn't go outside.
    A. because   B. so hard that   C. so that   D. too hard that

18. The Northern Hemisphere has mostly westerly winds _____ the rotation of the earth toward the east.
    A. due to   B. because   C. therefore   D. so

19. Great white sharks are dangerous to _____ will attack without warning.
    A. humans, they   B. humans
    C. humans. Because they   D. humans. They

20. _____ the need to finish this project soon, I want you to work on this overtime for the next few days.
    A. Because   B. So that   C. Because of   D. Inasmuch as

CHAPTER 9
Showing Relationships Between Ideas—Part II

◇ **PRACTICE 1—SELFSTUDY:** Using *even though* vs. *because.* (Chart 9-1)

Directions: Complete the sentences with *even though* or *because*.

1. I put on my sunglasses _____*even though*_____ it was a dark, cloudy day.

2. I put on my sunglasses _____*because*_____ the sun was bright.

3. _____ she has a job, she doesn't make enough money to support her four children.

4. _____ she has a job, she is able to pay her rent and provide food for her family.

5. I'm going horseback riding with Judy this afternoon _____ I'm afraid of horses.

6. I'm going horseback riding with Judy this afternoon _____ I enjoy it.

7. _____ you've made it clear that you don't want any help, I have to at least offer to help you.

8. I knew that I should get some sleep, but I just couldn't put my book down _____ I was really enjoying it.

9. I'm glad that my mother made me take piano lessons when I was a child _____ I hated it at the time. Now, I play the piano every day.

10. _____ Tom didn't know how to dance, he wanted to go to the school dance _____ he felt lonely sitting and staring blankly at the TV while all of his friends were having fun together.

11. Joe jumped into the river to rescue the little girl who was drowning _____ he wasn't a good swimmer.

12. My hair stylist subscribes to three different fashion magazines _____ she's not interested in clothes. She subscribes to them _____ her customers like them.

13. _____ the earthquake damaged the bridge across Skunk River, the Smiths were able to cross the river _____ they had a boat.

◇ **PRACTICE 2—GUIDED STUDY: Using *even though* vs. *because*. (Chart 9-1)**

Directions: Write sentences that include the given words. Use any tense or modal for the verb in parentheses.

Examples:

Because _____, I (*walk*) _____ all the way home.
→ *Because the bus drivers went on strike, I had to walk all the way home.*

Even though _____, I (*walk*) _____ all the way home.
→ *Even though I was dead tired, I walked all the way home.*

1. Because _____, I (*go*) _____ fishing.

2. Even though _____, I (*go*) _____ fishing.

3. I (*pay*) _____ for everyone's dinner because _____

4. I (*pay*) _____ for everyone's dinner even though _____

5. Even though there (*be*) _____ very few customers in the store, _____

6. Because there (*be*) _____ very few customers in the store, _____

7. I (*wear*) _____ heavy gloves because _____

8. Even though my feet (*be*) _____ killing me and my head (*be*) _____
   pounding, I _____

9. Even though _____, I (*get, not*) _____ a traffic ticket.

10. Even though I (*ask*) _____ him politely to speak more softly, _____

11. My friend (*subscribe*) _____ to three different fashion magazines because
    _____

12. When I (*open*) _____ the door, my roommate (*scream*)_____ because
    _____

13. Even though I (*be*) _____ tired, I _____ because _____

14. Even though _____ when _____, I _____ because
    _____

15. Because _____ while _____, I _____ even though
    _____

◇ **PRACTICE 3—SELFSTUDY: Showing opposition. (Chart 9-2)**

Directions: Complete the sentences with the given words. Pay close attention to the given punctuation and capitalization.

PART I: Complete the following with *but, even though,* or *nevertheless*.

1. Bob ate a large dinner. ____*Nevertheless*____, he is still hungry.

2. Bob ate a large dinner, ____*but*____ he is still hungry.

3. Bob is still hungry ____*even though*____ he ate a large dinner.

4. I had a lot of studying to do, _____ I went to a movie anyway.

5. I had a lot of studying to do. _____, I went to a movie.

6. _____ I had a lot of studying to do, I went to a movie.

7. I finished all of my work _____ I was very sleepy.

8. I was very sleepy, _____ I finished all of my work anyway.

9. I was very sleepy. _____, I finished all of my work.

10. All of my family friends have advised me not to travel abroad during this time of political turmoil. _____, I'm leaving next week to begin a trip around the world.

PART II: Complete the following sentences with *yet, although,* or *however*.

11. I washed my hands. _____, they still looked dirty.

12. I washed my hands, _____ they still looked dirty.

13. _____ I washed my hands, they still looked dirty.

14. Diana didn't know how to swim, _____ she jumped into the swimming pool.

15. _____ Diana didn't know how to swim, she jumped into the swimming pool.

16. Diana didn't know how to swim. _____, she jumped into the swimming pool.

17. I wouldn't trust Alan with my money _____ he seems to be trustworthy.

18. Alan seems trustworthy and capable as a financial advisor, _____ I wouldn't trust him with my money.

19. Alan seems capable as a financial advisor. _____, I wouldn't trust him with my money.

20. Some people think great strides have been made in cleaning up the environment in much of the world. _____, others think the situation is much worse than it was twenty years ago.

◇ **PRACTICE 4—SELFSTUDY: Showing opposition: punctuation. (Chart 9-2)**

Directions: Add commas, periods, and capital letters as necessary. Do not add or omit any words. Do not change the order of the words.

1. Anna's father gave her some good advice nevertheless she did not follow it.
   → *Anna's father gave her some good advice. Nevertheless, she did not follow it.*

2. Anna's father gave her some good advice but she didn't follow it.

3. Even though Anna's father gave her some good advice she didn't follow it.

4. Anna's father gave her some good advice she did not follow it however.

5. Thomas was thirsty I offered him some water he refused it.

6. Thomas refused the water although he was thirsty.

7. Thomas was thirsty he nevertheless refused the glass of water I brought him.

8. Thomas was thirsty yet he refused to drink the water that I offered him.

◇ **PRACTICE 5—SELFSTUDY:** *Despite/in spite of* vs. *even though/although.* **(Chart 9-2)**

Directions: Choose the correct completions.

1. a. (*Even though,*) *Despite* her doctor warned her, Carol has continued to smoke nearly three packs of cigarettes a day.

   b. *Even though,* (*Despite*) her doctor's warnings, Carol has continued to smoke nearly three packs of cigarettes a day.

   c. *Even though,* (*Despite*) the warnings her doctor gave her, Carol continues to smoke.

   d. *Even though,* (*Despite*) the fact that her doctor warned her of dangers to her health, Carol continues to smoke.

   e. (*Even though,*) *Despite* she has been warned about the dangers of smoking by her doctor, Carol continues to smoke.

2. a. *Although, In spite of* an approaching storm, the two climbers continued their trek up the mountain.

   b. *Although, In spite of* a storm was approaching, the two climbers continued their trek.

   c. *Although, In spite of* there was an approaching storm, the two climbers continued up the mountain.

   d. *Although, In spite of* the storm that was approaching the mountain area, the two climbers continued their trek.

   e. *Although, in spite of* the fact that a storm was approaching the mountain area, the two climbers continued their trek.

3. a. *Although, Despite* his many hours of practice, George failed his driving test for the third time.

   b. *Although, Despite* he had practiced for many hours, George failed his driving test for the third time.

   c. *Although, Despite* practicing for many hours, George failed his driving test again.

   d. *Although, Despite* his mother and father spent hours with him in the car trying to teach him how to drive, George failed his driving test repeatedly.

   e. *Although, Despite* his mother and father's efforts to teach him how to drive, George failed his driving test.

4. a. *Even though, In spite of* repeated crop failures due to drought, the villagers are refusing to leave their traditional homeland for resettlement in other areas.

   b. *Even though, In spite of* their crops have failed repeatedly due to drought, the villagers are refusing to leave their traditional homeland for resettlement in other areas.

   c. The villagers refused to leave *even though, in spite of* the drought.

   d. The villagers refuse to leave *even though, in spite of* the drought seriously threatens their food supply.

   e. The villagers refuse to leave *even though, in spite of* the threat to their food supply because of the continued drought.

   f. The villagers refuse to leave *even though, in spite of* the threat to their food supply is serious because of the continued drought.

   g. The villagers refuse to leave *even though, in spite of* their food supply is threatened.

   h. The villagers refused to leave *even though, in spite of* their threatened food supply.

◇ PRACTICE 6—SELFSTUDY: Using *in spite of/despite*, and *even though/though/although*. (Chart 9-2)

Directions: Complete the sentences. Place the letter of the completion in the blank space. Use each completion only one time.

   A. *its many benefits*
✔ B. *its inherent dangers*
   C. *it has been shown to be safe*
   D. *it has been shown to cause birth defects and sometimes death*
   E. *his fear of heights*
   F. *he is afraid of heights*
   G. *he is normally quite shy and sometimes inarticulate*
   H. *an inability to communicate well in any language besides English*
   I. *having excellent skills in the job category they were trying to fill*
   J. *he had the necessary qualifications*

1. In spite of __*B*__, nuclear energy is a clean and potentially inexhaustible source of energy.

2. In spite of _____, Carl enjoyed his helicopter trip over the Grand Canyon in Arizona.

3. Because of his age, John was not hired even though _____.

4. Although _____, Mark rode an elevator to the top of the World Trade Center in New York for the magnificent view.

5. Although _____, many people avoid using a microwave oven for fear of its rays.

6. Jack usually has little trouble making new friends in another country despite _____.

7. In spite of _____, the use of chemotherapy to treat cancer has many severe side effects.

8. Though _____, Bob managed to give an excellent presentation at the board meeting.

9. Jerry continued to be denied a promotion despite _____.

10. DDT is still used in many countries as a primary insecticide even though _____.

◇ **PRACTICE 7—SELFSTUDY: Direct opposition. (Chart 9-3)**

Directions: Choose the best completion.

1. Some people are tall, whereas others are ___C___.
   A. intelligent
   B. thin
   C. short
   D. large

2. A box is square, whereas _____.
   A. a rectangle has four sides
   B. my village has a town square in the center
   C. we use envelopes for letters
   D. a circle is round

3. While some parts of the world get an abundance of rain, others _____.
   A. are warm and humid
   B. are cold and wet
   C. get little or none
   D. get a lot

4. In some nations coffee is the favorite beverage, while _____.
   A. I like tea
   B. it has caffeine
   C. in others it is tea
   D. tea has caffeine too.

5. Some people like cream and sugar in their coffee, while _____.
   A. others drink hot coffee
   B. others like it black
   C. milk is good in coffee, too
   D. sugar can cause cavities

6. Jack is an interesting storyteller and conversationalist. His brother, on the other hand, _____.
   A. is a newspaper reporter.
   B. bores other people by talking about himself
   C. has four children
   D. knows a lot of stories, too

◇ **PRACTICE 8—GUIDED STUDY: Direct opposition. (Chart 9-3)**

Directions: Complete the sentences with your own words.

1. Some people really enjoy swimming, while others . . . *are afraid of water.*
2. In the U.S., people drive on the righthand side of the road. However, people in . . . .
3. While my apartment always seems to be a mess, my . . . .
4. Marge keeps to herself and has few friends. Carol, on the other hand, ...
5. People who grew up on farms are accustomed to dealing with various kinds of animals. However, city people like myself . . . .
6. Teak is a hard wood that is difficult to cut. Balsa, on the other hand, ...
7. My oldest son is shy, while my youngest son . . . .
8. I'm righthanded. That means that I can accomplish difficult manipulations with my right hand. However, ...

◇ **PRACTICE 9—SELFSTUDY: Cause/effect and opposition. (Charts 8-6 → 8-9 and 9-1 → 9-3)**

Directions: Choose the best completion.

Example:
   It was cold and wet. ___D___, *Bob put on his swimming suit and went to the beach.*
      A. Therefore   *B. Despite*   *C. Although*   *D. Nevertheless*

1. I can't ride my bicycle _____ there isn't any air in one of the tires.
      A. despite   B. because   C. although   D. but

2. I got to class on time _____ I had missed my bus.
      A. even though   B. nevertheless   C. because   D. despite

3. Brian used to be an active person, but now he has to limit his activities _____ problems with his health.
   A. nevertheless   B. because of   C. although   D. in spite of

4. It should be easy for Bob to find more time to spend with his children _____ he no longer has to work in the evenings and on weekends.
   A. even though   B. now that   C. due to   D. but

5. Jake is a very good student of languages. His brother Michael, _____, has never been able to master another language.
   A. therefore   B. even though
   C. whereas   D. on the other hand

6. The ancient Aztecs of Mexico had no technology for making tools from metal. _____, they had sharp knives and spears made from a stone called obsidian.
   A. Whereas   B. Although   C. Nevertheless   D. Despite

7. Roberta missed the meeting without a good reason _____ she had been told that it was critical that she be there. I wouldn't want to be in her shoes at work tomorrow.
   A. despite   B. despite the fact that   C. even   D. however

8. I usually enjoy attending amateur productions in small community theaters. The play we attended last night, _____, was so bad that I wanted to leave after the first act.
   A. therefore   B. however   C. whereas   D. even though

9. Some snakes are poisonous, _____ others are harmless.
   A. but   B. so   C. for   D. despite

10. Most 15th century Europeans believed that the world was flat and that a ship could conceivably sail off the end of the earth. _____, many sailors of the time refused to venture forth with explorers into unknown waters.
    A. Due to the fact that B. Nevertheless C. Therefore   D. Whereas

◇ **PRACTICE 10—GUIDED STUDY:** Cause/effect and opposition. (Charts 8-6 → 8-9 and 9-1 → 9-3)

Directions: Show the relationship between the ideas by adding any of the following expressions, as appropriate:

because	*because of*	*while/whereas*	*on the other hand*
since	*due to*	*nevertheless*	*in spite of*
now that	*even though*	*however*	*despite*
therefore	*although*		

1. It was still hot in the room ____**even though / although**____ I had turned on the air conditioner.

2. Several people in the crowd became ill and fainted _____**due to / because of**_____ the extreme heat.

3. The gardener trimmed the branches on the cherry tree _____ I asked him not to.

4. The meat of the puffer fish can cause paralysis or even death if it is improperly prepared. _____, it remains a delicacy in Japan for brave diners.

5. _____ everyone disagreed with him, Brian went ahead with his original plan for the company.

6. The first mention of the game of chess appears in an Indian text written almost 1500 years ago. _____ its ancient beginnings, it remains one of the most widely played games in the world today.

7. Alice heard a siren and saw the flashing lights of a police car in her rear-view mirror. _____, she quickly pulled over to the side of the road and stopped.

8. Most adults carry around certain attitudes and prejudices about the world around them. Most children, _____, enter new situations without such preconceived notions.

9. They often have to close all of the ski areas in the mountains _____ severe weather conditions and avalanche danger.

10. _____ paper was first developed by the ancient Chinese, its English name comes from the word *papyrus*, the name of an Egyptian water plant.

11. The supervisor must know what everyone in the department is doing _____ all responsibility for error will fall on her shoulders.

12. _____ aspirin is relatively safe for most adults, it should be administered very carefully to children, if at all. It can be dangerous to children's health.

13. The peanut is used today to make everything from cosmetics to explosives _____ the pioneering scientific work of George Washington Carver in the 1910s and 1920s.

14. In ancient China, yellow was considered to be an imperial color. _____, only the emperor was allowed to wear it. No one else could have yellow clothing of any kind.

15. _____ the abacus had been in use in Asia since ancient times, many in the Western world credited 19-year-old Blaise Pascal, a Frenchman, with inventing the first calculating machine in 1642.

16. _____ she thought she heard the telephone ringing, Marge turned the TV down—only to discover it had been a telephone on the show she was watching.

◇ **PRACTICE 11—GUIDED STUDY:** *"If* clauses." (Chart 9-4)

Directions: Using the given possibilities, make sentences using *if*. Pay special attention to verb forms.

1. My car will probably not start tomorrow morning.
   → *If my car **doesn't start** tomorrow morning, **I'll take** the bus to work.*
2. Sometimes my car doesn't start in the morning.
   → *If my car **doesn't start** in the morning, I **take** the bus to work.*

3. Sometimes I have free time.
4. Maybe I will have some free time tomorrow.
5. I might not be able to come to the meeting this afternoon.
6. Sometimes I can't attend a meeting at my office.
7. You will probably be too tired to finish your work this afternoon.
8. Perhaps I won't be able to get a ticket for Flight 605 Tuesday morning.
9. We might not have enough money to take our trip next month.
10. People might continue to destroy their environment.

◇ **PRACTICE 12—GUIDED STUDY:** Using *whether or not* and *even if*. (Chart 9-5)

Directions: Complete the sentences with your own words.

Examples:
  Even if . . . , I'm not going to go.
  → *Even if I get an invitation to the reception, I'm not going to go.*

  . . . whether I feel better or not.
  → *I have to go to work tomorrow whether I feel better or not.*

1. . . . even if the weather improves.
2. Even if . . . , you may not pass the course.
3. Getting that job depends on whether or not . . . .
4. Even if I have a lot of work to do, ...
5. . . . whether you want me to or not.
6. I won't tell you even if . . . .
7. . . . even if it's past midnight.
8. Please tell me soon whether or not . . . so that I can decide what I'm going to do.

◇ PRACTICE 13—SELFSTUDY: Using *in case* and *in the event that*. (Chart 9-6)

Directions: Complete the sentences by using ***in case***. Decide if it goes in the first blank or in the second blank. Add necessary punctuation and capitalization.

1. ____*In case*____ you need to get in touch with me _____,_____ I'll be in my office until late this evening.

2. _____*W*_____ we'll be at the Swan Hotel _____*in case*_____ you need to call us.

3. _____ you'd better take your raincoat with you _____ the weather changes. It could rain before you get home again.

4. Mary is willing to work with you on your design project. _____ you find that you need help with it _____ she'll be back in town next Monday and can meet with you then.

5. _____ my boss has to stay near a phone all weekend _____ the company wants him to go to London to close the deal they've been working on all month.

6. _____ I'm not back in time to make dinner _____ I put the phone number for carry-out Chinese food on the refrigerator. You can call and order the food for yourself.

Complete the sentences using ***in the event that***.

7. ____*In the event that*____ Janet is late for work again tomorrow _____ she will be fired.

8. Are you sure you're taking enough money with you? _____ you'd better take a credit card with you _____ you run out of cash.

9. The political situation is getting more unstable and dangerous. _____ my family plans to leave the country _____ there is a civil war.

10. Just to be on the safe side, _____ I always take a change of clothes in my carry-on bag _____ the airline loses my luggage.

11. The cheapest way to get from an airport to a hotel is to take an airport bus, but I'm not sure if River City has one. _____ there is no airport bus _____ you can always take a taxi.

12. Ann is one of five people nominated for an award to be given at the banquet this evening. _____ she has already prepared an acceptance speech _____ she wins it tonight.

◇ PRACTICE 14—SELFSTUDY: Using *unless* vs. *if* and *only if*. (Charts 9-7 and 9-8)

Directions: Choose the correct answer.

1. Most people you meet will be polite to you __*B*__ you are polite to them.
   A. unless   B. if

2. I can't buy a car _____ I save enough money.
   A. unless   B. only if

3. Eggs will not hatch _____ they are kept at the proper temperature.
   A. unless   B. only if

4. Our kids are allowed to watch television after dinner _____ they have finished their homework. Homework must come first.
   A. unless   B. only if

5. I'll give you a hand _____ you need it, but I hope I don't hurt my back.
   A. unless   B. if

6. I'm afraid the battery is dead. _____ I buy a new one, the car won't start.
   A. unless   B. if

7. My sister can fall asleep under any conditions, but I can't get to sleep _____ the light is off and the room is perfectly quiet.
   A. unless   B. if

8. There can be peace in the world _____ all nations sincerely lend their energy to that effort.
   A. unless   B. only if

9. Alice will tutor you in math _____ you promise to do everything she says.
   A. unless   B. only if

10. Oscar won't pass his math course _____ he gets a tutor.
    A. unless   B. only if

11. I won't be involved in this project _____ you assure me that we won't be violating any laws.
    A. unless   B. if

12. I'll prepare a really special dinner _____ you all promise to be home on time this evening. Let's plan on an old-fashioned sit-down dinner with the whole family at the table at once.
    A. unless   B. only if

◇ PRACTICE 15—SELFSTUDY: Using *if, only if, unless,* and *provided/providing that.* (Charts 9-7 and 9-8)

Directions: Choose the correct words in italics so that the sentences make sense.

1. I'm *going to go,* (*not going to go*) to the park unless the weather is nice.

2. I'm going to go to the park unless it *rains, doesn't rain*.

3. I'll pass the course provided that I *pass, don't pass* the final examination.

4. Tom doesn't like to work. He'll get a job *unless, only if* he has to.

5. I *always eat, never eat* breakfast unless I get up late and don't have enough time.

6. I always finish my homework *even if, only if* I'm sleepy and want to go to bed.

7. Grass grows provided that it *gets, doesn't get* enough water.

8. You *will, won't* learn to play the violin well unless you practice every day.

9. Even if the president calls, *wake, don't wake* me up. I don't want to talk to anyone. I want to sleep.

10. Jack is going to come to the game with us today *if, unless* his boss gives him the afternoon off.

11. *Borrow, Don't borrow* money from your friends unless you absolutely must.

12. I'll get tickets to the concert provided that there *are still some, aren't any* available.

◇ **PRACTICE 16—SELFSTUDY: Using** *only if* **vs.** *if*: **subject-verb inversion. (Chart 9-8)**

Directions: Change the position of the adverb clause to the front of the sentence. Make any necessary changes in the verb of the main clause.

1. I can finish this work on time only if you help me.
   → ***Only if*** *you help me* **can I finish** *this work on time.*

2. I can finish this work on time if you help me.
   → ***If*** *you help me,* **I can finish** *this work on time.*

3. I will go only if I am invited.

4. I will go if I am invited.

5. I eat only if I am hungry.

6. I usually eat some fruit if I am hungry during the morning.

7. You will be considered for that job only if you know both Arabic and Spanish.

8. John goes to the market only if the refrigerator is empty.

9. I will tell you the truth about what happened only if you promise not to get angry.

10. I won't discuss it any further if you get angry.

◇ **PRACTICE 17—GUIDED STUDY: Expressing conditions. (Charts 9-5 → 9-8)**

Directions: Complete the sentences using your own words.

Examples:
. . . only if you can prove to me that your assumptions are correct about next year's potential profits.
   → ***I will support your position with the boss*** *only if you can prove to me that your assumptions are correct about next year's potential profits.*

There's a 10 percent discount on everything today provided that . . . .
   → *There's a 10 percent discount on everything today provided that* **you have one of the coupons from today's newspaper.**

1. I'm never late to class unless . . . .
2. . . . only if I ask her to.
3. High school students shouldn't quit school even if . . . .
4. . . . providing that my flight leaves on time.
5. . . . unless the doctor says I shouldn't.
6. Mr. Crane will take the temporary assignment out of town only if . . . .
7. My neighbor will take care of my apartment while I'm out of town provided that . . . .
8. The price of oil will remain stable if . . . .
9. . . . only if you explain your reasons completely.
10. Providing that all of our work is finished, ...
11. I'm going to be gone for three days unless . . . .
12. I will interview for that job provided that . . . .

◇ **PRACTICE 18—SELFSTUDY: Using *otherwise*. (Chart 9-9)**

Directions: Make two sentences. Show the relationship between them by using *otherwise*. In the first sentence, use a modal auxiliary or similar expression: *should, had better, have to, must.*

1. If you don't eat less and get more exercise, you won't lose weight.
   → *You should (had better/have to/must) eat less and get more exercise. Otherwise, you won't lose weight.*

2. The children can watch TV tonight only if they finish all of their chores.
   → *The children have to (had better/should/must) finish all of their chores. Otherwise, they cannot watch TV tonight.*

3. Unless you speak up now, the boss will go ahead without knowing that you don't agree.

4. If you don't stop at the store on your way home from work, we won't have anything to eat for dinner tonight.

5. Unless you think it through very carefully, you won't come up with the right answer.

6. If we don't catch any fish this morning, we're going to have beans for dinner again.

7. It's going to be very difficult to finish on time if you don't get someone in to help you.

8. Maria is probably going to lose her job unless she finds a way to convince the boss that the error was unavoidable.

◇ **PRACTICE 19—SELFSTUDY: Expressing conditions. (Charts 9-5 → 9-8)**

Directions: Complete the sentences with any appropriate form of the verb "pass."

1. Keith will graduate if he _____ ***passes*** _____ all of his courses.

2. Sam won't graduate if he _____ ***doesn't pass*** _____ all of his courses.

3. Ed won't graduate unless he _____ all of his courses.

4. Sue will graduate only if she _____ all of her courses.

5. Jessica will graduate even if she _____ all of her courses.

6. Alex won't graduate even if he _____ all of his courses.

7. Jennifer will graduate provided that she _____ all of her courses.

8. Amy won't graduate in the event that she _____ all of her courses.

9. Jerry _____ all of his courses. Otherwise, he won't graduate.

10. Carolyn _____ all of her courses, or else she won't graduate.

◇ PRACTICE 20—GUIDED STUDY: Summary of relationship words. (Charts 8-5 and 9-10)

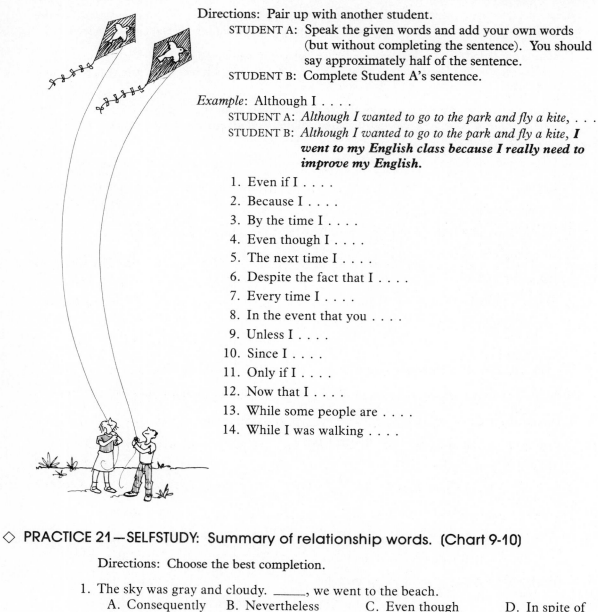

Directions: Pair up with another student.
STUDENT A: Speak the given words and add your own words (but without completing the sentence). You should say approximately half of the sentence.
STUDENT B: Complete Student A's sentence.

Example: Although I . . . .
STUDENT A: *Although I wanted to go to the park and fly a kite,* . . .
STUDENT B: *Although I wanted to go to the park and fly a kite,* **I went to my English class because I really need to improve my English.**

1. Even if I . . . .
2. Because I . . . .
3. By the time I . . . .
4. Even though I . . . .
5. The next time I . . . .
6. Despite the fact that I . . . .
7. Every time I . . . .
8. In the event that you . . . .
9. Unless I . . . .
10. Since I . . . .
11. Only if I . . . .
12. Now that I . . . .
13. While some people are . . . .
14. While I was walking . . . .

◇ PRACTICE 21—SELFSTUDY: Summary of relationship words. (Chart 9-10)

Directions: Choose the best completion.

1. The sky was gray and cloudy. _____, we went to the beach.
   A. Consequently   B. Nevertheless   C. Even though   D. In spite of

2. I turned on the fan _____ the room was hot.
   A. due to   B. despite   C. even though   D. because

3. Sam and I will meet you at the restaurant tonight _____ we can find a babysitter.
   A. although   B. unless   C. otherwise   D. only if

4. Carol showed up for the meeting _____ I asked her not to be there.
   A. even though   B. despite   C. provided that   D. because

5. You must lend me the money for the trip. _____, I won't be able to go.
   A. Consequently   B. Nevertheless   C. Otherwise   D. Although

6. The road will remain safe _____ the flood washes out the bridge.
   A. as long as   B. unless   C. providing that   D. since

7. The roles of men and women were not the same in ancient Greece. For example, men were both participants and spectators in the ancient Olympics. Women, _____, were forbidden to attend or participate.
   A. nevertheless   B. on the other hand   C. therefore   D. otherwise

8. The windows were all left open. _____, the room was a real mess after the windstorm.
   A. Nevertheless   B. However   C. Consequently   D. Otherwise

9. _____ I can't make the presentation myself, I've asked my assistant to be prepared to do it for me.
   A. For   B. In the event that   C. Only if   D. On the other hand

10. It looks like they're going to succeed _____ their present difficulties.
    A. despite   B. because of   C. even though   D. yet

11. _____ Marge is an honest person, I still wonder whether she's telling the truth about the incident.
    A. In spite of   B. Since   C. Though   D. In the event that

12. The professor told me that I was doing well, _____ my final grade was awful!
    A. so   B. therefore   C. in spite of   D. yet

13. _____ Beth has a new car, she no longer takes the commuter train to work. She drives to work every day.
    A. Now that   B. While   C. Although   D. In case

14. You'd better give me your answer quickly, _____ I'll withdraw the invitation.
    A. although   B. nevertheless   C. even though   D. or else

15. I have to go to the meeting _____ I want to or not.
    A. provided that   B. whether   C. even if   D. only if

16. What time do you expect Ted to be home? I must talk to him. I usually go to bed around ten, but tell him to call me tonight _____ it's past midnight.
    A. however   B. in case   C. even if   D. as long as

17. _____ you're going to the fruit market, would you please pick up a few apples for me?
    A. Even if   B. Although   C. So   D. As long as

18. I guess I'm a soft touch. I just lent Jan some money for lunch _____ she never paid me back my last loan.
    A. even though   B. unless   C. or else   D. only if

19. I think I did okay in my speech last night _____ I'd had almost no sleep for 24 hours.
    A. even   B. in spite of   C. unless   D. despite the fact that

20. I asked Angela to run the office while I'm gone _____ I know I can depend on her.
    A. unless   B. since   C. although   D. therefore

21. _____ the secret of how to make silk remained inside Asia, Europeans were forced to pay incredibly high sums of money for this mysterious material to be brought overland to Europe.
    A. Although   B. Only if   C. Due to   D. As long as

22. Ancient Egyptians mummified their dead through the use of chemicals, _____ ancient Peruvians mumified their dead through natural processes by putting dead bodies in extremely dry desert caves.
    A. whereas   B. because   C. even though   D. whether or not

◇ **PRACTICE 22—GUIDED STUDY:** Summary of relationship words. (Chart 9-10)

Directions: Form a group of 4 to 6 people. One of you should begin a "chain sentence" by speaking the given words plus one, two, or three additional words. Each of the others should add one, two, or three words until the sentence is completed. The maximum number of words a person can add is *three*. When you complete your sentence, one person in the group should write it down (with correct punctuation, spelling, and capitalization).

Example: Although education is . . . .
  STUDENT A : Although education is **important,** . . . .
  STUDENT B : Although education is important, **some students** . . . .
  STUDENT C : Although education is important, some students **would rather** . . . .
  STUDENT D : Although education is important, some students would rather **fly a kite** . . . .
  STUDENT A : Although education is important, some students would rather fly a kite **than** . . . .
  STUDENT B : Although education is important, some students would rather fly a kite than
      go to class.
  FINAL SENTENCE: → *Although education is important, some students would rather fly a kite than*
          go to class.

1. Because we are . . . .
2. Even though students don't . . . .
3. Unless students . . . .
4. In the event that an earthquake occurs in . . . .
5. Students have to study. Otherwise . . . .
6. In spite of the fact that students . . . .
7. Even if we . . . .
8. Only if . . . .
9. Being a student can be stressful. Therefore, ...
10. I was so confused when the teacher . . . .
11. Despite . . . .
12. Now that we . . . .

◇ **PRACTICE 23—GUIDED STUDY:** Summary of relationship words. (Chart 9-10)

Directions: Complete the sentences with your own words. Add necessary punctuation and capitalization.

Example:
  Mary has to wear glasses otherwise _____
  → *Mary has to wear glasses.* ***Otherwise, she can't see words clearly when she reads.***

1. _____ but I washed it anyway.

2. Only if _____ will I lend you the money for a red motorcycle.

3. I _____ only because I thought that everyone had already finished eating.

4. _____ although she had had a temperature and chills all night.

5. Next Monday is a national holiday therefore _____

6. _____ in the event that my suit isn't back from the cleaners.

7. As long as you have some extra money this month _____

8. I brought my brother with me just in case _____

9. Parents need to be involved in their children's education however _____

10. Inasmuch as _____ is my favorite color _____

11. I was so sure I was right that _____

12. The banana was brown and mushy nevertheless _____

13. _____ often have to work at odd hours of the day or night on the other hand _____ usually work daytime hours only.

14. Since I'm going to be out of town for the next two weeks _____

15. Since I came here _____

16. Most wild animals will attack a human being only if _____

17. There was a major accident on the interstate highway consequently _____

18. I wanted to relax so _____

19. The population of the city has increased so rapidly _____

20. I am getting an education so that _____

◇ **PRACTICE 24—GUIDED STUDY: Punctuation. (Chapters 6 → 9)**

Directions: Add appropriate punctuation and capitalization to clarify the following passages.

1. I did not expect to get a pay raise nevertheless I accepted when my boss offered it.

→ *I did not expect to get a pay raise. Nevertheless, I accepted when my boss offered it.*

2. Although a computer has tremendous power and speed it cannot think for itself a human operator is needed to give a computer instructions for it cannot initially tell itself what to do.

3. Being a lawyer in private practice I work hard but I do not go to my office on either Saturday or Sunday if clients insist upon seeing me on the weekend they have to come to my home.

4. Whenever my father goes fishing we know we will have fish to eat for dinner for even if he doesn't catch any he stops at the fish market on his way home and buys some.

5. The goatherd who supposedly discovered coffee is a legendary rather than historical figure no one knows for sure that the first coffee was discovered when an Ethiopian goatherd noticed that his goats did not fall asleep all night long after they had eaten the leaves and berries of coffee plants.

6. Whenever the weather is nice I walk to school but when it is cold or wet I either take the bus or get a ride with one of my friends even though my brother has a car I never ask him to take me to school because he is very busy he has a new job and has recently gotten married so he doesn't have time to drive me to and from school anymore I know he would give me a ride if I asked him to however I don't want to bother him.

7. The common cold which is the most widespread of all diseases continues to plague humanity despite the efforts of scientists to find its prevention and cure even though colds are minor illnesses they are one of the principal causes of absence from school and work people of all ages get colds but children and adults who live with children get the most colds can be dangerous for elderly people because they can lead to other infections I have had three colds so far this year I eat the right kinds of food get enough rest and exercise regularly nevertheless I still get at least one cold a year.

◇ PRACTICE 25—GUIDED STUDY: Showing relationships. (Chapters 8 and 9)

Directions: Using the words in parentheses, combine the following sentences to show the relationships between the ideas. Punctuate and capitalize correctly.

Example:
a. Jack hates going to the dentist.
b. He should see his dentist soon.
c. He has a very bad toothache.
(RELATIONSHIP WORDS TO USE: *even though, because*)
→ *Even though Jack hates going to the dentist, he should see his dentist soon because he has a very bad toothache.*

1. a. You may really mean what you say.
   b. I'll give you one more chance.
   c. You have to give me your best effort.
   d. You'll lose your job.
   (RELATIONSHIP WORDS: *if, but, otherwise*)

2. a. The weather is bad.
   b. I'm going to stay home.
   c. The weather may change.
   d. I don't want to go to the picnic.
   (RELATIONSHIP WORDS: *due to, even if*)

3. a. The children had eaten lunch.
   b. They got hungry in the middle of the afternoon.
   c. I took them to the market.
   d. They wanted to get some fruit for a snack.
   e. We went home for dinner.
   (RELATIONSHIP WORDS: *even though, therefore, so that, before*)

4. a. Robert is totally exhausted after playing tennis.
   b. Marge isn't even tired.
   c. She ran around a lot more during the game.
   (RELATIONSHIP WORDS: ***whereas, in spite of the fact that***)

5. a. My boss promised me that I could have two full weeks.
   b. It seems that I can't take my vacation after all.
   c. I have to train the new personnel this summer.
   d. I may not get a vacation in the fall either.
   e. I will be angry.
   (RELATIONSHIP WORDS: ***even though, because, if***)

6. a. Paul might finish his deliveries early this evening.
   b. He'll join us in time for dinner.
   c. You should make a reservation for him.
   d. The restaurant may not be able to accommodate all of us at the last minute.
   (RELATIONSHIP WORDS: ***in the event that, therefore, otherwise***)

7. a. Education, business, and government are all becoming more dependent on computers.
   b. It is advisable for all students to have basic computer skills.
   c. They graduate from high school and enter the work force or college.
   d. A course called "Computer Literacy" has recently become a requirement for graduation from Westside High School.
   e. Maybe you will want more information about this course.
   f. You can call the academic counselor at the high school.
   (RELATIONSHIP WORDS: ***inasmuch as, before, therefore, if***)

8. a. Many animals are most vulnerable to predators when they are grazing.
   b. Giraffes are most vulnerable when they are drinking.
   c. They must spread their legs awkwardly to lower their long necks to the water in front of them.
   d. It is difficult and time-consuming for them to stand up straight again to escape a predator.
   e. Once they are up and running, they are faster than most of their predators.
   (RELATIONSHIP WORDS: ***while, consequently, however***)

◇ PRACTICE 26—GUIDED STUDY: Showing relationships. (Chapters 6 → 9)

Directions: Write out the sentences, completing them with your own words. (Warning: Some of your sentences will have to get a little complicated.) Some punctuation is given; add other punctuation as necessary.

Example:

I have trouble _____, so I _____ when I _____
→ *I have trouble **remembering people's names**, so I **have to concentrate** when I **first meet someone.***

I wanted to _____. Nevertheless, I _____ because _____
→ *I wanted to **go to Chicago**. Nevertheless, I **stayed home** because **I had to study for final exams.***

1. _____ sore throat. Nevertheless, _____.

2. I _____. My _____, on the other hand, _____.

3. When a small, black insect _____, I _____ because _____.

4. I _____ because _____. However, _____.

5. Even though I told _____ that _____, _____.

6. According to the newspaper, now that _____. Therefore, _____.

7. Since neither the man who _____ nor _____, I _____.

8. _____, but in the event that _____, _____.

9. When people who _____, _____ because _____.

10. Since I didn't know whose _____, I _____.

11. Even though the book which _____, I _____.

12. What did the woman who _____ when you _____?

◇ PRACTICE 27—GUIDED STUDY: Giving examples. (Chart 9-11)

Directions: Add examples to the given sentences.

1. Countries such as _____ have large uninhabited areas. Other countries, such as _____, are densely populated.

2. Animals such as _____ make good house pets, but others such as _____ do not.

3. Colors that are bright and gaudy, such as _____, are best to wear when you want to stand out in a crowd. If you want to keep a low profile, however, colors such as _____ are more appropriate.

4. Hard metals and alloys such as _____ are used to produce exceptionally strong objects, while softer metals such as _____ are often shaped into jewelry or works of art.

5. Some things that we read, such as _____, engage our minds and make us think. Other things we read, however, such as _____, are strictly for entertainment.

6. There are many ways in which Paul could improve his health. For example, _____
_____.

7. Some television programs are educational, for example, _____.

8. We could get a fun gift for Anna on her birthday, something that would really surprise and delight her. For example, _____. Being a student, however, Anna would probably prefer something useful, such as _____.

9. An adjective (e.g., _____) usually describes a noun, but an adverb (e.g., _____) usually describes the action of a verb.

10. Some English words have the same pronunciation but different spelling, e.g., _____
_____.

◇ PRACTICE 28—SELFSTUDY: Continuing the same idea. (Chart 9-12)

Directions: Add *moreover/in addition/furthermore* where appropriate.

1. Government money is essential to successful research at our university. For example, much of the research in the medical school is funded by government grants. Such departments as physics, chemistry, computer science, and engineering now rely increasingly on government funding.

→ *Government money is essential to successful research at our university. For example, much of the research in the medical school is funded by government grants.* **Moreover/In addition/Furthermore,** *such departments as physics, chemistry, computer science, and engineering now rely increasingly on government funding.*

2. Applicants for the position must fulfill certain requirements. They need a college degree and two years' experience in the field. They must have computer skills. Two letters of recommendation should be submitted along with the application.

3. There are several reasons why I write in my diary every day. Writing a diary allows me to reflect on a day's events and their meanings. As the Greek philosopher Plato said, "A life that is unexamined is not worth living." I like the idea of keeping a record of my life to share with my children at a later date. Writing in a diary is calming. It forces me to take time out of my busy day to rest and think quiet thoughts.

4. If you are interested in the arts, you should come to visit my city, Montreal. Montreal is a leading cultural center in North America. You can go to the Museum of Fine Arts to see displays of works by Canadian artists, past and present. Montreal has a world-famous symphony orchestra. It has numerous theaters. One of them, the International Theater, performs plays in several languages.

Directions: The following passages are taken from student writing. Pretend you are the editor for these students. Rewrite the passages. Correct any errors and make whatever revisions in phrasing or vocabulary you feel will help the writers say what they intended to say.

Example:

My idea of the most important thing in life. It is to be healthy. Because a person can't enjoy life without health.

→ *In my opinion, the most important thing in life is good health, for a person cannot enjoy life fully without it.*

1. We went shopping after ate dinner. But the stores were closed. We had to go back home even we hadn't found what were we looking for.

2. I want explain that I know alot of grammars but is my problem I haven't enough vocabularies.

3. When I got lost in the bus station a kind man helped me, he explained how to read the huge bus schedule on the wall. Took me to the window to buy a ticket and showed me where was my bus, I will always appreciate his kindness.

4. I had never understand the important of know English language. Until I worked at a large international company.

5. Since I was young my father found an American woman to teach me and my brothers English, but when we move to other town my father wasn't able to find other teacher for other five years.

6. I was surprised to see the room that I was given at the dormitory. Because there aren't any furniture, and dirty.

7. When I met Mr. Lee for the first time, we played ping pong at the student center even though we can't communicate very well, but we had a good time.

8. Because the United States is a large and also big country. It means that there're various kinds of people live there and it has a diverse population.

9. My grammar class was start at 10:35. When the teacher was coming to class, she returned the last quiz to my classmates and I. After we have had another quiz.

10. The first time I went skiing. I was afraid to go down the hill. But somewhere from a little corner of my head kept shouting, "why not! Give it a try. You'll make it!" After stand around a couple of more minutes with my index finger in my mouth. Finally, I decided to go down that hill.

11. If a wife has a work, her husband should share the houseworks with her. If both of them help, the houseworks can be finish much faster.

12. This is a story about a man who had a big garden. One day he was sleeping in his garden. Then he woke up and he ate some fruit. Then he picked some apples and he walked to a small river and he saw a beautiful woman was on the other side. And he gave her some apples and then she gave him a loaf of bread. The two of them walked back to the garden. Then some children came and were playing games with him. Everyone was laughing and smiling. Then

one child destroyed a flower and the man became angry and he said to them, "Get out of here." Then the children left and the beautiful woman left. Then the man built a wall around his garden and would not let anyone in. He stayed in his garden all alone for the rest of his life.

◇ **PRACTICE TEST A—SELFSTUDY: Showing relationships between ideas. (Chapter 9)**

Directions: Choose the best completion.

Example:
___**C**___ *I heard the telephone ring, I didn't answer it.*
    A. *Because*   B. *Only if*   C. *Even though*   D. *Provided that*

1. _____ the salary meets my expectations, I will accept the job offer.
    A. Due to   B. Even if   C. Provided that   D. Unless

2. To power their inventions, people have made use of natural energy sources, _____ coal, oil, water, and steam.
    A. in addition to   B. as   C. and they use   D. such as

3. _____ excellent art museums, Moscow has a world-famous ballet company.
    A. Because of   B. In spite of   C. In case of   D. In addition to

4. It is still a good idea to know how to type. _____ the many technological advances in typewriters and word processors, a skilled operator remains indispensable.
    A. Because of   B. In spite of   C. In case of   D. In addition to

5. Even though a duck may live on water, it stays dry _____ the oil on its feathers. The oil prevents the water from soaking through the feathers and reaching its skin.
    A. due to   B. besides   C. in spite of   D. in the event of

6. Alex cannot express himself clearly and correctly in writing. He will never advance in his job _____ he improves his language skills.
    A. otherwise   B. if   C. only if   D. unless

7. _____ there was no electricity, I was able to read because I had a candle.
    A. Unless   B. Even though   C. Even   D. Only if

8. A fire must have a readily available supply of oxygen. _____, it will stop burning.
    A. Consequently   B. Furthermore   C. Otherwise   D. However

9. I studied Spanish for four years in high school. _____, I had trouble talking with people when I was traveling in Spain.
    A. Therefore   B. On the other hand   C. Moreover   D. Nevertheless

10. I'm sorry you've decided not to go with us on the river trip, but _____ you change your mind, there will still be enough room on the boat for you.
    A. even   B. nevertheless   C. in the event that   D. provided that

11. I like to keep the windows open at night no matter how cold it gets. My wife, _____, prefers a warm bedroom with all windows tightly shut.
    A. nevertheless   B. consequently   C. on the other hand   D. moreover

12. Some fish can survive only in salt water, _____ other species can live only in fresh water.
    A. whereas   B. unless   C. if   D. since

13. _____ Jason became famous, he has ignored his old friends. He shouldn't do that.
    A. If   B. Ever since   C. Even though   D. Due to

14. We're going to lose this game _____ the team doesn't start playing better soon.
    A. if   B. unless   C. although   D. whereas

15. My two children are cooking dinner for the family for the first time tonight. _____ the food is terrible, I'm going to enjoy this meal very much. It will be fun to have them cook for me for a change.
    A. Only if   B. If   C. Even if   D. Provided that

16. Jack insisted that he didn't need any help, _____ I helped him anyway.
    A. and   B. so   C. besides   D. but

17. Florida is famous for its tourist attractions. Its coastline offers excellent white sand beaches. _____, it has warm, sunny weather.
    A. Otherwise   B. Furthermore   C. Nevertheless   D. On the other hand

18. The flowers will soon start to bloom _____ winter is gone and the weather is beginning to get warmer.
    A. even if   B. now that   C. so   D. even though

19. Only if you promise to study hard _____ to tutor you.
    A. will I agree   B. agree I   C. I agree   D. I will agree

20. Camels have either one hump or two humps. The Arabian camel has one hump. The Bactrian camel, _____, has two humps.
    A. nevertheless   B. however   C. furthermore   D. otherwise

◇ **PRACTICE TEST B—GUIDED STUDY: Showing relationships between ideas. (Chapter 9)**

Directions: Choose the best completion.

Example:
    __C__ *I heard the telephone ring, I didn't answer it.*
    A. *Because*   B. *Only if*   C. *Even though*   D. *Provided that*

1. Mr. Jackson hopes to avoid surgery. He will not agree to the operation _____ he is convinced that it is absolutely necessary.
    A. in the event that   B. unless   C. if   D. only if

2. Some English words have the same pronunciation _____ they are spelled differently, for example, *dear* and *deer*.
    A. unless   B. even though   C. since   D. only if

3. Olives are a principal source of cooking oil, but by no means the only source. _____ olives, cooking oil can be extracted from coconuts, corn, and sunflower seeds.
    A. Because of   B. In spite of   C. In case of   D. In addition to

4. I couldn't use the pay phone, _____ I didn't have any coins with me.
    A. yet   B. despite   C. for   D. even though

5. I have to eat beakfast in the morning. _____, I get grouchy and hungry before my lunch break.
    A. Consequently   B. Furthermore   C. Otherwise   D. However

6. I need to find an apartment before I can move. _____ I can find one in the next week or so, I will move to Chicago the first of next month.
    A. Provided that B. Even if   C. Due to   D. Only if

7. Tom is trying to reduce the amount of fat he eats. Red meat is high in fat. Tom eats a lot of fish but avoids red meat _____ its high fat content.
    A. in the event of   B. besides   C. in spite of   D. because of

8. _____ want to take a train trip across western Canada, but my traveling companion wants to fly to Mexico City for our vacation.
    A. Although I   B. Even if I   C. I   D. Nevertheless I

9. Ms. Moore, the school counselor, has had years of experience dealing with student problems. _____, she is sometimes confronted by a problem that she cannot handle by herself.
     A. Therefore   B. Nevertheless   C. Otherwise   D. On the other hand

10. Right now all the seats on that flight are taken, sir. _____ there is a cancellation, I will call you.
     A. In the event that   B. Nevertheless   C. But   D. Even if

11. A newborn baby can neither walk nor crawl. A newborn antelope, _____, can run within minutes of birth.
     A. however   B. nevertheless   C. otherwise   D. even though

12. You must obey the speed limits on public roads. They are designed to keep you safe. You shouldn't exceed the speed limit _____ you are an experienced race car driver.
     A. only if   B. even if   C. if   D. provided that

13. My nose got sunburned _____ I wore a hat with a wide brim to shade my face.
     A. if   B. since   C. because   D. even though

14. Do you like jazz? You should go to the jazz festival _____ you like that kind of music.
     A. if   B. unless   C. although   D. while

15. Peter works hard at everything he does. His brother, _____, seldom puts out much effort.
     A. on the other hand   B. otherwise   C. furthermore   D. consequently

16. I don't understand why, but my neighbor Mr. Morrow doesn't seem to like me. He never smiles at me or speaks to me _____ the many efforts I have made to be friendly and neighborly.
     A. because of   B. in spite of   C. in case of   D. in addition to

17. The festival has many attractions. It will include contemporary orchestral music and an opera. _____, there will be poetry readings and theatrical presentations.
     A. Otherwise   B. Furthermore   C. Nevertheless   D. On the other hand

18. The bread was old and stale, _____ Martha ate it anyway.
     A. and   B. so   C. besides   D. but

19. Minerals _____ nickel, copper, and zinc can be found in sea water.
     A. as examples   B. such as   C. in an example   D. as

20. Only if you get to the theater early _____ a chance to get a ticket for tonight's performance.
     A. you will have   B. have   C. you have   D. will you have

CHAPTER *10*
Conditional Sentences

◇ **PRACTICE 1—SELFSTUDY: Conditional sentences. (Charts 10-1 → 10-4)**

Directions: Answer the questions about each conditional sentence with "yes" or "no".

1. *If the weather had been good yesterday, our picnic would not have been canceled.*
    a. Was the picnic canceled? _____**yes**_____
    b. Was the weather good? _____**no**_____

2. *If I had an envelope and a stamp, I would mail this letter right now.*
    a. Do I have an envelope and a stamp right now? _____
    b. Do I want to mail this letter right now? _____
    c. Am I going to mail this letter right now? _____

3. *Ann would have made it to class on time this morning if the bus hadn't been late.*
    a. Did Ann try to make it to class on time? _____
    b. Did Ann make it to class on time? _____
    c. Was the bus late? _____

4. *If I were a carpenter, I would build my own house.*
    a. Do I want to build my own house? _____
    b. Am I going to build my own house? _____
    c. Am I a carpenter? _____

5. *If the hotel had been built to withstand an earthquake, it would not have collapsed.*
    a. Was the hotel built to withstand an earthquake? _____
    b. Did the hotel collapse? _____

6. *If I didn't have any friends, I would be lonely.*
    a. Am I lonely? _____
    b. Do I have friends? _____

7. *If Bob had asked me to keep the news a secret, I wouldn't have told anybody.*
    a. Did I tell anybody the news? _____
    b. Did Bob ask me to keep it a secret? _____

8. *If Thomas had sold his car, he would have to take the subway to work every morning.*
    a. Does Thomas have a car? _____
    b. Does he take the subway to work? _____

9. *If Ann and Jan, who are twins, dressed alike and had the same hairstyles, I wouldn't be able to tell them apart.*
   a. Do Ann and Jan dress alike? _____
   b. Do they have the same hairstyles? _____
   c. Can I tell them apart? _____

◇ **PRACTICE 2—SELFSTUDY: Conditional sentences, present/future. (Charts 10-2 and 10-3)**

Directions: Complete the sentences with the correct form of the verbs in parentheses. Some of the sentences are "contrary to fact" and some are not.

1. I am not an astronaut. If I (be) _____**were**_____ an astronaut, I (take) _____**would**_____ _____**take**_____ my camera with me on the rocket ship next month.

2. Most people know that oil floats on water. If you pour oil on water, it (float)_____**floats/**_____ _____**will float**_____ .

3. If there (be) _____ no oxygen on earth, life as we know it (exist, not) _____ .

4. My evening newspaper has been late every day this week. If the paper (arrive, not) _____ on time today, I'm going to cancel my subscription.

5. If I (be) _____ a bird, I (want, not) _____ to live in a cage.

6. Sea water is salty. If the oceans (consist) _____ of fresh water, there (be) _____ plenty of water to irrigate all of the deserts in the world to provide an abundant food supply for the entire population of the earth.

7. It is expensive to call across the ocean. However, if transoceanic telephone calls (be) _____ cheap, I (call) _____ my family every day and (talk) _____ for hours.

8. Tom's hobby is collecting stamps from all over the world. If he (travel) _____ to a new country, he (spend, always) _____ time looking for new stamps. That's how he has acquired such a large collection of valuable stamps.

9. How old (live, human beings) _____ to be if all diseases in the world (be) _____ completely eradicated?

10. If you boil water, it (disappear) _____ into the atmosphere as vapor.

11. If people (have) _____ paws instead of hands with fingers, the machines we use in every day life (have to) _____ be constructed very differently. We (be, not) _____ able to turn knobs, push small buttons, or hold tools or utensils securely.

Directions: Complete the sentences with the words in parentheses. All of the sentences to complete are "contrary to fact."

1. I'm sorry you had to take a cab to the airport. I didn't know you needed a ride. If you (*tell*)
   _____**had told**_____ me, I (*give*) _____**would have given**_____ you a ride gladly.

2. You made a lot of unnecessary mistakes in your composition. If you (*use*) _____
   a dictionary to check your spelling, you (*receive*) _____ a better grade.

3. A: Shh! Your father is taking a nap. Oh-oh. You woke him up.

   B: Gee, I'm sorry, Mom. If I (*realize*) _____ he was sleeping, I (*make*,

   not) _____ so much noise when I came in. But how was I supposed to

   know?

4. Many people were not satisfied with the leader after he took office. If they (*know*)

   _____ more about his planned economic programs, they (*vote, not*)

   _____ for him.

5. Last night Alex ruined his sweater when he washed it. If he (*read*) _____ the

   label, he (*wash, not*) _____ it in hot water.

6. A: Ever since I broke my foot, I haven't been able to get down to the basement to wash my

   clothes.

   B: Why didn't you say something? I (*come*) _____ over and (*wash*)

   _____ them for you if you (*ask*) _____ me.

   A: I know you (*come*) _____ right away if I (*call*)

   _____ you. I guess I just didn't want to bother you.

   B: Nonsense! What are good neighbors for?

7. A: Oh, no! I've lost it!

    B: Lost what?

    A: The address for my job interview this afternoon. I wrote it on a match book.

    B: A match book! If you (*write*) _____ the address in your appointment book where it belongs, you (*lose, not*) _____ it. When are you going to get organized?

8. A: Ann, (*you, take*) _____ that job if you (*know*) _____ that you had to work nights?

    B: No way. I had no idea I'd have to work the late night hours they've had me working.

◇ **PRACTICE 4—SELFSTUDY: Conditional sentences. (Charts 10-1 → 10-4)**

  Directions: Complete the sentences with the words in parentheses.

1. If I (*have*) _____ wings, I (*have to, not*) _____ take an airplane to fly home.

2. This letter has got to be in Chicago in two days. I'm sure if I (*send*) _____ it today, it will arrive in time.

3. Hundreds of people became ill from eating contaminated meat during the last two weeks. If the government had responded more quickly to the crisis, fewer people (*suffer*) _____ _____ food poisoning.

4. (*People, be*) _____ able to fly if they (*have*) _____ feathers instead of hair?

5. What (*we, use*) _____ to look at ourselves when we comb our hair in the morning if we (*have, not*) _____ mirrors?

6. A: I don't understand anything in this class. It's boring. And I'm getting a failing grade.

    B: If I (*feel*) _____ the way you do about it, I (*drop*) _____ _____ the class as soon as possible.

7. It's been a long drought. It hasn't rained for over a month. If it (*rain, not*) _____ _____ soon, a lot of crops (*die*) _____. If the crops (*die*) _____, many people (*go*) _____ hungry this coming winter.

8. I didn't know the Newtons were going to bring two other people to dinner last night. If anyone else (*bring*) _____ extra guests, we (*have, not*) _____ _____ enough seats at the table.

9. If television (*invent*) _____ in the eighteenth century, George Washington (*interview*) _____ regularly on the evening news.

10. A: I'm exhausted, and we're no closer to a solution to this problem after nine hours of work.

    B: Why don't you go home and get some sleep, and I'll keep working. If I (*discover*)

    _____ a solution before morning, I (*call*) _____

    you immediately. I promise.

11. A: I can't believe that you haven't finished that report. What will I use in the committee

    meeting at noon today?

    B: I'm really sorry. If I (*know*) _____ you needed it today, I (*stay up*)

    _____ all night last night and (*finish*) _____ it.

12. According to one scientific theory, an asteroid collided with the earth millions of years ago,

    causing great changes in the earth's climate. Some scientists believe that if this asteroid

    (*collide, not*) _____ with the earth, the dinosaurs (*become, not*) _____

    _____ extinct. Can you imagine what the world (*be*) _____

    like today if dinosaurs (*exist, still*) _____? Do you think it (*be*) _____

    possible for dinosaurs and human beings to coexist on the same planet?

◇ **PRACTICE 5—SELFSTUDY: Conditional sentences. (Charts 10-1 → 10-4)**

Directions: Use the given information to make conditional sentences. Use *if*.

1. I was sick yesterday, so I didn't go to class.
   → *If I hadn't been sick yesterday, I would have gone to class.*
2. Because Alan never eats breakfast, he always overeats at lunch.
   → *If Alan ate breakfast, he wouldn't overeat at lunch.*
3. Peter didn't finish unloading the truck because John didn't help him.
4. Jack was late to his own wedding because his watch was ten minutes slow.
5. I don't ride the bus to work every morning because it's always so crowded.
6. I didn't bring extra money with me because you didn't tell me we were going to dinner after
   the movie.
7. Sam didn't know that highway 57 was closed, so he didn't take an alternative route.
8. Because I lost my key, I had to pound on the door to wake my roommate when I got home last
   night.

◇ **PRACTICE 6—GUIDED STUDY: Conditional sentences. (Charts 10-1 → 10-4)**

Directions: Make an "*if* clause" from the given information and then supply a "*result* clause" using
your own words.

Example:
   I wasn't late to work yesterday.
   → *If I had been late to work yesterday, I would have missed the regular morning meeting.*

   Tom asked my permission before he took my bicycle.
   → *If Tom hadn't asked my permission before he took my bicycle, I would have been angry.*

1. I wasn't absent from class yesterday.
2. I don't have enough energy today.
3. Ocean water is salty.

4. Our teacher likes his/her job.

5. I don't know how to swim.

6. You didn't ask for my opinion.

7. Water is heavier than air.

8. Most nations support world trade agreements.

◇ **PRACTICE 7—GUIDED STUDY: Conditional sentences. (Charts 10-1 → 10-4)**

Directions: Make a true statement about the given topic. Then make a contrary-to-fact conditional sentence about that statement.

Examples:
> yourself → *I am twenty years old. If I were seventy years old, I would already have lived most of my life.*
> ice → *Ice doesn't sink. If the polar ice caps sank, the level of the oceans would rise and flood coastal cities.*

Topics:

1. yourself	5. peace	9. your activities right now
2. fire	6. vegetables	10. your activities last night
3. a member of your family	7. air	11. dinosaurs
4. a famous person	8. a member of this class	12. space travel

◇ **PRACTICE 8—SELFSTUDY: Using progressive forms and mixed time in conditional sentences. (Charts 10-5 and 10-6)**

Directions: Using the given information, complete the conditional sentences.

1. It is raining, so we won't finish the game.
   → If it _____**weren't raining**_____, we _____**would finish**_____ the game.

2. I didn't eat lunch and now I'm hungry.
   → If I _____**had eaten**_____ lunch, I _____**wouldn't be**_____ hungry now.

3. Bob left his wallet at home this morning, and now he doesn't have any money for lunch.
   → If Bob _____ his wallet at home this morning, he _____
   _____ some money for lunch now.

4. Carol didn't answer the phone because she was studying.
   → Carol _____ the phone if she _____.

5. The sun was shining, so we went to the beach yesterday.
   → If the sun _____, we _____ to the beach yesterday.

6. Every muscle in my body aches today because I played basketball for three hours last night.
   → Every muscle in my body _____ today if I _____
   _____ basketball for three hours last night.

7. Barry stops to shake everyone's hand because he's running for political office.
   → Barry _____ to shake everyone's hand if he _____
   _____ for political office.

8. We didn't eat all of the turkey at dinner last night, so we have to have turkey again tonight.

→ If we _____ all of the turkey at dinner last night, we

_____ turkey again tonight.

9. The music was playing loudly at the restaurant, so I didn't hear everything Mr. Lee said during dinner.

→ If the music _____ loudly, I _____ everything Mr. Lee said during dinner.

10. The library is closing now, so we'll have to leave before finishing our research.

→ If the library _____ now, we _____ before finishing our research.

◇ **PRACTICE 9—SELFSTUDY:** Using progressive forms and mixed time in conditional sentences. (Charts 10-5 and 10-6)

Directions: Using the given information, make conditional sentences. Use *if*.

1. The wind is blowing hard, so I won't take the boat out for a ride.
   → *If the wind weren't blowing hard, I would take the boat out for a ride.*

2. I feel better now because you talked to me about my problems last night.
   → *I wouldn't feel better now if you hadn't talked to me about my problems last night.*

3. Gary carried heavy furniture when he helped Ann move. His back hurts now.

4. Paul is working on two jobs right now, so he doesn't have time to help you with your remodeling.

5. I wasn't working at the restaurant last night. I didn't wait on your table.

6. Because Diane asked questions every time she didn't understand a problem, she has a good understanding of geometry now.

7. A bulldozer was blocking the road, so we didn't arrive on time.

8. She is exhausted today because she didn't get any sleep last night.

9. They weren't paying attention, so they didn't see the sign marking their exit from the highway.

10. The doctor doesn't really care about his patients. He didn't explain the medical procedure to me before surgery.

◇ **PRACTICE 10—GUIDED STUDY:** Using *could, might,* and *should* in conditional sentences. (Chart 10-7)

Directions: Complete the following conditional sentences.

Examples:
Ann could have . . . if . . . .
→ *Ann could have made it to class on time if the bus hadn't been late.*

I might have helped . . . if . . . .
→ *I might have helped you if you had asked me earlier.*

If you should need . . . please . . . .
→ *If you should need more information, please give me a call.*

1. The situation might improve if . . . .
2. If anyone should get injured during the race . . . .
3. I couldn't have fixed the bicycle if . . . .
4. Mr. Swanson might have hired you for the summer if . . . .
5. If you should arrive at the meeting before I do . . . .
6. Some of the research might have been lost if . . . .
7. It looks like the catastrophe could have been avoided if . . . .
8. We could still get out of this mess if . . . .
9. If you should happen to . . . please . . . .
10. I might have . . . if I had . . . .
11. All things considered, I might not have succeeded if . . . .
12. . . . could have avoided the problem if . . . .
13. If your car should break down on the highway . . . .
14. I might understand your problem better if . . . .
15. You could have gotten the job if . . . .
16. . . . could have . . . if she had . . . .
17. If I could . . . I would . . . .
18. If I could have . . . I would have . . . .

◇ **PRACTICE 11—SELFSTUDY: Omitting *if*. (Chart 10-8)**

Directions: Make sentences with the same meaning by omitting ***if***.

1. *If you should need* more money, go to the bank before six o'clock.

    → _____***Should you need***_____ more money, go to the bank before six o'clock.

2. *If I were* you, I wouldn't do that.

    → _____***Were I***_____ you, I wouldn't do that.

3. *If they had realized* the danger, they would have done it differently.

    → _____***Had they realized***_____ the danger, they would have done it differently.

4. *If Alan had tried* to explain, I'm sure the professor would have given him another chance.

    → _____ to explain, I'm sure the professor would have given him another chance.

5. *If anyone should call*, would you please take a message?

    → _____, would you please take a message?

6. *If I were* your teacher, I would insist you do better work.

    → _____ your teacher, I would insist you do better work.

7. *If everyone had arrived* on time, none of these problems would have occurred.

    → _____ on time, none of these problems would have occurred.

8. *If the post office should close* before I get there, I'll mail your package in the morning.

    → _____ before I get there, I'll mail your package in the morning.

9. *If I had not opened* the door when I did, I wouldn't have seen you walk by.

→ _____ the door when I did, I wouldn't have seen you walk by.

10. *If she were* just a little older, I would start giving her driving lessons.

→ _____ just a little older, I would start giving her driving lessons.

11. *If you should change* your mind, please let me know immediately.

→ _____ your mind, please let me know immediately.

12. She would have gotten the job *if she had been* better prepared.

→ She would have gotten the job _____ better prepared.

◇ **PRACTICE 12—GUIDED STUDY: Omitting *if*. (Chart 10-8)**

Directions: Make sentences with the same meaning by omitting *if*.

1. If I were your age, I'd do things differently.
   → *Were I your age, I'd do things differently.*

2. If they had asked, I'd have had to tell them.
   → *Had they asked, I'd have had to tell them.*

3. If she were ever in trouble, I'd do anything I could to help her.

4. If Bob should show up, please give him my message.

5. If my uncle had stood up to sing, I'd have been embarrassed.

6. If you should hear the fire alarm, leave the building at once.

7. If I were the greatest scientist in the world, I still wouldn't be able to figure this out.

8. If you hadn't lent Jason your car, none of this would have happened.

9. If the president should question these figures, have him talk to the bookkeeper.

10. If my roommate had not mentioned your visit, I wouldn't have known about your new job.

◇ **PRACTICE 13—SELFSTUDY: Implied conditions. (Chart 10-9)**

Directions: Using the given information, complete the implied "*if* clauses."

1. I would have walked with you, but I twisted my ankle.

→ I would have walked with you if _____ **I hadn't twisted my ankle.** _____.

2. Sara's dad would have picked her up. However, I forgot to tell him that she needed a ride.

→ Sara's dad would have picked her up _____ **if I hadn't forgotten to tell him** _____
_____ **that she needed a ride.** _____

3. I couldn't have made it without your help.

→ I couldn't have made it if _____

4. Carol: Why didn't Bob tell his boss about the problem?

Alice: He would have gotten into a lot of trouble.

→ Bob would have gotten into trouble if _____

5. I opened the door slowly. Otherwise, I could have hit someone.

→ If _____, I could have hit someone.

6. The clerk would have bagged my groceries, but the woman behind me started yelling impatiently at him to check her out.

→ The clerk would have bagged my groceries if _____

7. I wanted everyone to know about it. Otherwise, I would have asked you to keep it to yourself.

→ If _____, I would have asked you to keep it to yourself.

8. Doug would have gone with me, but his boss wouldn't give him the time off.

→ Doug would have gone with me if _____

9. I would go back to the office and get your briefcase for you. However, the building is locked.

→ I would go back to the office and get your briefcase for you if _____

10. The business would never have gotten off the ground without Marge giving us the benefit of her expertise.

→ The business would never have gotten off the ground if _____

11. Sandra drove straight to the garage when the engine started making loud noises. Otherwise, she might have ended up stranded on the side of the road.

→ Sandra might have ended up stranded on the side of the road if _____

12. The cast had wanted to celebrate after the opening night's performance. However, the director made them all stay to rehearse some troublesome parts of the play.

→ If the director _____, they would have celebrated after the opening night's performance.

◇ PRACTICE 14—SELFSTUDY: Conditional sentences. (Charts 10-1 → 10-9)

Directions: Choose the correct completion.

1. If I could speak Spanish, I _____ next year studying in Mexico.
   A. would spend   B. would have spent   C. had spent   D. will spend

2. It would have been a much more serious accident _____ fast at the time.
   A. had she been driving   B. was she driving
   C. she had driven   D. she drove

3. "Can I borrow your car for this evening?"
   "Sure, but Nora's using it right now. If she _____ it back in time, you're welcome to borrow it."
   A. brought   B. would bring   C. will bring   D. brings

4. I didn't get home until well after midnight last night. Otherwise, I _____ your call.
   A. returned   B. had returned
   C. would return   D. would have returned

5. If energy _____ inexpensive and unlimited, many things in the world would be different.
   A. is   B. will be   C. were   D. would be

6. We _____ the game if we'd had a few more minutes.
   A. might have won   B. won   C. had won   D. will win

7. I _____ William with me if I had known you and he didn't get along with each other.
   A. hadn't brought   B. didn't bring
   C. wouldn't have brought   D. won't bring

8. The lecturer last night didn't know what he was talking about, but if Dr. Mason _____, I would have listened carefully.
   A. had been lecturing   B. was lecturing
   C. would lecture   D. lectured

9. If you _____ to my advice in the first place, you wouldn't be in this mess right now.
   A. listen   B. will listen   C. had listened   D. listened

10. _____ interested in that subject, I would try to learn more about it.
    A. Were I   B. Should I   C. I was   D. If I am

11. If I _____ the same problems you had as a child, I might not have succeeded in life as well as you have.
    A. have   B. would have   C. had had   D. should have

12. I _____ you sooner had someone told me you were in the hospital.
    A. would have visited   B. visited
    C. had visited   D. visit

13. _____ more help, I could call my neighbor.
    A. Needed   B. Should I need C. I have needed   D. I should need

14. _____ then what I know today, I would have saved myself a lot of time and trouble over the years.
    A. Had I known   B. Did I know   C. If I know   D. If I would know

15. Do you think there would be less conflict in the world if all people _____ the same language?
    A. spoke   B. speak   C. had spoken   D. will speak

16. If you can give me one good reason for your acting like this, _____ this incident again.
    A. I will never mention   B. I never mention
    C. will I never mention   D. I don't mention

17. I didn't know you were asleep. Otherwise, I _____ so much noise when I came in.
    A. didn't make   B. wouldn't have made
    C. won't make   D. don't make

18. Unless you _____ all of my questions, I can't do anything to help you.
    A. answered   B. answer   C. would answer   D. are answering

19. Had you told me that this was going to happen, I _____ it.
    A. would never have believed   B. don't believe
    C. hadn't believed   D. can't believe

20. If Jake _____ to go on the trip, would you have gone?
    A. doesn't agree   B. didn't agree
    C. hadn't agreed   D. wouldn't agree

◇ **PRACTICE 15—GUIDED STUDY: Expressing conditions. (Charts 10-1 → 10-9)**

Directions: Using the given information, make conditional sentences using "*if* clauses." Make two or more conditional sentences about each of the situations described below.

Example: Jan is working for a law firm, but she has been trying to find a different job for a long time. She doesn't like her job at the law firm. Recently she was offered a job with a computer company closer to her home. She wanted to accept it, but the salary was too low.

→ *If Jan liked her job at the law firm, she wouldn't be trying to find a different job.*
→ *Jan would have accepted the job at the computer company if the salary hadn't been too low.*

1. Jim: Why don't we go to the ball game after work today?
   Ron: I'd like to but I can't.
   Jim: Why not?
   Ron: I have a dinner meeting with a client.
   Jim: Well, maybe some other time.

2. Tommy had a pet mouse. He took it to school. His friend, Jimmy, took the mouse and put it in the teacher's desk drawer. When the teacher found the mouse, she jumped in surprise and tried to kill it with a book. Tommy ran to the front of the room and saved his pet mouse. Tommy got into a lot of trouble with his teacher.

3. My brother and I rented a truck and loaded up all of my furniture to move across town. I was driving the truck. When I heard something crashing around in the back, I turned around and, at that moment, went through a red light and crashed into a police car. Repairs to the truck and police car, the fine for breaking the law, and the damage to the furniture all cost a lot of money. In short, it would have been a lot less expensive to hire professional movers to take everything to the new house.

4. My ax was broken, and I wanted to borrow my neighbor's so that I could chop some wood. Then I remembered that I had already borrowed his saw and never returned it. I have since lost the saw, and I'm too embarrassed to tell him. Because of that, I decided not to ask him for his ax.

◇ **PRACTICE 16—GUIDED STUDY: Conditional sentences. (Charts 10-1 → 10-9)**

Directions: Using the given ideas, make conditional sentences.

Examples:
rain last Saturday/go (somewhere)
→ *If it hadn't been raining last Saturday, we could have gone on a picnic.*

be a magician/make (something/someone) disappear
→ *If I were a magician, I could make rabbits disappear into thin air.*

eat properly/run out of energy
→ *If I don't eat properly during the day, I always run out of energy late in the afternoon.*

1. know the answer/tell you
2. come to my house/cook dinner
3. be a teacher/teach
4. see a dragon/(do something)
5. be no fresh water/live
6. panic/die
7. listen/understand
8. score/win

9. make reservations/request a table for four
10. bus drivers be on strike/take a taxi
11. be no electricity/cook dinner
12. live in the city/raise horses
13. ten years old again/not have to (do something)
14. be a famous author/write about (something)
15. sit next to any famous person of my choosing on an airplane/sit next to (someone)

◇ **PRACTICE 17—GUIDED STUDY: Conditional sentences. (Charts 10-1 → 10-9)**

Directions: Answer the following questions.

1. If you could have free service for the rest of your life from a chauffeur, cook, housekeeper, or gardener, which would you choose? Why?

2. If you had to leave your country and build a new life elsewhere, where would you go? Why?

3. If you had control of all medical research in the world and, by concentrating funds and efforts, could find the cure to only one disease in the next 25 years, which disease would you select? Why?

4. If you could stay one particular age for a span of 50 years, what age would you choose? Why? (At the end of the 50 years, you would suddenly turn 50 years older.)

5. You have promised to spend an evening with your best friend. Then you discover you have the chance to spend the evening with _____ (*supply the name of a famous person*). Your friend is not invited. What would you do? Why?

6. Assume that you have a good job. If your boss told you to do something that you think is wrong, would you do it? Why or why not? You understand that if you don't do it, you will lose your job.

7. If you had to choose among good health, a loving family, and wealth (and you could have only one of the three during the rest of your life), which would you choose? Why?

8. Under what conditions, if any, would you . . .
   a. exceed the speed limit while driving?
   b. lie to your best friend?
   c. disobey an order from your boss?
   d. steal food?
   e. carry a friend on your back for a long distance?
   f. not pay your rent?
   g. (*make up other conditions for your classmates to discuss*)

◇ **PRACTICE 18—SELFSTUDY: Using *wish*. (Charts 10-10 and 10-11)**

Directions: Using the information in parentheses, complete the sentences.

1. (The sun isn't shining.) I wish the sun _____*were shining*_____ right now.

2. (I wanted you to go.) I wish you _____*had gone*_____ with us to the concert last night.

3. (John didn't drive.) I wish John _____ to work. I'd ask him for a ride home.

4. (I can't swim.) I wish I _____ so that I would feel safe in a boat.

5. (I want you to stop fighting.) I wish you _____ fighting and try to work things out.

6. (I wanted to win.) I wish we _____ the game last night.

7. (Bill didn't get the promotion.) I wish Bill _____ the promotion. He feels bad.

8. (I quit my job.) I wish I _____ my job until I'd found another one.

9. (It isn't winter.) I wish it _____ winter so that I could go skiing.

10. (I want Al to sing.) I wish Al _____ a couple of songs. He has a good voice.

11. (Diane can't bring her children.) I wish Diane _____ her children with her tomorrow. They would be good company for mine.

12. (No one offered to help.) I wish someone _____ to help us find our way when we got lost in the middle of the city.

◇ **PRACTICE 19—SELFSTUDY: Using *wish*. (Charts 10-10 and 10-11)**

Directions: Complete the sentences with the words in parentheses.

1. Tom's in trouble with the teacher. Now he wishes he (*miss, not*) _____*had not missed*_____ class three times this week.

2. A: It's raining. I wish it (*stop*) _____*would stop*_____.

   B: Me too. I wish the sun (*shine*)_____*were shining*_____ so that we could go swimming.

3. A: Alice doesn't like her job as a nurse. She wishes she (*go, not*) _____ to nursing school.

   B: Really? What does she wish she (*study*) _____ instead of nursing?

4. I wish I (*move, not*) _____ to this town. I can't seem to make any friends, and everything is so congested. I wish I (*take*) _____ the job I was offered in the small town near here.

5. I know I should quit smoking. I wish you (*stop*) _____ nagging me about it.

6. A: Did you get your car back from the garage?

   B: Yes, and it still isn't fixed. I wish I (*pay, not*) _____ them in full when I picked up the car. I should have waited to be sure that everything was all right.

7. A: I wish you (hurry) _____! We're going to be late.

   B: I wish you (relax) _____. We've got plenty of time.

8. I wish you (invite, not) _____ the neighbors over for dinner when you talked to them this afternoon. I don't feel like cooking a big dinner.

9. A: I know that something's bothering you. I wish you (tell) _____ me what it is. Maybe I can help you.

   B: I appreciate it, but I can't discuss it now.

10. A: My feet are killing me! I wish I (wear) _____ more comfortable shoes.

    B: Yeah, me too. I wish I (realize) _____ that we were going to have to walk this much.

11. A: How do you like the new president of our association?

    B: Not much. I wish he (elect, not) _____. I never should have voted for him.

    A: Oh, really? Then you probably wish I (vote, not) _____ for him. If you recall, he won by only one vote. You and I could have changed the outcome of the election if we'd known then what we know now.

12. A: I wish we (buy) _____ everything we wanted all the time.

    B: In that case, you probably wish money (grow) _____ on trees. We'd plant some in the back yard, and just go out and pick a little from the branches every morning.

13. A: My thirteen-year-old daughter wishes she (be, not) _____ so tall and wishes her hair (be) _____ black and straight.

    B: Really? My daughter wishes she (be) _____ taller and that her hair (be) _____ blond and curly.

14. A: I wish most world leaders (meet) _____ in the near future and reach some agreement on environmental issues. I'm worried the earth is running out of time.

    B:. I wish I (disagree) _____ with you and (prove) _____ your fears groundless, but I'm afraid you might be right.

◇ **PRACTICE 20—GUIDED STUDY: Using *wish*. (Charts 10-10 and 10-11)**

Directions: Using the given ideas, make sentences with **wish**. Add something that explains why you are making this wish.

Examples:
   be different → *I wish my name were different. I've never liked having "Daffodil" as my first name.*
   go to the moon → *I wish I could go to the moon for a vacation. It would be fun to be able to leap long distances, given the moon's lower gravity.*

1. be different
2. know several world leaders personally
3. speak every language in the world
4. be more patient and understanding
5. interview some great people in history

6. travel by instant teleportation
7. remember everything I read
8. be a big movie star
9. read people's minds
10. be born in the last century

◇ **PRACTICE 21—SELFSTUDY:** *As if/as though.* **(Chart 10-12)**

Directions: Using the information in parentheses, complete the sentences.

1. Tim acts as if he _____ ***were*** _____ the boss. (Tim isn't the boss.)

2. This hole in my shirt looks as if it ***had been made*** by a bullet. (The hole wasn't made by a bullet.)

3. Barbara looked at me as though she _____ never _____ me before. (She has met me many times before.)

4. They treat their dog as if it _____ a child. (The dog isn't a child.)

5. She went right on talking as though she _____ a word I'd said. (She heard everything I said.)

6. You look so depressed. You look as if you _____ a friend in the world. (You have many friends.)

7. He looked right through me as if I _____. (I exist.)

8. Craig bumped the other car and then continued as though nothing _____. (Something happened.)

9. A: Have Joe and Diane ever met?
   B: I don't think so. Why?
   A: He came in and started talking to her as if they _____ old friends. (They aren't old friends.)

10. I can hear his voice so clearly that it's as if he _____ here in this room. (He isn't here in this room; he's next door.)

11. It was so quiet that it seemed as if the earth _____. (The earth didn't stop.)

12. I turned, and there she was. It was as though she _____ out of nowhere. (She didn't appear out of nowhere.)

◇ **PRACTICE 22—GUIDED STUDY:** *As if/as though.* **(Chart 10-12)**

Directions: Complete the sentences with your own words.

Examples:
When I walked into the room, I felt as though . . . .
→ *When I walked into the room, I felt as though everyone were staring at me.*

I got angry at Mary. She talked to me as if . . . .
→ *I got angry at Mary. She talked to me as if I were a small child who needed discipline.*

1. Are you tired? You look as if . . . .
2. George only recently started piano lessons, but he plays as if . . . .
3. He's not very knowledgeable on the subject, but he speaks as though . . . .
4. Richard is very confident. He walks around as though . . . .

5. This meat is terrible. It tastes as if . . . .

6. You're looking at me as if . . . .

7. Bob is extremely pale. He looks as if . . . .

8. He's acting so nonchalant, as though . . . .

9. After he got knocked over, he got up as if . . . .

10. The child innocently whistled and looked around as though . . . .

◇ **PRACTICE 23—GUIDED STUDY: Conditionals. (Charts 10-1 → 10-12)**

Directions: Complete the sentences with the words in parentheses.

TOM: What's wrong, Bob? You look awful! You look as if you (*1. run*) _____
over by a truck!

BOB: Well, you (*2. look*) _____ this bad today, too, if you (*3. have*)
_____ a day like mine yesterday. My car slid into a tree because the
roads were icy.

TOM: Oh? I was driving on the icy roads yesterday, and I didn't slide into a tree. What
happened?

BOB: Well, I suppose if I (*4. drive, not*) _____ so fast, I (*5. slide, not*)
_____ into the tree.

TOM: Icy roads and speed don't mix. If drivers (*6. step*) _____ on the gas on
ice, they're likely to spin their car in a circle.

BOB: I know! And not only is my car a mess now, but I didn't have my driver's license with me,
so now I'll have to pay an extra fine when I go to court next month.

TOM: Why were you driving without your license?

BOB: Well, I lost my wallet a few days ago. It slipped out of my pocket while I was riding the bus
to work.

TOM: What a tale of woe! If you (*7. take, not*) _____ that bus, you (*8. lose,
not*) _____ your wallet. If you (*9. lose, not*) _____
your wallet, you (*10. have*) _____ your driver's license with you when
you hit a tree. If you (*11. have*) _____ your license with you, you
(*12. have to pay, not*) _____ a big fine when you go to court next week.
And of course, if you (*13. drive, not*) _____ too fast, you (*14. run into,
not*) _____ a tree, and you (*15. be, not*) _____ in
this mess now. If I (*16. be*) _____ you, I (*17. take*) _____
it easy for a while and just (*18. stay*) _____ home where you're safe and
sound.

BOB: Enough about me! How about you?

TOM: Well, things are really looking up for me. I'm planning to take off for Florida as soon as I finish my finals. I'm sick of all this cold, rainy weather we've been having. I (*19. stay*) _____ here for vacation if the weather (*20. be, not*) _____ so bad. But I need some sun!

BOB: I wish I (*21. go*) _____ with you. How are you planning on getting there?

TOM: If I have enough money, I (*22. fly*) _____. Otherwise, I (*23. take*) _____ the bus. I wish I (*24. drive*) _____ my own car there because it (*25. be*) _____ nice to have it to drive around in once I get there, but it's such a long trip. I've been looking for a friend to go with me and share the driving.

BOB: Hey, I have a super idea. Why don't I go with you? I can share the driving. I'm a great driver!

TOM: Didn't you just get through telling me that you'd wrapped your car around a tree?

◇ PRACTICE TEST A—SELFSTUDY: Conditional sentences. (Chapter 10)

Directions: Choose the correct answer.

Example:
If I _____ you, I would get some rest before the game tomorrow.
   A. am   *B. could be*   *C. were*   *D. had been*

1. When I stopped talking, Sam finished my sentence for me as though he _____ my mind.
   A. would read   B. had read   C. reads   D. can read

2. If you _____, I would have brought my friends over to your house this evening to watch TV, but I didn't want to bother you.
   A. had studied   B. studied
   C. hadn't been studying   D. didn't study

3. I wish I _____ you some money for your rent, but I'm broke myself.
   A. can lend   B. would lend   C. could lend   D. will lend

4. If someone _____ into the store, smile and say, "May I help you?"
   A. comes   B. came   C. would come   D. could come

5. "Are we lost?"
   "I think so. I wish we _____ a map with us today."
   A. were bringing   B. brought   C. had brought   D. would bring

6. "Here's my phone number."
   "Thanks. I'll give you a call if I _____ some help tomorrow."
   A. will need   B. need   C. would need   D. needed

7. If I weren't working for an accounting firm, I _____ in a bank.
   A. work   B. will work   C. have worked   D. would be working

8. Ed invested a lot of money with a dishonest advisor, and lost nearly all of it. Now he is having serious financial problems. He _____ in this position if he had listened to some of his friends.
   A. will be   B. wouldn't be   C. will be   D. hadn't been

9. The world _____ a better place if we had known a hundred years ago what we know today about the earth's environment.
    A. will be   B. was   C. should be   D. might be

10. The medicine made me feel dizzy. I felt as though the room _____ around and around.
    A. were spinning   B. will spin
    C. spins   D. would be spinning

11. "I'm really sorry about what happened during the meeting. I felt I had no choice."
"It's okay. I'm sure you wouldn't have done it if you _____."
    A. should have   B. had to
    C. hadn't had to   D. have to

12. _____ you, I'd think twice about that decision. It could be a bad move.
    A. If I had been   B. Were I
    C. Should I be   D. If I am

13. "Was Pam seriously injured in the automobile accident?"
"She broke her arm. It _____ much worse if she hadn't been wearing her seat belt."
    A. will be   B. would have been   C. was   D. were

14. If my candidate had won the election, I _____ happy now.
    A. am   B. would be   C. was   D. can be

15. I wish Janet _____ to the meeting this afternoon.
    A. came   B. will come   C. can come   D. could come

16. I _____ you to the woman I was speaking with, but I couldn't think of her name.
    A. will introduce   B. would introduce
    C. would have introduced   D. couldn't have introduced

17. "What _____ today if you hadn't come here this weekend?"
"I guess I'd be putting in extra hours at my office."
    A. did you do   B. can you do   C. will you be doing   D. would you be doing

18. Page 12 of the manual that came with the appliance says, "_____ any problem with the merchandise, contact your local dealer."
    A. You should have   B. Do you have
    C. Had you have   D. Should you have

19. Marge walked away from the discussion. Otherwise, she _____ something she would regret later.
    A. will say   B. said   C. might say   D. might have said

20. I would never have encouraged you to go into this field _____ it would be so stressful for you. I'm sorry it's been so difficult for you.
    A. had I known   B. and I had known
    C. should I know   D. but I knew

◇ **PRACTICE TEST B—GUIDED STUDY: Conditional sentences. (Chapter 10)**

Directions: Choose the correct answer.

Example:
If I __C__ you, I would get some rest before the game tomorrow.
    A. am   B. could be   C. were   D. had been

1. Please keep your voice down in this section of the library. If you _____ to talk loudly, I will have to ask you to leave.
    A. continued   B. could continue   C. will continue   D. continue

2. Gloria never seems to get tired. I sure wish I _____ her energy.
    A. would have   B. have   C. have had   D. had

3. "Why didn't Bill get the promotion he was expecting?"
   "He may not be qualified. If he were, he _____ that promotion last year."
    A. would have been given   B. were given
    C. would be given   D. was given

4. If I could find Rob's phone number, I _____ him about the change in plans. Maybe somebody else will call him.
    A. called   B. had called   C. could call   D. will call

5. "How do you like your new apartment?"
   "The apartment itself is great, but I wish I _____ used to the constant noise from the street below."
    A. got   B. could get
    C. had gotten   D. am

6. I was very engrossed in that presentation on Australia. The video tapes were so realistic that it was as though we _____ there, driving through the outback country.
    A. were   B. have been   C. are   D. will be

7. If I _____ following that other car too closely, I would have been able to stop in time instead of running into it.
    A. wasn't   B. would have been   C. was   D. hadn't been

8. "Why aren't you going mountain climbing with the rest of us next weekend?"
   "To be honest with you, I'm a coward. If I were brave, I _____ with you."
    A. would have gone   B. would go
    C. go   D. will go

9. "Will you see Tom at lunch today? I'd like you to give him a message for me."
   "I'm not going to lunch, but if I _____ him later, I'll give him your message."
    A. should see   B. will see   C. would see   D. could see

10. I'm really sleepy today. I wish I _____ Bob to the airport late last night.
    A. didn't have to take   B. weren't taking
    C. hadn't had to take   D. didn't take

11. Hurry! We've got to leave the house immediately. Otherwise, _____ the opening ceremony.
    A. we'd miss   B. we'd have missed
    C. we miss   D. we're going to miss

12. "Why didn't you tell me you were having so many problems?"
   "I _____ you, but I figured you had enough to worry about without my problems, so I said nothing."
    A. would tell   B. would have told   C. would be telling   D. had told

13. A nation's balance of trade is considered unfavorable if it _____ more money on imports than it gains from exports.
    A. will spend   B. would spend   C. can spend   D. spends

14. Many people who live near nuclear plants are concerned. _____ go wrong, the impact on the surrounding area could be disastrous.
    A. Something would   B. Something will
    C. Should something   D. Does something

15. Had I known the carpenter was going to take three days to show up, I _____ the materials and done the work myself. It would be finished by now.
    A. will get   B. would have gotten   C. might get   D. will have gotten

16. I wish you _____ making that noise. It's bothering me.
    A. would stop   B. are going to stop   C. stop   D. can stop

17. A huge tree crashed through the bedroom roof and broke my bed and most of the other furniture. _____ in the room, I would have been killed.
   A. Should I be   B. Had I been   C. Would I have been   D. Would I be

18. If everyone _____, how would we control air traffic? Surely, we'd all be crashing into each other.
   A. can fly   B. will fly   C. flies   D. could fly

19. If the world's tropical forests continue to disappear at their present rate, many animal species _____ extinct.
   A. became   B. would have become   C. will become   D. would become

20. When my lost briefcase was returned with my year-long research results intact, I felt tremendously relieved. It was as if a huge and heavy weight _____ from my shoulders.
   A. had been lifted   B. is being lifted
   C. would be lifted   D. is lifting

APPENDIX **1**
Supplementary Grammar Units

◇ **PRACTICE 1—SELFSTUDY: Subjects, verbs, and objects. (Chart A-1)**

Directions: Find the subject (**S**), verb (**V**), and object of the verb (**O**) in each sentence.

1. The <u>politician</u> <u>supported</u> new <u>taxes.</u>
          S   V   O
2. The mechanic repaired the engine.
3. Those boxes contain old photographs.
4. The teacher canceled the test.
5. An earthquake destroyed the village.
6. All birds have feathers.

List all of the nouns in the above sentences:

   politician, taxes, _____

◇ **PRACTICE 2—SELFSTUDY: Transitive vs. intransitive verbs. (Chart A-1)**

Directions: Find the verb in each sentence. Write **VT** if it is transitive. Write **VI** if it is intransitive.

1. Mr. West <u>repeated</u> his question.
                 VT
2. Smoke <u>rises.</u>
          VI
3. The children divided the candy.
4. I sneezed.
5. A strange thing happened.
6. The customer bought some butter.
7. Our team won the game.
8. Our team won yesterday.
9. Alice arrived at six o'clock.
10. I waited for Sam at the airport for two hours.
11. They're staying at a resort hotel in San Antonio, Texas.
12. The wind is blowing hard today.
13. I agree with you.
14. I walked to the theater, but Janice rode her bicycle.

◇ **PRACTICE 3—SELFSTUDY:** Identifying prepositions. (Chart A-2)

Directions: Find the prepositional phrases in the following. Identify the preposition (**P**) and the noun that is used as the object of the preposition (**O of P**).

  1. Grasshoppers destroyed the wheat $\underset{\text{P}}{\underline{\text{in}}}$ the $\underset{\text{O of P}}{\underline{\text{field.}}}$

  2. The waiter cleared the dirty dishes from our table.

  3. I parked my car in the garage.

  4. Trees fell during the violent storm.

  5. Cowboys depended on horses for transportation.

  6. We walked to the park after class.

◇ **PRACTICE 4—SELFSTUDY:** Sentence elements. (Charts A-1 and A-2)

Directions: Find the subjects (**S**), verbs (**VT** or **VI**), objects of verbs (**O**), and prepositional phrases (**PP**) in the following sentences.

  1. $\underset{\text{S}}{\underline{\text{Alex}}}$ $\underset{\text{VT}}{\underline{\text{needs}}}$ new $\underset{\text{O}}{\underline{\text{batteries}}}$ $\underset{\text{PP}}{\underline{\text{for his camera.}}}$

  2. A $\underset{\text{S}}{\underline{\text{bomb}}}$ $\underset{\text{VI}}{\underline{\text{exploded}}}$ $\underset{\text{PP}}{\underline{\text{in the road.}}}$

  3. Sally wore her blue suit to the meeting.

  4. Jim came to class without his books.

  5. Dark clouds appeared on the horizon.

  6. Plants need a reliable supply of water.

  7. Mary filled the shelves of the cabinet with boxes of old books.

  8. We enjoyed the view of snowy mountains from the window of our hotel room.

  9. The child sat between her parents on the sandy beach. Above her, an eagle flew across the cloudless sky.

◇ **PRACTICE 5—SELFSTUDY:** Nouns, verbs, adjectives, adverbs. (Charts A-1 → A-4)

Directions: Identify the adjectives (**ADJ**) and adverbs (**ADV**) in the following sentences.

  1. A $\underset{\text{ADJ}}{\underline{\text{terrible}}}$ fire spread $\underset{\text{ADV}}{\underline{\text{rapidly}}}$ through the $\underset{\text{ADJ}}{\underline{\text{old}}}$ house.

  2. A small child cried noisily in the third row of the theater.

  3. The eager player waited impatiently for the start of the game.

  4. An unusually large crowd came to the concert.

  5. Arthur carefully repaired the antique vase with special glue.

  6. On especially busy days, the telephone in the main office rings constantly.

The above six sentences have 10 adjectives and 7 adverbs.
Count the total number of nouns in the above six sentences: _____
Count the total number of verbs in the above six sentences: _____

◇ **PRACTICE 6—SELFSTUDY: Adjectives and adverbs. (Charts A-3 and A-4)**

Directions: Complete the sentence with the correct word (*adjective* or *adverb*).

1. *quick, quickly*   We ate __quickly__ and ran to the theater.
2. *quick, quickly*   We had a __quick__ dinner and ran to the theater.
3. *polite, politely*   I've always found Fred to be a _____ person.
4. *polite, politely*   He responded to my question _____.
5. *regular, regularly*   Mr. Thomas comes to the store _____ for cheese and bread.
6. *regular, regularly*   He is a _____ customer.
7. *usual, usually*   The teacher arrived at the _____ time.
8. *usual, usually*   She _____ comes to class five minutes before it begins.
9. *good, well*   Jennifer Cooper paints _____.
10. *good, well*   She is a _____ artist.
11. *gentle, gently*   A _____ breeze touched my face.
12. *gentle, gently*   A breeze _____ touched my face.
13. *annual, annually*   Many birds migrate _____ to a warm climate for the winter.
14. *annual, annually*   Many birds fly long distances in their _____ migration to a warm climate for the winter.
15. *bad, badly*   The audience booed the actors' _____ performance.
16. *bad, badly*   The audience booed and whistled because the actors performed _____ throughout the show.

◇ **PRACTICE 7—SELFSTUDY: Midsentence adverbs. (Chart A-4)**

Directions: Put the adverb in parentheses in its usual midsentence position.

1. *(always)*   Sue ∧ takes a walk in the morning.
   (always written above)
2. *(always)*   Tim is a hard worker.
3. *(always)*   Beth has worked hard.
4. *(always)*   Jack works hard.
5. *(always)*   Do you work hard?
6. *(usually)*   Taxis are available at the airport.
7. *(rarely)*   Tom takes a taxi to his office.
8. *(often)*   I have thought about quitting my job and sailing to Alaska.
9. *(probably)*   Cindy needs some help.
10. *(ever)*   Have you attended the show at the planetarium?
11. *(seldom)*   Al goes out to eat at a restaurant.

12. *(hardly ever)*   The students are late.

13. *(usually)*   Do you finish your homework before dinner?

14. *(generally)*   In India, the monsoon season begins in April.

15. *(usually)*   During the monsoon season, Mr. Singh's hometown receives around 610 centimeters (240 inches) of rain, an unusually large amount.

◇ PRACTICE 8—SELFSTUDY: Linking verbs. (Charts A-1 → A-6)

Directions: Some of the italicized words in the following are used as linking verbs. Identify which ones are linking verbs by underlining them. Also underline the adjective that follows the linking verb.

1. Olga *looked* at the fruit. *(no underline)*

2. It *looked* fresh.

3. Dan *noticed* a scratch on the door of his car.

4. Morris *tasted* the candy.

5. It *tasted* good.

6. The crowd *grew* quiet as the official began her speech.

7. Felix *grows* tomatoes in his garden.

8. Sally *grew* up in Florida.

9. I can *smell* the chicken in the oven.

10. It *smells* delicious.

11. Barbara *got* a package in the mail.

12. Al *got* sleepy after dinner.

13. During the storm, the sea *became* rough.

14. Nicole *became* a doctor after many years of study.

15. Diana *sounded* her horn to warn the driver of the other car.

16. Helen *sounded* happy when I talked to her.

17. The weather *turns* hot in July.

18. When Bob entered the room, I *turned* around to look at him.

19. I *turned* a page in the book.

20. It *appears* certain that Mary Hanson will win the election.

21. Dick's story *seems* strange. Do you believe it?

◇ PRACTICE 9—SELFSTUDY: Linking verbs; adjectives and adverbs. (Charts A-3 → A-6)

Directions: Complete the sentence with the correct word (*adjective* or *adverb*).

1. *clean, cleanly*   The floor looks __*clean*__.

2. *slow, slowly*   The bear climbed __*slowly*__ up the tree.

3. *safe, safely*   The plane landed _____ on the runway.

4. *anxious, anxiously*   When the wind started to blow, I grew _____.

5. *complete, completely*   This list of names appears _____. No more names need to be added.

6. *wild, wildly*   The crowd yelled _____ when we scored a goal.

7. *honest, honestly*   The merchant looked _____, but she wasn't. I discovered when I got home that she had cheated me.

8. *thoughtful, thoughtfully*   Jane looked at her book _____ before she answered the teacher's question.

9. *good, well*   Most of the students did _____ on their tests.

10. *fair, fairly*   The contract offer sounded _____ to me, so I accepted the job.

11. *terrible, terribly*   Jim felt _____ about forgetting his son's birthday.

12. *good, well*   A rose smells _____.

13. *light, lightly*   As dawn approached, the sky became _____.

14. *confident, confidently*   Beth spoke _____ when she delivered her speech.

15. *famous, famously*   The actor became _____ throughout much of the world.

16. *fine, finely*   I don't think this milk is spoiled. It tastes _____ to me.

◇ **PRACTICE 10—GUIDED STUDY:**   Nouns, verbs, adjectives, adverbs, prepositions.
(Charts A-1 → A-6)

Directions: Identify each underlined word as a NOUN, VERB, ADJECTIVE, ADVERB, or PREPOSITION.

      PREP.   **NOUN**

1. <u>Through</u> the centuries, many people have confused <u>whales</u> with fish.

2. <u>Whales</u> are <u>mammals</u>, not fish. They <u>breathe</u> <u>air</u> and give live birth to their young.

3. Orca whales, which are black and white, are <u>highly</u> <u>trainable</u>. They are also called "killer whales," but trainers tell us that these whales are <u>intelligent</u> and <u>sensitive</u>. One time, a newly captured male orca <u>refused</u> to eat for a long time. <u>Finally</u>, he took a fish from the trainer. However, he didn't eat the fish <u>immediately</u>; he <u>took</u> it to another recently captured whale, a female who had also refused to eat, and <u>shared</u> it with her.

4. Some species of whales <u>dive</u> <u>deeply</u> <u>beneath</u> the <u>surface</u> of the ocean in order to feed and can stay <u>under</u> the <u>water</u> for more than an hour. All whales, however, must come to the surface <u>for</u> air.

5. Whales make the longest <u>migrations</u> known <u>among</u> mammals. Gray whales <u>swim</u> <u>from</u> the Pacific coast of Mexico, where they give birth in winter, <u>to</u> the <u>icy</u> Arctic for the summer.

6. Whales do not have vocal chords, but they can communicate <u>with</u> each other. They have a <u>wide</u> range of <u>clicks</u>, <u>whistles</u>, and <u>songs</u>. When a whale is captured in a net, other whales <u>gather</u> <u>around</u> it and <u>communicate</u> <u>through</u> the net. They follow the captured whale for long distances.

◇ PRACTICE 11—SELFSTUDY: Personal pronouns. (Chart A-7)

Directions: Choose the correct pronoun in italics.

1. Please take these papers and give   *it, them*   to Mike.

2. Tom asked Ann and   *I, me*   about the new theater.

3. Janice and   *I, me*   live in an apartment.

4. Just between you and   *I, me* , I think Tom is going to lose   *him, his*   job.

5. When a player committed a foul, the referee blew   *him, his*   whistle and pointed at   *she, her*.

6. A boa constrictor, which is a very large snake, kills   *its, it's*   victims by strangling   *it, them*.

7. People can easily send a letter to another city.   *It, They*   simply have to drop   *it, them*   into a collection box.

8. The teacher said to the students, ''Throughout the semester, please write   *your, yours*   compositions on every other line, and be sure to write   *it, them*   in ink.''

9. Both Ron and   *I, me*   are expecting some mail. Are those letters for   *he, him*   or   *I, me* ?

10. *My, Mine*   roommate and   *I, me*   have to share a bookshelf.   *She, Her*   keeps   *her, hers*   books on the top two shelves, and I keep   *my, mine*   on the bottom two shelves.

11. *Our, Ours*   house is almost the same as   *our, ours*   neighbors' house. The only difference in appearance is that   *our, ours*   is gray and   *their, theirs*   is white.

12. When I was in Florida, I observed an interesting fish-eating bird called an anhinga.   *It, they*   dives into the water and spears   *it's, its*   prey on   *it's, its*   long, pointed bill. Upon emerging from the water,   *it, they*   will toss a fish into the air and catch   *it, them*   in mid-air, swallowing   *it, them*   headfirst.   *It's, Its*   interesting to watch anhingas in action. I enjoy watching   *it, them*.

◇ PRACTICE 12—SELFSTUDY: Personal pronouns, error analysis. (Chart A-7)

Directions: Find and correct the errors in pronoun usage in the following.

1. Some North American food is very good, but I don't like most of them.

2. When we were schoolgirls, my sister and me used to play badminton after school every day.

3. If you want to pass your exams, you had better study very hard for it.

4. The work had to be finished by my boss and I after the store had closed for the night.

5. A hippopotamus spends most of it's time in the water of rivers and lakes.

6. I studied English when I was in high school. But I haven't studied it since I graduated from high school ten years ago, so I've forgotten a lot of them.

7. I looked everywhere in my room for my keys, but I couldn't find it.

8. After work, Mr. Gray asked to speak to Tim and I about the company's new policies. He explained it to us and asked for ours opinions.

9. The first person I saw when I got off the plane was my sister. My father and her had come to the airport to greet me. My father was waiting for we in his car outside the airport.

10. A child should learn to respect other people. They need to learn how to treat other people nicely, including their playmates.

11. My friends asked to borrow my car because their's was in the garage for repairs.

◇ **PRACTICE 13—SELFSTUDY:** Contractions. (Chart A-8)

Directions: Write the contraction of the pronoun and verb if appropriate. Write Ø if the pronoun and verb cannot be contracted.

1. He is (___**He's**___) in my class.

2. He was (_____Ø_____) in my class.

3. He has (___**He's**___) been here since July.

4. He has (_____Ø_____) a dog.*

5. She had (_____) been there for a long time before we arrived.

6. She had (_____) a bad cold.

7. She would (_____) like to go to the zoo.

8. I did (_____) well on the test.

9. We will (_____) be there early.

10. They (_____) in their seats over there.**

11. It is (_____) going to be hot tomorrow.

12. It has (_____) been a long time since I've seen him.

13. A bear is a large animal. It has (_____) four legs and brown hair.

14. We were (_____) on time.

15. We are (_____) always on time.

16. She has (_____) a good job.

17. She has (_____) been working there for a long time.

18. She had (_____) opened the window before class began.

19. She would (_____) have helped us if we had (_____) asked her.

20. He could (_____) have helped us if he had (_____) been there.

_____
*NOTE: **has, have,** and **had** are NOT contracted when they are used as main verbs. They are contracted only when they are used as helping verbs.
****They're, their,** and **there** all have the same pronunciation.

Directions: From the underlined sentences, make questions for the given answers. Fill in the blank space with the appropriate words. If no word is needed, write Ø.

1. *Bob can live there.*

	Question word	Auxiliary verb	Subject	Main verb	Rest of question	→	Answer
1a.	Ø	**Can**	Bob	*live*	there ?	→	Yes.
1b.	Where	*can*	Bob	*live*	Ø ?	→	There.
1c.	Who	*can*	Ø	*live*	there ? ?	→	Bob.

2. *Don is living there.*

	Question word	Auxiliary verb	Subject	Main verb	Rest of question	→	Answer
2a.	Ø		Don		there ? ?	→	Yes.
2b.	Where		Don		Ø ?	→	There.
2c.	Who		Ø		there ? ?	→	Don.

3. *Sue lives there.*

	Question word	Auxiliary verb	Subject	Main verb	Rest of question	→	Answer
3a.	Ø		Sue		there ? ?	→	Yes.
3b.	Where				Ø ?	→	There.
3c.	Who				there ? ?	→	Sue.

4. *Ann will live there.*

	Question word	Auxiliary verb	Subject	Main verb	Rest of question	→	Answer
4a.	Ø				there ? ?	→	Yes.
4b.	Where				Ø ?	→	There.
4c.	Who				there ? ?	→	Ann.

5. *Jack lived there.*

	Question word	Auxiliary verb	Subject	Main verb	Rest of question	→	Answer
5a.	Ø				there ? ?	→	Yes.
5b.					Ø ?	→	There.
5c.					there ? ?	→	Jack.

6. *Mary has lived there.*

	Question word	Auxiliary verb	Subject	Main verb	Rest of question	→	Answer
6a.					?	→	Yes.
6b.					?	→	There.
6c.					?	→	Mary.

◇ PRACTICE 15—SELFSTUDY: Yes/no and information questions. (Charts B-1 and B-2)

Directions: Make questions to fit the dialogues. There are two speakers in each dialogue: A and B. Notice in the examples that in each dialogue there is a short answer and then in parentheses a long answer. The question you create should produce those answers.

1. A: __*When are you going to the zoo?*__
   B: Tomorrow. *(I'm going to the zoo tomorrow.)*

2. A: __*Are you going downtown later today?*__
   B: Yes. *(I'm going downtown later today.)*

3. A: _____
   B: Yes. *(I live in an apartment.)*

4. A: _____
   B: In a condominium. *(Sue lives in a condominium.)*

5. A: _____
   B: Jack. *(Jack lives in that house.)*

6. A: _____
   B: Yes. *(I can speak French.)*

7. A: _____
   B: Don. *(Don can speak Arabic.)*

8. A: _____
   B: Two weeks ago. *(Olga arrived two weeks ago.)*

9. A: _____
   B: Ali. *(Ali arrived late.)*

10. A: _____
    B: The window. *(Ann is opening the window.)*

11. A: _____
    B: Opening the window. *(Ann is opening the window.)*

12. A: _____
    B: Her book. *(Mary opened her book.)*

13. A: _____
    B: Tom. *(Tom opened the door.)*

14. A: _____
    B: Yes. *(The mail has arrived.)*

15. A: _____
    B: Yes. *(I have a bicycle.)*

16. A: _____
    B: A pen. *(Alex has a pen in his hand.)*

17. A: _____
    B: Yes. *(I like ice cream.)*

18. A: _____
    B: Yes. *(I would like an ice cream cone.)*

19. A: _____

    B: A candy bar. *(Joe would like a candy bar.)*

20. A: _____

    B: Ann. *(Ann would like a soft drink.)*

◇ **PRACTICE 16—SELFSTUDY: Yes/no and information questions. (Charts B-1 and B-2).**

Directions: Make questions to fit the dialogues. There are two speakers in each dialogue: A and B. Notice in the examples that in each dialogue there is a short answer and then in parentheses a long answer. The question you create should produce those answers.

1. A: ___***How long has Pierre been living here?***___

   B: Since last September. *(Pierre has been living here since last September.)*

2. A: I need some information. Maybe you can help me. ___***Which (city) is***___
   ___***farther north, London or Paris?***___

   B: London. *(London is farther north than Paris.)*

3. A: Is that your umbrella?
   B: No.

   A: _____
   B: Jane's. *(It's Jane's.)*

4. A: I haven't seen you for weeks. How are you? _____
   B: Going to school and studying hard. *(I've been going to school and studying hard.)*

5. A: Did you call Sally?
   B: Yes, but she wasn't in.

   A: _____
   B: Her roommate. *(Her roommate answered the phone.)*

6. A: Do the villagers have tractors in the rural areas?
   B: No. They don't have any modern farm machinery.

   A: _____
   B: With oxen or water buffaloes. *(They plow their fields with oxen or water buffaloes.)*

7. A: I really like having my own computer.
   B: _____
   A: Since last December. *(I've had it since last December.)*

8. A: _____ I've never seen one quite like it.
   B: A myna. It's common in warm climates. *(That kind of bird is a myna.)*

9. A: _____
   B: I missed my bus. *(I was late for work this morning because I missed my bus.)*

10. A: Last summer we painted the outside of our house.

   B: That must have been a big job. _____

   A: About four days. *(It took us about four days.)*

11. A: Jack was late last night, wasn't he? _____

   B: At 11:30. *(He finally got home at 11:30.)*

12. A: Would you like a cup of coffee?

   B: Thanks. That sounds good.

   A: _____

   B: With cream and sugar. *(I take it with cream and sugar.)*

13. A: _____

   B: Around 250 million. *(The population of the United States is around 250 million.)*

14. A: _____

   B: The red one. *(Of those two coats, I like the red one better than the black one.)*

15. A: We spent a relaxing weekend in a small village in the mountains.

   B: _____

   A: By bus. *(We got there by bus.)*

16. A: I'm sending a letter to the consulate about the problem I'm having with my visa. _____

   _____

   B: Mr. Ho. *(You should address it to Mr. Ho.)*

17. A: _____

   B: Over 800 miles. *(It's over 800 miles from here to Los Angeles.)*

18. A: _____

   B: Ann, Susan, and Alice. *(Ann, Susan, and Alice are going to be at the meeting tonight.)*

19. A: In my country, we eat rice every day. _____

   B: About once a week. *(People in my country have rice about once a week.)*

20. A: _____

   B: Silly looking hat?! I think it's a great hat! I got it at the shopping mall. *(I got that silly looking hat at the shopping mall.)*

21. A: _____

   B: Twelve. *(There are twelve edges on a cube.)*

   A: _____

   B: Eight. *(There are eight edges on a pyramid.)*

22. A: _____

   B: To say you're sorry. *("Apologize" means "to say you're sorry.")*

23. A: I've never met Bob. _____

   B: He *has dark hair, a mustache, wears glasses, and is about average height.*

24. A: You know Ann Green, don't you? _____

   B: She's *energetic, bright, very friendly. A really nice person.*

◇ PRACTICE 17—GUIDED STUDY: Information questions. (Charts B-1 and B-2)

Directions: Make questions from the following sentences. The italicized words in parentheses should be the answer to your question.

1. I take my coffee *(black)*. → *How do you take your coffee?*
2. I have *(an English-English)* dictionary.
3. He *(runs a grocery store)* for a living.
4. Margaret was talking to *(her uncle)*.
5. *(Only ten)* people showed up for the meeting.
6. *(Due to heavy fog)*, none of the planes could take off.
7. She was thinking about *(her experiences as a rural doctor)*.
8. I was driving *(sixty-five miles per hour)* when the policeman stopped me.
9. I like *(hot and spicy Mexican)* food best.
10. *(The)* apartment *(at the end of the hall on the second floor)* is mine.
11. Oscar is *(friendly, generous, and kindhearted)*.
12. Oscar *(is tall and thin and has short black hair)*.
13. *(Ann's)* dictionary fell to the floor.
14. Abby isn't here *(because she has a doctor's appointment)*.
15. All of the students in the class will be informed of their final grades *(on Friday)*.
16. I feel *(awful)*.
17. Of those three books, I preferred *(the one by Tolstoy)*.
18. I like *(rock)* music.
19. The plane is expected to be *(an hour)* late.
20. The driver of the stalled car lit a flare *(in order to warn oncoming cars)*.
21. I want *(the felt-tip)* pen, *(not the ballpoint)*.
22. The weather is *(hot and humid)* in July.
23. I like my steak *(medium rare)*.
24. I did *(very well)* on the test.
25. There are *(31,536,000)* seconds in a year.

◇ PRACTICE 18—GUIDED STUDY: Information questions. (Charts B-1 and B-2)

Directions: Make questions from the given sentences. (Suggestion: Ask a classmate or friend to read what is written for each item. Then you, with your book closed, make an appropriate question.)

1. The teacher. The teacher opened the door. → *Who opened the door?*
2. Talking on the phone. Bob is talking on the phone. → *What is Bob doing?*
3. My friend. That letter is from my friend.
4. Mary. Mary wrote that letter.

5. My mother's. That is my mother's coat.

6. In August. Alice and John are going to get married in August.

7. Ours. Our team won, not their team.

8. Gray. Her eyes are gray.

9. Black. Her hair is black.

10. Herb tea. That kind of tea is herb tea.

11. Coffee. I usually drink coffee with my breakfast.

12. Ten minutes. It usually takes me ten minutes to eat breakfast.

13. By taxi. I got to the airport by taxi.

14. Four. I have four brothers and sisters.

15. Florida. I grew up in Florida.

16. Five hours. It takes five hours to get there by plane.

17. Historical novels. I like to read historical novels.

18. Chapters 2 and 3. The test will cover Chapters 2 and 3.

19. Because he wanted to travel around the world. Frank quit school because he wanted to travel around the world.

20. For three days. She's been sick for three days.

21. Twenty. I'm going to invite twenty people to my party.

22. This one. You should buy this camera, not that one.

23. Marie Curie. Marie Curie discovered radium.

24. Practicing asking questions. I'm practicing asking questions.

25. Great. Everything's going great.

◇ **PRACTICE 19—GUIDED STUDY:** Information questions. (Charts B-1 and B-2)

Directions: Create dialogues between A and B in which the following are the answers to questions. Make up any question that would produce the given answer.

Example:
   Next week.
   A: When are we going to have a test on this chapter?
   B: Next week.

1. Blue.
2. Two years.
3. Cold and wet.
4. The one on the red chair.
5. Chris's.
6. With two "t's".
7. Andy and Ed.
8. Two million.
9. Once a week.
10. Five blocks.
11. 1979.
12. Fine.
13. Biochemistry.
14. Reading.
15. Saudi Arabia.
    In the Middle East.
    Over twelve million.
    Islam.
    Oil.
    Riyadh.

◇ **PRACTICE 20—GUIDED STUDY:**   Asking questions. (Charts B-1 and B-2)

Directions: Pair up with another student. Together create a dialogue for the given situation in one or more of the following. One of you is Speaker A and the other is Speaker B. (Note to the student: If you don't have a partner, write dialogues as you would imagine the conversation to go.) The beginning of each dialogue is given.

1. *The following conversation takes place after class is over.*
   Speaker A, you are a student. You have a problem.
   Speaker B, you are a teacher. You try to solve the problem.

   A: Excuse me, _____. Do you have a few minutes?

   B: Certainly.

   A: I'd like to talk to you about _____.

   B: _____.

   etc.

2. *The following conversation takes place on the telephone.*
   Speaker A, you work for a travel agency.
   Speaker B, you want to take a trip.

   A: Hello. Worldwide Travel Agency. May I help you?

   B: Yes. I need to make arrangements to go to _____.

   (etc.)

3. *The following conversation takes place at a department store.*
   Speaker A, you are a salesperson.
   Speaker B, you are trying to decide whether or not to buy something.

   A: Could I help you?

   B: Yes. I'm thinking about buying _____, but _____.

   (etc.)

4. *The following conversation takes place at a job interview.*
   Speaker A, you are the interviewer.
   Speaker B, you are the interviewee.

   A: Mr./Ms. _____, isn't it?

   B: Yes.

   A: I'm Mr./Ms. _____. It's nice to meet you. Come in and have a seat.

   (etc.)

5. *Assign yourselves roles, and make up your own conversation.*

◇ **PRACTICE 21—GUIDED STUDY:**   Shortened yes/no questions. (Chart B-1)

Directions: Sometimes in spoken English, the auxiliary and the subject *you* are dropped from a yes/no question. Notice the following examples:
   (a) Going to bed now? = Are you going to bed now?
   (b) Finish your work? = Did you finish your work?
   (c) Want to go to the movie with us? = Do you want to go to the movie with us?
Find the shortened questions in the following, and then give the complete question form.

1. A: Need some help?
   B: Thanks.

2. A: Why do you keep looking out of the window? Expecting someone?
   B: I'm waiting for the mail.
3. A: You look tired.
   B: I am.
   A: Stay up late last night?
   B: Yup.
4. A: I'm looking forward to going to Colorado over spring vacation.
   B: Ever been there before?
5. A: Why are you pacing the floor? Nervous?
   B: Who me?
6. A: Want a cup of coffee?
   B: Only if it's already made.
7. A: Heard any news about your scholarship?
   B: Not yet.
8. A: Hungry?
   B: Yeah. You?

◇ PRACTICE 22—SELFSTUDY: Negative questions. (Chart B-3)

Directions: In the following dialogues, make negative questions from the words in parentheses, and determine the expected response.

1. A: Your infected finger looks terrible. *(You, see, not)* _____***Haven't you seen***_____ a doctor yet?

   B: ___***No***___. But I'm going to. I don't want the infection to get any worse.

2. A: I can't understand why David isn't here yet. *(He, say, not)* _____ _____ he would be here by 4:00?

   B: _____. Something must have delayed him. I'm sure he'll be here soon.

3. A: Did you see Mark at the meeting?

   B: No, I didn't.

   A: Really? *(He, be, not)* _____ there?

   B: _____.

   A: That's funny. I've never known him to miss a meeting before.

4. A: Why didn't you come to the meeting yesterday afternoon?

   B: What meeting? I didn't know there was a meeting.

   A: *(Mary, tell, not)* _____ you about it?

   B: _____. No one said a word to me about it.

5. A: What's the matter? Everyone else at the party seems to be having fun, but you look bored.

   (You, have, not) _____ a good time?

   B: _____. I'm thinking about going home pretty soon.

6. A: I have a package for Janet. *(Janet and you, work, not)* _____

   _____ in the same building?

   B: _____. I'd be happy to take the package to her tomorrow when I go to work.

7. A: Frank didn't report all of his income on his tax forms.

   B: *(That, be, not)* _____ against the law?

   A: _____. And that's why he's in a lot of legal trouble. He might even go to jail.

8. A: Did you know that the Missouri River is the longest river in the United States?

   B: Are you sure? *(The Mississippi, be, not)* _____

   the longest?

   A: _____. The Missouri is around 2,565 miles (4,130 kilometers) long. The Mississippi is around 2,350 miles (3,800 kilometers).

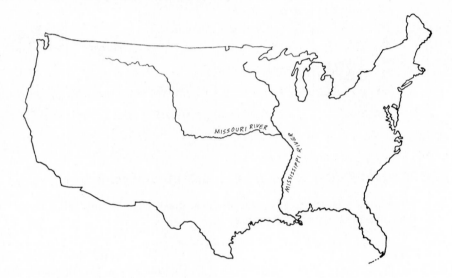

◇ **PRACTICE 23—SELFSTUDY:** Tag questions. (Chart B-4)

Directions: Add tag questions to the following.

1. You live in an apartment, ___*don't you*___?

2. You've never been in Italy, ___*have you*___?

3. Sally turned in her report, _____?

4. There are more countries north of the equator than south of it, _____?

5. You've never met Jack Freeman, _____?

6. You have a ticket to the game, _____?

7. You'll be there, _____?

8. Tom knows Alice Reed, _____?

9. We should call Rita, _____?

10. Monkeys can't sing, _____?

11. These books aren't yours, _____?

12. That's Bob's, _____?

13. No one died in the accident, _____?

14. I'm right, _____?

15. This grammar is easy, _____?

◇ PRACTICE 24—SELFSTUDY: Using *not* and *no.* (Chart C-1)

Directions: Complete the sentences with ***not*** or ***no.***

1. There are ___*no*___ mountains in Iowa. You will ___*not*___ see any mountains in Iowa.

2. Fish have _____ eyelids. They are _____ able to shut their eyes, but they do rest or sleep regularly.

3. _____ automobiles are permitted in the park on Sundays.

4. I can do it by myself. I need _____ help.

5. The operation was _____ successful. The patient did _____ survive.

6. When I became ill, I had _____ choice but to cancel my trip.

7. The opera *Rigoletto* was _____ composed by Mozart; it was composed by Verdi.

8. I have _____ patience with cheaters.

9. Ask me _____ questions, and I'll tell you _____ lies.

10. You should _____ ask people embarrassing questions about their personal lives.

11. "Colour" is spelled with a "u" in British English, but there is _____ "u" in the American English spelling ("color").

12. I excitedly reeled in my fishing line, but the big fish I had expected to find did _____ appear. Instead, I pulled up an old rubber boot.

◇ PRACTICE 25—SELFSTUDY: Avoiding "double negatives." (Chart C-2)

Directions: Correct the errors in the following sentences, all of which contain double negatives.

1. We don't have no time to waste.

   → *We have no time to waste.*   OR: *We don't have any time to waste.*

2. I didn't have no problems.

3. I can't do nothing about it.

4. You can't hardly ever understand her when she speaks.

5. I don't know neither Ann nor her husband.

6. Don't never drink water from that river without boiling it first.

7. Because I had to sit in the back row of the auditorium, I couldn't barely hear the speaker.

◇ **PRACTICE 26—SELFSTUDY: Beginning a sentence with a negative word. (Chart C-3)**

Directions: Change each sentence so that it begins with a negative word.

1. I had hardly stepped out of bed when the phone rang.

→ *Hardly had I stepped out of bed when the phone rang.*

2. I will never say that again.

3. I have scarcely ever enjoyed myself more than I did yesterday.

4. She rarely makes a mistake.

5. I will never trust him again because he lied to me.

6. It is hardly ever possible to get an appointment to see him.

7. I seldom skip breakfast.

8. I have never known a more generous person than Samantha.

◇ **PRACTICE 27—SELFSTUDY: Using articles. (Charts D-1 and D-2)**

Directions: Complete the sentences with *a/an, the,* or Ø.

1. __Ø__ lightning is __a__ flash of light. It is usually followed by __Ø__ thunder.

2. Last night we had __a__ terrible storm. Our children were frightened by __the__ thunder.

3. _____ circles are _____ round geometric figures.

4. _____ circle with _____ slash drawn through it is an international symbol meaning "Do not do this!" For example, _____ circle in _____ illustration below means "No smoking."

5. _____ milk I put on my cereal this morning was sour because someone forgot to put it in _____ refrigerator after dinner last night.

6. _____ milk is an important source of _____ protein and _____ calcium.

7. Do you ever gaze into _____ space and wonder if _____ other life forms exist in _____ universe?

8. We need to get _____ new phone.

9. Alex, would you please answer _____ phone?

10. _____ wisdom comes more from _____ understanding than from _____ knowledge.

11. I always appreciate _____ wisdom of my mother's advice.

12. In class yesterday, I sat next to two women. _____ woman on my right had _____ right answer to _____ teacher's question about verb forms.

13. Maria is _____ independent young woman who knows her own mind.

14. We flew to Dallas and then rented _____ car. On _____ second day we had _____ car, it wouldn't start, so the rental agency provided us with another one.

15. _____ people use _____ plants in _____ many different ways. Plants supply us with _____ oxygen. They are a source of _____ lifesaving medicines. We use plant products to build _____ houses and to make _____ paper and _____ textiles.

◇ **PRACTICE 28—GUIDED STUDY: Using articles. (Charts D-1 and D-2)**

Directions: Complete the sentences with *a/an, the,* or Ø.

1. Have you met Mr. and Mrs. Smith? Mrs. Smith used to be _____ teacher, but now she is _____ computer programmer. Mr. Smith is _____ architect. The Smiths used to live in _____ apartment, but recently they have built _____ house.

2. Frank Lloyd Wright is _____ name of _____ famous architect. He is _____ architect who designed the Guggenheim Museum in New York. He also designed _____ hotel in Tokyo. _____ hotel was designed to withstand _____ earthquakes.

3. When you look at _____ sandy shore, it might seem practically empty of _____ animals. This appearance is deceptive, however. Beneath _____ surface, the sand is full of _____ life. It is teeming with _____ crabs, _____ shrimp, _____ worms, _____ snails, and _____ other kinds of _____ marine animals.

4. Our children enjoyed going to the beach yesterday. When they dug in _____ sand, they found various kinds of _____ animals. Susie found _____ crab, and so did Johnny. _____ crab Johnny found pinched him, which made him cry. But he had _____ good time at _____ beach anyway.

5. The biggest bird in the world is the ostrich. It eats just about anything it can reach, including _____ stones, _____ glass, and _____ keys. It can kill _____ person with one kick.

6. In _____ recent newspaper article, I read about _____ Australian swimmer who was saved from _____ shark by _____ group of dolphins. When _____ shark attacked _____ swimmer, _____ dolphins chased it away. They saved _____ swimmer's life.

7. I heard on the radio that there is _____ evidence that _____ dolphins suffer in captivity. Dolphins that are free in _____ nature live around 40 years. Captive dolphins live _____ average of 12 years. It is believed that some captive dolphins commit _____ suicide.

8. According to today's paper, the mayor has appointed _____ committee to study what improvements need to be made in the city. _____ committee, which plans to continue its study through the rest of this year, will discuss _____ following proposals: (1) to build _____ new sewage disposal plant and (2) to create _____ new park. In _____ present proposal, _____ new park would have _____ swimming pool.

9. The large oak tree growing at _____ southeast corner of Vine Avenue and Pine Street has been _____ landmark since pioneer days. Unfortunately, it was shattered by _____ bolt of lightning during the thunderstorm last night.

10. My uncle's hobby is restoring _____ old cars. Right now he's working on _____ 1922 automobile. It's _____ antique car and has great value.

11. My aunt's new car has _____ power windows, _____ cassette player, and _____ multi-adjustable driver's seat.

12. Patty is my ten-year-old daughter. She likes to play _____ jokes on people. Yesterday she put _____ frog into _____ lunchbox she saw sitting on _____ table in _____ school lunchroom.

13. _____ most mirrors are made from _____ glass to which _____ thin layer of _____ silver or _____ aluminum has been applied.

14. Long-term exposure to _____ sun between _____ hours of 10 AM and 3 PM can be harmful. _____ person's skin will eventually become wrinkled and more susceptible to _____ cancer.

15. _____ phonograph records have become old-fashioned. They have been supplanted by _____ compact discs, which are commonly referred to as CDs.

16. Yesterday I locked my keys in my car. Using _____ coat hanger, I tried to reach _____ lock inside _____ window next to _____ driver's seat, but I couldn't get _____ door to unlock. I thought about calling _____ police, but finally decided to call my wife. I suggested she take _____ taxi and bring her keys to open _____ car for me.

17. Look. There's _____ fly walking on _____ ceiling. It's upside down. Do you suppose _____ fly was flying rightside up and flipped over at _____ last second, or was it flying upside down when it landed on _____ ceiling?

18. This sentence is _____ last sentence in this exercise. This is _____ end.

Index

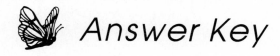 **Answer Key**

Answers to the Selfstudy Practices

To the student: To make it easy to correct your own answers, remove this answer key along the perforations and make a separate answer key booklet for yourself.

Chapter 1: VERB TENSES

◇ **1 (p. 1):**   1. do you do ... eat   2. did you do ... ate ... visited ... wrote   3. are you doing ... am talking ... am answering   4. was looking   5. have I asked ... have asked   6. have you been doing ... have been talking   7. will you be (OR: are you going to be) ... will be (OR: am going to be)   8. will you be doing ... will be sitting   9. had you done ... had eaten
10. will you have done ... will have eaten

◇ **2 (p. 2):**   1. simple present   2. simple past   3. present progresive   4. past progressive
5. present perfect   6. present perfect progressive   7. simple future   8. future progressive   9. past perfect   10. future perfect   11. past perfect progressive
12. future perfect progressive

◇ **3 (p. 4):**   1. eats   2. ate   3. will eat (OR: is going to eat)   4. am eating   5. was eating   6. will be eating   7. have already eaten   8. had already eaten   9. will have already eaten (OR: will already have eaten)   10. has been eating   11. had been eating   12. will have been eating

◇ **4 (p. 6):**

PART A	PART B	PART C	PART D	PART E
1. shouting, shouted	11. pointing	21. bothered	31. dreaming	41. combed
2. sloping, sloped	12. beating	22. blurred	32. filing	42. wrapped
3. stopping, stopped	13. betting	23. scared	33. filling	43. groaned
4. stooping, stooped	14. exciting	24. scarred	34. failing	44. occupied
5. answering, answered	15. exiting	25. feared	35. annoying	45. sprayed
6. referring, referred	16. regretting	26. starred	36. denying	46. wiped
7. returning, returned	17. attempting	27. stared	37. scrubbing	47. whipped
8. enjoying, enjoyed	18. shouting	28. ordered	38. draining	48. accepted
9. copying, copied	19. flitting	29. suffered	39. fanning	49. permitted
10. dying, died	20. interesting	30. occurred	40. interrupting	50. merited
				51. whispered
				52. inferred

◇ **5 (p. 7):** 1. isn't shining   2. own   3. am trying   4. belongs   5. sleep   6. is bleeding   7. am failing   8. shrinks   9. is biting   10. isn't blowing   11. are always fighting   12. is he screaming   13. means   14. are you whispering   15. is taping

◇ **6 (p. 8):** 1. has   2. is having   3. weighs   4. is weighing . . . needs   5. am doing . . . consists   6. am thinking . . . think   7. is looking . . . look   8. is being . . . doesn't want . . . is always

◇ **9 (p. 13):** 1. swore   2. shook   3. drew   4. burst   5. hid   6. stuck   7. slit   8. slid   9. spread   10. won   11. dug   12. bought

◇ **10 (p. 13):** 1. bit   2. clung   3. meant   4. blew   5. quit   6. felt   7. stung   8. swam   9. paid   10. caught   11. shed   12. wove

◇ **11 (p. 14):** 1. spent   2. led   3. bet   4. wept   5. upset   6. split   7. sank   8. flew   9. spun   10. rang   11. chose   12. froze

◇ **12 (p. 15):** 1. fell   2. struck   3. broadcast   4. sought   5. lost   6. dealt   7. held   8. shot   9. cost   10. swept   11. stole   12. fled

◇ **14 (p. 16):** 1. raises   2. rose   3. set   4. sat   5. lays   6. lying   7. lay   8. laid   9. hung   10. lies   11. lies

◇ **15 (p. 16):** 1. had   2. were at home having   3. was in his garage working . . . exploded . . . caused . . . lit (OR: lighted)   4. didn't see . . . was thinking . . . were you thinking   5. didn't want . . . was waiting   6. didn't hear . . . was in her room listening   7. stopped . . . fell . . . spilled   8. came . . . didn't hear . . . was in her room drying   9. served . . . went   10. looked . . . was sleeping . . . was dreaming . . . was smiling

◇ **18 (p. 18):** 1. have already eaten   2. have won   3. haven't written   4. has improved   5. hasn't started   6. have already swept   7. have you known   8. have made   9. have never ridden   10. Have you ever swum   11. has grown   12. have driven   13. has forgotten   14. has cost . . . have saved

◇ **19 (p. 19):** 1. for . . . since   2. since   3. for   4. for . . . since   5. for   6. since   7. for   8. since   9. for . . . for   10. since   11. since . . . since   12. since

◇ **20 (p. 20):** 1. knew . . . have known   2. agreed . . . have agreed   3. took . . . has taken   4. has played . . . played   5. wrote . . . has written   6. sent . . . have sent   7. has flown . . . flew   8. overslept . . . has overslept   9. has drawn . . . drew   10. has called . . . called   11. has worn . . . wore   12. has risen . . . rose

◇ **22 (p. 21):** 1. have been playing   2. has played   3. has been sleeping   4. has slept   5. haven't flown   6. have been flying   7. have been searching   8. has raised   9. has been lecturing   10. has never missed   11. have finally made . . . have chosen   12. has been driving

◇ **25 (p. 24):** 1. had already finished   2. turned on   3. had already invented   4. had burned   5. had never spent   6. stung   7. had never designed   8. helped   9. had never been   10. had flown   11. had not taught   12. had already left

◇ **26 (p. 24):** 1. went . . . had never been . . . didn't take . . . was   2. ate . . . had never eaten   3. was . . . studied . . . had never had . . . spoke . . . enjoyed   4. saw . . . did . . . Had you ever acted . . . started   5. went . . . moved . . . took . . . had arrived . . . laughed . . . invited . . . was   6. traveled . . . had never lived . . . had . . . became . . . had never lived   7. emigrated . . . had never traveled . . . settled . . . grew . . . went . . . had always wanted

◇ **28 (p. 26):** 1. had been listening to . . . have been dancing . . . singing   2. have been waiting   3. had been waiting   4. has been training   5. had been running   6. had been trying . . . has been teaching   7. has been performing   8. have been working . . . had been building

◇ **30 (p. 27):** 1. will   2. are going to   3. will   4. Are you going to . . . are going to   5. am going to   6. will   7. will   8. am going to

◇ **32 (p. 29):** 1. [when you arrive tomorrow.]   2. [After the rain stops,]   3. [before my wife gets home from work today.]   4. [As soon as the war is over,]   5. [until Jessica comes.]   6. [when the tide comes in,]

◇ **33 (p. 29):** 1. will not/are not going to return . . . get   2. gets . . . will be/is going to be   3. will lend . . . finish   4. hear . . . will let   5. isn't going to be/won't be . . . learns . . . comes . . . asks   6. returns . . . will start/is going to start   7. is going to build/will build . . . will be/is going to be . . . complete   8. will be/is going to be . . . is

◇ **35 (p. 30):** 1. am meeting   2. am taking   3. are having . . . are coming   4. am seeing   5. is picking up   6. are driving   7. is playing   8. am quitting

◇ **37 (p. 32):** 1. heals . . . will be playing   2. clear . . . will be standing   3. start . . . will be attending   4. have . . . will be shopping   5. will be attending . . . return   6. will be living . . . will be driving

◇ **38 (p. 33):** 1. will already have risen (OR: will have already risen)   2. will have been riding   3. will already have arrived (OR: will have already arrived)   4. will have been listening   5. will have smoked   6. will have been flying   7. will have saved   8. will have taught

◇ **40 (p. 34):** 1. had been   2. met   3. had missed   4. was   5. got   6. took   7. was   8. had grown   9. was   10. was wearing   11. had changed   12. was still   13. asked   14. had gained   15. had turned   16. looked   17. were

◇ **41 (p. 34):** 1. will have been   2. will meet   3. will have missed   4. will be   5. get   6. will take   7. will no longer be   8. will have grown   9. will be   10. will probably be wearing   11. will have changed   12. will still be   13. will ask   14. will probably have gained   15. will have turned   16. will look   17. will be

◇ **44 (p. 38):** 1. I **have been** studying . . . .
2. . . . to my country, I **will have been** away . . . .
3. As soon as I **graduate**, I **am** going to return . . . .
4. . . . scientists will **have** discovered the cure . . . .
5. . . . but I **haven't met** the right . . . .
6. I **have seen** that movie . . . , and now I **want** to see . . . .
7. Last night, I **had** dinner with two friends. I **have known** both of . . . .
8. I **do** not like my job . . . .   I **think** he is right.
9. . . . the teachers **have given** us . . . .
10. There **have been** fewer than . . . .   George Washington **was** the first . . . .   He **became** the president . . . .
11. . . . when he **felt** a sharp . . . .
12. . . . I **used** my key . . . .   I **tried** my key . . . .   So I **knocked** on the door . . . the door **opened**, but I **didn't see** my wife . . . .   I **had been trying** . . . .   I quickly **apologized** and **went** to . . . .

◇ **PRACTICE TEST A (p. 39):**   1. C   2. C   3. A   4. A   5. B   6. C   7. C   8. C   9. B   10. C   11. D   12. A   13. D   14. A   15. B   16. B   17. D   18. B   19. D   20. C

Chapter 2: MODAL AUXILIARIES AND SIMILAR EXPRESSIONS

◇ **1 (p. 43):** 1. C 2. C 3. C 4. B 5. C 6. C 7. C 8. C 9. C 10. C 11. C
12. C

◇ **2 (p. 44):** 1. Would you (please) hand me that book? 2. Could you (please) give me some advice about buying a computer? 3. Could I (please) borrow your wheelbarrow? 4. May I (please) have a cup of coffee? 5. Can I (please) use your bicycle tomorrow? 6. Would you (please) read over my composition for spelling errors? 7. Would you mind opening the door for me? 8. Would you mind if I left early?

◇ **3 (p. 44):** 1. opening 2. if I opened 3. taking 4. if I showed 5. drying 6. finishing
7. if I used 8. waiting 9. if I borrowed 10. if I gave

◇ **7 (p. 47):** 1. B 2. A 3. A 4. B 5. A 6. C 7. B 8. C 9. A 10. B

◇ **8 (p. 48):** 1. Do you have to . . . have to 2. had to . . . . Did you have to 3. doesn't have to
4. don't have to (OR: won't have to) 5. have had to 6. did Tom have to 7. don't have
to (OR: won't have to) 8. Did John have to 9. has had to 10. will have had to
11. Don't you have to 12. will have to (OR: is going to have to) . . . . Does she have to (OR:
Will she have to) 13. didn't have to 14. haven't had to

◇ **16 (p. 54):** 1. B 2. A 3. A 4. B 5. B 6. A 7. B 8. A 9. B 10. A 11. B
12. B

◇ **20 (p. 57):** 1. a. Fred 2. a. Jane 3. a. a rat 4. a. Mark 5. a. Janet 6. a. the breeze
b. Tom b. Don b. a cat b. my neighbor b. Sally b. Bobby
c. Alice c. Sue c. a mouse c. Carol c. Bob c. The cat
d. Ann d. Andy

◇ **21 (p. 59):** 1. may have been attending 2. shouldn't be watching 3. might have been washing
4. must be waiting 5. shouldn't have left 6. could be visiting 7. should watch
8. must have thrown 9. should be working . . . shouldn't be wasting (OR: shouldn't waste)
10. might be traveling 11. might have borrowed 12. must be playing 13. might have
been washing . . . may have already left 14. must not have been expecting (OR: must not have
expected)

◇ **24 (p. 62):** 1. used to live 2. am used to living 3. used to work 4. am used to working 5. used
to have . . . . am not used to seeing 6. used to think 7. used to take 8. is used to
flying 9. used to give 10. is used to taking

◇ **26 (p. 63):** 1. would always yell . . . would come 2. would fall . . . would throw 3. would never call
. . . wouldn't even knock 4. would always bring 5. would take 6. would always wipe
7. would tell . . . would listen 8. would drive

◇ **28 (p. 64):** 1. could stay 2. went (*could* is not possible) 3. managed to complete (*could* is not
possible) 4. finished (*could* is not possible) 5. watched (*could* is not possible) 6. could
ride 7. managed to get (*could* is not possible) 8. rode (*could* is not possible) 9. enjoyed
(*could* is not possible) 10. got (*could* is not possible) 11. could swim

◇ **PRACTICE TEST A (p. 70):** 1. B 2. D 3. D 4. A 5. B 6. B 7. D 8. C 9. D
10. A 11. D 12. C 13. C 14. D 15. C 16. A 17. D
18. C 19. D 20. A

Chapter 3: THE PASSIVE

◇ **1 (p. 74):** 1. are 2. is being 3. has been 4. was 5. was being 6. had been 7. will be 8. is going to be 9. will have been 10. has been 11. was 12. are being 13. will be 14. had been 15. will have been 16. are 17. is going to be 18. were being

◇ **3 (p. 75):** 1. was . . . discovered 2. was written 3. won't be paid 4. was refilled 5. Was . . . knocked 6. wasn't broken 7. am not impressed 8. is being taped 9. is . . . being flown 10. will be won 11. won't be influenced 12. is going to be decided 13. has been discovered 14. hasn't been taught 15. had . . . been delivered 16. was being affected

◇ **4 (p. 77):**

	VERB	OBJECT OF VERB	PASSIVE SENTENCE
1.	will pay	the bill	The bill will be paid by Al.
2.	will come	Ø	Ø
3.	supplies	towels	Towels are supplied by the hotel.
4.	happen	Ø	Ø
5.	noticed	my mistake	My mistake was noticed by everyone.
6.	arrived	Ø	Ø
7.	didn't surprise	me	I wasn't surprised by the news.
8.	Did . . . surprise	you	Were you surprised by the news?
9.	wasn't shining	Ø	Ø
10.	interrupted	my story	My story was interrupted by Ann.
11.	Do . . . exist	Ø	Ø
12.	fly	Ø	Ø
13.	Will . . . come	Ø	Ø
14.	died	Ø	Ø
15.	Did . . . throw	the ball	Was the ball thrown by Bob?
16.	laughed	Ø	Ø
17.	told	the story	The story was told by an old man.
18.	rained	Ø	Ø

◇ **5 (p. 77):** 1. You will be met at the airport by my uncle. 2. (*no change*) 3. The food will be prepared by the chef. 4. (*no change*) 5. The fire wasn't caused by lightning. 6. (*no change*) 7. The subway is ridden by thousands of people every day. 8. (*no change*) 9. (*no change*) 10. (*no change*) 11. (*no change*) 12. The dispute is going to be settled by a special committee. 13. (*no change*) 14. (*no change*) 15. (*no change*) 16. Was the enemy surrounded by the army? 17. (*no change*) 18. Windmills were invented by the Persians around 1500 years ago. (OR: Windmills were invented around 1500 years ago by the Persians.)

◇ **6 (p. 78):** 1. will be notified 2. didn't remember 3. is being restored 4. was built 5. was ruled . . . walked . . . stood 6. is visited 7. do not use 8. do not agree 9. will be invaded (OR: are going to be invaded) 10. live . . . lives 11. Had you already been accepted 12. was being followed . . . felt 13. was felt 14. died 15. is influenced 16. was stolen . . . was caught

◇ **7 (p. 79):** 1. Rice is grown in India. 2. This rug was made by my aunt. 3. My car is being fixed today. 4. French is spoken in Quebec. 5. That bridge was designed by Mr. Eads in the 1870s. 6. The wheel was invented thousands of years ago. 7. Was the telephone invented by Thomas Edison? 8. A new hospital is going to be built just outside of town. 9. How are candles made? 10. That TV show is watched by very few people. 11. Look! The seals are being fed.

◇ **9 (p. 81):** 1. (I.O. = Jack) Jack is going to be served breakfast in bed on his birthday.   2. (I.O. = Mike) Mike has been offered the opportunity to study abroad.   3. (I.O. = babysitters) Babysitters aren't paid a lot of money.   4. (I.O. = me) When I was living in Kuwait, I was taught Arabic by my neighbor.   5. (I.O. = Jason) Jason was awarded a medal for distinguished service in the military.   6. (I.O. = you) You will be sent a copy of the sales contract by the real estate office.   7. (I.O. = me) I was handed a telegram when I answered the door.   8. (I.O. = the schoolchildren) The schoolchildren are going to be given a special tour of the modern art exhibit by the director of the museum, Ms. Cynthia Hall.   9. (I.O = Mr. French) Mr. French was given a gold watch upon his retirement from the company.

◇ **10 (p. 81):** 1. will be told   2. completed   3. was assisted   4. was being ignored (*also possible*: had been ignored)   5. did you buy…didn't buy…was given.… Do you like   6. applied …was hired   7. lie…are fed   8. will probably be eroded (OR: is probably going to be eroded)   9. had already been rented   10. were introduced…were eaten…are exported …are enjoyed   11. is going to be interviewed (OR: will be interviewed)…has collected 12. is circled…are held…are circled   13. worshiped (*alternative spelling:* worshipped)

◇ **12 (p. 84):** 1. redecorated   2. threading   3. smuggled   4. dragged   5. exposed   6. scrubbing 7. wound   8. broadcast   9. shoved   10. financed   11. leaning   12. mined 13. stretched   14. bred

◇ **14 (p. 85):** 1. Pandas should be saved from extinction.   2. All traffic laws must be obeyed.   3. This broken window ought to be repaired.   4. The hotel guests should have been supplied with clean towels.   5. This garbage had better be taken to the dump soon.   6. Tomatoes can be picked before they are completely ripe.   7. The profits are supposed to be divided among the shareholders.   8. Bob's feelings must have been hurt.   9. This work has to be finished today.   10. The accident ought to have been reported to the police.   11. Bananas shouldn't be put in the freezer.

◇ **15 (p. 86):** 1. be told   2. repeated   3. be wrapped   4. forgotten   5. been discovered   6. sew 7. been replaced   8. cost   9. whisper   10. be polluted   11. be considered   12. be worn   13. be signed   14. read

◇ **17 (p. 89):** 1. are excited   2. are covered   3. is cracked   4. are exhausted   5. Are…finished 6. was insured   7. is polluted   8. is closed   9. is stuck   10. is dressed   11. am …confused   12. are buried

◇ **19 (p. 91):** 1. about   2. with   3. for   4. to   5. with   6. against   7. to   8. with   9. in 10. with   11. to   12. to   13. of   14. with   15. of   16. with   17. to…in 18. in…with   19. to…of

◇ **20 (p. 91):** 1. with   2. for   3. from   4. with   5. in   6. to   7. to   8. with   9. with 10. with   11. of   12. to   13. with   14. to   15. for   16. with   17. in…to… with   18. with…in…to

◇ **22 (p. 93):** 1. got torn   2. get broken   3. got lost   4. get hired   5. get hurt   6. was getting worried   7. got…soaked   8. get started   9. got buried   10. got stuck

◇ **24 (p. 95):** 1. (a) interesting (b) interested   2. (a) irritating (b) irritated   3. (a) tired (b) tiring 4. (a) boiling (b) boiled   5. (a) upset (b) upsetting   6. (a) confusing (b) confused 7. (a) disappointing (b) disappointed   8. (a) reassuring (b) reassured   9. (a) frustrating (b) frustrated   10. (a) disturbing (b) disturbed   11. (a) convincing (b) convinced 12. (a) moving (b) moved   13. (a) shocking (b) shocked   14. (a) depressed (b) depressing   15. (a) humiliated (b) humiliating   16. (a) intriguing (b) intrigued

◇ **25 (p. 96):** 1. Polluted   2. furnished   3. dividing   4. running   5. invited   6. elected
7. suggested   8. written   9. exhausting   10. stimulating   11. spoken   12. falling
13. Frozen   14. invading   15. thrilling

◇ **28 (p. 100):**
   1. The children were **frightened** by....
   2. Two people got **hurt** in the accident and were **taken** to....
   3. The movie was so **boring** that....
   4. The students **were** helped by....
   5. That allloy is **composed of** iron and tin.
   6. The winner of the race hasn't been **announced** yet.
   7. If you are **interested** in....   It is **fascinating.**
   8. Progress is **being** made every day.
   9. When, where, and by whom **was** the automobile **invented?**
   10. ...have always been **interested** in learning....
   11. I **do** not agree with...think you'll **ever convince** me.
   12. ...it is **accompanied** by....
   13. Arthur was **given** an award by....
   14. ...I was getting very **worried** about my son.
   15. The problem was very **puzzling.** I couldn't figure it out.
   16. Many strange **things happened** last night.

◇ **PRACTICE TEST A (p. 101):** 1. A   2. C   3. A   4. C   5. D   6. D   7. C   8. D   9. C
10. B   11. A   12. C   13. B   14. D   15. B   16. C   17. A
18. B   19. D   20. A

Chapter 4: GERUNDS AND INFINITIVES

◇ **1 (p. 105):** 1. of asking   2. to seeing   3. of washing   4. for breaking   5. from opening   6. of talking   7. like having   8. to killing   9. about finishing   10. for locking...(for) making   11. of practicing

◇ **4 (p. 106):** 1. B   2. B   3. A   4. A   5. B   6. B   7. A   8. B   9. B   10. A   11. B
12. A   13. A   14. A   15. B   16. B   17. B   18. B   19. A   20. A

◇ **5 (p. 107):** 1. asked Jim to give   2. were warned not to park   3. reminded him to brush   4. are required to wear   5. advised me to consult   6. was ordered to leave   7. are expected to complete   8. reminded my husband to buy   9. advised me to get   10. were warned not to be   11. is permitted to use   12. asked her father to buy   13. encouraged our grandfather to write   14. was ordered not to shout

◇ **7 (p. 109):** 1. B   2. A, B   3. A, B   4. A, B   5. A, B   6. B   7. A, B   8. B   9. A, B
10. A, B   11. A   12. B   13. A, B   14. A, B   15. B   16. A   17. B   18. A
19. B   20. A   21. A   22. B   23. A   24. B   25. A   26. B

◇ **9 (p. 111):** (The answers are included in the Practice.)

◇ **10 (p. 111):** 1. to refund   2. to be   3. to buy   4. throwing   5. to get   6. to wear   7. to visit
8. to be   9. thinking   10. to attend   11. to leave   12. to cut   13. to ignore
14. singing   15. avoiding   16. to count   17. painting   18. to get   19. paying
20. to keep   21. taking   22. to know   23. moving   24. to watch   25. to keep

◇ **11 (p. 113):** 1. to operate   2. to shoot   3. having   4. to go   5. getting   6. to attend   7. to come   8. to turn   9. to tell   10. practicing   11. to clean   12. reading   13. sending   14. to see   15. to go   16. taking   17. to speak   18. receiving   19. to meet   20. getting   21. staying   22. to apologize   23. to obey   24. seeing   25. to take

◇ **12 (p. 114):** 1. A   2. B   3. A   4. A   5. B   6. A   7. B   8. B   9. A   10. A   11. B   12. B   13. A   14. B   15. B

◇ **16 (p. 116):** 1. in order   2. ∅   3. ∅   4. in order   5. ∅   6. in order   7. in order   8. in order   9. ∅   10. in order   11. in order   12. ∅   13. in order   14. in order   15. in order   16. ∅   17. in order   18. ∅

◇ **18 (p. 117):** 1. very   2. too   3. too   4. very   5. too   6. too   7. very   8. too   9. very   10. very   11. very...too   12. too   13. very   14. too   15. too

◇ **19 (p. 118):** 1. B   2. B   3. A   4. B   5. B   6. B   7. B   8. A   9. B   10. B

◇ **20 (p. 119):** 1. B   2. A   3. B   4. B   5. A   6. B   7. B   8. B   9. A   10. B

◇ **21 (p. 119):** 1. B   2. D   3. A   4. C   5. B   6. A   7. B   8. C   9. B   10. D   11. A   12. A   13. B   14. B   15. D

◇ **22 (p. 120):** 1. B   2. C   3. D   4. D   5. C   6. D   7. B   8. B   9. A   10. A

◇ **23 (p. 121):**
1. My mother was angry about **my losing** (OR: **having lost**) my new watch.
2. We look forward to **their spending** their vacation with us.
3. No one can understand **Tony's failing** (OR: **having failed**) the economics test even though . . . .
4. I am upset about the **students' being required** to pay an extra fee to use the laboratory.
5. The supervisor appreciated **Mary's working** (OR: **having worked**) late to finish the project.
6. I will no longer tolerate **your being** late to work every morning.

◇ **24 (p. 121):** 1. D   2. A   3. C   4. A   5. A   6. D   7. B   8. C   9. D   10. B   11. D   12. C   13. B   14. C   15. A

◇ **26 (p. 123):** 1. practice   2. open   3. prevent   4. win   5. snoring   6. arrive   7. emerge (*also possible:* emerging)   8. perform (*also possible:* performing)   9. climb (*also possible:* climbing)   10. chirp (*also possible:* chirping)   11. explain   12. melt

◇ **28 (p. 124):** 1. C   2. A, B   3. A   4. A   5. C   6. B   7. A   8. A, B   9. A   10. A

◇ **31 (p. 125):** 1. B   2. A   3. B   4. C   5. C   6. D   7. D   8. B   9. B   10. C   11. B   12. A   13. A   14. C   15. D   16. D   17. D   18. B   19. D   20. C

◇ **32 (p. 127):** 1. to buy   2. opening   3. being asked   4. having   5. to wear...dressing   6. being allowed   7. jumping...falling   8. being taken   9. Observing...climb (OR: climbing) ...realize   10. to stop delivering...to fill   11. gazing...(in order) to cheer   12. to have been performed   13. wash...come   14. having   15. being surprised (OR: having been surprised)...planning   16. being   17. to move   18. to help...resolve (OR: to resolve) ...not to interfere   19. to be identified   20. to apply   21. to learn...to discover... promoting   22. reminding...to lock...trying to remember   23. to pick   24. meeting (OR: having met)...to be introduced   25. asking...forgetting   26. to be considered (OR: to have been considered)   27. not to sign   28. to sleep...thinking   29. notifying ...to call   30. burning...coming

◇ **34 (p. 132):**   1. Please promise not **to tell** anybody. . . .
2. I would appreciate **hearing** from you soon.
3. . . . let very young **children stay** at home alone.
4. . . . complained about **having** a handicap.
5. Mr. Lee didn't remember **to bring** his passport . . . .
6. Lillian deserves to be **told** the truth . . . .
7. Ali **doesn't** speak Spanish, and Juan **doesn't** know Arabic. But they communicate well by **speaking** English when they **are** together.
8. I enjoyed **talking** to her. . . .   I look forward to **seeing** her next week.
9. . . . everyone is required **to leave** the building.
10. **Attending** the premiere of the new . . . .
11. Don't keep **asking** me the same . . . .
12. I anticipate **arriving** at the airport . . . .
13. Let **me help** you **carry** that table upstairs.
14. . . . I found my young son **standing** on . . . .

◇ **PRACTICE TEST A (p. 134):** 1. A   2. B   3. D   4. A   5. B   6. D   7. C   8. D   9. D
10. A   11. B   12. D   13. B   14. B   15. C   16. C   17. D
18. C   19. A   20. B

Chapter 5: SINGULAR AND PLURAL

◇ **1 (p. 137):**   1. care**s** . . . feather**s**   2. occupation**s** . . . Doctor**s** . . . Pilot**s** . . . airplane**s** . . . Farmer**s** . . . crop**s** . . . Shepherd**s**   3. design**s** . . . building**s** . . . dig**s** . . . object**s**   4. computer**s** . . . computer**s**   5. factor**ies** . . . employ**s**   6. Kangaroo**s** . . . animal**s** . . . continent**s** . . . zoo**s**
7. Mosquito**s**/Mosquito**es**   8. tomato**es**   9. Bird**s** . . . insect**s** . . . mammal**s** . . . form**s** . . . characteristic**s**   10. creature**s** . . . five sense**s** . . . these sense**s** . . . Bird**s** . . . Animal**s** . . . dog**s** . . . human being**s**

◇ **2 (p. 138):**   1. men   2. boxes . . . oxen   3. teeth   4. matches   5. mice   6. potatoes
7. beaches . . . cliffs   8. leaves   9. attorneys   10. discoveries . . . laboratories
11. fish   12. wolves . . . foxes . . . deer . . . sheep   13. children . . . bushes
14. ducks . . . geese   15. echoes   16. pianos

◇ **3 (p. 139):**   1. theses   2. phenomena   3. hypotheses   4. crises   5. memoranda   6. media
7. criteria   8. curricula   9. stimuli   10. bacteria   11. oases   12. data

◇ **4 (p. 139):**   1. friends'   2. friend's   3. father's   4. aunts' . . . mother's   5. aunt's
6. astronauts'   7. children's   8. child's   9. secretary's   10. people's   11. Bill's
12. Bess's (OR: Bess')   13. diplomats'   14. diplomat's

◇ **5 (p. 140):**   1. Mary**'s** father. . . He**'s** a dentist.   **2.** Jack**'s** parents live . . . His parents**'** home   3. Our teacher**'s** last name . . . She**'s** one of the best teachers   4. Our teachers**'** last names . . . They**'re** all good teachers.   5. Ms. Wells**'** (OR: Wells**'s**) husband . . . Ms. Hunt**'s** husband
6. It**'s** well known that a bear likes   7. Ann**'s** telephone number [NOTE: No apostrophes are used with possessive pronouns (e.g., *hers, ours*). See Appendix 1, Chart A-7.]   8. Although it**'s** found . . . our children**'s** and grandchildren**'s** lives . . . .

◇ **7 (p. 140):**   1. They sell **shoes** . . . a **shoe** store   2. I like **tomato** salads . . . contain **tomatoes**   3. from black **beans** . . . black **bean** soup   4. for **babies** . . . **baby** food   5. a **vegetable** garden . . . kinds of **vegetables**   6. addicted to **drugs** . . . **drug** addicts   7. from **mosquitoes**/**mosquitos** . . . a **mosquito** net   8. for **salads** . . . a **salad** fork

◇ **8 (p. 141):** 1. a **two-hour** wait . . . for **two hours**   2. is **ten years old** . . . a **ten-year-old** brother   3. had only **two lanes** . . . a **two-lane** highway   4. a **five-minute** speech . . . for **five minutes**   5. a **sixty-year-old** house . . . is **sixty years old**   6. **ten** different **speeds** . . . a **ten-speed** bike   7. won **six games** . . . a **six-game** winning streak   8. **three-letter** words . . . has **three letters**

◇ **9 (p. 142):** 1. a bank robber   2. a bullfighter   3. a stamp collector   4. an animal trainer   5. a storyteller   6. a tax collector   7. a can opener   8. a windshield wiper   9. a wage earner   10. an office manager   11. a computer programmer   12. a bookkeeper   13. a spot remover   14. a pot holder   15. a troublemaker   16. a mind reader   17. a hair dryer (OR: hair drier)   18. a potato peeler   19. a tennis player   20. a firefighter   21. a mail carrier

◇ **10 (p. 143):** 1. **A** bird   2. **An** animal   3. Ø Food   4. **A** concert   5. **An** opera   6. Ø Music   7. **A** cup   8. Ø Milk   9. **An** island   10. Ø Gold   11. **A** bridge   12. **A** valley   13. Ø Health   14. **An** adjective   15. Ø Knowledge   16. Ø Gold   17. **A** professional golfer   18. **A** tree   19. Ø Water   20. Ø Homework   21. Ø Grammar   22. **A** sentence   23. Ø English   24. **A** leaf   25. **An** orange   26. Ø Fruit   27. Ø Iron   28. **An** iron   29. **A** basketball   30. Ø Basketball

◇ **11 (p. 144):** 1. **an** announcement   2. **a** bird   3. **some** birds   4. **some** money   5. **an** accident   6. **some** homework   7. **a** table   8. **some** furniture   9. **some** chairs   10. **some** advice   11. **a** suitcase   12. **some** luggage   13. **an** earthquake   14. **some** letters   15. **a** letter   16. **some** mail   17. **a** machine   18. **some** new machinery   19. **Some** machines   20. **some** junk   21. **an** old basket   22. **some** old boots

◇ **13 (p. 145):** 1. [*no change*] . . . eyes   2. [*no change*]   3. [*no change*]   4. sandwiches   5. [*no change*]   6. [*no change*]   7. photographs   8. [*no change*]   9. ideas   10. [*no change*]   11. [*no change*]   12. [*no change*]   13. words   14. [*no change*]   15. [*no change*]   16. [*no change*]   17. gloves   18. cars . . . minutes . . . [*no change*]   19. [*no changes in whole sentence*]   20. [*only one change*]: customs

◇ **15 (p. 146):** 1. many cities   2. much money   3. is too much furniture   4. aren't many hotels   5. much mail   6. many letters   7. isn't much traffic   8. aren't many cars   9. much work   10. many sides [*Answer: A pentagon has five sides.*]   11. much information   12. much homework   13. many people   14. much postage   15. is too much violence   16. much patience   17. many patients   18. many teeth [*Answer: The average person has 32 teeth.*]   19. isn't much international news   20. many fish are   21. many continents are [*Answer: There are 7 continents: Africa, Antarctica, Asia, Australia, Europe, North America, and South America.*]   22. much progress

◇ **16 (p. 147):**

1. lamps	4. Ø	7. sleep	10. patience
Ø	loaves of bread	information	wealth
Ø	Ø	facts	Ø
necklaces	jars of honey	help	Ø
2. Ø	5. novels	8. women	11. luck
salt	Ø	movies	money
equipment	poems	scenes	advice
Ø	Ø	Ø	Ø
3. stamps	6. orange juice	9. shirts	12. ideas
rice	light bulbs	Ø	theories
stuff	hardware	pens	hypotheses
things	computer software	Ø	Ø

◇ **17 (p. 148):** 1. a little   2. (very) few   3. A little   4. (very) little   5. a few   6. (very) few   7. a few   8. a little   9. (very) little   10. a little   11. a few   12. (Very) Few

◇ **18 (p. 149):** 1. Ø 2. of 3. Ø 4. of 5. Ø 6. of 7. of 8. Ø 9. Ø 10. of 11. Ø 12. Ø 13. of 14. Ø 15. of 16. Ø 17. Ø 18. of OR: Ø 19. of OR: Ø 20. Ø 21. of 22. Ø 23. Ø...Ø 24. of 25. Ø 26. Ø 27. of 28. Ø 29. Ø 30. of

◇ **21 (p. 150):** 1. student 2. students 3. room 4. rooms 5. window 6. windows 7. item 8. items 9. country 10. countries 11. person 12. question 13. children... child 14. problems 15. applicants

◇ **23 (p. 151):** 1. are 2. vote 3. have 4. was 5. leads 6. consists 7. is 8. Isn't 9. speak and understand 10. are 11. do 12. are 13. have 14. continues 15. confirms 16. is...is 17. are 18. were 19. is 20. was 21. contain 22. Are 23. is 24. are [*Answer: The population of Canada is over 27 million.*] 25. is 26. begin [*Answer: Four (Alabama, Alaska, Arkansas, and Arizona).*] 27. is [*Answer: Antarctica is the only uninhabited continent.*] 28. is [*Answer: Approximately 3% of all the water in the world is fresh water.*] 29. is 30. have [*Answer: The only places in the world where snakes do not live are New Zealand, Ireland, the North Pole, the South Pole, and a few islands in the South Pacific.*]

◇ **25 (p. 155):** 1. his/her; his or her; his 2. their 3. their 4. his/her; his or her; his 5. his/her; his or her; his; her 6. their 7. them OR: him/her 8. their OR: his/her; his or her; his; her 9. Their 10. They have...they 11. They 12. It was

◇ **26 (p. 155):** 1. himself 2. myself 3. himself 4. yourself 5. yourselves 6. themselves 7. myself 8. themselves 9. myself 10. herself 11. himself 12. yourself 13. ourselves 14. myself 15. himself

◇ **27 (p. 157):** 1. ourselves...we are...our 2. yourself...you are...your 3. yourselves...you are...your 4. themselves...they are...their 5. INFORMAL: themselves...they are... their/FORMAL: himself...he is...his OR: herself...she is...her (*Also possible*: him/ herself...s/he is...his/her)

◇ **29 (p. 158):** 1. another 2. Others 3. The other 4. another 5. the others 6. the other [*Answer: The other states are Oregon, California, Hawaii, and Alaska.*] 7. other 8. others...others...Other 9. another 10. another 11. the others 12. other

◇ **32 (p. 160):**
1. In my country, there **are** a **lot** of [OR: are **lots** of] schools.
2. Writing compositions **is** very hard for me.
3. The front-page articles in the daily newspaper **have** the most important news.
4. Besides the zoo and the art museum, I have visited many **other** places in this city.
5. It's difficult for me to understand English when people **use** a lot of **slang**.
6. **Students** ... and hand in **their** assignments on time. [OR: **A student** ... and hand in **his/her** assignments on time.]
7. In the past, horses **were** the principal **means** of transportation.
8. In my opinion, [Ø] **English** is **an** easy language to learn.
9. There **are** many different **kinds** of **animals** in the world.
10. They want to move to **another** city because they don't like [Ø] cold weather.
11. I like to travel because I like to learn about other **countries** and **customs**.
12. Collecting stamps is one of my **hobbies**.
13. Chicago has many tall **skyscrapers**.
14. I came here three and a half **months** ago. I think I have made [Ø] good progress in English.
15. I was looking for my clothes, but I couldn't find **them**.

◇ **PRACTICE TEST A (p. 161):** 1. C   2. D   3. A   4. C   5. C   6. B   7. B   8. C   9. A
10. C   11. A   12. A   13. D   14. A   15. A   16. B   17. C   18. D
19. D   20. B

Chapter 6: ADJECTIVE CLAUSES

◇ **1 (p. 165):** 1. a. that are marked with a small red dot . . .   b. which are marked with a small red dot
2. a. who sits at the first desk on the right . . .   b. that sits at the first desk on the right
3. a. that I bought . . .   b. which I bought . . .   c. I bought   4. a. that I met at the
meeting . . .   b. who(m) I met at the meeting . . .   c. I met at the meeting   5. a. we listened
to last night . . .   b. that we listened to last night . . .   c. which we listened to last night . . .
d. to which we listened last night   6. a. I told you about . . .   b. who(m) I told you
about . . .   c. that I told you about . . .   d. about whom I told you   7. whose parents you
just met   8. who played at the concert last night   9. a waiter has to serve at a restaurant
10. Bob recommended   11. whose book on time and space has been translated into dozens
of languages   12. who lives next door to us

◇ **2 (p. 166):** 1. who(m)/that/Ø   2. who/that   3. which/that/Ø   4. which   5. who(m)/that/Ø
6. who/that   7. whose   8. whom   9. which/that

◇ **3 (p. 167):** 1. which/that   2. who/that   3. which/that   4. which/that   5. who/that
6. which/that/Ø   7. who(m)/that/Ø   8. which/that/Ø   9. which   10. which/that/Ø
11. whom   12. who(m)/that/Ø

◇ **4 (p. 168):** 1. Louis knows the woman **who/that is meeting us at the airport.**
2. The chair **which/that/Ø Sally inherited from her grandmother** is an antique.
3. The bench **which/that/Ø I sat on** was wet./The bench **on which I sat** was wet.
4. The man **who(m)/that/Ø I hired to paint my house** finished the job in four days.
5. I miss seeing the old woman **who/that used to sell flowers on that street corner.**
6. The architect **who(m)/that/Ø Mario works with** is brilliant./The architect **with whom
Mario works** is brilliant.
7. Mary tutors students **who/that need extra help in geometry.**
8. I took a picture of the rainbow **which/that appeared in the sky after the shower.**

◇ **5 (p. 169):** 1. I spoke to the man whose wife had been admitted to the hospital.
2. I read about a child whose life was saved by her pet dog.
3. The students whose names were called raised their hands.
4. Jack knows a man whose name is William Blueheart Duckbill, Jr.
5. The police came to question the woman whose purse was stolen outside the supermarket.
6. We live in a small town whose inhabitants are almost invariably friendly and helpful.
7. The day care center was established to take care of children whose parents work . . . .
8. We couldn't find the person whose car was blocking our driveway.
9. Tobacco is a plant whose large leaves are used for smoking or chewing.
10. The professor told the three students whose reports were turned in late that he would
accept the late papers this time but never again.

◇ **6 (p. 169):** 1. A,D   2. B,C,D   3. C,D   4. B   5. D   6. B,C   7. A   8. C,D
9. B,C,D   10. B   11. A   12. A

◇ **7 (p. 170):** 1. speak   2. speaks   3. are . . . don't   4. offers . . . are   5. measures . . . walks
6. suffer   7. were   8. have   9. have   10. work   11. are   12. state . . . wish

◇ **8 (p. 171):** 1. In our village, there were many people **who/that** didn't have much money. OR: In our village, many people didn't have much money.   2. I enjoyed the book that you told me to read (*omit "it"*).   3. I still remember the man who (*omit "he"*) taught me to play the violin when I was a boy.   4. I showed my father a picture of the car I am going to buy (*omit "it"*) as soon as I save enough money.   5. The woman about **whom** I was talking (*omit "about"*) suddenly walked into the room. OR: The woman **who(m)/that/Ø** I was talking about suddenly....   6. Almost all of the people **who/that** appear on television wear makeup. 7. My grandfather was a community leader whom everyone in our town admired (*omit "him"*) very much.   8. I don't like to spend time with people **who/that lose** (*omit final "-s"*) their tempers easily.   9. I sit next to a person **whose** name is Ahmed.   10. In one corner of the marketplace, **there was** an old man who was playing a violin. OR: In one corner of the marketplace, an old man (*omit "who"*) was playing a violin.

◇ **9 (p. 171):** 1. That is the place **where** the accident occurred.   2. There was a time **when** movies cost a dime.   3. A cafe is a small restaurant **where** people can get a light meal.   4. Every neighborhood in Brussels has small cafes **where** customers drink coffee and eat pastries. 5. There was a time **when** dinosaurs dominated the earth.   6. The house **where** I was born and grew up was destroyed in an earthquake ten years ago.   7. Summer is the time of year **when** the weather is the hottest.   8. The miser hid his money in a place **where** it was safe from robbers.   9. There came a time **when** the miser had to spend his money.   10. . . . so Dan took it back to the store **where** he'd bought it.

◇ **12 (p. 172):** 1. NO   2. YES . . . Paul O'Grady, who died two years ago, was a kind and loving man. 3. NO   4. YES . . . I made an appointment with Dr. Raven, who is considered an expert on eye disorders.   5. NO   6. NO   7. YES . . . Bogota, which is the capital of Colombia, is a cosmopolitan city.   8. YES . . . They climbed Mount Rainier, which is in the state of Washington, twice last year.   9. YES . . . Emeralds, which are valuable gemstones, are mined in Colombia.   10. YES . . . The company offered the position to John, whose department performed best this year.   11. YES . . . On our trip to Africa we visited Nairobi, which is near several fascinating game reserves, and then traveled to Egypt to see the pyramids.   12. NO 13. NO   14. YES . . . Larry was very close to his only brother, who was a famous social historian.   15. NO   16. NO   17. YES . . . A typhoon, which is a violent tropical storm, can cause great destruction.   18. NO

◇ **13 (p. 173):** 1. A   2. A,D   3. C   4. A   5. A,B,D,E   6. B   7. A   8. C   9. A,D 10. A   11. A,D   12. A   13. C,D,E

◇ **14 (p. 174):** 1. a   2. b   3. a   4. b   5. b   6. a   7. b   8. a

◇ **15 (p. 174):** 1. YES . . . Thirty people, two of whom were members of the crew, were killed in the ferry accident.   2. NO   3. YES . . . Over 500 students took the entrance examination, the results of which will be posted in the administration building at the end of the month. 4. YES . . . My instructor assigned 150 pages of reading for tomorrow, which is too much. I won't have time to do it.   5. NO   6. YES . . . The Caspian Sea, which is bounded by the Soviet Union and Iran, is fed by eight rivers.   7. YES . . . The supervisor was not happy with his work crew, none of whom seemed interested in doing quality work.   8. YES . . . My oldest brother, in whose house I lived for six months when I was ten, has been a father to me in many ways.   9. YES . . . Tom is always interrupting me, which makes me mad.   10. NO 11. YES . . . To express the uselessness of worrying, Mark Twain once said, "I've had a lot of problems in my life, most of which never happened."

◇ **16 (p. 175):** 1. . . . offers, **neither of which** I accepted.   2. . . . three brothers, **two of whom** are professional athletes.   3. . . . business ventures, **only one of which** is profitable. 4. . . . fifty states, **the majority of which** are located . . . .   5. The two women, **both of whom** are changing careers, have already dissolved . . . .   6. . . . success, **much of which** has been due to hard work, but **some of which** has been due to good luck.

◇ **17 (p. 175):** 1. Sally lost her job, which wasn't surprising.   2. She usually came to work late, which upset her boss.   3. So her boss fired her, which made her angry.   4. She hadn't saved any money, which was unfortunate.   5. So she had to borrow some money from me, which I didn't like.   6. She has found a new job, which is lucky.   7. So she has repaid the money she borrowed from me, which I appreciate.   8. She has promised herself to be on time for work every day, which is a good idea.

◇ **20 (p. 177):** 1. Only a few of the *movies* **shown at the Gray Theater** are suitable . . . .
2. *Jasmine*, **a viny plant with fragrant flowers,** grows only in warm places.
3. The *couple* **living in the house next door** are both college professors.
4. A throne is the *chair* **occupied by a queen, king, or other rulers.**
5. A knuckle is a *joint* **connecting a finger to the rest of the hand.**
6. We visited *Belgrade*, **the capital city of Yugoslavia.**
7. . . . by a huge *ice cap* **containing 70 percent of the earth's fresh water.**
8. *Astronomy*, **the study of planets and stars,** is one of the world's oldest sciences.
9. Only a small fraction of the *eggs* **laid by a fish** actually hatch and survive to adulthood.
10. Our solar system is in a *galaxy* **called the Milky Way.**
11. Two out of three *people* **struck by lightning** survive.
12. *Arizona*, **once thought to be a useless desert,** is today a rapidly growing . . . .
13. *Simon Bolivar*, **a great South American general,** led the fight for . . . .
14. . . . people enjoy *lemonade*, **a drink made of lemon juice, water, and sugar.**
15. . . . the sound of *laughter* **coming from the room next door to mine at the motel.**
16. Few tourists ever see a *jaguar*, **a spotted wild cat native to tropical America.**

◇ **21 (p. 178):** 1. . . . Martin Luther King, Jr., the leader of the . . . .   2. Neil Armstrong, the first person to set foot on the moon, reported . . . .   3. Susan B. Anthony, the first and only woman whose picture appears on U.S. money, worked tirelessly . . . .   4. (no commas)   5. . . . Abraham Lincoln, one of the truly great presidents of the United States, ran for public office 26 times and lost 23 of the elections. Walt Disney, the creator of Mickey Mouse and founder of his own movie production company, once got fired by a newspaper editor because he had no good ideas. Thomas Edison, the inventor of the light bulb and phonograph, was believed by his teachers to be too stupid to learn. Albert Einstein, one of the greatest scientists of all time, performed badly in almost all of his high school courses and failed his college entrance exam.

◇ **22 (p. 178):** 1. . . . Everest, the second highest mountain in the world, is . . . .   2. . . . Baghdad, the capital of Iraq.   3. . . . seismographs, sensitive instruments that measure the shaking of the ground.   4. . . . Dead Sea, the lowest place on the earth's surface, is . . . . [NOTE: The shoreline of the Dead Sea is about 400 meters/1310 feet below sea level.]   5. . . . Buenos Aires, the capital of Argentina.   6. . . . lasers, devices that produce a powerful beam of light.   7. Mexico, the northernmost country in Latin America, lies . . . .   8. . . . Nigeria, the most populous country in Africa.   9. . . . Mexico City, the largest city in the Western Hemisphere, and New York City, the largest city in the United States, face . . . .   10. . . . mole, a small animal that spends its entire life underground, is almost blind. The aardvark, an African animal that eats ants and termites, also lives . . . .

◇ **26 (p. 181):** 1. . . . people **who(m)/that/Ø** I admire most is . . . .
2. . . . the only sport in which I am interested (*omit "in it"*). OR: . . . the only sport **which/that/Ø** I am interested in (*omit "it"*).
3. My favorite teacher, Mr. Peterson, (*omit "he"*) was always . . . .
4. . . . people in the government who **are** trying . . . .
5. . . . anyone who (*omit "he"*) wants to learn . . . . OR: . . . anyone **wanting** to learn . . . .
6. . . . Carver Hall, **which** is a large brick building . . . . OR: . . . Carver Hall, (*add comma, omit "that is"*) a large brick building . . . .
7. . . . a lot of people **waiting** in a long line . . . .
8. Students who **live** on campus . . . . OR: Students (*omit "who"*) **living** on campus . . . .
9. A myth is a story **which/that** expresses . . . . OR: A myth is a story **expressing** . . .

10. . . . the librarian **who/that** sits at . . . OR: the librarian **sitting** at . . . .

11. . . . sister is Anna, **who** is 21 years old. OR: . . . sister, Anna, is 21 years old.

12. . . . in Sapporo, **which** is a city . . . OR: . . . in Sapporo, (*omit "that is"*) a city . . . .

13. Patrick, who is my oldest brother, is married and . . . . OR: Patrick, my oldest brother, is married and . . . .

14. The person **who sits/sitting** next to me is someone **who(m)/that/Ø** I've never met (*omit "him"*).

15. . . . a small city (*omit "is"*) located . . . . OR: . . . a small city **which/that** is located . . . .

◇ PRACTICE TEST A (p. 182): 1. D 2. A 3. B 4. D 5. B 6. A 7. C 8. D 9. C
10. A 11. C 12. B 13. C 14. D 15. D 16. B 17. D 18. B
19. A 20. C

Chapter 7: NOUN CLAUSES

◇ 1 (p. 186): 1. Q(?) 2. N.Cl.(.) 3. Q(?) 4. N.Cl.(.) 5. Q(?) 6. N.Cl.(.) 7. N.Cl.(.)
8. Q(?) 9. Q(?) 10. N.Cl.(?) [NOTE: *"who she is" is a noun clause; the whole sentence is a question.*] 11. Q(?) 12. N.Cl.(.)

◇ 2 (p. 186): 1. Where(?) 2. I don't know(.) 3. I don't know(.) 4. What(?) 5. How(?)
6. I don't know(.) 7. Where(?) 8. I don't know(.) 9. I don't know(.)
10. Why(?) 11. I don't know(.) 12. Who(?) 13. When (?) 14. I don't know(.)
15. Who(?) 16. I don't know(.)

◇ 3 (p. 187): 1. When will Tom be here? . . . when Tom will be here. 2. Why is he coming? . . . why he is coming. 3. Which flight will he be on? . . . which flight he will be on. 4. Who is going to meet him at the airport? . . . who is going to meet him at the airport. 5. Who is Jim Hunter? . . . who Jim Hunter is. 6. What is Tom's address? . . . what Tom's address is.
7. Where does he live? . . . where he lives. 8. Where was he last week? . . . where he was last week. 9. How long has he been working for IBM? . . . how long he has been working for IBM? 10. What kind of computer does he have at home? . . . what kind of computer he has at home? 11. What does he need? . . . what he needs? 12. When did he call? . . . when he called. 13. What does he want to do after he gets here? . . . what he wants to do after he gets here? 14. Whose idea was it to have a party? . . . whose idea it was to have a party?

◇ 4 (p. 188): 1. A: did Ruth go . . . B: Ruth went 2. A: He's looking for . . . B: are you looking for
3. A: is my eraser . . . B: it is 4. A: did he decide . . . B: he decided 5. A: is this . . .
B: it is 6. A: did he buy . . . B: he bought 7. A: didn't Fred lock . . . B: he didn't lock 8. A: have they been . . . B: he and his family have lived . . . 9. A: John's tutor is . . . B: is John's tutor 10. A: you are taking . . . B: are you taking 11. A: didn't you study . . . B: I didn't study 12. A: are we supposed . . . B: we're supposed

◇ 6 (p. 190): 1. if/whether it will rain 2. when it will rain 3. if/whether Sam is 4. where Sam is
5. if/whether Jane called 6. what time Jane called 7. why the earth is called 8. how far it is 9. if/whether Susan has ever been 10. if/whether she speaks 11. who Ann played 12. who won 13. if/whether Ann won 14. if/whether all creatures, including fish and insects, feel 15. where the nearest post office is 16. if/whether there is a post office 17. if/whether birds can communicate 18. how birds communicate

◇ 7 (p. 192): 1. Please tell me what **your name is**. 2. No one seems to know when **Maria will** arrive.
3. I wonder why **Bob was** late for class. 4. I don't know **what that word means.**
5. I wonder **if/whether the teacher knows** the answer. 6. What **they should** do about the hole in their roof is their most pressing problem. 7. I'll ask her **if/whether she would** like some coffee. 8. Be sure to tell the doctor where **it hurts**. 9. Why **I am** unhappy is

something I can't explain.   10. I wonder **if/whether** Tom knows about the meeting.
11. I need to know who **your teacher is**.   12. I don't understand why **the car is not** running properly.

◇ **8 (p. 192):**   1. where to buy   2. whether to stay...go   3. how to fix   4. whether (or not) to look   5. where to get   6. whether (or not) to go   7. what time to pick   8. who to talk   9. whether to take...to do   10. how to solve   11. where to tell   12. how long to cook   13. what to wear   14. how much coffee to make   15. which essay to use   16. whether to take...travel...(to) keep...save

◇ **10 (p. 194):**   1. *Regardless of the fact that I studied for three months for the examination*, I barely passed.   2. There's nothing we can do *about the fact that Jim lost our tickets to the concert.*   3. *The fact that we are going to miss one of the best concerts of the year because of Jim's carelessness* makes me a little angry.   4. *In view of the fact that we can't go to the concert*, let's plan to go to a movie.   5. *Except for the fact that I couldn't speak a word of Italian and understood very little*, I had a wonderful time visiting my Italian cousins in Rome.   6. When I first visited Florida, I was surprised *by the fact that many people living in Miami speak only Spanish.*   7. *The fact that Bobby broke my grandmother's antique flower vase* isn't important.   8. *The fact that he lied about it* is what bothers me.   9. At first, some of us objected *to the fact that Prof. Brown, who had almost no teaching experience, was hired to teach the advanced physics courses*, but she has proven herself to be one of the best.   10. I am impressed *by the fact that that automobile has the best safety record of any car manufactured this year* and would definitely recommend that you buy that make.

◇ **11 (p. 194):**
1. The athlete said, "**W**here is my uniform?"
2. "Who won the game?" asked the spectator.
3. "Stop the clock," shouted the referee. "**W**e have an injured player."
4. "I can't remember," Margaret said, "where I put my purse."
5. Sandy asked her sister, "**H**ow can I help you get through this difficulty?"
6. "I'll answer your question later," he whispered. "**I**'m trying to hear what the speaker is saying."
7. As the students entered the room, the teacher said, "**P**lease take your seats quickly."
8. "Why did I ever take this job?" Barry wondered aloud.
9. After crashing into me and knocking all of my packages to the ground, the man stopped abruptly, turned to me, and said softly, "**E**xcuse me."
10. "I'm going to rest for the next three hours," she said. "I don't want to be disturbed." "That's fine," I replied. "**Y**ou get some rest. I'll make sure no one disturbs you."
11. "Do we want four more years of corruption and debt?" the candidate shouted into the microphone.
    "No!" the crowd screamed.
12.   The woman behind the fast-food restaurant counter shouted, "**W**ho's next?"
       "I am," three people replied all at the same time.
       "Which one of you is really next?" she asked impatiently.
       "I was here first," said a young woman elbowing her way up to the counter. "I want a hamburger."
       "You were not!" hollered an older man standing next to her. "I was here before you were. **G**ive me a chicken sandwich and a cup of coffee."
       "Wait a minute! I was in line first," said a young man. "**G**ive me a cheeseburger and a chocolate shake."
       The woman behind the restaurant counter spotted a little boy politely waiting his turn. **S**he turned to him and said, "Hi, Sonny. **W**hat can I get for you?"

◇ **12 (p. 196):** 1. was   2. needed   3. was having   4. had finished   5. had finished   6. would arrive   7. was going to be/ would be   8. could solve   9. might come   10. might come   11. had to leave   12. had to leave   13. should go   14. ought to go   15. to stay   16. not to move   17. was   18. had arrived

◇ **13 (p. 196):** 1. if/whether she was planning   2. what time the movie begins   3. if/whether we could still get   4. how he can help   5. if/whether he could help   6. when the final decision would be made   7. where she had been   8. what Kim's native language is   9. what the problem was   10. if/whether I was doing   11. when this terrible drought is going   12. what time he had   13. who(m) she should give the message to   14. (that) we would be leaving   15. why we hadn't called

◇ **14 (p. 197):** 1. could still get . . . had already bought   2. had to clean up . . . empty . . . could leave . . . would   3. still smoked . . . had tried . . . didn't seem   4. was going . . . didn't know . . . worked   5. what the capital of Australia was/is . . . wasn't . . . thought it was   6. where the next chess match would take . . . hadn't been decided   7. would be . . . would . . . left   8. was . . . didn't think . . . would ever speak . . . was getting . . . would be speaking   9. . . . was pouring . . . had better take . . . would stop . . . didn't need   10. were . . . might be . . . could develop

◇ **18 (p. 201):**
1. What **the president is** going to say . . . .
2. I asked Paul **to** help me . . . .
3. My friend asked me, "What are you going to do Saturday**?**" I replied, "**It** depends on the weather." OR: My friend asked me what **I was** going to do Saturday. I replied (that) it **depended** on the weather.
4. What my friend and I did (*omit "it"*) was our secret. We . . . parents what **we did.**
5. The doctor asked **if/whether** I felt okay. I told him that I **didn't** feel well.
6. **It** is clear that the ability to use a computer (*omit "it"*) is an important skill . . . .
7. They asked us **to** be sure (OR: **if we would** be sure) to turn out the lights when we leave/**left.**
8. "Is **it** true you almost drowned?" my friend asked me.
   "Yes," I said. "I'm really glad to be alive. It was really frightening."
9. **The** fact that I almost drowned makes . . . .

◇ **20 (p. 201):** 1. organize   2. be divided   3. call   4. be told   5. open   6. take   7. be   8. be mailed   9. obey   10. be given

◇ **21 (p. 202):** 1. whenever   2. wherever   3. whatever   4. whichever   5. whatever   6. who(m)ever   7. whichever   8. Whoever   9. whatever   10. wherever

◇ **PRACTICE TEST A (p. 203):**   1. B   2. C   3. B   4. D   5. A   6. A   7. D   8. D   9. A   10. B   11. B   12. A   13. D   14. D   15. D   16. B   17. C   18. C   19. A   20. B

Chapter 8: SHOWING RELATIONSHIPS BETWEEN IDEAS—PART I

◇ **1 (p. 206):** 1. fresh and sweet   2. apples and pears   3. washed and dried   4. am washing and drying   5. happily and quickly   6. biting and tasting   7. to bite and (to) taste   8. delicious but expensive   9. apples, pears, and bananas   10. red, ripe, and juicy

◇ **2 (p. 206):**
1. **I:** for his intelligence, cheerful disposition, and **honesty**
2. **C:** was a lawyer and a politician
3. **I:** she had to rent an apartment, make new friends, and **find** a job
4. **C:** Barbara studies . . . and works
5. **C:** is plentiful and relatively inexpensive
6. **I:** enjoy visiting Disneyland and **touring** movie studios
7. **C:** are usually interested in but a little frightened by
8. **I:** Fainting can result from **either** a lack of oxygen or a loss of blood

9. **I**: how to write . . . , organize . . . , and **summarize**
10. **I**: sailed . . . smoothly and **quietly**
11. **C**: not coffee but chocolate
12. **I**: Not only universities **but also many government agencies** support medical . . . .
13. **C**: explains why water freezes and how the sun produces heat
14. **C**: need light, a suitable climate, and an ample supply ALSO: of water and minerals
15. **C**: With their keen sight, fine hearing, and refined sense of smell ALSO: hunt day or night
  ALSO: of elk, deer, moose, or caribou

◇ **3 (p. 207):**   1. knows   2. know   3. knows   4. know   5. know   6. wants   7. like   8. has
  9. agrees   10. are   11. realizes   12. think

◇ **4 (p. 207):**   1. Many people drink **neither coffee nor alcohol**.   2. Barbara is fluent in **not only Chinese but also Japanese**.   3. I'm sorry to say that Paul has **neither patience nor sensitivity** to others.   4. She can **both sing and dance**   5. . . . you should talk to **either your teacher or your academic counselor**. OR: . . . talk **either to your teacher or to your academic counselor**.   6. Diana is **both intelligent and very creative**.   7. You may begin working **either tomorrow or next week**.   8. Michael told neither his **mother nor his father** . . .
  9. . . . requires **not only balance and skill but also concentration and mental alertness**.

◇ **7 (p. 210):**   1. . . . cooking. **M**y wife . . . .   2. . . . cooking, [*optional comma*] but my wife . . . .   3. . . . that book. **I**t's very good.   4. . . . that book, but I didn't like it.   5. [*Add no punctuation.*]   6. . . . the door. **M**y sister answered . . . .   7. . . . the door, [*optional comma*] and my sister answered . . . .   8. . . . materials. **T**hey are found in rocks and soil.   9. . . . are minerals. **T**hey are found in rocks, soil, and water.   10. . . . by plane, [*optional comma*] or you can go . . . .   11. [*Add no punctuation.*]   12. . . . all night, so he declined . . . .   13. . . . invitation to dinner. **H**e needed to . . . .   14. . . . howling outside, yet it was warm and comfortable indoors.   15. . . . answer the phone, for I didn't want . . . .   16. . . . went camping. **I**t rained the entire time.   17. . . . under construction, so we had to take . . . .   18. . . . win the championship, yet our team won . . . .   19. . . . at the theatre late, but the play had not yet begun. **W**e were quite surprised.   20. . . . from one central place. **M**ost central heating systems service only one building, but some systems heat a group of buildings, such as those at a military base, a campus, or an apartment complex.

◇ **9 (p. 211):**   1. A hurricane's force begins to diminish as soon as it strikes land.   2. When I reached my 21st birthday, I didn't feel any older.   3. Before I left for work, I had a cup of tea.   4. I like to read the evening newspaper after I get home from work.   5. I have been late to work three times since my watch broke.   6. Whenever it rains, my cat hides under the house.   7. Once I finish school, I'm going to get a job.   8. I heard a gunshot while I was waiting for my bus.   9. Until a new generator is installed, the village will have no electric power.   10. I saw Mr. Wu the last time I was in Taipei.   11. I didn't have to stand in line at the airline counter because I already had my boarding pass.   12. If the workplace is made pleasant, productivity in a factory increases.

◇ **10 (p. 211):**   1. The lake was calm. Tom went fishing.   2. Because the lake was calm, Tom went fishing.   3. Tom went fishing because the lake was calm. **H**e caught two fish.   4. Tom went fishing because the lake was calm and caught two fish.   5. When Tom went fishing, the lake was calm. **H**e caught two fish.   6. The lake was calm, so Tom went fishing. **H**e caught two fish.   7. Because the lake was calm and quiet, Tom went fishing.   8. The lake was calm, quiet, and clear when Tom went fishing.

◇ **12 (p. 212):**   1. C   2. C   3. D   4. C   5. C   6. D   7. B   8. B   9. C   10. A
  11. A   12. A   13. A   14. C   15. B

◇ **14 (p. 214):** 1. As soon as the other passengers get on the bus, we'll leave. 2. I turned off the lights before I left the room. 3. Whenever Susan feels nervous, she chews her nails. 4. The first time I saw the great pyramids of Egypt in the moonlight, I was speechless. 5. The frying pan caught on fire while I was making dinner. 6. As soon as I finish working on the car, we'll take a walk in the park. 7. After Ceylon had been independent for 24 years, its name was changed to Sri Lanka. 8. By the time Shakespeare died in 1616, he had written more than 37 plays. 9. Since Douglas fell off his bicycle last week, he has had to use crutches to walk. 10. Ms. Johnson will return your call as soon as she has some free time. 11. Once John learns how to use a computer, he'll be able to work more efficiently. 12. I won't return my book to the library until I have finished my research project. 13. Sue dropped a carton of eggs as she was leaving the store. 14. The next time Sam goes to the movies, he'll remember to take his glasses. 15. When the flooding river raced down the valley, it destroyed everything in its path.

◇ **16 (p. 215):** 1. A,B 2. B 3. A,D 4. B 5. C 6. A,B,C,D 7. B,C 8. C 9. A,D 10. B 11. D 12. A

◇ **17 (p. 216):** 1. We can go swimming every day *now that the weather is warm.* 2. *Since all of the students had done poorly on the test,* the teacher decided to give it again. 3. Cold air hovers near the earth *because it is heavier than hot air.* 4. *Because our TV set was broken,* we listened to the news on the radio. 5. *Now that Larry is finally caught up on his work,* he can start his vacation tomorrow. 6. *Inasmuch as you have paid for the theater tickets,* please let me pay for our dinner. 7. *Since 92,000 people already have reservations with Pan Am for a trip to the moon,* I doubt that I'll ever get the chance to go on one of the first tourist flights. 8. *As long as our flight is going to be delayed,* let's relax and enjoy a quiet dinner. 9. My registration is going to be canceled *because I haven't paid my fees.* 10. *Now that Erica has qualified for the Olympics in speedskating,* she must train even more vigorously.

◇ **18 (p. 217):** 1. because of 2. because 3. because 4. because of 5. Because of 6. Because 7. because 8. because of 9. because of 10. because 11. because 12. Because of

◇ **20 (p. 218):** 1. [*no changes*] 2. ... wouldn't start. **T**herefore, he couldn't pick .... 3. ... an inquisitive student, he was always .... 4 [*no changes*] 5. ... our head. **T**herefore, it is important .... 6. ... the eighth inning. **T**herefore, most of the audience .... 7. When I was in my teens and twenties, it was easy for me to get into an argument with my father because both of us .... 8. Robert did not pay close attention to what the travel agent said when he went to see her at her office last week. **T**herefore, he had to ask many of the same questions again the next time he talked to her.

◇ **21 (p. 218):** **Part I**: 1. Because 2. ... rained. Therefore, we .... 3. because of 4. ... town. Therefore, all .... 5. because of 6. Because the hurricane ... town, all .... 7. because of 8. because 9. ... courageous. Roman soldiers, therefore, ate .... **Part II**: 1. Due to his poor eyesight, John .... 2. Since John has poor eyesight, he .... 3. ... eyesight. Consequently, he .... 4. ... heights. Consequently, she .... 5. due to 6. Since a camel ... ten days, it is .... 7. ... overweight. Consequently, his doctor .... 8. Since a diamond ... hard, it can .... 9. Due to consumer demand for ivory, many ... ruthlessly. Consequently, people who ....

◇ **22 (p. 219):** 1. so 2. such 3. so 4. so 5. such 6. such 7. so 8. so 9. so 10. such 11. so 12. so 13. So 14. so 15. such 16. so

◇ **24 (p. 221):** 1. (G) ... I could listen to the news. 2. (I) ... he can become a Canadian citizen. 3. (A) ... she could read the fine print at the bottom of the contract. 4. (C) ... she can fix her own car. 5. (H) ... he will be considered for a promotion at this company.

6. (J)...she can graduate early.   7. (B)...he can travel in Europe.   8. (F)...it would not disturb her roommate.   9. (D)...she could see the dancers in the street.   10. (E) ...we can get expert advice on our itinerary.

◇ **27 (p. 223):** 1. Since opening....   2. ...before leaving the room.   3. While herding his goats....
4. Before marching into battle,....   5. After meeting/having met the movie star....
6. ...keys after searching through....   7. When first brought....   8. Since (being) imported into Australia many years ago, the rabbit....

◇ **28 (p. 224):** 1. [*no change*]   2. After stopping the fight, the police arrested two men and a woman.
3. Since opening his new business, Bob has been working 16 hours a day.   4. [*no change*]
5. While driving to work, Sam had a flat tire.   6. [*no change*]   7. [*no change*]   8. After working hard in the garden all afternoon, Tom took a shower and then went to the movies with his friends.   9. [*no change*]   10. [*no change*]   11. [*no change*]   12. Emily always straightens her desk before leaving the office at the end of the day.
13. [*no change*]

◇ **29 (p. 224):** 1. a. leaving ... b. left   2. a. invented/had invented ... b. inventing/having invented
3. a. working ... b. was working   4. a. flies ... b. flying   5. a. studied/had studied ...
b. studying/having studied   6. a. learning ... b. learned   7. a. is taken ...
b. taken   8. a. taking ... b. are taking   9. a. was driving ... b. driving

◇ **30 (p. 225):** 1. **Keeping** one hand on the steering wheel, **Anna** opened a can of soda pop with her free hand.   2. [*no change*]   3. **Misunderstanding** the directions to the hotel, **I** arrived one hour late for the dinner party.   4. [*no change*]   5. **Misunderstanding** my directions to the hotel, **the taxi driver** took me to the wrong place.   6. **Living** a long distance from my work, **I** have to commute daily by train.   7. **Living** a long distance from her work, **Heidi** has to commute daily by train.   8. [*no change*]   9. **Picking** strawberries in the garden, **Martha** was stung by a bumblebee.   10. **Remembering** that she hadn't turned off the oven, **Ann** went directly home.   11. **Tripping** on the carpet, **Jim** spilt his coffee.   12. **Having recognized** his face but having forgotten his name, **I** just smiled and said, "Hi."   13. [*no change*]   14. **Lying** by the swimming pool, **I** realized I was getting sunburned.   15. [*no change*]   16. **Living** in the Pacific Northwest, where it rains a great deal, **my family and I** are accustomed to cool, damp weather.

◇ **31 (p. 226):** 1. E   2. J   3. A   4. G   5. B   6. L   7. I   8. H   9. C   10. K   11. F
12. D

◇ **33 (p. 227):** 1. Upon arriving at the airport....   2. Upon reaching the other side of the lake....
3. Upon discovering it was hot....   4. Upon hearing my name called....   5. Upon hearing those words....   6. upon investigating the cause....   7. Upon learning the problem was not at all serious....   8. Upon being told that she had gotten (had got) it....

◇ **34 (p. 228):** 1. After spending some time in a cocoon, a caterpillar....   2. [*no change*]   3. Upon entering the theater, we handed....   4. Being unprepared/Unprepared for the test, I didn't do well.   5. Before leaving on my trip, I checked....   6. [*no change*]   7. Not having understood/Not understanding the directions, I got lost.   8. My father reluctantly agreed to let me attend the game after having talked/after talking it over with my mother.   9. Upon discovering I had lost my key to the apartment, I called....   10. [*no change*]   11. Garcia Lopez de Cardenas accidentally discovered the Grand Canyon while looking for....   12. [*no change*]   13. After having waited/After waiting for over a half an hour, we were finally....
14. Before getting accepted on her country's Olympic running team, Maria had spent....
15. Not paying attention to his driving, George didn't see....

◇ **36 (p. 230):** 1. **I**   2. **C**   3. **I**   4. **C**   5. **I**   6. **I**   7. **I**   8. **C**   9. **I**   10. **C**   11. **I**
12. **I**   13. **I**   14. **I**   15. **C**

◇ 37 (p. 231):
1. I was very tired, **so I went** to bed.
2. Because our leader could not attend the meeting, (*omit "so"*) it was canceled. OR: (*omit "Because"*) Our leader could not attend the meeting, so it was canceled.
3. **My wife and I like** to travel.
4. I always fasten my seatbelt before **starting/I start** the engine.
5. I don't like our classroom **b**ecause it is hot and crowded. I hope we can change....
6. The day was very warm and humid, **so** I turned on the air conditioner.
7. Upon **learning** that my car couldn't be repaired for three days, I **was** very distressed.
8. **Because I (had)** missed the final examination, the teacher gave me a failing grade.
9. Both my sister and my brother **are** going to be at the family reunion.
10. I hope my son will remain in school until he **finishes** his degree.
11. My brother has succeeded in business because (*omit "of"*) he works hard.
12. Luis stood up, turned toward me, and **spoke** so softly that I couldn't hear what he said.
13. I was lost. I could find **neither** my parents **nor** my brother.
14. When I traveled through Europe, I visited England, France, Italy, Germany, and **Switzerland.**

◇ PRACTICE TEST A (p. 232):   1. B   2. A   3. B   4. D   5. C   6. D   7. A   8. C   9. B
10. A   11. B   12. C   13. A   14. A   15. B   16. D   17. A   18. C
19. C   20. C

Chapter 9: SHOWING RELATIONSHIPS BETWEEN IDEAS—PART II

◇ 1 (p. 235):   1. even though   2. because   3. Even though   4. Because   5. even though
6. because   7. Even though   8. because   9. even though   10. Even though...
because   11. even though   12. even though...because   13. Even though...because

◇ 3 (p. 236):   **Part I**: 1. Nevertheless   2. but   3. even though   4. but   5. Nevertheless   6. Even
though   7. even though   8. but   9. nevertheless   10. Nevertheless
Part II: 11. However   12. yet   13. Although   14. yet   15. Although
16. However   17. although   18. yet   19. However   20. However

◇ 4 (p. 237):   1. ...good advice. **N**evertheless, she....   2. ...good advice, but she....   3. Even
though...good advice, she....   4. ...good advice. **S**he did not follow it, however.
5. Thomas was thirsty. **I** offered him some water. **H**e refused it.   6. [*no change*]
7. Thomas was thirsty. **H**e, nevertheless, refused the glass of water I brought him.
8. Thomas was thirsty, yet he refused to drink the water that I offered him.

◇ 5 (p. 238):
1. a. Even though	2. a. In spite of	3. a. Despite	4. a. In spite of
b. Despite	b. Although	b. Although	b. Even though
c. Despite	c. Although	c. Despite	c. In spite of
d. Despite	d. In spite of	d. Although	d. even though
e. Even though	e. In spite of	e. Despite	e. in spite of
			f. even though
			g. even though
			h. in spite of

◇ 6 (p. 239):   1. B   2. E   3. J   4. F   5. C   6. H   7. A   8. G   9. I   10. D

◇ 7 (p. 240):   1. C   2. D   3. C   4. C   5. B   6. B

◇ 9 (p. 240):   1. B   2. A   3. B   4. B   5. D   6. C   7. B   8. B   9. A   10. C

◇ **13 (p. 244):** 1. In case you need . . . with me, I'll . . . . 2. **W**e'll . . . in case you need to call us.
3. **Y**ou'd better . . . with you in case the weather changes. 4. . . . design project. **I**n case you
find that you need help with it, she'll be . . . . 5. **M**y boss . . . in case the company . . . .
6. **I**n case I'm not back to make dinner, I put the . . . . 7. **I**n the event that Janet . . .
tomorrow, she will . . . . 8. **Y**ou'd better . . . in the event that you run out . . . . 9. **M**y
family . . . the country in the event that there is a civil war. 10. . . . safe side, I always . . .
carry-on bag in the event that the airline loses . . . . 11. In the event that there is no airport
bus, you can always . . . . 12. . . . evening. **S**he has already . . . speech in the event that she
wins it tonight.

◇ **14 (p. 244):** 1. B 2. A 3. A 4. B 5. B 6. A 7. A 8. B 9. B 10. A 11. A
12. B

◇ **15 (p. 245):** 1. not going to go 2. rains 3. pass 4. only if 5. always eat 6. even if
7. gets 8. won't 9. don't wake 10. if 11. Don't borrow 12. are still some

◇ **16 (p. 246):** 1. Only if you help me can I finish this work on time. 2. If you help me, I can finish this
work on time. 3. Only if I am invited will I go. 4. If I am invited, I will go. 5. Only
if I am hungry do I eat. 6. If I am hungry during the morning, I usually eat some fruit.
7. Only if you know both Arabic and Spanish will you be considered for that job. 8. Only if
the refrigerator is empty will John go to the market. 9. Only if you promise not to get angry
will I tell you the truth about what happened. 10. If you get angry, I won't discuss it any
further.

◇ **18 (p. 247):** 1. You should (had better/have to/must) eat less and get more exercise. Otherwise, you won't
lose weight. 2. The children have to (had better/should/must) finish all of their chores.
Otherwise, they cannot watch . . . . 3. You have to (must/should/had better) speak up now.
Otherwise, the boss will go ahead . . . . 4. You must (had better/should/have to) stop at the
store on your way home from work. Otherwise, we won't have anything . . . . 5. You had
better (have to/should/must) think it through very carefully. Otherwise, you won't come up
with . . . . 6. We have to (had better/should/must) catch fish this morning. Otherwise, we're
going to have beans . . . . 7. You should (had better/have to/must) get someone to help you.
Otherwise, it's going to be very . . . . 8. Maria had better (should/has to/must) find a way to
convince the boss that the error was unavoidable. Otherwise, she'll probably lose her job.

◇ **19 (p. 247):** 1. passes 2. doesn't pass 3. passes 4. passes 5. doesn't pass 6. passes
7. passes 8. doesn't pass 9. must/has to pass 10. had better (must/has to) pass

◇ **21 (p. 248):** 1. B 2. D 3. D 4. A 5. C 6. B 7. B 8. C 9. B 10. A 11. C
12. D 13. A 14. D 15. B 16. C 17. D 18. A 19. D 20. B
21. D 22. A

◇ **28 (p. 255):** 1. Government money is essential to successful research at our university. For example, much
of the research in the medical school is funded by government grants. **Moreover/In addition /
Furthermore,** such departments as physics, chemistry, computer science, and engineering now
rely increasingly on govenment funding.
2. Applicants for the position must fulfill certain requirements. They need a college degree and
two years' experience in the field. **In addition (Furthermore/Moreover),** they must have
computer skills. **Furthermore (Moreover/In addition),** two letters of recommendation should
be submitted along with the application.
3. There are several reasons why I write in my diary every day. Writing in a diary allows me to
reflect on a day's events and their meanings. As the Greek philosopher Plato said, ''A life that
is unexamined is not worth living.'' **In addition (Furthermore/Moreover)** I like the idea of
keeping a record of my life to share with my children at a later date. **Furthermore (In
addition/Moreover),** writing in a diary is calming. It forces me to take time out of my busy day
to rest and think quiet thoughts.

4. If you are interested in the arts, you should come to visit my city, Montreal. Montreal is a leading cultural center in North America. You can go to the Museum of Fine Arts to see displays of works by Canadian artists, past and present. **Moreover (In addition/Furthermore),** Montreal has a world famous symphony orchestra and numerous theaters. One of them, the International Theater, performs plays in several languages.

◇ **PRACTICE TEST A (p. 257):** 1. C   2. D   3. D   4. B   5. A   6. D   7. B   8. C   9. D   10. C   11. C   12. A   13. B   14. A   15. C   16. D   17. B   18. B   19. A   20. B

Chapter 10: CONDITIONAL SENTENCES

◇ **1 (p. 260):**
1. a. yes
   b. no
2. a. no
   b. yes
   c. no
3. a. yes
   b. no
   c. yes
4. a. yes
   b. no
   c. no
5. a. no
   b. yes
6. a. no
   b. yes
7. a. yes
   b. no
8. a. yes
   b. no
9. a. no
   b. no
   c. yes

◇ **2 (p. 261):**   1. were . . . would take   2. floats/will float   3. were . . . would not exist   4. doesn't arrive   5. were . . . wouldn't want   6. consisted . . . would be   7. were . . . would call . . . (would) talk   8. travels . . . always spends   9. would human beings live . . . were   10. disappears/will disappear   11. had . . . would have to . . . would not be

◇ **3 (p. 262):**   1. had told . . . would have given   2. had used . . . would have received   3. had realized . . . wouldn't have made   4. had known . . . wouldn't have voted   5. had read . . . wouldn't have washed   6. B: would have come . . . (would have) washed . . . had asked . . .   A: would have come . . . had called   7. had written . . . wouldn't have lost   8. would you have taken . . . had known

◇ **4 (p. 263):**   1. had . . . wouldn't have to   2. send   3. would have suffered   4. Would people be . . . had   5. would we use . . . didn't have (possible: hadn't)   6. felt . . . would drop   7. doesn't rain . . . will die . . . die . . . will go   8. had brought . . . would not have had   9. had been invented . . . would have been interviewed   10. discover . . . will call   11. had known . . . would have stayed up . . . (would have) finished   12. had not collided . . . would not have become . . . would be . . . still existed . . . would be

◇ **5 (p. 264):**   1. If I hadn't been sick yesterday, I would have gone to class.   2. If Alan ate breakfast, he wouldn't overeat at lunch.   3. Peter would have finished unloading the truck if John had helped him.   4. Jack wouldn't have been late to his own wedding if his watch hadn't been ten minutes slow.   5. I would ride the bus to work every morning if it weren't always so crowded.   6. I would have brought extra money with me if you had told me we were going to dinner after the movie.   7. If Sam had known that highway 57 was closed, he would have taken an alternative route.   8. If I hadn't lost my key, I wouldn't have had to pound on the door to wake my roommate when I got home last night.

◇ **8 (p. 265):**   1. weren't raining . . . would finish   2. had eaten . . . wouldn't be   3. hadn't left . . . would have   4. would have answered . . . hadn't been studying   5. hadn't been shining . . . wouldn't have gone   6. wouldn't ache . . . hadn't played   7. wouldn't stop . . . weren't running   8. had eaten . . . wouldn't have to have   9. hadn't been playing . . . would have heard   10. weren't closing . . . wouldn't have to leave

◇ **9 (p. 266):** 1. If the wind **weren't blowing** hard, I **would take** the boat out for a ride. 2. I **wouldn't feel** better now if you **hadn't talked** to me about my problems last night. 3. If Gary **hadn't carried** heavy furniture when he helped Ann move, his back **wouldn't hurt** now. 4. If Paul **weren't working** on two jobs right now, he **would have time** to help you with your remodeling. 5. If I **had been working** at the restaurant last night, I **would have waited** on your table. 6. If Diane **hadn't asked questions** every time she didn't understand a problem, she **wouldn't have** a good understanding of geometry now. 7. If a bulldozer **hadn't been blocking** the road, we **would have arrived** on time. 8. She **wouldn't be** exhausted today if she **had gotten** some sleep last night. 9. If they **had been paying** attention, they **would have seen** the sign marking their exit from the highway. 10. If the doctor really **cared** about his patients, he **would have explained** the medical procedure to me before surgery.

◇ **11 (p. 267):** 1. Should you need 2. Were I you 3. Had they realized 4. Had Alan tried 5. Should anyone call 6. Were I 7. Had everyone arrived 8. Should the post office close 9. Had I not opened 10. Were she 11. Should you change 12. had she been

◇ **13 (p. 268):** 1. I hadn't twisted my ankle 2. I had not forgotten to tell him that she needed a ride 3. you hadn't helped me 4. he had told his boss about the problem 5. I hadn't opened the door slowly 6. the woman behind me hadn't started yelling impatiently at him to check her out 7. I hadn't wanted everyone to know about it 8. his boss had given him the time off 9. the building weren't locked 10. Marge hadn't given us the benefit of her expertise 11. she hadn't driven straight to the garage when the engine started making loud noises 12. hadn't made the cast stay to rehearse some troublesome parts of the play

◇ **14 (p. 269):** 1. A 2. A 3. D 4. D 5. C 6. A 7. C 8. A 9. C 10. A 11. C 12. A 13. B 14. A 15. A 16. A 17. B 18. B 19. A 20. C

◇ **18 (p. 273):** 1. were shining 2. had gone 3. had driven 4. could swim 5. would stop 6. had won 7. had gotten 8. hadn't quit 9. were 10. would sing 11. could bring 12. had offered

◇ **19 (p. 273):** 1. hadn't missed 2. would stop . . . were shining 3. hadn't gone . . . had studied 4. hadn't moved . . . had taken 5. would stop 6. hadn't paid 7. would hurry . . . would relax 8. hadn't invited 9. would tell 10. had worn (*also possible*: were wearing) . . . had realized 11. hadn't been elected . . . hadn't voted 12. could buy . . . grew 13. weren't . . . were . . . were . . . were 14. would meet . . . disagreed . . . could prove

◇ **21 (p. 275):** 1. were 2. had been made 3. had (never) met 4. were 5. hadn't heard 6. didn't have (OR: hadn't) 7. didn't exist 8. had happened 9. were 10. were 11. had stopped 12. had appeared

◇ **PRACTICE TEST A (p. 277):** 1. B 2. C 3. C 4. A 5. C 6. B 7. D 8. B 9. D 10. A 11. C 12. B 13. B 14. B 15. D 16. C 17. D 18. D 19. D 20. A

Appendix 1: SUPPLEMENTARY GRAMMAR UNITS

◇ **1 (p. 281):**

SUBJECT	VERB	OBJECT
1. politician	supported	taxes
2. mechanic	repaired	engine
3. boxes	contain	photographs
4. teacher	canceled	test
5. earthquake	destroyed	village
6. birds	have	feathers

List of all of the nouns: politician, taxes, mechanic, engine, boxes, photographs, teacher, test, earthquake, village, birds, feathers.

◇ **2 (p. 281):** 1. repeated (**VT**)   2. rises (**VI**)   3. divided (**VT**)   4. sneezed (**VI**)   5. happened (**VI**)
6. bought (**VT**)   7. won (**VT**)   8. won (**VI**)   9. arrived (**VI**)   10. waited (**VI**)
11. are staying (**VI**)   12. is blowing (**VI**)   13. agree (**VI**)   14. walked (**VI**) . . . rode (**VT**)

◇ **3 (p. 282):**

PREPOSITION	OBJECT OF PREPOSITION
1. in	field
2. from	table
3. in	garage
4. during	storm
5. on	horses
for	transportation
6. to	park
after	class

◇ **4 (p. 282):**

```
      S     VT        O          PP
1. Alex  needs  new batteries  for his camera.
```
```
       S     VI       PP
2. A bomb  exploded  in the road.
```
```
      S    VT        O            PP
3. Sally  wore  her blue suit  to the meeting.
```
```
     S    VI      PP           PP
4. Jim  came  to class   without his books.
```
```
        S       VI          PP
5. Dark clouds  appeared  on the horizon.
```
```
      S     VT          O           PP
6. Plants  need  a reliable supply  of water.
```
```
      S     VT       O          PP          PP          PP
7. Mary  filled  the shelves  of the cabinet  with boxes  of old books.
```
```
    S     VT       O          PP            PP            PP
8. We  enjoyed  the view  of snowy mountains  from the window  of our hotel room.
```
```
        S    VI       PP              PP
9. The child  sat  between her parents  on the sandy beach.
```
```
      PP         S     VI        PP
Above her,  an eagle  flew  across the cloudless sky.
```

◇ **5 (p. 282):**

```
     ADJ              ADV            ADJ
1. A terrible  fire spread  rapidly  through the  old  house.
```
```
     ADJ              ADV          ADJ
2. A small  child cried  noisily  in the  third  row of the theater.
```
```
        ADJ                ADV
3. The  eager  player waited  impatiently  for the start of the game.
```

         ADV   **ADJ**
4. An <u>unusually</u> <u>large</u> crowd came to the concert.

          ADV   **ADJ**   **ADJ**
5. Arthur <u>carefully</u> repaired the <u>antique</u> vase with <u>special</u> glue.

         ADV   **ADJ**   **ADJ**   **ADV**
6. On <u>especially</u> <u>busy</u> days, the telephone in the <u>main</u> office rings <u>constantly.</u>

Total number of nouns: 16. *Total number of verbs:* 6.

◇ **6 (p. 283):**   1. quickly   2. quick   3. polite   4. politely   5. regularly   6. regular   7. usual   8. usually   9. well   10. good   11. gentle   12. gently   13. annually   14. annual   15. bad   16. badly

◇ **7 (p. 283):**
1. Sue **always takes** a walk in the morning.
2. Tim **is always** a hard worker.
3. Beth **has always worked** hard.
4. Jack **always works** hard.
5. **Do you always work** hard?
6. Taxis **are usually** available . . . .
7. Tom **rarely takes** a taxi . . . .
8. I **have often thought** about . . . .
9. Cindy **probably needs** some help.
10. **Have you ever attended** the show . . . ?
11. Al **seldom goes** out . . . .
12. The students **are hardly ever** late.
13. **Do you usually finish** your . . . ?
14. In India, the monsoon season **generally begins** in April.
15. . . . Mr. Singh's hometown **usually receives** around . . . .

◇ **8 (p. 284):**

LINKING VERB + ADJECTIVE	LINKING VERB + ADJECTIVE
1. Ø *(no linking verb in the sentence)*	12. got . . . . sleepy
2. looked . . . . fresh	13. became . . . . rough
3. Ø	14. Ø
4. Ø	15. Ø
5. tasted . . . . good	16. sounded . . . . . . happy
6. grew . . . . quiet	17. turns . . . . hot
7. Ø	18. Ø
8. Ø	19. Ø
9. Ø	20. appears . . . . certain
10. smells . . . . delicious	21. seems . . . . strange
11. Ø	

◇ **9 (p. 284):**   1. clean   2. slowly   3. safely   4. anxious   5. complete   6. wildly   7. honest   8. thoughtfully   9. well   10. fair   11. terrible   12. good   13. light   14. confidently   15. famous   16. fine

◇ **11 (p. 286):**   1. them   2. me   3. I   4. me . . . his   5. his . . . her   6. its . . . them   7. They . . . it   8. your . . . them   9. I . . . him . . . me   10. My . . . I . . . . She . . . her . . . mine   11. Our . . . our . . . ours . . . theirs   12. It . . . its . . . its . . . it . . . it . . . it . . . It's . . . them

◇ **12 (p. 286):**
1. . . . but I don't like most of **it**.
2. . . . my sister and **I** used to play . . . .
3. . . . study very hard for **them**.
4. . . . by my boss and **me** after . . . .
5. . . . most of **its** time . . . .
6. . . . so I've forgotten a lot of **it**.

7. ...but I couldn't find **them**.

8. ...speak to Tim and **me** about.... He explained **them** to...and asked for **our** opinions.

9. My father and **she** had come.... was waiting for **us**....

10. ...respect other people. **He** (OR: **She, S/he, He or she**) needs to...including **his** (OR: **her, his or her**) playmates. [NOTE: *The masculine-feminine pronoun problem can be avoided by using a plural noun:* **Children** should learn to respect.... **They** need...**their** playmates.]

11. ...because **theirs** was in the garage....

◇ **13 (p. 287):** 1. He's 2. Ø 3. He's 4. Ø 5. She'd 6. Ø 7. She'd 8. Ø 9. We'll 10. They're 11. It's 12. It's 13. Ø 14. Ø 15. We're 16. Ø 17. She's 18. She'd 19. She'd...we'd 20. Ø...he'd

◇ **14 (p. 288):**

	Question word	Auxiliary verb	Subject	Main verb	Rest of question
1a.	Ø	**Can**	Bob	**live**	there?
1b.	Where	**can**	Bob	**live**	Ø ?
1c.	Who	**can**	Ø	**live**	there?
2a.	Ø	**Is**	Don	**living**	there?
2b.	Where	**is**	Don	**living**	Ø ?
2c.	Who	**is**	Ø	**living**	there?
3a.	Ø	**Does**	Sue	**live**	there?
3b.	Where	**does**	**Sue**	**live**	Ø ?
3c.	Who	Ø	Ø	**lives**	there?
4a.	Ø	**Will**	Ann	**live**	there?
4b.	Where	**will**	Ann	**live**	Ø ?
4c.	Who	**will**	Ø	**live**	there?
5a.	Ø	**Did**	Jack	**live**	there?
5b.	**Where**	**did**	Jack	**live**	Ø ?
5c.	**Who**	Ø	Ø	**lived**	there?
6a.	Ø	**Has**	Mary	**lived**	**there?**
6b.	**Where**	**has**	Mary	**lived**	Ø ?
6c.	**Who**	**has**	Ø	**lived**	**there?**

◇ **15 (p. 289):** 1. When are you going to the zoo? 2. Are you going downtown later today? 3. Do you live in an apartment? 4. Where does Sue live? 5. Who lives in that house? 6. Can you speak French? 7. Who can speak Arabic? 8. When did Olga arrive? 9. Who arrived late? 10. What is Ann opening? 11. What is Ann doing? 12. What did Mary open? 13. Who opened the door? 14. Has the mail arrived? 15. Do you have a bicycle? 16. What does Alex have in his hand? 17. Do you like ice cream? 18. Would you like an ice cream cone? 19. What would Joe like? 20. Who would like a soft drink?

◇ **16 (p. 290):** 1. How long has Pierre been living here? 2. Which (city) is farther north, London or Paris? 3. Whose is it? 4. What have you been doing? 5. Who answered the phone? 6. How do they plow their fields? 7. How long have you had it? 8. What kind of bird is that? 9. Why were you late for work this morning? (OR: How come you were late for work this morning?) 10. How long did it take you? 11. What time/When did he finally get home? 12. How do you take it? 13. What is the population of the United States? 14. Which (coat/one) do you like better (, the red one or the black one)? 15. How did you get there? 16. Who(m) should I address it to? (*Formal:* To whom should I address it?) 17. How far (How many miles) is it from here to Los Angeles? 18. Who is going to be at the meeting tonight? 19. How often (How many times a week) do people in your country have rice?　20. Where did you get that silly looking hat?　21. How many edges are there on a cube?　....　How many edges are there on a pyramid?　22. What does "apologize" mean?　23. What does he look like?　24. What is she like?

◇ **22 (p. 295):**　1. Haven't you seen...?　No　2. Didn't he say...?　Yes　3. Wasn't he...?　No
4. Didn't Mary tell...?　No　5. Aren't you having...?　No　6. Don't Janet and you work
...?　Yes　7. Isn't that...?　Yes　8. Isn't the Mississippi...?　No

◇ **23 (p. 296):**　1. don't you　2. have you　3. didn't she　4. aren't there　5. have you　6. don't you
(*possible but less common:* haven't you)　7. won't you　8. doesn't he　9. shouldn't we
10. can they　11. are they　12. isn't it　13. did they　14. aren't I/am I not
15. isn't it

◇ **24 (p. 297):**　1. no...not　2. no...not　3. No　4. no　5. not...not　6. no　7. not
8. no　9. no...no　10. not　11. no　12. not

◇ **25 (p. 297):**　1. We **have no** time to waste.　OR:　We **don't have any** time to waste.　2. I **didn't have any** problems.　OR:　I **had no** problems.　3. I **can't do anything** about it.　OR:　I **can do nothing** about it.　4. You **can hardly ever understand** her when she speaks.　5. I **know neither** Ann **nor** her husband.　OR:　I **don't know either** Ann **or** her husband.　6. **Don't ever drink** water from....　OR:　**Never drink** water from....　7. ...I **could barely hear** the speaker.

◇ **26 (p. 298):**　1. **Hardly had I stepped** out of bed....　2. **Never will I say** that again.　3. **Scarcely ever have I enjoyed** myself more....　4. **Rarely does she make** a mistake.　5. **Never will I trust** him again because....　6. **Hardly ever is it** possible to get....　7. **Seldom do I skip** breakfast.　8. **Never have I known** a more....

◇ **27 (p. 298):**　1. Ø Lightning...**a** flash...Ø thunder　2. **a** terrible storm...**the** thunder　3. Ø Circles ...Ø round geometric figures　4. **A** circle...**a** slash...**the** circle...**the** illustration
5. **The** milk...**the** refrigerator　6. Ø Milk...Ø protein...Ø calcium　7. Ø space...Ø other...**the** universe　8. **a** new phone　9. **the** phone　10. Ø Wisdom...Ø understanding ...Ø knowledge　11. **the** wisdom　12. **The** woman...**the** right answer...**the** teacher's question　13. **an** independent young woman　14. **a** car...**the** second day...**the** car
15. Ø People...Ø plants...Ø many different ways...Ø oxygen...Ø lifesaving medicines...Ø houses...Ø paper...Ø textiles.